The Arab World

The Arab World

Society, Culture, and State

HALIM BARAKAT

University of California Press

BERKELEY   LOS ANGELES   OXFORD

University of California Press
Berkeley and Los Angeles, California

University of California Press, Ltd.
Oxford, England

© 1993 by
The Regents of the University of California

Library of Congress Cataloging-in-Publication Data
Barakat, Halim Isber.
    The Arab world : society, culture, and state / Halim Barakat.
    p.   cm.
    Includes bibliographical references and index.
    ISBN 0-520-07907-8 (alk. paper)
    1. Civilization, Arab—20th century.
  DS36.88.B36   1993
  909'.0974927—dc20   92-23342

Printed in the United States of America
9   8   7   6   5   4   3   2   1

The paper used in this publication meets the minimum requirements of
American National Standard for Information Sciences—Permanence of
Paper for Printed Library Materials, ANSI Z39.48-1984. ∞

To Umm Halim, Hayat, and Beshara

Contents

Preface

The intention of this book is to present a comprehensive portrait of Arab society without overlooking its complexity, specificity, and inner dynamics. In the last analysis, the purpose is to provide a new theoretical framework that contributes to a deeper understanding of Arabs and their place in the modern era; this task must be achieved through a combination of concerted scholarly analysis and social criticism from an Arab perspective. For me, scholarship is inseparable from genuine concern over issues of social and political transformation.

Given this context, I should begin by saying that I view the Arab world as a single, overarching society rather than a collection of several independent nation-states that increasingly, and particularly in times of crisis, assert their differences and separate identities. In other words, my analytical starting point is social rather than political reality. This social reality differs dramatically from the picture presented by Orientalist scholars in the West: Arab society is not a mere mosaic of sects, ethnic groups, tribes, local communities, and regional entities. Rather, it carries within it the potential for both unity and divisiveness. My focus encompasses all of that potential rather than assuming one or the other is necessarily dominant over time. This focus recognizes conditions that constantly pull contemporary Arab society between all sorts of polarities and conflicting orientations: unity versus fragmentation, tradition versus modernity, sacred versus secular, East versus West, local versus national.

The book explores the range of issues posed by social and political diversity and integration; only in this way may we understand the challenges facing Arabs as they try to define national identity and struggle to overcome their difficulties. A critical analysis of Arab consciousness of identity, however, must also lead us to discard idealist views emphasizing uniformity or similarity and to substitute an emphasis on the common destiny and distinctive characteristic features that Arabs share in the context of their place in history and networks of human relationship. The dilemma confronting Arabs in modern times is one of combining plurality and unity. A lasting challenge for Arabs, since the political fragmentation of the region after the collapse of the Ottoman empire, has been to create one out of many without compromising the richness of diversity. A central flaw in the thinking of Arabs about themselves is the traditional idealist tendency to conceive of identity as something that is already completely formed and not something to be achieved.

Forces of unity and divisiveness are described here in relation to each other, within the context of underlying contradictions and specific historical conditions. The book investigates the nature of existing social structures and institutions—that is, social classes, family, religion, and politics. In contrast to societal fragmentation, the social institutions of the Arab world are dominated either by a single patriarchal figure—the father in the family; the ruler in politics; and God in monotheistic religion—or by a few elites. As we examine the specifics of Arab society, we shall search as well for the potential for a plural unity that is inherent in these social institutions.

Arab culture is also explored in this book. I argue the need for a dual process of analysis, in which we deconstruct the static and oversimplified views prevalent in Western scholarship on the Arab World and reconstruct a dynamic approach to a highly complex and contradictory reality. Finally, the book expounds the thesis that there is a crisis of civil society in Arab countries and a desperate search to transcend conditions of alienation. Chapters 1 and 2 delineate the methodology and underlying assumptions that lead to this thesis, as well as my prognosis for the daring and fundamental changes necessary to address this crisis.

Many of my ideas and observations in this book evolved from teaching a course on contemporary Arab society that I have offered since the beginning of my career as a professor of sociology in 1966. Conversations and discussions with my students, friends, and colleagues contributed greatly to the development of my understanding of Arab society. I am indebted to them all. In particular I wish to express my appreciation to Adonis, Hisham Sharabi, Munir Bashshur, Kamal Boullata, Samih Farsoun, Sandria Freitag, and Beshara Doumani. I wish also to acknowledge the valuable editorial help of Mary Ann Faye, Garay Menicucci, and Beshara Doumani. My book in Arabic *Al-Mujtama' al-'arabi al-Mu'asir* (Contemporary Arab Society), first published by The Center for Arab Unity Studies, Beirut, in 1984, served as a prelude to the present book.

At the time of writing this preface, the ruins of Iraq and Kuwait are still smoldering. The Arab world is living one of the darkest moments of its modern history. The causes of the Gulf War and the immensity of its consequences can be systematically traced to the conditions discussed in this book, which was completed immediately prior to the Gulf crisis. The tragic irony is that just as Arabs were approaching the horizon of the twenty-first century, the Gulf War seems to have returned them full circle to the beginnings of a century of foreign domination that they had been hoping to erase from memory. Once again Arab society is being fragmented, and it will now have to confront the replacement of European imperial power by that of the United States of America. This is the kind of reality Arabs will have to deal with for some time to come, burdened with calamities of great magnitude.

PART ONE

Arab Identity and Issues of Diversity and Integration: Out of Many, One

1 Social and Political Integration
Alternative Visions of the Future

One highly distinctive feature of contemporary Arab society is the alarming gap between reality and dream. Pan-Arabism is the proclaimed ideal among the ruling classes and the prevailing sentiment among the Arab masses, but Arab society continues to suffer from the erosion of civil life and profound fragmentation. Efforts at social and political integration have been frustrated by regionalism, the pursuit of idiosyncratic interests by the established ruling classes in separate Arab countries, dependency, colonization, the power of traditional loyalties (religious, ethnic, kinship), urban-rural-nomadic differences, and repressive conditions. What adds to the complexity of the problem is the lack of understanding both of these divisive forces and of their interactions and mutual reinforcement. For example, in Arab society there is a congruence between social class and communal cleavages, with some ethnic, religious, tribal, and regional communities enjoying more wealth, power, and prestige at the expense of others. Although the distinctions relating to these different types of cleavages are now blurred beyond recognition, analysts persist in describing the problem with a vocabulary that emphasizes sectarian identity above all other forms of affiliation. Without clear analysis that grasps and conveys the complexities involved, Arabs can never address the gap between this reality and the dream of national unity.

At the same time, there are a number of very real forces and conditions making for unity; their existence partly explains the dynamism of Arab society and its continuous struggle. This book proposes a theory of transformation predicated on the development, among Arabs, of higher forms of awareness or consciousness of the problems they face in achieving the dream of unity. In the model I propose here, transformation will be achieved through the profound reconstruction—even re-creation—of Arab reality. The analysis that informs this book thus also leads to a theory of action for the future. It does more than this, however, by focusing on the basic building blocks of Arab society. This analytical focus enables us to understand the dynamics of popular movements for national unity, as well as the efforts that have sought to redefine national identity through establishment of a more effective, democratic model of civil society.

The analytical approach proposed here is crucial, because the failure of those seeking political unity to achieve their goal so far has not been caused by the ideals they set for themselves, but by their inability to devise the necessary rational structures and strategies. That is, the problem lies, not in the ideal itself, but in the gap or imbalance between this goal and actions designed to achieve the historical task of achieving unity. Some objective conditions for unity do exist, to a greater extent than has been the case in other societies that have already succeeded in achieving unity. These building blocks of unity include the Arabic language and shared culture; the Arabs' sense of their place in history, and their sense of belonging; similar economic interests; and the looming presence of external threats and challenges that face Arab society, regardless of nation–state boundary lines.

Even in instances where local or regional identities become very strong because of systematic cultivation, as in Egypt under President Anwar Sadat, Arab nationalism seems to remain alive. The Egyptian scholar Gamal Hamdan has emphasized the uniqueness of Egyptian identity, but points out that Egypt has always been the meeting place of the Arab family. He argues that "Egypt in the Arab world is like Cairo in Egypt": that it is the "cultural hub" and "oasis" of Arabs, and that "it cannot but be a nucleus of Arab unity." As Arabs, moreover, Egyptians share the responsibility to solve larger Arab problems. "Perhaps the final test of Egyptian leadership may lie in whether it is able to face the responsibility of regaining Palestine for the Arabs," Hamdan says. "If it is true that there is no Arab unity without Egyptian leadership, it is probably as true to say that Egypt would lose its leadership among the Arabs by failing to regain Palestine for the Arabs." At the root of Hamdan's argument is his distinction between *wataniyya* (patriotism to the homeland) and *qawmiyya* (nationalism or loyalty to the larger Arab nation). He sees Egypt as the homeland and the Arab world as the nation, and argues that an emphasis on the homeland does not conflict with loyalty to the nation (*al-watan al-'arabi al-kabir*). "We do not see the Egyptian personality, no matter how distinct it may be, as anything other than a part of the personality of the greater Arab homeland," he concludes.[1]

Similarly, the Egyptian anthropologist Laila El-Hamamsy examined Egyptian identity and concluded that "it is not surprising, then, in the light of their history, that Egyptians . . . should be conscious of their national identity and consider themselves, above all, Egyptians." El-Hamamsy then asks: "How is the Egyptian, with this strong sense of Egyptian identity, able to look on himself as an Arab, too?" Her answer is that Egyptianization has meant Arabization as well: "The result has been an increased tempo of Arabization, for facility in the Arabic language opened windows into the rich legacy of Arabic culture. . . . Thus in seeking a cultural identity, Egypt has revived its Arab cultural heritage."[2]

Consequently, during a period of systematic efforts by the Sadat government to separate Egypt from the rest of the Arab world, a number of articles by prominent Egyptian intellectuals reasserted the Arabism of Egypt. Between October 1978 and January 1979, for instance, the London-based weekly *Al-Dastour* serialized a study entitled "The Arabism of Egypt" by the famous Egyptian poet 'Abd Al-Mu'ti Hijazi, and Hijazi's argument was subsequently reflected in an article by Al-Sayyid Yassin, who writes:

> We can conclude that there are several factors on the basis of which we can talk with certainty about the existence of one Arab nation. These factors are the common historical experience, the Arabic language, and the common cultural heritage. . . . Though all these factors are . . . superstructural, they are the cover of a substructure that has grown and developed along largely similar lines in the different regions of the Arab homeland.[3]

The nature of Arabism and Egyptian separatism have been analyzed by another Egyptian sociologist, Saad Eddin Ibrahim, who scrutinized the dialogue among seventeen Egyptian intellectuals generated by Tawfiq al-Hakim's call on March 3, 1978, for the neutrality of Egypt in the ongoing Arab conflicts with Israel and the West. Of thirty-one articles published between March 3, 1978, and May 11, 1978, eight articles (by two authors, Tawfiq al-Hakim and Hussein Fawzi) called for neutrality yet acknowledged the Arab identity of Egypt; three articles (by Louis Awad) opposed neutrality and denied Egypt its Arab identity; eighteen articles, by such writers as Yusuf Idriss, Ahmed Baha' Eddin, Bint Ash-Shati', 'Abd El-Azim Ramadan, Raja' an-Naqqash, Al-Sayyid Yassin, and Saad Eddin Ibrahim, disapproved of the call for neutrality and asserted Egypt's Arab identity; and two articles wavered between the second and third stands.[4]

It is gradually becoming apparent, particularly in view of the Arab-Israeli conflict, the Lebanese and Sudanese civil wars, the Iran-Iraq war, and the Gulf War, that Arabs are essentially faced with two alternative visions, and consequently two designs for their future. One vision accepts the present reality and proposes to preserve the status quo or even to dismantle Arab society further by legitimizing or establishing sovereign states as national homes for the different ethnic and religious communities in the area. This design provides advantages to certain Western centers of power. It is being promoted by Zionism because it would legitimize an expanding Israel while maintaining Western hegemony.

The other design envisages a radical transformation of the existing order through the establishment of an overarching, unified, democratic, secular, and egalitarian Arab nation. This dream contrasts sharply with the present reality. How is it possible to achieve unity, democracy, secularism, and social justice in a society burdened with fragmentation, authoritarianism, traditionalism, religious fundamentalism, patriarchy, erosion of a sense of shared civil society, pyramidal social class structure, and dependency? Are such dreams the product of hopelessly romantic, utopian, and idealist minds? To answer this question, we must understand the historical context in which Arabs have made decisions, and the special role played by Israel in this context.

Historical Context

Meddling in Arab affairs by European powers, and later by the United States, accelerated after Britain dishonored her World War I pledges to the Arabs. Instead of permitting Arab unity, Britain issued the Balfour Declaration, which promised a homeland for the Jews in Palestine, and the Sykes-Picot Agreement, which led to the partitioning of geographical Syria into British and French spheres of control. The subsequent period saw further attempts to establish fragmented pieces of the Arab world as separate states. These states were based on the Western Orientalist "mosaic" perceptions: they defined as "national" constituents a few particular subgroups in Arab society. For example, states were proposed for Alawites and Druze in Syria, Berbers in North Africa, and Kurds in Iraq. New states, such as Israel, were created. Parts of one country were annexed to another (for example, Iskenderun to Turkey). Certain communities were imposed on others within the same country (for example, the Maronites in Lebanon). 'Ali Eddin Hilal argued that this imperialist policy of fragmentation aimed at several interconnected goals pursued by the West. First, it led to the establishment of ruling classes and systems that would stand to benefit from continued disunity. Second, it produced better circumstances for manipulating internal differences and conflicts among the Arabs, in keeping with the policy of divide and rule. Third, it created economically and socially incomplete entities that would, therefore, remain perpetually dependent on the imperialist powers in order to function in the global world order.[5]

The establishment of Israel furthered this policy, while creating a national home for the Jews. Since its inception, Israel has served both as a base and a model. As a base, it has worked to preserve the existing order. Examples of such activity include its participation in the attack on Egypt in 1956 to reverse the nationalization of the Suez canal; its invasion of Lebanon in 1982; its continual threats to interfere with any serious attempts to alter existing socio-political arrangements, on the pretext that they might undermine Israeli security; and its reminders to the West, and particularly the United States, of Israel's strategic role in preserving the status quo in the area.

As a model, Israel has provided the necessary assistance to, as well as the inspiration for, sectarian and religiously or ethnically oriented regimes and movements. In covering the Lebanese civil war, for instance, the American journalist Jonathan Randal discovered the presence of a sustained collaboration between Maronite rightists, Israelis, and some others who believed in the "theory of mosaic states."[6] The personal diary of Moshe Sharett, a former foreign minister and prime minister of Israel, exposed a 1954 proposal by David Ben-Gurion to encourage "the Maronites . . . to proclaim a Christian state. . . . The creation of a Christian state is . . . a national act; it has historical roots and it will find support in wide circles in the Christian world. . . . In normal times this would be almost impossible. First and foremost because of the lack of initiative and courage of the Christians. But at times of confusion or revolution or civil war, things take on another aspect, and even the weak declares himself to be a hero." Sharett also wrote that Moshe Dayan expressed his enthusiastic support for the proposal, saying that "the only thing that is necessary is to find an officer . . . to make him agree to declare himself the savior of the Maronite population. Then the Israeli army will enter Lebanon, will occupy the necessary territory, and will create a Christian regime which will ally itself with Israel. The territory from the Litani southward will be totally annexed to Israel."[7] In the same year (1954), Pierre Gemayel, the founder and the head of the Kata'ib (Phalangist) party, threatened Lebanese Muslims by saying that the Christians were "ready when necessary to cooperate with the devil itself [code for Israel]."[8]

This is the context in which Western studies of minorities in the Arab world need to be placed. In their introduction to two issues of the *Middle East Review* devoted to the subject of ethnic and religious minorities in the area, Anne Sinai and Chaim Waxman argued that

> the current civil war in Lebanon is but the latest and most publicized in a broad range of events and situations which belie the contention that the Middle East is a unitary world of Arabs with a common background, culture, language and identity. The Middle East in fact consists of an intricate mosaic of different peoples. . . . There are Shi'ites . . . Alawites, Druze, Yazidis, Isma'ilies and followers of various other Muslim denominations, who cling determinedly to their own style of faith and their own set of beliefs. They are not

even necessarily ethnically "Arab," being the descendants of many different peoples conquered and converted by the Islamic armies. . . . The first of the three great monotheistic religions, Judaism, and the people with whom it is identical, have been part of the Middle East mosaic from their beginning. . . . There are, in addition . . . other small religious groupings, each clinging to its own distinctive identity. No Arab state, thus, can claim societal homogeneity and all consist of major and minor religious, linguistic and ethnic groupings. . . . Many of the minority communities have resisted Arabization.[9]

In the same issue, R. Hrair Dekmejian noted:

While few generalizations are valid for the Middle East as a whole, two realities stand out as being beyond question. (1) No single state in the Middle East can claim societal homogeneity. All Middle Eastern states consist of several major and minor religious, linguistic, and/or tribal collectivities; hence the use of the term mosaic to describe the region's cultural diversity. (2) In modern times as well as historically, the Middle Eastern milieu has been singularly inhospitable to its ethnic minorities.[10]

Thus Zionist scholarship, as well as research sponsored by the United States, continues to assert the Orientalist notion of a mosaic society. The 1988 edition of *Syria: A Country Study* in the Area Handbook Series asserts that "Syrian society is a mosaic of social groups of various sizes that lacks both a consistent stratification system linking all together and a set of shared values and loyalties binding the population into one nation. Distinctions of language, region, religion, ethnicity, and way of life cut across the society, producing a large number of separate communities, each marked by strong internal loyalty and solidarity. Although about two-thirds of the people are Arabic-speaking Sunni Muslims, they do not constitute a unitary social force because of the strongly felt differences among bedouin, village, and urban dwellers. A perceptive observer has spoken of the " 'empty center' of Syrian society, a society lacking an influential group embodying a national consensus."[11]

Even many of those who worry about the effects of fragmentation proffer solutions rooted in the paradigm of a mosaic society. These analysts often propose the use of conflict-management practices devised for "integrating" divided societies. For example, Eric A. Nordlinger recommended "those decision-making procedures, political arrangements, and behavioral rules which are potentially capable of accommodating antagonistic groups to one another, thereby providing the framework within which severe conflicts are regulated."[12] Another example of the conflict-management theory, although focused on an outcome that moves beyond the current limitations found in

Arab society, is the consociational democracy model of Arend Lijphart, which calls for governance by an elite cartel designed to turn a democracy with a fragmented political culture into a stable democracy.[13] Lijphart at least assumes that Arab society seeks genuine transformation rather than the mere management of divisiveness and fragmentation. These proposed solutions are likely to be ineffective in the long run, however, because they do not create an environment for true social and political integration.

At this point, let us return to the question of whether those who pursue liberation and the creation of a unified, secular, democratic, and egalitarian Arab society have fallen prey to idealism, romanticism, and utopian thinking. Having a dream and a set of ideals for a society constitutes romanticism only if one is unable to devise effective, relevant, and rational structures and strategies for its implementation. The issue is not really one of realism versus idealism. Indeed, modern history provides ample evidence that authentic transformation is possible under certain conditions, and that the application of conflict-management practices in divided societies might be ineffective in the long run. Consider Lebanon's two civil wars since independence as an example. The Arab progressive nationalist movement, despite its imperfections, is developing a better understanding of the divisive forces and contradictions within Arab society. Its adherents increasingly perceive the immensity of the burden and the challenge they face in transforming reality. Successive failures have been disheartening and frustrating at times, but they have also served as an incentive for more serious reflection and for attaining greater readiness for self-transformation and the confrontation of reality. The progressive nationalists are coming to realize that bridging the gap between reality and the dream is a long-term goal achievable only by a popular national movement that undertakes to change the fundamental social structures that order society. Only in this way can the appropriate building blocks be introduced in lieu of existing structures that only promote traditional values and loyalties.

Yet we must move beyond these initial attempts to diagnose and propose remedies for the ailments of the Arab society. We need to raise a series of important questions that have not yet been faced: what conditions have contributed to the survival and intensification of traditional loyalties and cleavages? What kinds of socioeconomic structures and interests promote traditionalism? In what ways do these cleavages coincide with and reinforce one another? To what extent do vertical loyalties (such as religious and ethnic ties) constitute disguised forms of socioeconomic discrimination and distinction? In what ways do traditional loyalties serve as mechanisms of adjustment to, or reconciliation with, situations of deprivation and domination? How can movements for change combat the manipulation of traditional loyalties by foreign powers and ruling classes? To what extent does a fair distribution of wealth, power, and social status presently exist in the Arab world? Our analysis of existing Arab society must answer these questions before we can fully understand the issues to be addressed by successful strategies for transformation.

Then we face another set of questions, this time concerning the process of transformation itself. Who is likely to carry out the historical task of creating national unity by transcending traditional loyalties? Why is it that Arab nationalists have failed so far to genuinely concern themselves with problems of social liberation and secularism? What forces hinder the process of transformation? What are the sources of the crisis of civil society? On what level should change begin? Should the prevailing traditional loyalties be accepted as permanent, and managed by conflict-regulating practices, or should they be transformed and replaced with higher forms of consciousness? What kinds of goals need to be incorporated into an ideology of progressive Arab nationalist movements? Under what conditions can social integration be achieved? What sort of integration is required?

Conclusion

To succeed, the Arab nationalist movement must formulate a more progressive and realistic program for unity. The movement must continue to pressure Arab governments. Its long-term goals should be the achievement of unity, democracy, social justice, and secularism. In order to attain these ends, the Arab nationalist movement will have to redefine itself more fully by incorporating some basic elements into its ideology:

1. Secularism has to become a genuine and integral part of Arab nationalist ideology, given the urgent need to transcend traditional loyalties and break the vicious circle of communal rivalries. Through secularism, governments must end discrimination and enable political representation on a nonsectarian basis, making all citizens equal before the law regardless of affiliations and gender. Such equality must be accompanied by the creation of institutional structures that will bring about the emergence of a central state and leadership that represent all, rather than just a segment, of the population.

2. Arab nationalist ideology must take cognizance of the camouflaged class divisions that exist in Arab society. One of these camouflages is the identity of regional nationalisms. As Samir Amin points out, "The framework within which class struggle occurs is a national framework and the oppression of the peoples of the region is not only economic, but national." [14]

3. If social integration is to be achieved, the Arab nationalist movement must address itself to the task of transforming the existing social class structure and bridging the gap between the rich and the poor. Extreme concentration of national wealth in a few hands has prevailed in most Arab countries, and

disparities are increasing. Moreover, national liberation from foreign domination is inseparably linked to liberation from internal economic exploitation because of the alliance between neocolonialists and the Arab ruling classes.

4. The Arab nationalist movement needs to become more genuinely concerned with the problem of alienation and lack of civil society. The Arab masses are powerless vis-à-vis their institutions—the state, family, school, religious establishments, and places of work. Numerous movements for national independence have succeeded in liberating Arab countries from foreign control, only to result in the establishment of authoritarian systems of repression, exploitation, and degradation.

5. Social integration and national unity are increasingly understood by progressive Arab movements to mean harmony with adversity rather than the imposition of cultural uniformity. Arab society is pluralistic in a variety of ways, which should enrich its well-being. In any case, efforts to impose unification from the top have proved unsuccessful.

These five elements must become an integral part of the ideology of the Arab nationalist movement if the movement hopes to achieve political and social integration. Secularism, democracy, social justice, individual freedom, and unity with diversity are not a list of separate requirements. They have to be taken or rejected all together, for they are interconnected and represent different aspects of the same struggle for human liberation. If reformers focus firmly on these five elements, they will readily see the kinds of strategies they must adopt in order to pursue such aims as liberalization through modernization; industrialization; the creation of appropriate political and social institutions; the improvement of communication among Arab countries; the end of censorship; the establishment of facilities for cultural and economic exchange; the reduction of travel and residence restrictions on other Arabs; the provision of relevant and readily accessible education; and the protection of human rights. All of these aims are important in achieving successful integration of the Arab world. But they are only manifestations of deeper commitments and a broader vision of a new and integrated Arab society—a society that will only emerge if the five elements delineated here are placed at the center of reform activity.

The present situation and the immediate future look bleak indeed (particularly in the aftermath of the Gulf War). Yet the struggle will go on, sustained by a strong belief that in the long run there is no acceptable alternative to the comprehensive transformation of Arab society. As a first step toward transformation, we turn now to analysis of the fundamental building blocks of Arab society.

2   Arab Society

Basic Characteristic Features

Stretching some 5.25 million square miles between the Gulf and the Atlantic, the Arab world is officially composed of twenty-one states and inhabited by a mostly young population expected to number over 200 million before the end of the twentieth century. Besides linking Asia and Africa, it has long served as the gateway to Europe. It is not unusual for scholars and laity alike to wonder whether this Arab world constitutes a society. Skeptics conceive of the Arab world as a collection of independent states increasingly asserting their differences, peculiarities, and separate identities, an image reinforced during periods of intra-Arab conflict. It is important to note, however, that this model bases itself on states formed in very recent times and uses "national" boundaries and political configurations to prove its point, rather than looking at the social and cultural connections within Arab society.

Views emphasizing the mosaic nature of Arab society have also been reinforced over time by the transitions experienced by contemporary Arab society since the collapse of the Ottoman Empire initiated a desperate search for a new order. The emerging Arab society has been in flux, pulled constantly between opposite poles: past versus future, East versus West, tradition versus modernity, sacred versus secular, ethnicity versus class solidarity, unity versus fragmentation, and so on. It appears to be in conflict with itself and with other societies. These internal contradictions are perhaps responsible for the various characterizations of Arab society in the West—such as mosaic, segmentary, mercantilistic and agricultural, patriarchal, patrimonial, tribal, inherently religious, Asiatic in its mode of production, dependent, underdeveloped, or stratified.

Nevertheless, deriving their overarching identity from shared social patterns and culture, rather than from an artificially imposed polity or religion, the inhabitants of Arab countries overwhelmingly perceive themselves, and are perceived by others, as Arab. The Moroccan sociologist Abdelkebir Khatibi has observed that Arab identity is shaped by where Arabs stand in time and space, by their history, by their memory, by the places in which they have lived and died.[1] This basic identity, rooted in territory and civilization, is reconstituted in individuals and in the collective memory. It is perpetuated from one century to the next, feeding on nostalgia for the past as well as on dreams of the future.

Before we can analyze the potential of the Arab world to use this shared sense of identity to constitute an integrated society, we need to know more about the distinctive national identity or identities of Arabs. In addition to the coincidence of communal and class cleavages, this inquiry will reveal the interplay of the social and political realities of the Arab world, and the new and old dynamic forces that have shaped and reshaped it. Let us turn first, however, to the methodologies that will enable us to make this examination.

A Critical Approach: Some Methodological Observations

This study may be described as critical and dynamic. Unlike Orientalism (Western scholarship on "the Orient" from the perspective of "the Occident"), my criticism of Arab society is deeply embedded in a sense of belonging and of commitment to its transformation. I identify with the forces of change in opposition to those upholding the status quo. My approach may also be characterized as sociological, analytical, structural, and dialectical. Regardless of the labels used to describe the type of analysis used in the pages that follow, I have undertaken to explore the total Arab situation, guided by these principles:

1. The phenomena under study are examined in their social and historical contexts. The starting point is society in history, rather than polity (particular nation-state boundaries) or religion (Islam). This principle is diametrically opposed to the assumption that guides Orientalist studies—namely, the perception of Arab society as a collection of political entities and of Islam as a peculiar religion superimposed on society rather than emerging out of a certain social reality. Orientalists have emphasized texts rather than actual behavior in everyday life and have tended to see society as a product of religion rather than the other way around.

2. I seek to portray society as changing rather than static. The forces of change are explained in terms of internal and external contradictions, renewed historical challenges, encounters with other societies, the discovery and development of new resources, and invented or borrowed innovations. In this process, the West has served more as a challenge than as a model to be emulated. This, too, contrasts with the Orientalist approach, which has essentialized the social and political characteristics of Arab society (that is, sees them as inherent).

3. My investigation emphasizes social class and analysis of the structures

ordering Arab society. The communal strife existing in some parts of the Arab world is examined in a socioeconomic context as a form of conflict masking deeper structures of stratification. Furthermore, class contradictions are linked to external pressures as well as internal differentiation among Arabs. Indeed, class and nationalistic struggles are inexorably linked by the dual nature of internal and external domination and exploitation.

4. I treat behavior as a complex network of relationships to be examined in holistic and integrative ways. Aspects of human behavior, group formation, institutions, culture, and so on, are explored, not as separate entities, but in terms of the relationships among them. Separate chapters are devoted to social class, family, politics, religion, and culture only for ease of analysis; we must always keep in mind the interrelationships among these aspects of Arab society.

5. The prevailing conditions and the dominant culture render Arabs alienated. Although many have sought self-deliverance from this state of alienation through compliance or escape, the struggle to transform reality and achieve the *nahda* (Arab renaissance) continues unabated in many forms. This book attempts to explain the sources of alienation and the forces sustaining the struggle against it.

My approach may be described as dynamic because, in contrast to the Orientalist construction of Arab society as static, it portrays Arab society as being in a state of constant change; as analytical because it attempts to explain rather than merely describe the phenomena under study; as dialectical because it emphasizes the social contradictions at the root of the ongoing struggle to transcend dehumanizing conditions; as sociological because it examines human behavior and issues in a social and historical context; and as critical because, out of deep concern and affinity, it calls for the replacement of the prevailing order with a new one.

Simply put, Arab society is presented in this analysis from a self-critical Arab perspective. This effort constitutes an integral part of the task of developing an Arab sociology free both from the metaphysical thinking that traditionally prevails in the Arab world and from Western knowledge rooted in relations of domination (that is, "Orientalism"). In urging the decolonization of Arab sociology, Khatibi calls this process "double criticism."[2] Another Moroccan writer, Taher ben Jelloun, also calls for the liberation of sociology from its colonial legacy, which he sees as emanating from the need of a colonial administration "to know perfectly the society it had decided to dominate. Sociology was the part of the colonial strategy of penetration and pacification."[3] Hence the dual task undertaken here of unlearning and relearning.

Some Characteristic Features of Arab Society

Chapter 3 includes a comprehensive analysis of Arab identity in its many aspects. We need to begin, however, with an overview of contemporary Arab society. The most important thing to remember about the characteristics summarized below is that they constitute interrelated features, not elements to be considered in isolation.

Social Diversity. The literature on social diversity and cleavages in Arab society and the Middle East as a whole suffers from several fallacies, two of which are most pertinent here. One is the tendency, particularly among Orientalists, to speak both of the mosaic nature of Arab society and of the existence of a unified mentality, or one Arab mind, without any awareness of the contradiction between these two abstractions. The other is the emphasis either on communal cleavages or on class conflicts, with the result that one becomes explanatory while the other is ignored. The interplay and coincidence of these two cleavages are rarely examined in their historical and social contexts. The diversity that characterizes Arab society needs to be analyzed within a three-dimensional framework: (a) a homogeneity-heterogeneity continuum; (b) the processes of conflict-accommodation-assimilation; and (c) social class cleavages.

The continuum that covers the range from a completely homogeneous society to one of great heterogeneity encompasses a complex system of vertical loyalties and communal differentiations (ethnic, linguistic, sectarian, tribal, local, regional, and the like) that coincides as well as conflicts with social class cleavages. Arab society has historically been highly heterogeneous. Certainly, one may argue that there has recently been a resurgence of communal loyalties and mobilization, confirming the mosaic and segmentary structures of society. What cannot be granted is the static conception of these loyalties and cleavage as permanent, unchanging forms of differentiation.

The characterization of Arab society as heterogeneous, however, needs to be accompanied by an explicit clarification that not all Arab countries are similar in this respect. In fact, they differ widely in regard to their positions on the homogeneity-heterogeneity continuum. Compared to other Arab countries, Egypt and Tunisia, for instance, may be described as rather homogeneous as far as communal cleavages are concerned. These two countries tend to have fewer ethnic, religious, and tribal differences (and, hence, conflicts) than other Arab societies, and are characterized more by social complexity and social class cleavages. A second group of Arab countries, such as Lebanon and Sudan, occupy a position close to the opposite end of the continuum, each being more of a mosaic in structure and social composition. A third set, such as Syria,

Algeria, Arabia, and Morocco, tend to occupy positions more in the middle of the continuum.

The application of the conflict-accommodation-assimilation model reveals great diversity in Arab society in the handling of ethnic or class conflicts. Highly heterogeneous Arab countries like Lebanon and Sudan have fluctuated between accommodation and conflict, including sustained violent encounters between self-assertive communities. Here *accommodation* means adoption by the elites representing the different communities of a policy of coexistence without compromising their separate identities. Such communities achieved accommodation, for instance, in the Lebanese national pact of 1943. By contrast, attempts at maintaining stability through the use of some conflict-regulating practices, the management of differences, and consociational democracy have not been successful. Success eluded Lebanese and Sudanese elites because they failed to accommodate the divergent interests of their communities. Moreover, their commitment to the maintenance of the status quo—and their own power bases—reflects a lack of concern about growing socioeconomic inequalities. These elites never intended to concern themselves with the task of transcending cleavages or with the need to meld conflicting private identities into a more comprehensive national identity. On the contrary, they attempted to suppress any popular movements working toward such goals.

How do these lenses help us understand what we see when we look at the Arab world? If the two continua of homogeneity-heterogeneity and conflict-accommodation-assimilation are applied simultaneously to an analysis of Arab society, some tentative generalizations can be made. A few Arab countries—including Egypt and, to some extent, Tunisia and Libya—may be characterized as relatively homogeneous. Without communal fragmentation to focus conflict, it has been possible to foster a shared social identity. The historian Gamal Hamdan has argued that Egypt has certain historically significant features that make it a peculiar example of the Hegelian synthesis, combining thesis and antithesis in a "balanced and authentic composition" and rendering Egypt "the master of moderate solutions" and a "centrist nation in the full sense of the word." It is important to note the complex interactions necessary to achieve this balance. The basic elements contributing to this synthesis, according to Hamdan, are a relatively homogeneous population, centralized political unity, historical continuity, and geographical uniformity (that is, a single agricultural region extending along the Nile river and one desert oasis). "Egypt is the strongest force among Arab countries twice: once by its mere size, and once by its absolute homogeneity," Hamdan concludes.[4] Another Egyptian historian, Hussein Fawzi, has addressed himself to the same issue, noting that Egypt's homogeneity explains the continuous, unified way of life "underlying all those successive civilizations" that made Egypt "the most ancient of nations on the surface of the planet."[5]

This unique, agriculturally based social homogeneity may at least partly explain the presence of a highly centralized political system. This is reinforced by extreme bureaucratization and a strong consensus among Egyptians on issues of national identity, as well as on political issues and national heroes—such as Ahmad 'Arabi, Sa'ad Zaghloul, and Gamal Abdel Nasser—in modern history. The appearance of perhaps the first form of monotheism under Akhenaton in 1379–1362 B.C., and the ease with which internal uprisings have been crushed, have contributed as well. As a result of all these characteristics, a strong sense of Egyptian identity developed at the expense of other loyalties, including even Arab and Islamic affinities.

In contrast, and representative of a mosaic society par excellence, Lebanon and its elites managed with external support to impose a discriminatory political system on the country. This system ensured the dominance of private over public identities, and of the few over the many. Composed of several religious minorities, none of which constituted a majority, Lebanon devised a political system that gives one community (the Maronites) predominance over others. Exacerbating this religious (or, more accurately, sectarian) divisiveness were growing socioeconomic disparities. Hence, intercommunal relations oscillated between conflicts and elite attempts at accommodation. As a highly stratified communal society, Lebanon failed to establish a consensus on national identity or to reform its rigid, confessional (that is, sectarian) political system.[6] Aggravated by regional and domestic problems, the country suffered two civil wars during less than a half-century of independence.

Sudan also continues to suffer from recurrent civil wars and political crises. Social cleavages, political rivalries, and regional as well as ethnic and tribal disparities were exacerbated by the colonial legacy and regional conflicts. The resulting Sudan became a mosaic society unable to achieve national integration. The north-south civil war and the violent struggle for power between rival northern groups have been further complicated lately by attempts at the Islamization of Sudanese laws.[7]

With Egypt and Sudan marking the ends of the continuum, a number of Arab countries fall midway between relatively homogeneous societies and mosaic ones. These countries include Syria, Algeria, and Morocco, which despite their heterogeneity or pluralistic structures have managed to accommodate divergent communities and groups within relatively unified social and national orders. While their diverse communities—delineated by ethnic, sectarian, tribal, and local boundaries—continued to maintain their private and distinctive identities, a public national identity was forged and a strong central state was formed (or imposed) to ensure the reconciliation of private and public identities. The failure to democratize their political systems and to prevent the monopolization of power by certain elites, however, threaten these nationalistic achievements.

In the case of Syria, being socially heterogeneous (that is, composed of several religious, sectarian, ethnic, tribal, and local communities) has not undermined a strong sense of Arab identity and Syria's sense of historic responsibility as the citadel of the Arab world. Both the minorities in power and those without power have outdone one another in defending what are rhetorically defined as Arab causes.

Modern Algeria has been molded by a traumatic and unusual historical experience—a century and a quarter of national resistance culminating in a revolution that finally liberated the country from one of the harshest forms of colonization, that of French imperialism. This revolutionary legacy has enabled the society to overcome its ethnic and tribal differences but not its social disparities. Currently, bilingualism and hierarchical communal relationships are being slowly but steadily undermined by an active process of Arabization that will reinforce the dominant ideal that the "Algerian personality is an Arab personality and an integral part . . . of the Arab nation."[8] To be complete, however, I think this process needs to be accompanied by an equally significant process of democratization to favor diversity rather than imposed uniformity. Lack of democracy and centralized state capitalism have undermined civil society and contributed to the emergence of a militant Islamic movement.

Morocco historically has been more isolated and less vulnerable to foreign control than the other North African countries, and it has thus been conceptually and normatively unified. Yet the central authority could not exert its control over the whole country. Consequently, it was divided into at least three zones or concentric circles of power. The first circle, Bled el-Makhzen, represented the locus of power and was based in urban areas. The second circle represented subject tribes in intermediary zones surrounding the cities. The third circle, Bled es-Siba, represented peripheral and dissident tribes.[9] The concepts of tripartism and dualism are expressed in Abdallah Laroui's *The History of the Maghrib*. He concludes that social diversity changed its form and meaning from stage to stage, but "the image we retain of the Maghrib is one of a pyramid with different levels: anthropological, linguistic, socio-economic, in short historical, and at each level lies the sediment of an unresolved contradiction."[10] At the present time, Morocco continues to be highly pluralistic in structure and orientation.

These pluralistic societies and others such as Iraq and Yemen have managed in their modern history to achieve consensus occasionally on some fundamentals such as national identity. They have asserted the need for social and political integration and have created unified educational systems. Yet internal crises and divisiveness continue to characterize their history. These negative outcomes may be attributed mainly to a combination of external interventions, vertical loyalties, class cleavages, and, certainly, the lack of democracy. The observation of Hanna Batatu on the coincidence of communal and class divisions prior to the 1958 Iraqi revolution still applies today. He notes "a great degree of coincidence between all these hierarchies; that is, those who stood, say, at the top in the scale of power tended also to stand at the top with respect to wealth or in terms of religious, sectarian, ethnic, or status affiliation."[11] The coincidence of these communal and class divisions must still be seen today as providing the roots of Iraqi upheavals in the aftermath of the Gulf War.

Pyramidal Class Structure. Conventional Western literature on Arab and other Middle Eastern societies has persistently avoided any serious discussion of social class structure. Instead, it has conceived of Arab societies simply as a mosaic. At the margin of this mainstream discourse, however, there has been some occasional speculation on problems of social stratification. Whenever a discussion of this nature has taken place, it has evolved into a heated exchange. One point of view reaffirms the conclusions of the mosaic model and questions the relevance of class analysis. For instance, C. A. O. van Niewenhuijze and James Bill, in separate works, dismiss class analysis in economic terms and instead use Weberian concepts of status and power.[12] Similarly, Iliya Harik has more recently dismissed the thesis put forward by some writers that the Lebanese civil war is actually a class struggle and expressed his "belief that class distinctions in Lebanon are too obscure to sustain the class struggle argument."[13]

Bryan S. Turner, by contrast, has pointed out that anyone "who wants to develop a Marxist analysis of North Africa and the Middle East must start with a critique of the mosaic theory and all its related assumptions." Such a critique, he explains, is required because mosaic analysts believe "that traditional Middle Eastern societies were not 'class dominated' and that in the modern Middle East 'social class' is only in the process of emerging alongside other forms of social stratification."[14] Nicholas S. Hopkins has applied ideas of class derived from the Marxist tradition to changes in the social structure of an agricultural town in Tunisia, concluding that essential changes in the mechanization of agriculture and in the improvement of communications "led to a shift in the organization of work away from a pattern based on mobilization of labor within the household or the extended kindred . . . and toward a pattern of labor determined by wage labor." Consequently, this Tunisian agricultural town has shifted from a society in which rank was based "on vertical rather than on horizontal links" to one "based on class." Hopkins argues further that not only is there class in the objective sense, "there is also class consciousness, at least in embryonic, symbolic form."[15]

My own view is that the persistence of communal cleavages complicates rather than nullifies social class consciousness and struggle. This persistence of communal cleavages and vertical loyalties in some Arab countries is owing to the perpetuation of traditional systems in which communities are linked to their local *za'ims* (traditional leaders) through patron-client relationships. To the extent that constructive change can be introduced in these areas, such traditional systems will give way, increasingly, to other social and class relationships.

To Marxists, sectarianism, tribalism, and the like constitute false consciousness that masks class interests and mystifies class struggle. Western functionalists, by contrast, view these communal cleavages as "a premodern phenomenon, a residue of particularism and ascription incompatible with the trend toward achievement, universalism and rationality supposedly exhibited by industrial societies."[16] Western sociologists whose point of departure is a sociobiological paradigm have argued that ethnic and racial solidarity are extensions of kinship sentiments. For instance, Pierre van den Berghe asserts that there "exists a general behavioral predisposition, in our species as in many others, to react favorably toward other organisms to the extent that these organisms are biologically related to the actor. The closer the relationship is, the stronger the preferential behavior." He concludes, therefore, that "ethnic solidarity is an extension of kin-based solidarity—that is, of nepotism." But he realizes that as human societies grow, the boundaries of ethnicity become "increasingly manipulated and perverted to other ends, including domination and exploitation."[17] I would argue, however, that just because ethnicity is more primordial than class does not mean that it is always more salient. As distinct principles of social organization, class and ethnicity interpenetrate in complex and varying ways. This interplay becomes one of the most difficult problems facing sociological analysis of complex societies.

Nevertheless, examination of the Arab situation in depth reveals a clearly pyramidal social class structure. This means that the majority of the people are relatively poor. The middle class, in turn, is significantly small in size. Wealth and power are concentrated in few hands. This kind of triangular class structure differs sharply from the diamond-shaped structure that indicates the presence in society of a significantly large middle class—the configuration for which Westerners interested in class analysis always look. In both structures, however, social class formations proceed from contradictory relationships and antagonistic interests.

How do class-based configurations relate to the continua discussed earlier? Social class cleavages based on social contradictions, divergent positions in the socioeconomic structures, and control or lack of control over the means of production are more relevant than communal cleavages in relatively homogeneous Arab societies such as Egypt and Tunisia. In more pluralistic societies, such as Syria and Algeria, where class is becoming increasingly relevant, there is some coincidence of class and communal cleavages. In mosaic societies such as Lebanon, there is much greater evidence, not of communal cleavages as such, but of communal stratification. This means that besides class cleavages, one or a few communities enjoy more power, wealth, and status than others. In a previous study on the relationship between religious affiliations and political orientations among university students in Lebanon, I concluded that strong ideological positions can be analytically connected to class origins if these connections are examined in their historical and socioeconomic contexts. One basic finding of this study was that "those students who come from deprived families and deprived religious communities—such as the poor Shi'ite students—showed the most significant inclination to adopt the leftist ideology. In contrast, those students who came from privileged families and privileged religious communities—such as the rich Maronite students—showed the most significant inclination to adopt the rightist ideology." [18]

One may also suggest that the greater the socioeconomic inequalities in mosaic societies, the more the likelihood of uprisings. However, such uprisings are more likely to result in civil wars (in which one controlling elite is substituted for another), rather than popular revolutions (in which society is transformed, and the dominant order is replaced by a new order). The reverse pattern is more likely to emerge in relatively homogeneous societies. In the latter, the greater the inequalities, the greater the class solidarity, mobilization, and prospect of revolution. If these assumptions are correct, one should expect the first Arab popular revolution to take place in Egypt or Tunisia. This does not, however, exclude the possibility that revolutions may occur in more pluralistic societies as well.

Social Complementarity. This sociological analysis begins with the assumption that the Arab world constitutes a single society rather than a disparate collection of sovereign states. The latter view is often advanced by Western mainstream scholars and the mass media, but it ignores the artificial nature of many of these recently created political entities. If one begins by looking at social organization rather than political structures, one discovers that social diversity and local or regional peculiarities do not preclude Arab commonalities, especially in those areas addressed by this book—such as family, social class structure, religious and political behavior, patterns of living, change, and the impact of economic development. Many of these commonalities will be discussed in the next chapter. Here, the point is that political fragmentation has been caused by the interplay of internal and external forces. Current political configurations—the array of particular states born of specific international circumstances—thus cannot be expected to reflect social and cultural complementarity, however strong its presence may be. Nor are common Arab interests and shared aspirations for unity provided with an outlet in contemporary political configurations. Thus the bewilderment with which Arab intellectuals have looked at their society after the defeats in the Six-Day War of June 1967 and the 1991 Gulf War is an expression of concern, rather than a farewell to the renaissance (*nahda*) of Arab society or an announcement of the death of Arab civilization.[19] Yet the Gulf War may prove much more devastating than Arabs can admit.

Transition and the Arab Renaissance. One of the basic contradictions of mainstream Western scholarship is its simultaneous emphasis on the complexity of Arab conflict on the one hand and its portrayal of Arab society as constant and static on the other. In fact, some Arab intellectuals have themselves deplored the lack of change and lamented the futility of struggle. A more sober sociohistorical examination of Arab society, coupled with contextualized interpretations of Arab writers' reflections, would show that Arabs have actively struggled for a century and a half to meet the challenges of modern times. The result has been a battle between the old and the new in every aspect of human life. Confrontations between vehemently opposed forces have led to a strenuous process of rebirth.

The intensely transitional nature of contemporary Arab society makes generalization difficult. Arab society today is neither traditional nor modern, old or new, capitalist or socialist or feudal, Eastern or Western, religious or secular, particularistic or universalistic in its cultural orientations. It is this very complexity that led to my definition of Arab society as an association of all these contradictions and several others in a contradictory world. Nevertheless, crises are ever-present, equaled only by dreams of overcoming them.

The tendency in mainstream Western literature to ignore the complex transitional situation of the present-day Middle East may explain some of the prevailing oversimplifications and misconceptions. Of particular significance in this respect are those oversimplifications pertaining to structural change and the definition of Arab identity. Since the establishment of Israel and the emergence of a large body of literature to legitimize its existence and territorial expansions, these oversimplifications of Arab society have grown even wilder. Development in the Middle East, we are told, is hampered largely by resistance to change, and the root of this vehement resistance lies in cultural attitudes and in the individual and collective psyche. This view ignores the significance of the prevailing relationships of dependency, as well as the existing socioeconomic and political structures, and reveals the animosity toward Arabs (and especially toward Muslims) that underlies many scholarly pretensions. Thus Menahem Milson asserts, for example, that there is a need "to take into consideration certain cultural attitudes to power and government deeply rooted in Islamic tradition, which tend to discourage resistance to the incumbent government, no matter how it assumed power. The very possession of coercive power becomes, as it were, a source of political legitimation."[20]

Patriarchal Relations. The family is the basic unit of social organization and production in traditional and contemporary Arab society, and it remains a relatively cohesive institution at the center of social and economic activities. It is patriarchal; pyramidally hierarchical, particularly with respect to sex and age; and extended. Yet the Arab family has been undergoing significant changes as a result of structural change at the level of production and needs to be examined carefully. It must be placed in the context of the transitional nature of Arab society. Both the internal and external confrontations that Arab families are facing and the struggle for social transformation that Arab society is waging emerge clearly from such an examination.

The traditional Arab family constitutes an economic and social unit in all three Arab patterns of living—bedouin, rural, and urban—in the sense that all members cooperate to secure its livelihood and improve its standing in the community. Farms, shops, businesses, and herds are commonly owned and managed for the benefit of all. The success or failure of an individual member becomes that of the family as a whole. This centrality of the family as the basic socioeconomic unit is now being increasingly challenged by the state and other social institutions. But the network of interdependent kinship relations continues to prevail. In this network, the father continues to wield authority, assume responsibility for the family, and expect respect and unquestioning compliance with his instructions. Thus the continued dominance of the family as the basic unit of social organization and production has contributed to the diffusion of patriarchal relations and to their application to similar situations within other social institutions. Specifically, the same patriarchal relations and values that prevail in the Arab family seem also to prevail at work, at school, and in religious, political, and social associations. In all of these, a father figure rules over others, monopolizing authority, expecting strict obedience, and showing little tolerance of dissent. Projecting a paternal image, those in positions of responsibility (as rulers, leaders, teachers, employers, or supervisors) securely occupy the top of the pyramid of authority. Once in this position, the patriarch cannot be dethroned except by someone who is equally patriarchal.

Hisham Sharabi points out that because of the prevailing patriarchy, modernization could only be "dependent modernization," that is, distorted and inverted modernity. In other words, this modernization has not only failed to break down patriarchal relations and forms, it has provided the ground for producing a hybrid—the present neopatriarchal society, which is neither modern nor traditional, but which limits participation by its members because of the continued dominance exercised by single leaders.[21]

Primary Group Relations. A highly distinctive feature of Arab society is the continuing dominance of primary group relations—that is, those characterized by intimate, personal, informal, noncontractual, comprehensive, and extensive relations. By entering into these primary relations, which they do freely and spontaneously, individuals engage in an unlimited commitment to one another. They derive satisfaction from extensive affiliations and develop a sense of belonging. These relations, however, though they result in lifelong friendships, may also contribute to the development of repressed hostilities and jealousies. They are centered in the extended family and in the communal system typical of bedouin, agricultural, and service-oriented societies. Thus, in contrast to the atomized industrial and capitalist societies of the West, social relations in mercantilistic and agricultural Arab society exhibit the following characteristics.

First, Arabs tend to interact as committed members of a group, rather than as independent individuals who constantly assert their apartness and privacy. My own experience upon my arrival in the United States illustrates this. One of the first things I observed was that Americans travel on their own, hardly relating to one another. This is in sharp contrast to Arabs, who almost always travel in the close company of two or more people, intimately and spontaneously engaged in lively conversation. Finding myself in the moving crowds of New York City, however, I realized I had to view the people around me in new ways. I realized that what I saw in America were crowds not groups. What you have is a mass of individuals who maintain their psychological distance in spite of their spatial closeness. What I observed was people colliding into each other rather than relating to each other. In fact, some seemed to be speaking audibly or even loudly, but to themselves, almost completely oblivious of others. Since then I have been intrigued by the loneliness that exists in the midst of city crowds. Personal space seems to be narrowing, in sharp contrast to the social psychological distance, which continues to expand.

Second, Arabs, even in big cities, experience a strong sense of belonging through sustained commitments and loyalties to family, community, and friends. What seems to be the source of this sense of well-being is affiliation rather than the individual achievement that characterizes Western capitalist societies. Yet both orientations can have negative consequences. Arabs, especially the young, complain a great deal about family and community pressures and the constant interference in their private lives. Citizens of capitalist, atomized societies complain of the lack of family life, while insisting on narrowly defined contractual commitments and cherishing their privacy.

Spontaneity and Expressiveness. Notwithstanding religious taboos and social and political repression, Arabs tend to express themselves spontaneously and freely in several areas of life, particularly in those related to human emotions and the arts. Undeterred by their need for affiliation and group solidarity, they openly express their likes and dislikes. Joy and sadness, hope and despair, satisfaction and discontent, congeniality and aggression all characterize their art. Hence, there is the perception by themselves and others that they tend to be emotional rather than rational and calculating.

Of course, to overstate this tendency and to make such generalizations without appropriate qualifications may border on the stereotyping of a whole culture. A keen observer, however, cannot fail to take note of such spontaneity and intensity of feelings, particularly in times of stress or joy and in areas of interpersonal relationships. To balance this, such an observer would also have to notice the existence of religious and political taboos and the tendency toward conformity. Moreover, self-censorship and the practice of *taqiyya* (dissembling—the denial of certain feelings and beliefs—in order to avoid certain persecution) also constrain emotional expression. Spontaneity and expressiveness encourage the Arab inclination toward the arts, particularly literature and poetry, at the expense of the sciences. To the extent that this is so, present-day Arab culture seems to be more literary than scientifically oriented.

Two related phenomena need to be mentioned. One manifestation of expressiveness is the emphasis on the significance of "the word" in Arab culture. Besides the role played by the word in literature and, especially, poetry, words are the most celebrated artistic elements in music and drawing (see Chapter 10). Another manifestation is the great stress on symbolism, imagery, and metaphor in everyday ordinary communication. As an example, an American receiving condolences on the death of his young daughter was moved when an Arab friend said, "Life is God's garden out of which, now and then, He picks the most beautiful flower."

Continuing Dependency and Underdevelopment. Arab society continues to suffer from dependency as well as widening gaps or disparities between the privileged few and the deprived classes. These disparities also emerge between rich and poor Arab countries and between Arab society and the developed societies of the West. Being increasingly integrated into the global capitalist economic system and locked into a network of dependent relations, the Arab world seems to lack control over its resources and destiny. Oil-wealth, neopatriarchal relations, and external control have all resulted in the emergence of marginal ruling families and classes, and a distorted development directed toward consumption rather than production. As indicated earlier, Arab society today is neither traditional nor modern. One feature of neopatriarchal societies, Hisham Sharabi has noted, is "the absence equally of genuine traditionalism and authentic modernity."[22] This distorted duality is made even more complex by another duality, the intra-Arab and inter-Arab stratification systems. The growing disparities between the lavishly rich and the desperately poor within the boundaries of specific countries are manifested either in great wealth enjoyed by the few in the midst of acute poverty (Egypt, Morocco) or unwavering poverty in the midst of unusual wealth (oil-producing countries).[23] The same patriarchal and neopatriarchal relations continue to prevail in both sets of countries. Nevertheless, rich Arab countries conduct themselves as regional powers by imposing a system of local dependency on poor countries. This intra-Arab stratification system results in a dual or even triple dependency, which weighs heavily on impoverished countries.

What adds to the complexity of this situation is the pressing need to cope with formidable modern challenges from within highly rigid systems. While there seems to be a strong determination to adopt and imitate the most fashionable and technologically sophisticated innovations, the process of development continues to be hindered by prevailing socioeconomic and political structures and by a network of authoritarian relationships.[24]

Alienation and the Lack of Civil Society. The conditions described above— dependency, underdevelopment, patriarchal and authoritarian relationships, social and political fragmentation, class distinctions, successive historical defeats, and a generalized state of repression—have rendered the Arab people and society powerless. Having lost control over its resources and destiny, and failing to develop a vision for the future, the society seems to lack a core and a will of its own. Instead, it drifts at the mercy of historic challenges and events. Its material and human resources have been harnessed for the benefit of a small segment of the population and on behalf of antagonistic external forces.

The Arab world does not seem to be a society that functions well. This is so because, in order for civil society to function properly, its affairs must be the affairs of the people themselves and not merely of the ruler and the state. Basic human rights and vital functions of society have been constantly undermined and curtailed by authoritarian regimes. Arabs have become powerless and subordinated to the whims of their rulers. Consequently, Arab states represent a force directed against society, and Arab society has been unable to cope with disasters. It needs to develop a will of its own if it is to confront trying historical challenges. Instead of realizing the dreams they have set for themselves for a century and a half, Arabs have undergone shockingly bitter experiences and setbacks. Goals such as national unity and state-building have eluded them. Equally unachievable has been the establishment of democratic institutions and associations. Even economic goals such as comprehensive development and the overcoming of socioeconomic disparities remain out of reach. In short, Arabs lack control over their destiny (see Chapter 12).

Successive failures to achieve such goals have reinforced the other conditions that continue to contribute to the strong sense of alienation. Arabs, as will be shown, have become powerless, not just in relation to the state, but even in relation to their own institutions. They are alienated from, and within, religious and family structures, institutions of learning, places of work, political parties, unions, and other sorts of social organizations. In all these instances, people are excluded from participation in the making of their own futures and the shaping of their own destinies; hence the growing gap between dream and reality.

The characteristic features noted above, and others that will be discussed in the next chapter, should be perceived as interrelated aspects of the present Arab social situation and should be seen in their social and historic contexts. To focus on them out of context or by separating out a few as independent variables is to miss what constitutes a distinctive Arab whole. One other point needs to be reasserted. These characteristic features are constantly changing, which requires us to use a dynamic rather than a static approach to the study of Arab society. Thus, what we might conclude at this stage is that fragmentation, disparities, dependency, alienation, underdevelopment, and the like represent major obstacles to the effective functioning of contemporary Arab society.

Basics of the Physical Setting, Demography, and Ecology

Some basic facts pertaining to the physical environment, demography and ecology of the Arab world need to be briefly described at this stage in preparation for a fuller discussion of issues of social diversity and integration in the next two chapters.

Physical Environment. The Arab homeland extends from the Gulf and the Zagros mountains on the Iranian frontier in the east to the Atlantic Ocean in the west, and from the Taurus range on the Turkish border in the north to Central Africa beyond the Sahara and the Horn of Africa in the south. This vast region is one of contrasting natural habitats, geological and topographic configurations, climates (mostly hot and deficient in rain), and patterns of settlement. This physical variation encompasses a wide range.[25] For instance, desert and semidesert areas that are virtually uninhabited (except for scattered oases) constitute more than 80 percent of the total area of the Arab homeland. The climate of the desert (a high-pressure area) is characterized by extremes in temperature, lack of rain, and the bedouin way of life, with its legacy of authentic tribalism. By contrast, the coastal strips of land that embrace the Mediterranean and extend on both sides of the Red Sea to the Arabian Sea and the Gulf are mostly low-pressure areas of moderate temperature (rainy during the winter, and rainless and hot during the summer). There are also plateaus, rising less than 1,500 feet (492 meters), in the Maghrib, the Fertile Crescent, and Arabia. Moreover, great mountain ranges separate the cultivable lands and coastal strips from the deserts. The peaks of the Atlas range of the Maghrib and the Zagros ranges reach over 13,000 feet (4,000 meters). The Taurus range separating Syria and Turkey, the Yemen Highlands, and Jabal al-Sheikh

(Mount Hermon) rise over 12,000 feet (3,700 meters). A range of mountains in the Levant overlooks the Mediterranean and separates the coastal strip from the arid interior. The inhabitants of these mountainous areas are peasants, villagers, and minorities whose relative isolation, communal relations, and tribal social organization have made them historically less accessible and vulnerable to invaders and central government control.

Also present are the river valleys of the Nile and the Tigris-Euphrates, which are agrarian and densely populated. In contrast to the mountainous areas, river irrigation requires centralized planning and government regulation. This made the inhabitants highly accessible to government control. The peasants of Egypt and Mesopotamia (homelands of the most ancient civilizations and empires) have had a totally different pattern of living in comparison with the bedouin of the deserts and the peasants of the mountainous areas of the Levant, the Maghrib, and Yemen.

Small valleys and plains overshadowed by mountains, steppes, and plateaus exist in different parts of the Arab homeland, particularly in the Levant, Yemen, and the Maghrib. In addition, there are a few lowland areas, such as that of the Dead Sea (395 meters below sea level). These contrasting environmental settings and climates have contributed historically to the emergence of contrasting patterns of living (see Chapter 4 on bedouin, rural, and urban patterns of living) and have endowed them with distinctive cultural identities.

Population. The numbers presented here are estimates that indicate certain trends. Demographic trends, however, need to be examined in the context of more comprehensive social structures. The population of the Arab countries was estimated to exceed 175 million in the 1980s and is expected to reach almost 300 million early in the twenty-first century. A century earlier, the total Arab population was estimated at around 22 million, and increased to 38 million by the beginning of the twentieth century. The population of Egypt increased from 2.5 million in 1820 to 5 million in 1860, 9.6 million in 1897, 21 million in 1952, and 48 million in 1985. It is expected to reach 67 million by the end of this century. [26]

Other basic demographic trends and indicators, not unlike those of other Third World countries, may be briefly described. For instance, the population increase has been the result of a sustained high birthrate and declining death rate. Since the beginning of the second half of the twentieth century, the average annual rate of population growth has ranged between 2.5 percent and 3 percent owing to a crude birthrate ranging between 28 and 50 per thousand and a declining death rate currently ranging between 3 and 20 per thousand. How is this population distributed? Population density in the Arab world must be seen in terms of the large stretches of uninhabited desert and semidesert, or arid, areas. Estimates disregarding this fact were as low as 12/km^2 in the early

1980s, ranging between 1/km² in Libya and 437/km² in Bahrain. These estimates become totally different once desert areas have been taken into consideration. The rates jumped to 1,049 per km² in Egypt (some estimates are as high as 1,200 and 1,400), 750 in Qatar and Bahrain, 395 in Saudi Arabia, 132 in Kuwait, 90 in Jordan, 47 in Iraq, and 53 in Syria.

This Arab population may be described as young in age and as dependent. Estimates show that 45 percent of the population are below 15 years of age, that half are between 15 and 65 years old, and that only 5 percent are over 65 years old. In contrast, the average rate of population below 15 years of age is estimated to be 37 percent for the whole world, 28 percent for the developed societies, and 42 percent for the less developed societies. Life expectancy in the 1980s averaged about 55 years in the Arab world, ranging from 46 in Somalia to 72 in Kuwait.

Quantitatively, Arab education has changed dramatically since the middle of the twentieth century. By the late 1970s, enrollment in elementary schools increased for all Arab countries, from 39 percent of children 6–11 years old (28 percent for girls and 50 percent for boys) in 1960 to 48 percent in 1965, 51 percent in 1975, and 60 percent in 1977 (46 percent for girls and 72 percent for boys). The trend has continued, especially in some countries, such as Oman, where rates of elementary school enrollment increased from 3 percent in 1970 to 69 percent in 1980; in Algeria, where this rate changed from 36 percent in 1960 to 60 percent in 1970 and 81 percent in 1980; and in Syria, where it went from 51 percent in 1960 to 80 percent in 1970 and 99 percent in 1980. These rates continued to be relatively low in some countries, among them Sudan (from 12 percent to 24 percent to 37 percent), Morocco (from 33 percent to 34 percent to 46 percent), and Somalia (from 4–5 percent to 48 percent). On the whole, taking 1960 as a base line (100 percent), the number of elementary students in all Arab countries increased 349 percent in 1977 (in comparison to an increase of 528 percent in intermediary and 700 percent in secondary schooling). Qualitatively, education also improved; it was extended to poor and rural areas as well as to women; it was made public rather than private; and it was Arabized.[27]

A similar trend is reflected in the ongoing urbanization process. Because of natural growth and rural–urban migration, the percentage of urban population increased from 10 percent at the beginning of the twentieth century to 40 percent in the 1970s and is expected to reach 70 percent by the end of the century. The rates of urbanization, however, differ widely in different Arab countries. Some of them are closer to city states, with an urbanization rate of over 80 percent (95 percent in Kuwait, and about 80 percent in both Bahrain and the United Arab Emirates). Some others continue to be essentially rural, with an urbanization rate as low as 30 percent or less, including Yemen,

Oman, and Sudan. In between, there are those Arab countries that are about equally divided between rural and urban, such as Syria, Egypt, and Tunisia. As will be shown in Chapter 4, rural-urban migration has developed into an issue of grave concern because among other things it both reflects and influences socioeconomic inequalities. Underdevelopment, the decline of agriculture, and food dependency are affected as well. Other results of urbanization include the increased availability of social services, the centralization of power, and the intensification of social and political tensions. Thus the phenomenon of rural-urban migration can be understood only in its social structural and historical contexts.

Another vital demographic issue is labor migration. As pointed out by Fred Halliday, "We are seeing a process of increased inequality and deterioration in the productive and human resources of the Arab world: first, between the oil-rich and population-rich states; and second, between the Arab world as a whole and the industrialized economies." By 1980 more than 3 million Arabs had migrated to other Arab states, and since 1945 more than 15 million have migrated to Europe, where they currently form minority groups vulnerable to acute discrimination (850,000 Algerians, 250,000 Moroccans, and 60,000 Tunisians have settled in France).[28] An issue of grave concern is the magnitude of Arab labor migration to Arab oil-producing countries, estimated to have doubled between 1973 and 1975, and reaching four and a half million by the mid 1980s. At issue also is the fact that Arab and non-Arab labor migrants constitute over half of the populations of some oil-producing countries.[29]

One final demographic issue of great significance is the confinement of women to family and domestic production. In addition to being occupied with housework, women have been active participants in such economic activities as cloth-making, weaving, sewing, livestock care, farming, and the fetching of water. More recently, they have worked outside their homes as secretaries, teachers, nurses, cleaners, factory workers, shop saleswomen, and the like. Yet, as pointed out by Huda Zurayk and several others, such as Fatima Mernissi, their varied and complex work has gone largely unacknowledged. So far, "the nature of women's work places it largely outside the production boundary, and thus it goes largely unmeasured, unrecognized, and unacknowledged in systems of economic and social accounting."[30]

Ecology. Some unique phenomena have emerged as a result of the historical interplay between the two constituent elements (of people and geography) in Arab society. One of the most visible is the relationship between contrasting natural habitats, or physical variations, and patterns of settlement. It is no accident that desert and semidesert areas have been the homelands of the bedouin. Rather, human adjustment to contrasting environmental settings resulted in the formation of contrasting patterns of living (bedouin, rural, and urban), each with its own distinctive social organization and value orientations.

It also determined to a great extent the nature of the relationships among them. Conflicting interests often resulted in violent encounters and the development of negative images and perceptions of one another (see Chapter 4).

In addition to settlement patterns, forms of rule have varied under ecological influences. We have noted that in contrast to rain-fed areas (Syria, Maghrib, Yemen), the river-irrigated valleys of the Nile and the Tigris-Euphrates required the development of centralized rule. The rain-fed areas, on the other hand, have been inhabited by relatively isolated and diverse communities. Their location made them less accessible to government control and to outside invasions. This also explains why minorities sought refuge or survived in mountainous areas—such as the Berbers in the Maghrib, the Zaydis in Yemen, the Kurds in Iraq, the Maronites in Lebanon, and the Alawites in Syria.

Factors like geographic centrality, the struggle against aridity and desolation, internal strife, and external invasions may have resulted in the appearance of the three great religions of the area. Perhaps one of the most relevant phenomena is the emergence of monotheism in Egypt, a development that could not have occurred in a fragmented society (see Chapter 7).

Successive civilizations, such as the Sumerian, Babylonian, Assyrian, Egyptian, Aramaean, and Canaanite, appeared in this area, expanded to their natural limits, and then declined. By doing so, they unified the region and left a legacy of great historical consequence to the world that endures to the present. A part of this process was the human migration from Arabia to the Fertile Crescent, Egypt, Sudan, and the Maghrib that facilitated Arabization and, later, Islamization. The historic interplay between geographical habitats and inhabitants also contributed to the emergence of the four distinctive regional identities of the present Arab world: the Maghrib, extending over 4,715,443 km^2 and constituting half the area of the Arab homeland; the Nile Valley; the Fertile Crescent; and Arabia.

Conclusion

The centrality of the Arab world in ancient and modern times has qualified it to serve as an important nodal point in human history. It has acted as a passage connecting Asia, Africa, and Europe. It has produced some of the most important intellectual, cultural, and religious contributions of recorded history. It is this position at human and geographic crossroads, and not merely its oil and other resources, that makes the Arab world so strategically significant.

This chapter serves as a prelude to further exploration of the issues of social and political integration analyzed in the following chapters. It also provides, along with the remaining chapters of this section, a framework of analysis for a more comprehensive examination of the structures and dynamics of society, culture and state in the Arab world that are undertaken in Parts II and III.

3   Arab Identity

E pluribus unum

A critical study of Arab consciousness of a sense of identity begins by discarding idealist views of identity that overemphasize similarities. My analysis is dialectical, attaching greater significance to common characteristics and interests in the context of history and networks of relationships. Contextualization allows us to connect similarities as well as distinctive differences.

From this perspective, identity refers to the sharing of essential elements that define the character and orientation of people and affirm their common needs, interests, and goals with reference to joint action. At the same time it recognizes the importance of differences. Simply put, a nuanced view of national identity does not exclude heterogeneity and plurality. This is not an idealized view, but one rooted in sociological inquiry, in which heterogeneity and shared identity together help form potential building blocks of a positive future for the Arab world.

Yet the dilemma of reconciling plurality and unity constitutes an integral part of the definition of Arab identity. In fact, one flaw in the thinking by Arabs about themselves is the tendency toward an idealized concept of identity as something that is already completely formed, rather than as something to be achieved. Hence, there is a lack of thinking about the conditions that contribute to the making and unmaking of national identity. The belief that unity is inevitable, a foregone conclusion, flows from this idealized view of it.

Another equally serious flaw is the tendency among Arab nationalists to think in terms of separate and independent forces of unity and forces of divisiveness, ignoring the dialectical relationship between these forces. Thus, we have been told repeatedly that there are certain elements of unity (such as language, common culture, geography, or shared history) as well as certain elements of fragmentation (such as imperialism, sectarianism, tribalism, ethnic solidarity [*shu'ubiyya*], localism, or regionalism). If, instead, we view these forces from the vantage point of dialectical relations, the definition of Arab identity involves a simultaneous and systematic examination of both the processes of unification and fragmentation. This very point makes it possible to argue that Arabs can belong together without being the same; similarly, it can be seen that they may have antagonistic relations without being different. Furthermore, under certain specific conditions that must be consciously created by Arabs themselves, old identities may fade and new ones emerge.

Thus, it is necessary to describe the forces of unity and the forces of divisiveness in relation to each other. These forces operate within the context of underlying conflicts and confrontations and under certain specific conditions. Arab identity is therefore developed to the extent that it manifests itself through a sense of belonging and a diversity of affiliations. Arab identity relies, as well, on a shared culture and its variations. Arabs also recognize a shared place in history and common experiences. Similarly, social formations and shared economic interests have helped to shape Arab identity. And, finally, Arab identity is shaped by specific, shared external challenges and conflicts.

The Arab Sense of Belonging

The great majority of the citizens of Arab countries view themselves and are viewed by outsiders as Arabs. Their sense of Arab nationhood is based on what they have in common—namely, language, culture, sociopolitical experiences, economic interests, and a collective memory of their place and role in history. This sense of nationhood is constantly being formed and reformed, reflecting changing conditions and self-conceptions; together these exclude complete separation as well as complete integration. In all instances, the way communities relate to one another is reinforced by shared images and conceptions, and not merely by what they actually are. As a result of the combined influence of these conditions and orientations, identity may acquire narrower or wider meanings in particular historical circumstances.

Since its inception, Arab national identity has been seen as based primarily on language. Albert Hourani began his most famous book, *Arabic Thought in the Liberal Age*, with the statement that Arabs are "more conscious of their language than any people in the world."[1] This notion is asserted even more strongly by Jacques Berque, who points out that "the East is the home of the word," that "the Arabic language scarcely belongs to the world of men; rather, it seems to be lent to them," and that "Arabic writing is more suggestive than informative."[2]

It has often been stated that the great majority of Arabs speak Arabic as their mother tongue and thus feel that they belong to the same nation regardless of race, religion, tribe, or region. This explains the tendency to dismiss the existing states as artificial and to call for political unity coinciding with linguistic identity. The prevailing view is that only a small minority of the citizens of Arab countries do not speak Arabic as their mother tongue and lack a sense of being Arab; this minority category includes the Kurds, Berbers, Armenians, and the ethnolinguistic groups of southern Sudan.[3] Fewer still are those who speak Arabic as their mother tongue without sharing with the majority a sense of nationhood, a trend that may exist among the Maronites of Lebanon in times of conflict. Most other minority groups, such as the Orthodox Christians, Shi'ites, Alawites, and Druze, consider themselves Arabs with some qualifications and reservations.

There is, in fact, unanimous agreement among theoreticians of Arab nationalism on the great significance of language. The Iraqi historian Abd al-Aziz Duri has observed that it was language that historically contributed to the development of Arab consciousness prior to the emergence of Islam.[4] Initially, Arabism "had an ethnic focus, but [it] later took on a linguistic and cultural connotation. The two currents, Islam and Arabism, were closely linked at first, but subsequently followed separate courses. While both remained important to Arab development, it was the successes and failures of Arabism that determined the eventual geographic and human boundaries of the Arab nation."[5]

This relationship between language and national identity is stressed more emphatically by another Iraqi scholar and ideologue, Sati' al-Husari, who dismisses several other elements, including religion, economy, and geography, as irrelevant to the formation of nationalism. For him, only language and history define national identity. The former is "the heart and spirit of the nation," and the latter is its "memory and feeling." Consequently, those "people who speak one language must have one heart and one spirit, and so they must constitute one nation and therefore one state."[6] (Language, it should be noted here, is not a mere instrument of communication or container of ideas and feelings; it is the embodiment of a whole culture and a set of linkages across time and space.)

The conception of Arab identity as being primarily linguistic lends itself to several criticisms. First, some other basic elements have to be taken into account in any serious and systematic attempt at defining national identity. These other elements are many and varied; they include social formations, economy, geography, culture in a broad sense, ethnicity, regionalism, external challenges and conflicts, and religion. (I shall have more to say about each of these in the following chapters.) Second, a definition of Arab identity in linguistic terms would have to demonstrate the uniqueness of the Arabic language in comparison to those of other societies in which groups shared the same language but evolved into different nationalities. Third, a definition of Arab identity rooted primarily or solely in language tends to ignore several aspects of the present state of the Arabic language—such as the continuing gap between written and spoken Arabic, the different Arab dialects, the bilingualism in some Arab countries, and the limited literacy of the Arab masses. It is true that literary Arabic "tends to become the spoken language of the whole of the Arab world"[7]—a development that took Arabic in the opposite direction from Latin, which evolved into separate languages—but these aspects cannot be ignored. Fourth, the Arab sense of belonging has to be assessed in the light of overlapping and conflicting affiliations. Among the most significant of these overlapping identities are religious, regional, kinship or tribal, and ethnic affiliations. Let us look briefly at each of these identities in turn.

Since the overwhelming majority of Arabs are Muslim, the two identities are often viewed as inseparable. Indeed, the people of the Maghrib hyphenated the two in an attempt to assert their distinctive character vis-à-vis the European invaders. In the eastern Arab world, however, there have been two divergent currents within Arabism—one essentially religious and the other more secular. In comparison to Islamic reformers like Jamal Eddin al-Afghani, Muhammed Abdu, and Rashid Rida, early Muslim and non-Muslim Arabists viewed Arab nationalism as a secular alternative to the Islamic Ottoman caliphate. The concept of *umma* (nation) began to lose its religious meaning and to refer to solidarity based on common language, territory, economic interests, culture, history, and destiny. As the demand for Arab rights within the Ottoman caliphate grew, some of these early Arabists, such as Abd al-Rahman al-Kawakibi, began "to promote the notion of a secular Arab nationalism, claiming that Arabic-speaking Muslims, Christians and Jews were 'Arab' before they were members of their respective religious communities."[8]

Yet, most Arabists, especially today in response to the emergence of Islamic fundamentalism, continue to assert the complementarity, if not the synonymity, of Islam and Arabism. For example, Abd al-Aziz Duri has concluded that "Islam unified Arabs and provided them with a message, an ideological framework, and a state." He also noted that "the Islamic movement came about as Arab in its environment and leadership," and that Arabs in the formative era of Islam had "a strong sense of their unity and distinctiveness, for the state was Arab, the language was Arabic, and Arabs were the carriers of the message of Islam."[9] As pointed out earlier, Duri himself has indicated that Islam and Arabism "were closely linked at first, but subsequently followed separate courses."[10]

Another prominent Arab historian, Constantine Zurayk, argues that tensions have existed between Islam and other forms of solidarity throughout its history. Tribal, ethnic, and nationalist loyalties have remained alive, undermining the establishment of genuine unity within the *umma*. With respect to the relationship between Islam and Arabism, Zurayk concludes that "from the beginning a certain ambivalence existed between Islam and Arabism. Islam is a universal religion, but it was revealed to an Arab prophet through the Arabic tongue, and its rise and early spread beyond Arabia were due to Arab zeal, energy and struggle. The Umayyad rule in Damascus was, to a large extent, Arab in attitude and policy. The non-Arab converts, largely of Persian stock, were reduced to the ranks of clients (*mawali*), which caused them to become disaffected, to seek to vindicate (in the name of Islam) their claim to equality with the Arabs, and to work for the overthrow of Arab dominance." These very conditions contributed to the emergence of *shu'ubiyya* (peoplehood or ethnicity). Islamic political life became "an arena of conflict between Arabs, Persians, Turks, Kurds, and Berbers." [11]

Such developments, Duri points out, "furthered the idea that the *umma* was something based on the Arabic language and Arab culture. This was often stated by writers of the third/ninth century and after. Jahiz, for example, considered Arabic the most important tie. . . . Ibn Qutaiba defended Arabic and the Arabs as being a nation before Islam and after. Farabi found that language, natural traits, and character comprised formative elements of the *umma*. . . . He distinguished the human *umma* from the *milla* based on religion. Mas'udi talked of the major nations (*umam*) in history, and indicated their formative elements: (a) geographic conditions , . . and (b) language . . . Ibn Khaldun . . . generally used *umma* to mean nation and *milla* to mean religious community." [12]

What does "community" mean in the distinction between Arabism and nationalism? The twentieth century witnessed the collapse of the Ottoman Islamic caliphate and the rise of nationalism. The conflict between the two currents, however, has continued unabated to the present time, when Islamic fundamentalism is posing itself as an alternative to secular nationalism (see Chapters 7 and 8). Indeed, the new emergence of fundamentalism has now problematized the relationship between nationalism and religious identity. The predominance of Islam (90 percent of Arabs are Muslims) and the rise of religious fundamentalism since the Iranian revolution in 1979 do not in the long run mean a downgrading of secular nationalism. Religious fundamentalism lends itself to many conflicting interpretations. It is also responsible for the creation of opposed forces within its ranks, and for internal and external as well as conservative and radical manipulations. Furthermore, as will be demonstrated in a separate chapter on religious behavior, social analysis reveals the predominance of sect over religion per se. The prevailing socioeconomic structures and political arrangements promote sectarian and communal affiliations within the same society at the expense of a more general and shared religiosity, as well as of national and class interests.

Thus the relationship between sectarianism and Arabism is also important to sort out. Persons and groups in the eastern Arab world see themselves and are seen by others in religious terms—as Sunnis, Shi'ites, Druze, Alawites, and Maronites. They are not merely members of a certain religion, however, but first and foremost are seen as Arabs. In fact, the social-pyschological distances between some sects within the same religion may be greater than the distance perceived between different religions. This situation is not exclusively confined to Lebanon. The Kuwaiti sociologist Muhammed Rumayhi detected such distances between Sunnis and Shi'ites in the Gulf states even before the Iraq-Iran war, noting that in the 1970s "no Sunni candidate who ran for elections could win in electoral districts inhabited mostly by Shi'ites. Similarly, no Shi'ite candidate could win in Sunni electoral districts. . . . It has become a tradition that electoral districts are closed circles for specific tribes and sects." [13] These sectarian solidarities have to be examined in the larger context of social and political organization, as well as patterns of hierarchical arrangements. As will be shown later, sectarianism is a mechanism for maintaining certain privileges or for redressing grievances.

What is the place of minorities in the use of sectarianism as identity? It may be argued that the above analysis cannot be applied to the Maghrib, because only Sunnis are present there. Instead, a more abstract characterization is made in the Maghrib of its identity as Islamic-Arab, using the motto of the Algerian revolution, "Islam is our religion, Arabic is our language, and Algeria is our homeland." Yet, on an intra-Arab or intra-Islamic level, even an open-minded and enlightened Moroccan intellectual and political leader such as 'Allal al-Fassi could not transcend sectarianism. This is shown in his explanation of why the Fatimids (a Shi'ite dynasty that ruled portions of northern Africa in A.D. 909–1171), who maintained that the caliph must be a descendant of the Prophet through his daughter Fatima, did not last long in Morocco. He says it was "because the idea they supported disagrees with the spirit of freedom that the nature of the land required . . . as well as with the Islamic model . . . which does not recognize the racial supremacy of a family or an individual." [14]

Beyond sectarianism is local or regional identity. A persistently strong affiliation undermining Arab national identity is *wataniyya* (regionalism or patriotism). Even artificially created countries seem to be developing identities of their own. Jordan, Kuwait and the Gulf states, Lebanon, and others have managed through the formation of sovereign orders and socialization to create separate identities. Increasingly, citizens of these countries define themselves and are defined by others in terms of their local affiliations. Nonetheless, they continue to assert their Arab identity and lament Arab disunity and divisiveness, while clinging to their existing local identities. In times of crisis and intra-Arab conflicts (such as the 1990–91 Gulf crisis), however, local identities tend to prevail only at the expense of Arab nationalism. In this context, local ruling families and classes lack legitimacy. Nevertheless, they have become increasingly entrenched through regional and international alliances and through the development of vested interests among influential segments of population who want to preserve the status quo. On normative and rhetorical levels, local leaders continue to assert their Arab identity and the need for Arab unity. They refer to the Arab world, and not their own countries, as constituting the *umma*. Yet they follow their own separate courses at the expense of Arabism.

Another ironic development is the peculiar brand of Arabism practiced by some pan-Arab regimes. Roger Owen has observed that control over mass media and education by these pan-Arab regimes was used to promote a "brand of Arabism designed to suggest that only the local regime was properly Arab or capable of acting in a truly Arab interest. Little by little the vocabulary of Arabism was altered to accommodate ideas and concepts designed to highlight regional difference and local particularity." [15]

Thus, besides the gap between words and deeds, there have been throughout the modern era three major nationalist orientations in the Arab world. As we have seen, one is pan-Arabism, which dismisses existing sovereign states as artificial creations and calls for Arab unity. Another is the local nationalist orientation, which insists on preserving the independence and sovereignty of existing states. In between these two is a regional nationalist orientation that seeks to establish some regional unity, such as a greater Syria or a greater Maghrib, either permanently or as a step toward a larger Arab unity.

The presence of these various national trends and the emergence of conflicts between *wataniyya* (patriotism) and *qawmiyya* (nationalism) have encouraged the development of scholarly investigations of the relationship between "Arab personality" and "regional personalities." For instance, the Egyptian sociologist El-Sayyid Yassin asks: "Is there one Arab national personality in spite of the multiplicity and variance of Arab regions from the [Atlantic] ocean to the Gulf? What are the characteristic features of this Arab personality? If there were an Arab national personality, how can we explain the psychological, civilizational, and social differences between the Iraqi personality and the Egyptian personality and the Tunisian personality?" [16] Attempting a normative and conciliatory conclusion, Yassin says that the Arab personality constitutes "the primary pattern," while "regional personalities" constitute "the secondary patterns."

Reconciling these varieties of nationalism continues to be the most challenging task confronting Arabs in their attempt to achieve the *nahda*. So far the efforts made to legitimize the status quo continue to work against an ability to transcend and to synthesize conflicting or overlapping affiliations.

The fact that the family constitutes the basic unit of social organization in traditional contemporary Arab society (see Chapter 6) may explain why it continues to exert so much influence on identity formation. At the center of social and economic activities, it remains a very cohesive social institution, exerting the earliest and most lasting impact on a person's affiliations.

Tribalism, too, continues to undermine the unity of the *umma* in both its Islamic and secular nationalist versions. As the prominent Lebanese Shi'i spiritual leader Muhammed Mahdi Shamseddin has pointed out, Islam has "attempted to destroy tribal solidarity by diverse means in order to establish a community based on unity of belief."[17] The triumph of Islam in unifying conflicting tribes into an *umma* of believers does not mean that it has managed to eliminate tribalism. Tribes themselves have also managed to use Islam in diverse ways. The Egyptian scholar Muhammed 'Amara notes that since the earliest period of Islamic history, the state has tended to resort to tribalism as a means of balancing society's conflicting forces.[18] A similar conclusion is reached by Zurayk, who writes that whereas Arabs were able to transcend their old religious beliefs in favor of Islam, "it was not as easy for them . . . to rid themselves of their loyalties to tribe and clan for the sake of the new loyalty to the *umma*. During the whole of the formative period, and indeed throughout Islamic history to the present day, tension has persisted between tribal and Islamic affiliations."[19]

The same tension exists between tribalism and secular nationalism in contemporary Arab society. Both popular nationalist movements and ruling regimes have attempted to combat or use tribalism to advance their causes. This is particularly true in Arab countries that are more tribally constituted than others, such as Arabia, Sudan, and the Maghrib. The Saudi family, itself a branch of the 'Aneza tribe, has attempted to stitch together a mosaic of tribes into a nation-state. Through all sorts of inducements and confrontations, tribes have been contained in a stable political system. Yet the tribes continue to distinguish between two aspects of this political system: the *dawla*, or modern state bureaucracy, and the *hukuma*, or members of the Saudi royal family. Their allegiance is to the latter rather than the former.[20] A second example is the Arab Maghrib, where process of transition from tribal societies to nation-states is evidenced by the disappearance of the traditional circles of power referred to earlier, the Bled el-Makhzen, or intermediary tribes allied with the central government, and the Bled es-Siba, or dissident tribes. Yet tribal organization has continued to "constitute an obstacle to the political unification" of Maghribi societies.[21] Another case in point is the unique coincidence of sect, tribe, and political movements in the Sudan. The Umma party has represented the Mahdiyya or Ansar religious order of the Mahdi family. Similarly, the National Unionist party has represented the Khatmiyya religious order of the Al-Hindi family. This recalls the coincidence of religion (Wahabi sect) and family (Al-Saud) in Arabia and of the characterization of the various Lebanese religious sects as "tribes in disguise."[22]

The intensity of the conflict between tribalism and nationalism, as well as the coincidence of sect, regionalism, tribe, and rural-urban divisions, is highly acute in Yemen, where political loyalties have coincided with and reinforced sectarian and tribal divisions. The former socialist order in southern Yemen could not avoid the transformation of political rivalries into violent tribal confrontations. These illustrations and others attest to the continuation of tribalism as a force opposed to the concept of the *umma* in both its Islamic and secular nationalist versions.

Ethnicity is defined in cultural and linguistic terms as well as in terms of descent from distant common ancestors. Occasionally, Arab identity is linked to the descent of the Arabs from the 'Adnanites, Qahtanites, and other tribes, and to their constituting an ethnic group. Once this definition is made, however, the dilemma emerges of reconciling it with other ethnic groups within the Arab world—such as the Kurds, Berbers, Circassians, Assyrians, Chaldaeans, Jews, Armenians, and the African communities of southern Sudan. For example, there are about 572 tribes and 56 ethnic groups in the Sudan. In "each region there is one major ethnic group dominating the others, i.e., the Arabs in Blue Nile, Khartoum, Kordofan, Northern and Kassala provinces, the Fur in Darfur province, the Nilotics in Bahr el-Ghazqal and upper Nile provinces and the Nilo-Hamites in Equatoria province."[23]

The Berbers of the Maghrib, who call themselves Imazighen (singular, Amazigh), are related to one another by a common language with different dialects as well as by claims of bedouin and tribal origins—claims that facilitated Islamization and Arabization. Some estimates indicate that they constitute about 40 percent of the population of Morocco and two-thirds of its rural population; they are about 30 percent in Algeria. The Islamic conquest resulted in the total Islamization of the Berbers and their partial Arabization. Attempts at imposing an Arab identity on the Berber population led to its seclusion in the Rif and Atlas mountains. This isolation "allowed the Berber language to survive and preserve its vitality and folklore."[24]

By contrast, European colonization cultivated Arab-Berber differences. This included attempts to de-Arabize Algeria and to establish a separate Berberistan, while maintaining Islam. As noted by the Tunisian sociologist Elbaki Hermassi, the French policy "developed the Kabyle myth in Algeria. The Algerian Berbers were considered more assimilable than the Moroccan Berbers because they were assumed to be more 'superficially Islamic.' Because of this distinction, the French permitted them their local assemblies, their customs, and representation . . . the whole policy was designed to prevent the two peoples of Algeria from growing accustomed to contact with each other."[25]

The Kurds also define themselves in linguistic and cultural terms. Their tribes speak different dialects and form the local majority in northern and north-eastern Iraq. Based on their ethnic distinctiveness, they have been seeking self-rule for Kurdistan (including parts of Turkey, Iraq, and Iran). This desire has put them in open conflict with the states of the area, which insist on their own national territorial integrity. Though several plans have been proposed to accommodate them, Kurdish grievances continue to foster their restlessness and efforts for independent self-expression.[26] Their uprisings have collapsed amid desperate feelings of betrayal by Western and regional instigators.

These kinds of ethnic and other affiliations coincide with several vertical and horizontal forces undermining Arab national identity. Religious, regional, tribal and ethnic, and other cleavages have been constantly exacerbated by conditions of underdevelopment, socioeconomic inequalities, political repression, and foreign intervention. Constituting a unique system of multiple affiliations, they have hindered efforts at Arab unity. We turn now to other variables and affinities before reaching relatively definitive conclusions on the nature of Arab identity and prospects for social and political integration.

Shared Culture and Its Variations

Next to language, a single, shared culture has often been cited as the most basic element in Arab national identity. One implicit assumption here is that the great majority of the population in the Arab world "is Arabic in language and therefore to a great extent in culture."[27] Another basic assumption of this literature is that a common culture is derived from the fact that more than 90 percent of Arabs are Muslim by faith. Implicitly, then, Arab culture is viewed as basically religious in form and literary in expression. It is what most Arabs share, regardless of their diverse affiliations.

Yet in assessing the role of such common culture in the formation of Arab national identity, one needs to take note of some special considerations. First, the most commonly accepted operational definition of culture in the social sciences refers to three aspects: (a) the entire or total way of life of people, including a shared social heritage, visions of social reality, value orientations, beliefs, customs, norms, traditions, skills, and the like; (b) artistic achievements; and (c) knowledge or thought and the sciences. (These aspects of culture are acquired through human association or communication with others in society. In Part III of this book, separate chapters are devoted to these aspects of Arab culture.) Second, the culture of any society is characterized by specificity and distinctiveness—or uniqueness owing to social formations, patterns of living, modes of production, socialization, and adjustment to the environment by a community of people. In other words, culture represents the complete design for living of a community of people inhabiting a particular environment.

Culture is rarely characterized by complete uniformity. On the contrary, its dynamism reflects diversity, pluralism, and contradictions. In the Arab case, this includes several different levels of cultural foci. Not unlike others, Arab society has its own dominant culture, constructed from what is most common and diffused among Arabs. In addition, it has its subcultures, those peculiar to some communities, and its countercultures, those of alienated and radical groups. Arab dominant culture is derived from interaction among these levels of culture, and from Arab collective memory, but it is constantly reinterpreted and cultivated by those in control of the resources of society, at the expense of others. The process of socialization in this case is often based on repression and inducements. Subcultures are represented by different patterns of living (such as rural, urban, or bedouin); by social formations (such as mercantilist or agricultural); by social class differences and contradictions (such as high, bourgeois, and mass cultures); by religious and sectarian affiliations (such as Sunni, Shi'ite, Druze, Alawi, Isma'ili, Copt, Orthodox, Maronite, Catholic, Protestant, or Jewish); and by ethnicity (such as Kurd or Berber). Countercultures are represented in Arab society by alienated intellectuals, uprooted communities, and radical movements.

Thus Arab culture is in a constant state of becoming. This state results from internal contradictions, new social formations and the utilization of resources such as oil, encounters with other cultures, and innovativeness. There would not have been any need to assert this fact were it not for the misrepresentation of reality by both Western Orientalists and traditional Arab scholars. Western Orientalists have tended to emphasize the "constant" rather than the "changing" nature of Arab culture and the "oneness" of the "Arab mind" rather than the "pluralism" inherent in a distinctive Arab culture. Similarly, traditional Arab scholars have tended to emphasize some sort of traditional values and to focus on conforming to a traditional model rather than what actually exists. In such a traditional view, authenticity is deprived of creativity, genuineness, and open-mindedness. The contemporary discourse in Islamist circles reduces authenticity to a dismissal of ideas and innovations considered alien (*dakhil, wafid, majlub, bud'a*) to Arab culture. Notions such as nationalism, democracy, socialism, class analysis, secularism, and several others are dismissed as being borrowed or imported from the West. The Egyptian scholar Tariq al-Bushri, for instance, has described secularism as an alien plant, *nabt wafid*, which did not begin to grow in the Arab "intellectual and civilizational environment" before the beginning of the twentieth century.[28] Using more sophisticated notions, the Moroccan scholar Muhammed Abed al-Jabri describes secularism as originating in European civilization and hiding "behind the mask of nationalist discourse."[29] In reply to these characterizations, I would argue that the distinctiveness of Arab cultural identity needs to take account of a highly complex human reality as it now exists.

The Place of Arabs in History and Their Common Experiences

Intra-Arab conflicts and the reinforcement of the boundaries that separate Arab countries stand in sharp contrast to the place of Arabs in history and their sense of common historical experiences. All sorts of barriers have hindered the free movement of people, products, and ideas across heavily guarded artificial borders. More often than not, the closer Arab countries are geographically, the greater the conflicts and the less the communication between them. Political disagreements over minor and major issues may develop into open conflicts even at times of external threat and acute national crisis. Domestic as well as foreign policies are increasingly being determined by immediate rather than long-term local interests.

In fact, one of the obstacles to Arab unity is the growing social-psychological distance resulting from a lack of communication. First, there has been a process of economic disintegration. Each Arab country is being increasingly—and separately—integrated into the world capitalist system. So the greater the dependency of the peripheral Arab countries on the centers of this capitalist system, the less the economic exchanges and links among the Arab countries themselves. Second, except for decreasing labor migration between oil-producing and non-oil-producing countries, travel across Arab borders has been made extremely difficult. Even when allowed, travel between Arab countries has been frustrating and humiliating. Third, a strict process of censorship undermines cultural exchange among Arab countries. A policy of cultural self-sufficiency is in effect almost everywhere. Governmental control over the mass media and culture is accompanied by the banning of publications produced in other Arab countries. Each government has its own publishing houses and publications. Unlike in earlier times, when literature in Arabic was discussed and referred to as Arabic, increasingly it is being presented and promoted by literary critics as Egyptian, Iraqi, Syrian, Lebanese, Algerian, Jordanian, Kuwaiti, Saudi, Tunisian, Qatari, and the like. Fourth, censorship is encompassing ever-broader areas and topics. Lists of taboos are growing to include wider political, religious, and sexual topics and terms or even criticisms of other rulers and governments that are friendly.

These instances of lack of communication cannot be explained by the absence or weakness of Arab national feelings among the people. On the contrary, they might be interpreted as indicative of the strength of such feelings in the face of the insecurity and illegitimacy of the Arab regimes themselves. Evidence supporting this interpretation is the gap between the words and deeds of Arab rulers and officials and between their public and private statements. On a normative level, their words and public statements continue to proclaim their unwavering commitment to "the causes of the Arab nation" and to lament deteriorating relationships. They do so without acknowledging their own responsibility, instead blaming the deterioration completely on other Arabs and antagonistic external forces. This disunity occurs despite the fact that the Arab people themselves share common historical experiences. National disasters such as the exile of the Palestinians in 1948, the defeat of the Arabs in the Six-Day War of 1967, and the Gulf War have become an integral part of the Arab psyche and its collective consciousness. The same is true of both ancient and contemporary victories. In recent times, the heroic Egyptian defense of the Suez Canal in 1956, the Lebanese resistance following the Israeli invasion of 1982, and the Algerian war of liberation of 1954–62 have been sources of inspiration and pride for the great majority of Arabs. Contacts with fellow Arabs, no matter how geographically distant, almost always lead to the development of strong negative or positive rather than neutral feelings toward one another. This strong feeling can only be attributed to the identification and mutual expectations generated by a common history and destiny. Moreover, the sense of common identity has been strengthened in modern times by opposition to Western penetration.

Shared Economic Interests

Studies of the nature of the relationship between economic life and the emergence or weakening of Arab national identity have reached almost diametrically opposed conclusions. Defining Arab nationalism in linguistic and cultural terms, Sati' al-Husari warns against "the consideration of economic interests as a basic element in the formation of nationalism," which he considers contrary to "requisites of reason and logic."[30] For him, the assignment of the country into agricultural, industrial, commercial, and tourist areas sets them apart. The assumption here is that national unity is based on similarity, rather than on the interdependence or complementarity of a division of labor. Another Arab nationalist, Adib Nassur, has warned that notions of economic inequalities and class analysis will eventually lead to splitting the ranks of Arab nationalists into opposing camps.[31]

In contrast, another body of literature on the formation and decline of Arab nationalism highlights the relevance of the economic variable. Samir Amin, for instance, emphasizes the historical significance of mercantile relations and long-distance trade in the formation of the Arab nation. It was this urban commercial class that controlled the central state apparatus and ensured economic and political unity. Once the power of this social class faded, the nation began to "regress into a formless conglomeration of more or less related ethnicities"; the decline of commerce "had caused the Arab world to lose its previous unity."[32] Similarly, Walid Kaziha concludes that Arab nationalism represents "an expression of the ambitions of certain social forces" and that its decline came about as a result of the weakening of those forces.[33] Zurayk also stresses the significance of the economic variable as a unifying force. The future trend of human development, he points out, "is toward larger and larger societies, and not toward narrow, powerless, and confined societies which cannot confront the complex economic and political situations and necessities of the scientific and technological revolution. Modern life . . . requires accumulation of natural resources, human skills and expertise. . . . Hence the limitation of small states . . . in meeting the necessities of modern life."[34]

Cultural and economic analysts might agree, however, that certain economic conditions can contribute to social and political fragmentation. For instance, growing disparities between rich and poor Arab countries have created further rifts between them, notwithstanding labor migration and other forms of interdependency between oil-producing and non-oil-producing Arab countries.[35] Another instance of how economic factors may contribute to Arab national fragmentation is the expansion of European commerce in the nineteenth century to the benefit of certain minorities at the expense of the majority of the population. Philip Khoury has pointed out that during the twenty years leading up to the events of 1860 in Lebanon and Syria, the economic impact of Europe was heightened in that some religious groups "enriched themselves by serving as agents of European interests."[36]

External Challenges and Political Unity

A classic sociological principle proposes a positive relationship between external conflicts and internal cohesion, but an exclusive focus on the integrative function of external conflicts represents a one-sided analysis.[37] One such exclusive focus is the constantly expressed view that the only thing Arabs agree on is hatred of Israel. A more systematic application of the theory of conflict to the Arab situation has been attempted by Nadim Bitar, who holds that the Palestinian problem has generated movement in the direction of revolutionary Arab unity.[38]

A closer reexamination of the Arab situation would, however, show that under certain conditions, external conflicts and challenges may actually lead to further fragmentation and disruption. The creation of artificial states in the Arab world has rendered it more vulnerable to disruption when confronting intense external challenges. Furthermore, against the background of continuing Arab dependency on the West, as well as the emergence of nation-states and established ruling groups, external conflicts have proved very disruptive.

Contrary to repeated claims, events have demonstrated that the establishment of Israel and the ensuing related conflicts contributed to further political fragmentation. Both Arab regimes and the Palestinian leadership have been divided over such issues as the nature of the confrontation with Israel and the resolution of the Palestinian problem. One source of divisiveness since the inception of the Palestinian problem has been the split between those who favor negotiations and a peaceful solution (in spite of dim prospects) and those who favor armed struggle against all odds. This split is further compounded by accompanying conflicts between old and new orders, repressive regimes and popular movements, pro-Western and nationalist as well as reactionary and progressive forces, and moderate and rejectionist camps.

Conclusion

A critical approach to the study of Arab national identity, such as that attempted here, reveals that it has been undergoing a process of continuous change. The presence of conflicting affiliations and threatening challenges may attest to its dynamism rather than to its static nature. This very dynamic quality means, however, that Arab society may or may not succeed in its struggle to achieve political and social integration. Success will be determined by the will of Arabs to attend precisely to this historical task. Although they have failed miserably to achieve their objectives so far, their struggle has not necessarily been in vain. It is a fact that the *nahda* continues to be unfulfilled and that a gap separates the dream from reality. Hence, one witnesses deep and comprehensive alienation. Strong feelings of anger and cynicism have emerged over the marginalization of the Arab world, once located at the very center of human affairs. Arabs feel strongly, too, about deprivation in the midst of unprecedented wealth, and about the impotence of ruling groups in times of trying challenges. True, the Arab world in its present circumstances does not constitute a single coherent system or civil society as much as a multiplicity of societies. Besides the growing development of local and regional identities at the expense of a more comprehensive nationalism, all the existing nation-states function independently of one another and rarely in terms of Arab national interests.

These conditions of alienation and the lack of civil society do not necessarily constitute an Arab retreat from historical challenges. (I say this because there are those who see expressions of alienation on the part of Arab intellectuals as a sign of retreat: the bewilderment with which contemporary writers have been looking at their society has in recent years prompted some scholars to announce the death of Arab nationalism.) [39] On the contrary, I see such expressions of bewilderment as a sign of vitality and dynamism in Arab culture.

It is out of deep identification that these writers speak of the stark reality confronting Arab society. The world for them always indicates a new beginning. Each genuinely expresses the outcry of the Arab people, searching constantly for unity and the will to change in order to attain true nationhood. They know full well that it is not impossible to transcend the present reality and to remake their society.

4 The Continuity of Old Cleavages

Tribe, Village, City

The old *badu-hadar* (bedouin-sedentary) divisions in Arab society and culture have not disappeared. The renowned Arab sociologist-historian Ibn Khaldun (1332–1406) first interpreted Arab history in terms of *badu* versus *hadar* conflicts and struggles for power. For Ibn Khaldun, the difference between such communities "arises out of the difference in their means of livelihood" (*ikhtilaf nihlatihim min al-ma'ash*).[1] Consequently, he characterized *badu-hadar* relationships as confrontational because of their intrinsic conflict of interests. The bedouin, he explained, cannot accept the fact that city people enjoy so much affluence while they continue to retreat into their desolate deserts. Since the bedouin possess strength and courage as rugged warriors, it becomes inevitable that one day they will attack the city people, whom they consider weak, cowardly, and affluent. However, once they conquer cities and establish ruling dynasties, they settle down to enjoy the new wealth and power and eventually lose their courage and solidarity. This state of "weakness" in turn invites attacks by other waves of bedouin seeking to establish their own rule. Thus, society goes through cycles of conquest, enjoyment of power and affluence, and decline.[2] We need to continue investigating these ancient cleavages, which still influence struggles for social and political integration in the Arab world.

In fact, we need to expand our analysis beyond the structure provided by Ibn Khaldun—by identifying village or peasant life as a third, distinct pattern of living. That is, rather than relying on the cliché of *badu-hadar* conflict to understand contemporary Arab society, we should utilize recent social science research on the village to characterize a triad of distinctive social patterns rooted in tribal, village, and urban life. This new view will enable us to explore bedouin-rural-urban relationships, not merely as contradictory forces undermining efforts at national construction, but also as sources of diversity that could be used as building blocks for a new Arab world. Such an approach, however, will differ from the social science literature itself; modern analysts have tended to dwell on what they see as exotic cultural variations, rather than on the social contradictions underlying these patterns of living. They have lost sight of the potential complementarity inherent in the essential elements characterizing bedouin-rural-urban relationships.

A number of developments in the twentieth century have begun to break down the spatial as well as psychological barriers between these ancient forms of community. Chief among these developments has been the transition from tribal or communal societies to nation-states, with a concomitant end put to the relative isolation and self-sufficiency of communities, and the opening up of communication networks among them. The settlement of bedouin, rural-urban migration, and the imposition of a central state's sovereignty over distant districts have also contributed. Important economic factors include opportunities for government employment, integration into the world market, and the formation of new social classes in response to political and economic developments. Yet the process of integration has proven uneven among Arab societies. While some barriers have been removed, new contradictions and disparities seem to have emerged or become increasingly visible. For instance, the Egyptian sociologist Mahmoud 'Awda has pointed out that the transformations just described have led, among other things, to the lack of a "formal feeling of land ownership" among peasants. This is because they possess only the power of their labor and because old skills and industries such as weaving have disappeared.[3] Assessments have also shown that within a decade (1975–1985), the average annual income in urban areas, initially measured as 5.8 times that in rural areas, has increased to 14.5 times.[4]

In order to understand the nature of these transformations and their relationship to processes of social and political integration, we need to focus on the three patterns of living that we have identified in contemporary Arab society. Once we understand the nature of tribe, village, and city life, we can investigate the nature of their interrelationships, mutual images, and sources of shared values and norms.

The Bedouin Way of Life

While some continue to portray bedouin as a menace to civilization and a source of values and norms that hinder the assertion of a shared Arab culture (Ali al-Wardi; Faruq al-Kilani),[5] others romanticize them as representative of certain essential Arab characteristics—the spirit of independence, integrity, and generosity.[6] An accurate description would define *badawa* (the nomadic style of life) by its social organization, as a pastoral and tribally organized pattern of living in the *badia* (the beginning of life in the desert). This particular human form of settlement resulted from a prolonged historical process of adaptation to the harsh conditions of the desert environment. For instance, regular movement in search of water and pasture was imperative. Similarly, certain institutions and forms of organization for purposes of defense and for the distribution of scarce resources made sense in the desert environment. Indeed, it was this peculiarly hard life in a harsh environment that necessitated a tribal social organization regulated by norms of solidarity, equality, and chivalry. Such an ecological analysis was clearly reflected in Ibn Khaldun's definition of the bedouin as those who cooperated in securing the bare necessities of life by leading a simple pastoral life and engaging in warfare and occasional cultivation.

The most nomadic of the bedouin are those who secure their livelihood by raising camels and roaming deeply into the desert. Another type of bedouin includes those who raise sheep and cattle; these move less often and less deeply into the desert. There are also nomads who secure their livelihood by combining pastoralism and land cultivation, and who are thus more inclined to settle down.[7] Similar criteria continue to be used in classifying present-day bedouin as roaming pastoralists (inhabiting Arabia, the Syrian desert, Sinai, some parts of the Sudan and Somalia, and the great Sahara) and semi-pastoralists (practicing some cultivation in oases and small village settlements and seasonally roaming the desert).[8] In a few instances, bedouin are ethnically classified as being Arab or non-Arab (for example, in the Sudan). Bedouin themselves are more inclined to assert internal equality and solidarity, but insist on distinguishing among tribes on the basis of considerations of nobility. Some nomadic tribes trace their descent from the most ancient Arab nobility, including the tribes of 'Aneze, Rwala, Shammar, Al-Murrah, and Beni Khalid. Other groups are seen as having less status because they cannot trace their origins to ancient Arab tribes. In this respect, some are treated as outcast bedouin and known as *mualin* because they are attached to or under the protection of noble tribes. Some outcast groups (such as the *bedoon,* who are without citizenship and thus considered stateless in Kuwait) only emerged into public consciousness during the 1990–91 Gulf crisis.

Bedouin Social Organization. The most distinctive features of bedouin social organization, then, are tribal solidarity based on blood and symbiotic ties, and what the anthropologist William Lancaster has called "premises of equality, autonomy and the acquisition of reputation."[9] As noted, these features are directly and closely related to the harshness of desert life, which necessitates militancy and constant movement in search of water and pasture.

The basic units of such bedouin social organization may be seen as a series of concentric circles, including (from the outermost circle) the *qabila* (tribe) or *'ashira* (clan); *hamula, fakhdh, batn,* or *far'* (subtribes); and family, including both the *beit, ahl,* or *'aila* (extended family), and the *usra* (nuclear family). At the center is the circle of the extended family, which has its own private herd and is the focus of daily activities. The next circle is the subtribe, which is composed of a number of extended families tracing themselves to one distant patrilineal father, going back five generations or so. This subtribe constitutes a defense unit, usually entrusted with ownership and defense of common wells and herds. The same premises of equality and freedom enjoyed by the inner circle of the *beit* are extended to subtribes. Decisions are normally made by the consensus of the extended families constituting the subtribe. The most inclusive circle (*qabila* or *'ashira*) consists of a number of subtribes, usually from four to six, and may trace itself to a real or fictional grandfather. The tribe's activities are mainly political, consisting of the management of relations with other tribes and governments. At this level, the tribe is led by a powerful sheikh or emir advised by a tribal council. Finally, some confederation, *ittihad,* of tribes may emerge such as the 'Aneze confederation referred to as "the tribes of 'Aneze." [10] Class differences are less developed among bedouin than in other sectors of Arab society. In spite of the prominence and wealth of the sheikhs, emirs, and a few other wealthy families within each tribe, socioeconomic disparities are minimized by the importance attributed to blood and symbiotic ties as well as the concept of communal ownership. The main production and consumption activity in the economy is herding, and each *beit* has its own herd, which is often held communally by the group as a whole. The relative equality in wealth and status and the lack of class distinctions are reinforced by the value attributed by bedouin to egalitarianism and consensual decision-making.

A hierarchy of status and power has nevertheless always characterized intertribal relations. Bedouin tribes are known to have forced less powerful tribes to pay *khuwa* (protection money). They are also known to have had slaves and outcasts. One other distinctive feature is the fact that there is very little intermarriage between tribes of varying degrees of nobility. For instance, the Beni Rwala look down on Beni Atieh and the Huwaitat, who in turn look down on the Beni 'Ugla. Some tribes are considered to have lost their nobility because of intermarriage with lower-status tribes. It is said that the Suleitat tribe, for example, lost their nobility because they supposedly descended from a man of the 'Aneze, who had married a lower-status Sliba woman.

The bedouin lack the religious establishment so preponderant in urban centers. As a consequence, urbanites tend to accuse the bedouin of a "lack of an inhibiting religious conscience," [11] and of applying their own tribal customs (*'araf*) at the expense of the Islamic shari'a (law). Yet, a relationship can be argued between bedouin patriarchy and the bedouin's intense faith in God's overwhelming power. Moreover, the Islamic image of heaven as a place of rivers, greenery, and shade seems to be a desert dweller's dream. Thus religion differs in its meaning and explication for bedouin, but shares fundamental assumptions with the Islam of city dwellers.

In regard to bedouin political structure, tribes have always been inclined to affirm their independence and to resist external control or infringements on their cherished autonomy. Ibn Khaldun observed that bedouin were the least inclined to be governed. As noted earlier, Islam managed to unify conflicting tribes and to establish an *umma* (community of believers). But as courageous warriors, the bedouin somehow partly regained their control over the new society in Islamic guise. More recently, nation-states have been forged out of tribally segmented societies in several parts of the Arab world. In Arabia, for instance, the Saudi family, itself a branch of the 'Aneze tribe, had to resort to the Islamic tradition of *hijra*, as well as the use of force and material inducements, to secure bedouin support. According to the *hijra* tradition, Islam encouraged the bedouin to desert their tribes and join the Islamic community. Before the conquest of Mecca, Islam proclaimed the bedouin way of life (*badawa*) as part of the *jahiliyya* (the pre-Islamic period of paganism and polytheism) and considered *hijra* the duty of every Muslim. The Saudi government benefited from this tradition by naming modern bedouin settlements *hajr* and its residents *ikhwan* (brothers). Yet, bedouin sheikhs continue to base their power on their ability to gain concessions from the central government, to reconcile conflicts, and to serve as intermediaries between members of the tribe and state rulers. Lancaster has pointed out that the emir of the Rwala tribe lived in Syria during the 1970s, although it would have been financially well worth his while to live in Saudi Arabia; by staying outside the kingdom, he could act more freely on behalf of his tribe.[12]

In other Arab countries, such as Sudan and Yemen, tribes continue to enjoy much greater autonomy. A study of tribal structure in Yemen has shown that bedouin as well as village tribes in the northern and eastern parts of the country continue to enjoy a high degree of political and economic autonomy. They claim sovereignty over the land they inhabit, considering it to be the private property of the tribe. The Yemeni tribes, we are told, "continue to reject complete submission to the authority of the central state"; since 1962, in fact, the revolutionary government has returned to the tribes some of the powers they had lost under the repressive rule of Imam Ahmed Yahia Hamid Eddin (1948–1962).[13]

Bedouin Value Orientations. The tendency to romanticize or condemn bedouin culture seems to overlook the notion that bedouin value orientations have their origins in the peculiar desert milieu and the requisite social organization described earlier. Five value orientations seem to distinguish bedouin culture: tribal solidarity, chivalry, hospitality, individuality, and simplicity.

It is not accidental that tribal cohesion (*'asabiyya*) is an important value in bedouin culture. Both the survival and advancement of the bedouin require it in the harsh desert environment. Vulnerability to external threats and relative isolation have led to self-sufficiency, communal ownership, and small-sized groups, as well as the premium placed on the ability to exact tribute through invasion and to assert tribal power. Tribal *'asabiyya* is based on both blood and symbiotic ties, highlighting the significance of *nasab* (kinship ties). Ibn Khaldun tells us that *'asabiyya* is based on *nasab* ("Al-'asabiyya inama takun min al-iltiham bil-nasab" ["Cohesion is formed through attachment to kinship"]), and that *nasab* have been "a natural disposition in human beings since they existed" (*naz'a tabi'iyya fi al-bashar mudh kanu*).[14]

For similar social and ecological reasons, bedouin society attaches great importance to socializing its members into the values of chivalry (*furussiyya*) from early childhood, emphasizing courage, gallantry, power, fierce vitality, confrontation, attachment to and mastery of arms, manhood, pride, rivalry, defiance, heroism, and austerity. The fear this orientation invokes in the *hadar* has led them occasionally to present some of these values in negative terms. The Iraqi sociologist Ali al-Wardi, for instance, has described bedouin as "knowing nothing of their world except knighthood, pride of overcoming, and competition to be chiefs. . . . Bedouin way of life is nothing but raids and wars, and it is most shameful for a bedouin to earn his living by the labor of his hand and the sweat of his forehead."[15]

The bedouin are widely known for their legendary attachment to the values of hospitality and generosity (*dhiafa, karam*), reflected in the overwhelming number of stories and anecdotes that equate the bedouin way of life with these values. Their domination of bedouin culture is also associated with a complex set of traditions and manners involving coffee rituals, artful conversation, sacrifices, and the protection of those seeking refuge.

An integral part of the particular form of solidarity emphasized by bedouin is the emphasis on individual independence, autonomy, freedom, and dignity. Bedouin are also egalitarian and tend to express themselves freely and to honor their word no matter what the cost. Persons are also valued as individuals who despise pettiness, refuse any jobs that require services to others, and insist on their rights.

The bedouin lifestyle is also considered synonymous with simplicity, austerity, and the dignified control over desire in public situations. Al-Marzuqi's study of Tunisian bedouin noted that one field of competitiveness is the demonstration of endurance of thirst and hunger. For Ibn Khaldun, it was these values, in contrast to the affluence of city life, that partly explained bedouin success in conquest.

The Future of the Bedouin Way of Life. Modern nation-states and political movements have used every sort of pressure and enticement to encourage bedouin to abandon "their primitive way of life" and settle down. Some Arab governments have devised settlement projects, relying on urban and foreign experts, planners, and developers—all people who have had little contact with nomads.[16] The degree of success of these settlement projects, and consequently the future of nomadism, have been the subject of constant speculation. Some have concluded that the bedouin are threatened with extinction. Muhammed al-Marzuqi has observed that education, roads, electricity, employment in the city, and other aspects of modern civilization in postindependence Tunisia have resulted in the disappearance of nomadic culture and "whatever remains of its traces will vanish with the disappearance of the old generation."[17] A 1978 study of the Jordanian bedouin concluded somewhat sardonically that sooner or later the bedouin lifestyle would disappear because the camel was no match for airplanes and Landrovers.[18]

The opposite conclusion was reached in the early 1980s by Saad Eddin Ibrahim, who pointed out that efforts to incorporate nomads into modern sectors of Saudi society had succeeded in only two areas: the oil fields and the Saudi National Guard. "In both cases, however, the individual Bedouin remains strongly committed to his tribe and to its nomadic life-style," Ibrahim noted.[19] In an earlier study, Ibrahim and Donald Cole argued that "the Bedouins are far from being incorporated into modern economic sectors," that they "are still locked up in a subsistence-like economy," and that the "youngest age groups in our samples showed less disposition toward settling than their elders."[20] This would seem to contradict Al-Marzuqi's assertion that the bedouin way of life would vanish with the older generation.

These studies thus suggest on balance that, although the bedouin way of life may be threatened, they continue to resist total integration. William Lancaster concludes his study of the Rwala with the observation that:

> Some [tribesmen] . . . feel that the end of the road has been reached and that, despite their best efforts, the tribe will break down and disappear in the face of modernization; a few feel that before this happens it would be better to defy modernity militarily and vanish in a blaze of glory; yet others feel that it is nothing to do with them and simply get on with their own lives. However, the most respected and influential of [them] . . . reckon that they are capable of further adaptation yet and are actively exploring the means of doing so.[21]

The Peasantry and the Village

Until the middle of the twentieth century, almost three-quarters of the inhabitants of Arab countries lived in villages.[22] Some of these countries—such as Egypt, Sudan, Morocco, and Yemen—continue to be considered predominantly agricultural societies. Peasants derive their identity from the land and village life. Their relationship to the land is inseparable from their intimate and interdependent kinship relationships. So the village may be described as a community of extended families securing their livelihood through agricultural and other directly related activities. What differentiates bedouin from peasants is the latter's relationship to the land rather than kinship ties. The bedouin view attachment to the land as a source of humiliation (*al-dhul fi al-ard*). They look down on peasants and see them as slaves of the land and of those who have control over it. The peasants, by contrast, seek land and consider it to be the source of their dignity (*al-karama fi al-ard*). They see bedouin who do not own land as irresponsible, uprooted vagabonds bent on raids and thievery.

Village Social Organization. Village social organization is an intricate net of interrelationships of extended families. To be landless or detached from family is to be uprooted until death. To die is to return to the land like seeds, whose planting—that is, burial—begins the process of renewal and rebirth. Death, as clearly reflected in so many peasant folktales and legends, is defined by continuity in land cultivation. What may take precedence over notions of death and fertility is the linkage between femaleness and the land in peasant imaginations and collective memory.

Many villages in parts of the Arab world are referred to as *beit*, *kafr*, or *beni*, which indicates some historical relationship between the social organization in agricultural communities and that in bedouin tribes. This relationship continues to be visible, for example, in the shared social organizational forms of north and northeastern Yemen. The harshness of the environment there has contributed to the perpetuation of kinship solidarity and tribal conflicts, as well as of other characteristics that we often think of as tribal—such as patriarchal relations, endogamous marriages, and congruence between tribe and locale. There remains, as well, some synonymity between *beit*, extended family, and village. The study of tribal social structure in Yemeni society by Abu Ghanim has shown that the concept of tribe in Yemen does not necessarily refer to the presence of nomadic tribes (as in northern Arabia or as in the case of the Awlad Ali tribes in the western Egyptian Sahara). Instead, "for the individual member of the Yemeni tribe, the concept of tribal solidarity ['*asabiyya*] is shaped by belief in the independent ancestral origins [*nasab*] of each tribe, as well as in the tribe's sovereignty over the land it inhabits, including the right to independent control of economic resources and perception of the land as the tribe's private property."[23]

Generally speaking, however, the basic kinship unit among peasants in villages is the extended family rather than the tribe. The family structure is based on a web of relations centered on land cultivation. As such, it constitutes the basic socioeconomic unit in the villages. Family members are bound by an intricate and complex net of interdependent relations and have to function as a team according to a strict division of labor based on gender and age. Rosemary Sayigh pointed out in the 1970s, for instance, that the Palestinian village constituted a "family of families," which could be interpreted as being "almost a counter society in its strength." Yet the respective solidarities of village and family were not in contradiction. On the contrary, they "reinforced each other. Quarrels and feuds were part of the stuff of village life and never seriously threatened economic cooperation or social cohesion."[24]

Given the importance of ties to the land, we should look briefly at the various forms that the relationship to land, or land tenure, may take. *Mulk*, or privately owned land, has become the most prevalent type of land tenure since the early nineteenth century. Prior to that, agricultural land belonged in principle to the state or ruler. The Egyptian sociologist Mahmoud 'Awda has pointed out that from pharaonic times up to the rule of Muhammad Ali and the British occupation, "the basic source of Egyptian wealth, namely land, was the property of the absolute ruler."[25] The second type of land tenure, *miri* (*al-ard al-amiriyya*), is state land. Direct state ownership of land underwent some changes in the seventeenth and eighteenth centuries. A peculiar feudal system emerged as a result of the development of the *timar* and *iltizam* (discussed below), which meant that agricultural land was granted to individuals in return for certain services to the state. *Waqf* (land held by endowment) is property set aside for religious or charitable purposes (*waqf khairi*). Tenants or sharecroppers work these properties, and the proceeds are designated to the support of mosques, schools, hospitals, monasteries, shrines, and the like. A *waqf dhurri* (private family) keeps property within the family but provides conditions for its beneficiaries and use.[26] A fourth type of land tenure is *musha'* (communal land), which is commonly used in villages for pasture and woodland. Finally, *mawat* (wasteland) is unclaimed, deserted, or unexploited land.[27]

The village class structure emanates correspondingly from social distinctions based on land ownership and the related tenure systems. Essentially, rural society has been divided into "a few who own but do not work and a majority who work but do not own."[28] We may take the case of Egypt as illustrative of this pattern. Before 1952, 64.4 percent of the cultivable land in Egypt was owned by 6 percent of all owners. The great majority of the rural population were landless peasants. Land reforms in 1954 and 1961 resulted in only minor changes to this situation. At the root of these disparities in land distribution was the emergence of the peculiar feudal landholding systems of *timar* and *iltizam* prior to Muhammad Ali's rule (1805–48). In accordance with the *timar* system, agricultural land was granted to certain individuals in return for specific services to the state, which reserved the right to reclaim its ownership. Under the *iltizam* system, state land was turned over to families who paid a fixed price for the right to collect taxes from the peasants. Although these two systems were abolished by Muhammad Ali in 1811 and direct state ownership was instituted, the new situation did not contribute much toward resolving the acute problems of the peasantry. As a result of the transition from a subsistence economy to a cash-crop economy, the situation of the peasants became more complex and precarious. Subsequently, peasants were "subjected to both the central government and local big owners" as well as to the volatility of the world market.[29] The new situation gave rise to new bases for social stratification and the emergence of such social classes as city-dwelling landlords, small landowners, landless tenants and sharecroppers, and landless wage laborers.[30]

Rural politics is conspicuously class-based. At the center of local politics is the tense rivalry between notable families who try to balance their local obligations and interests with their outside commitments. This task is an integral part of their role as intermediaries between village and district, and between the village and the national centers of power. The official intermediary role of the local notable (called *mukhtar* in the Fertile Crescent, *'umda* in Egypt and Sudan, and *amin* or *kadi* in North Africa) is not separate from the informal roles played by notables in controlling local politics. This pattern does seem to be eroding, however; recently political parties and central governments have made much greater headway in villages at the expense of local notables.

Finally, it should be noted that the nature of the irrigation system plays a significant role in determining village social organization. Hence, there is a need to distinguish between river- and rain-irrigated rural areas. Social organization in river-irrigated areas, such as Egypt and Iraq, is much more likely to be guided by central planning, government control, and teamwork, given the need to organize externally for distribution, access, and maintenance. By contrast, social organization in rain-irrigated villages, such as in Syria, Yemen, and North Africa, is much more likely to be characterized by local autonomy, relative isolation, and diversification, since rainwater can be managed and distributed on a very local basis.

Peasant Value Orientations. This brief overview makes it clear that the basic value orientations in Arab peasant culture pertain directly to land, family, the local community, religion, social class, and time. This list obviously differs in important ways from the one I have given for bedouin, although certain congruences will also prove significant to my analysis.

The land is the source of peasants' most cherished values. Besides being their livelihood, it provides them with a deep sense of well-being and continuity. To own land brings security and belonging; to lose it represents defeat and uprootedness. Directly associated with the land are such peasant values as fertility, continuity, patience, and spontaneity.

Land features abundantly and spontaneously in peasants' imaginations and in their collective memory; it is celebrated in their songs, poetry, folktales, and dreams. Certain natural phenomena, such as rain, springs, valleys, mountains, trees and flowers, fruits and herbs (grapes, figs, dates, almonds, oranges, olives, pomegranates, thyme, and so on), have special meanings for Arab peasants and evoke deep feelings among them. This is particularly true in the case of those who have lost their land or have found themselves in exile, such as the Palestinians. The Palestinian sociologist Salim Tamari refers to "olive Palestinians" (those from rural areas inland) and "orange Palestinians" (those from the coastal areas). The land of Palestine and the lover become one and the same in the writings of the Palestinians Ghassan Kanafani and Mahmoud Darwish. The former, from a coastal city, entitled a collection of his short stories *The Sad Orange*. The latter, from a village, has enriched the Arabic language with a new vocabulary and imagery derived from the peasant environment, using evocative phrases like "trees of exile," "the wedding of grapevines," "the land we carry in our blood," "heroes in distant fields," and "the carrier of the agony of land." "My skin is the cloak of every peasant who comes from the fields . . . to eliminate centers of power," Darwish writes. "I call land the extension of my soul"; "I call birds almonds and figs"; "I call my ribs trees." He apostrophizes and identifies with the Palestinian earth: "Trees are feathers in your wings," he says, and it proclaims: "I am the land, plow my body."[31]

The peasants' sense of belonging is defined as much by attachment to the family home (*beit*) as it is by attachment to the land. Honor and security are deeply rooted in land and family. An uncomfortable situation for a peasant is being forced to choose between them. Palestinian peasants found themselves in this situation during the Arab-Israeli wars. Fearing threats to the honor of their family and women (*'ird*), they had to choose between leaving their land and village or staying. Those who chose *'ird* over *ard* (land) continue to experience remorse and guilt feelings. Home (*beit*) like land is a symbol of identity that must be maintained and never sold or rented. Another important family value in peasant culture is motherhood, which, like the land, symbolizes fertility and unlimited generosity. Other family values include brotherhood, marriage, children, respect for parents and the elderly, obedience, patience, spontaneity, simplicity, cooperation, and neighborliness. Peasants may engage in intense rivalries and feuds when land or family values are threatened. Thus, irrigation and water disputes traditionally have been the most troublesome in village life. Yet peasant culture is also distinguished by its emphasis on neighborliness as a significant value (in contrast to bedouin culture). This emphasis is reflected in often-repeated proverbs such as "Al-jar qabl ad-dar" ("The neighbor before the homefolk") and "Jarak al-qareeb wala akhouk al-ba'id"

("Your close neighbor and not your distant brother"); community affiliation is given priority over individual achievement and power. Indeed, *najda* (mutual support) is a critical concept in the villagers' value system. Cooperation and competition thus exist in a complex and subtle combination, as reflected in such peasant dances as the *debkeh*, a group dance widely performed in the Fertile Crescent (variations are also known in Turkey, Greece, and eastern Europe).

These community-oriented values are an integral part of the village ethos. This is not unusual in light of the composition of the village as a family of extended families. This emphasis on family—held together by informal ties—also explains the dominance of informal over contractual commitments, and the use of mediation and reconciliation to resolve conflicts in lieu of reliance on formal legal action. Disputes in rural communities are resolved, as among bedouin, informally and outside the official courts, according to customary law.

Village life accords a significant role to clerics, but is structured primarily around popular or folk religion. The *sadah* or *ashraf* subclass (those who claim descent from the family of the Prophet Muhammad) and the shrines of saints have been central to village life (see Chapter 7). This is because the religious values of peasants derive from their immediate environment rather than from texts and religious institutions or establishments, and from concrete expressions of faith rather than from abstract philosophical notions. Their deep religiousness centers on saints, shrines, and rituals. It serves as a mechanism for relating to (even controlling) their environment, and for overcoming daily problems. Thus, there is a contrast or even conflict between official religion centered in cities and the folk religion of the villages. Among the most dominant religious values in the village is *baraka* (blessedness), which emanates naturally from dependence on seasonal harvests and direct exposure to environmental forces. Closely connected to this orientation are devotion, patience, reverence, and contentment. These latter values should not be confused with submissiveness or resignation, which are often wrongly attributed to peasant culture.

In terms of the complexity of social class formation in Arab society, the village occupies a middle position between tribe and city. Its land-based class structure has promoted teamwork, as well as intra- and interfamily interdependence. The emphasis is on hard work, simplicity of lifestyle, humility, and intimacy. Compared to the city, there is less of a gender-based division of labor. As indicated earlier, such values do not exclude subtle rivalry and competition. Overt hospitality and unusual lavishness in welcoming guests within limited means are similar to those of the bedouin and may be understood as closely related to the environment and to status-seeking. In this respect, notable peasant families are known for their whole-hearted adoption of the symbols of status and power, and for the prominence they accord to their family home (*beit*).

Peasants are not haunted by time but are much more aware of the seasons and seasonal events than are city people. Three particular values dominate such awareness: endurance, mixed with anxiety for the renewal of life and new opportunities; the struggle with time, which is usually perceived as being for or against you (*ma'ak* or *'alik*); and patience in commemorating and celebrating time (*as-sabr 'ala az-zman*).

Villagers are naturally attracted to the cities by prospects of employment and prosperity (whether illusory or realistic), and rapid population growth, diminishing resources, lack of development in rural areas, the absence of new cultivable land, and the great disparities in land distribution have also served to draw people out of the villages. Janet Abu-Lughod speaks of the "urbanization of large segments of . . . peasant folk" and "continual ruralization of the cities," suggesting that a certain degree of integration is taking place,[32] but just as the settlement of bedouin on the land does not represent a process of integration, the movement of peasants from the countryside to the cities may pose more problems for national unity than it solves. Under the wrong conditions, the encounter may reinforce old conflicts rather than producing a national consensus.

Be this as it may, the enticements and services of urban life, including improved and expanding means of communication, have everywhere resulted in a massive influx of villagers to the cities. The more educated villagers are able to join the ranks of the emerging middle classes as government employees, self-employed shopkeepers, skilled wage workers, teachers, professionals, and army officers, but vast masses of poor peasants have been converted into a lumpenproletariat, composed of occasional laborers, street vendors, porters, shoe shiners, garbage collectors, garage attendants, domestic servants, drivers, soldiers and gatemen, who inhabit cramped slum areas surrounding the cities.

The consequences of these structural changes in Arab societies have been far-reaching. "All the important radical parties and movements . . . had their roots [in them]," Hanna Batatu has pointed out. "From the same sources flowed the insurrectionary trend which had its most powerful expressions in this century" in a number of Arab revolutions, upheavals, guerrilla risings, and civil wars.[33]

On the cultural level, village life has been profoundly threatened by these changes. Anis Frayha long ago pointed out that the spiritual and mental virtues of the Lebanese village had been eroded as a result of "the Western civilizational invasion [by way of the urban centers] of the majority of Lebanese villages including the distant ones."[34] (This observation is, however, more of an expression of concern about the fate of the village than an announcement of the end of a changing way of life.)

The City: Urbanization of Society

The urban pattern is best defined in terms of its distinctive functions rather than mere population size, although the size of urban populations clearly distinguishes cities from tribal and village clusters. City functions include serving as the center of economic, political, religious, and cultural activities. The Arabic word for city, *medina*, connotes the center of political and economic power or the seat of the ruler or judge who passes judgment *(dana)* on others. *Din* (religion) is derived from the same root and has the same connotation. Some classical and contemporary definitions suggest that cities, as a result of their economic functions, have served as centers of power or control as well as of religious and cultural activities. Ibn Khaldun defined the *hadar* (city dwellers) as those who cooperate in securing affluence in food, shelter, and clothing and who specialize in commerce and manufacturing.[35] Albert Hourani notes that a "town or city comes into existence when a countryside produces enough food beyond its requirements to enable a group of people to live without growing their own crops or rearing their own livestock, and devote themselves to manufacturing articles for sale or performing other services for the hinterland."[36]

Defining the city in terms of its political and commerical functions underscores its integrative role internally, as well as on the level of the larger society. Internally, neighborhood communities (in comparison to the tribe of the bedouin and the extended families in villages) may be relatively self-sufficient or more integrated, depending on the strength of the state and the dominance of some communities or classes over others. Within the larger structure of the nation-state and Arab society in general, cities play an integrative role to the extent that they dominate villages and tribes.

These urban functions have implications for the size of urban centers; the greater the centralization of such functions in particular cities, the greater their size. It is mainly this fact that accounts for the phenomenal rate of urban growth and the development of primary cities in Arab countries. The proportion of Arabs living in cities has increased from 10 percent at the beginning of the twentieth century to more than 40 percent in the 1970s, and is expected to reach about 70 percent by the end of the century. Some Arab countries, like the Gulf states, are close to being city-states. Others, such as Yemen and the Sudan, are essentially rural. The great majority are more or less evenly divided between rural and urban centers.

Besides this phenomenal rate of growth, Arab cities are also demographically characterized by (1) a selectivity in rural–urban migration that favors young males; (2) the dominance of primary cities (one or two large cities dominating others and the rest of the country); (3) a lack of city planning; (4) a duality between old and new cities (for example, coexistence of *casba* and new cities in the Maghrib); and (5) the emergence of slums and "hut and tin" cities.

City Social Organization. What the tribe is to the bedouin and the extended family is to the village, neighborhoods and institutions are to the city. As the tribe and the extended family give way to more elaborate forms of economic and social organization, a clearer social class structure begins to take shape. The complex network of interrelated functions (be these commercial, political, religious, educational, social, or cultural) requires the development of particular forms of organization. Essentially, these forms involve the emergence of factories, markets, government bureaucracies, houses of worship, educational institutions, mass media and related communication and transportation networks, hospitals, entertainment industries, and hotels and other tourist facilities. The specific social formations that have emerged with these specialized sectors may be seen as characteristic of Arab urban society. Yet what are peculiar to Arab cities are those features that cannot be understood on their own or in isolation, even for the purpose of analysis. It is necessary to identify and describe features in relationship to each other and to the overall structure.

Arab cities are often described as a mosaic of neighborhoods based mainly on their religious, ethnic, and socioeconomic composition. This characteristic is slowly being undermined, but many cities continue to exhibit aspects of it. Cairo, for instance, preserves some of the old divisions in separate quarters and subquarters based on ethnic and socioeconomic groupings. While each quarter increasingly shares many common features with the rest of the city, some of its identifying marks have survived modernization and economic reorganization. In the early 1970s, in an attempt to distinguish areas of contemporary Cairo from neighboring communities with which they seldom interacted, Janet Abu-Lughod was able to differentiate thirteen major subcities or "cities within the city": the slum of Bulaq; Shubra, a lower-middle-class mélange; the northern farmland wedge; the strip city of the urban working class; the old and the new middle-class sectors; Imbabah and the western rural fringe; the "gold coast" adjacent to the center of the city, which includes some of the wealthiest and most Westernized residents; the "silver coast," including the western bank of the Nile and the southern island of Rawdah; the city of the dead inhabited by tomb and cemetery dwellers on the eastern fringe; medieval Cairo; the transitional zone of osmosis; the old Cairo (Misr al-qadimah); and the southern rural fringe. In each of these areas, residents shared common lifestyles that were distinctive from those pursued by residents of the neighboring communities, with whom they seldom interacted. [37]

Similarly, the link between neighborhoods and important ethnic, sectarian, and social class divisions was clearly visible in the city of Beirut during and prior to the present civil war. Some quarters and suburbs of Beirut were predominantly inhabited (and quite often named for) Sunnis, Shi'ites, Orthodox Christians, Maronites, Druze, Armenians, Kurds, and other groups. Similar linkages characterize most other eastern Arab cities of the Fertile Crescent, such as Damascus, Baghdad, Aleppo, Jerusalem, and Amman. The neighborhoods of North African cities are distinguished mainly by socioeconomic differentiation, old city neighborhoods versus new areas, and, in some instances, by traditional guild systems. Some peripheral zones of North African cities, such as Tunis, have become the residential areas of poor rural migrants and the homeless. In this example, such settlements, called *gourbivilles* (from *gourbi*, a French term for Arab shacks), began to take hold in the late 1920s. By independence in 1956, the most populous *gourbivilles* of Tunis included Djebel Lahmar, Mellassine, Saida Manoubia, and Bordj Ali Rais.

Social relationships in subneighborhoods (*hara*) continue to be regulated by primary group norms. The Egyptian anthropologist Nawal Nadim has described several aspects of primary group relations within the *hara* in Cairo, such as the identification of the residents with their subculture, intimate interpersonal and kinship relations, minimal privacy, and limited residential mobility. The manner and form with which intimate activities are carried out in the *hara* "make it evident that the alley is actually considered by both sexes to be a private domain. Members of the two sexes in the *hara* treat each other with familiarity similar to that existing among members of the same family."[38] Such relations are reflected in several of Naguib Mahfouz's novels set in traditional neighborhoods of Cairo, such as *Zuqaq al-Midaqq* (Midaq Alley), *Awlad haratina* (The Children of Geblawi), and his famous Cairo trilogy, *Al-Thulthiyya*, published 1956–57 *(Baina al-qasrain, Qasr al-showq,* and *Al-Sukkarriyya*). Almost self-sufficient relationships within the *hai* (another word for neighborhood) are also depicted by the Moroccan novelist Abdulkarim Ghallab in a novel set in preindependence Fez entitled *Dafanna al-madi* (We Buried the Past). In it, Ghallab writes that "many hardly knew anything except the neighborhood their families had lived in for decades."[39] The process of simultaneously maintaining both traditional values and modernization has intensified since the encounter with the West at the beginning of the nineteenth century. This tension has contributed to the emergence of a duality characteristic of some Arab cities, particularly those in North Africa. In these cities two basic districts emerged—the old city (*medina, casba*) and the new. The two exist side by side, overlapping other social divisions and specialized functions.

Arab cities are most often described as "Islamic" by Orientalists, who draw upon one another's work and upon a small sample of premodern cities. Janet

Abu-Lughod has deconstructed the idea of the Islamic city as advanced by Western scholars. Cities have been depicted by these authorities as a product of three Islamic elements: a distinction between the members of the *umma* and outsiders; the segregation of the sexes; and a legal system that left to the litigation of neighbors the adjudication of mutual rights over space and use. In confining themselves to these elements, scholars ignore other equally significant historical facts and geographical characteristics. For Arab cities have been "deeply influenced by such non-Islamic factors as climate, terrain, technologies of construction, circulation, and production, as well as political variables such as the relation between rulers and the ruled, the general level of intercommunal strife, and fluctuations in the degree of internal and external security."[40]

Moreover, the Orientalist view has reversed the historical process by arguing a particular cause-and-effect relationship to Islam. They have ignored the fact that Islam itself emerged in an urban setting and should be characterized as an urban religion. By reversing the emphasis, Orientalists reveal a basic flaw in this school of thought, which treats Islam almost exclusively as the independent variable that shapes society, instead of as a characteristic that has been shaped by the societies into which it has been introduced.

Urban Value Orientations. City dwellers' values are clearly embedded in an intricately balanced social structure based on the interrelationship of class, family, and religious establishment. The traditional urban bourgeoisie in Arab countries such as Morocco, Jordan, and Saudi Arabia constitutes a well-developed class of notable families that controls the religious establishment and the political system. Since independence, a new national bourgeoisie has taken over the political system in several Arab countries, such as Egypt, Syria, and Iraq, and is seeking new sources of legitimacy. A more balanced rivalry between the old bourgeoisie and the new exists in some other Arab countries, such as Lebanon, Tunisia, Sudan, and Yemen. In all instances, the impoverished masses continue to be attached to different sets of values than those held by these two types of elites.

The first elite, composed of the traditional bourgeoisie of notable families (including particularly the merchant class), has placed a high value on "strife and struggle; not daydreaming" in its search for material profits and power.[41] Such strife emphasizes realistic evaluations, moderation, cunning, cleverness, opportunism, and innovativeness. The ultimate objectives have always been expressions of affluence and the trappings of power, such as possessing palaces, jewelry, servants, and women. The novel by the Moroccan writer Abdulkarim Ghallab mentioned above contains an excellent portrayal of such notable families. Having ample wealth and status, they adhere to modes of traditional behavior, seeking stability even in the midst of the struggle for independence. Using religion as a mechanism of control, they preach loyalty and obedience.

Hajj Muhammed, the patriarch of such a notable family, believes that what he owns has been given to him by God. "What my right hand possesses is part of what God has rendered *halal* [allowed]," this "pious" man says.[42] "God granted him her [a concubine's] neck," the novel comments, and his "respected" wife had to accept it. (The same attitudes on the part of the traditional bourgeoisie are also explored in the works of Naguib Mahfouz; see Chapter 10.) Ghallab's characterization is only one example of the delicate balance achieved by the elite through use of class, family, and religion to legitimize domination. All three institutions continue to be central to the prevailing social organization in societies in which the traditional bourgeoisie remains in control.

The new bourgeoisie constitutes a second type of elite. Composed mainly of professionals, it adheres to a different set of values and increases its power through education and professional work. Members of this group have tended to follow one of two courses. In some Arab countries, they have emphasized nationalist and socialist values and managed to seize power through military coups (Egypt, Syria, Iraq) or national liberation movements (in Algeria and among the Palestinians). In others, they have followed the course of Western liberalism, emphasizing the values of success, ambition, achievement, self-reliance, pragmatism, a free economy, consumption, Western education, and individuality.

Both the old bourgeoisie and the new have dissociated themselves from the impoverished masses, who tend, particularly in difficult times, to attach more value to personal and kinship relations than the elite and to seek solace in their religious faith, vacillating between desperate struggle to change their conditions and patient compliance. Their preoccupation with pressing daily needs has undermined their struggle and forced them to seek satisfaction in interdependent family relations that may also connect them in some protective way to these emerging elites. In such situations, they may also find in religion a source of satisfaction and a way to reconcile themselves to their miserable reality.

Nature of the Relationships between Tribe, Village, and City

The examination of tribe, village, and city in the context of social integration requires us to explore the nature of their interrelationships. In this respect, three issues present themselves as relevant: the extent to which these interrelationships are characterized by conflict or cooperation; the images exchanged by these three groups; and sources of common values and norms.

The literature on the nature of the relationships between tribe, village, and city tends to emphasize complementarity, separateness and contradictions.

Some studies tend to focus on the more cooperative aspects of their relationships, such as the trade or exchange of basic commodities. Bedouin, for instance, depend on villages and cities for their supplies of rice, flour, coffee, tea, sugar, clothes, and the like. They also depend on them for educational, health, religious, and political services. Villagers and city people depend on bedouin for cattle, the transportation of their products (camel caravans), and protection against raids and invasions. More recently, bedouin have served in Arab armies, national guards, and security forces. Similar examples of cooperation and interdependence between villages and cities also exist. On the one hand, peasants depend on the city for many of their supplies and for markets for their products. As large-scale farming has become more complex and mechanized, they have needed to borrow money from urban banks and to buy machinery manufactured in cities. On the other hand, city people have bought land and invested money in rural areas. In some areas, villages serve as summer resorts and tourist spots. In fact, some cities have emerged and continue to survive at the crossroads of caravan routes (such as Riyadh, Palmyra, Petra) or at the center of agricultural areas (such as Homs and Hama in Syria, Tripoli in Lebanon, Mosul in Iraq, and Constantine in Algeria).

Other studies concern themselves mainly with the contradictions and conflicts in bedouin-rural-urban relations. As indicated earlier, Ibn Khaldun saw Arab and Islamic history as essentially a *badu-hadar* struggle. Other analyses of the contradictions and conflicts between bedouin, peasants, and city people are numerous. As a result of the need to control the land and its products, city dwellers have always attempted to dominate villages. In some instances, they used bedouin tribes to do the job. This alliance ensured urban dominance of the peasants in the Fertile Crescent, Yemen, the Nile valley, and the greater Maghrib. Urban dominance resulted in the imposition of a feudalistic system, taxation, and absentee landlords residing in urban centers, and led to the emergence of landless peasants.

Several Arabic literary works vividly portray these contradictions and conflicts. In 1954 the Egyptian writer Abdel Rahman al-Sharqawi published *Al-Ard* (The Earth), a novel that portrays peasants in a state of rebellion against feudal lords and the central government. Yusif Idriss's novella *Al-Haram* (The Sin) and play *Malik al-qutn* (The King of Cotton) describe the complexity of class structure and resulting social contradiction. The novel *Dafanna al-madi* (We Buried the Past) by Abdulkarim Ghallab of Morocco exposes the notable families of Fez bent on enslaving village girls even during the war for independence. Since they owned the land and the villages, they felt entitled to own the people. Reflecting the overwhelming differences in access to power, Ghallab depicts peasants as reconciled to this reality.

These contradictory relationships and attitudes are also reflected in several scholarly studies, including that of As-Sayyid al-Husseini. Commenting on rural-urban migration, he concludes: "The village supplies the city not only with food, but with people also."[43] Before modern states acquired control over their territories, Frank H. Stewart points out, "When the central governments were weak, Bedouin tribes were able to take over large parts of the countryside. The area under cultivation shrank dramatically, and numerous villages vanished from the map. Those that survived often had to pay tribute to the nomads, and the sedentary population was in many places deeply influenced by the culture of tribes."[44]

From the 1950s on, however, these relationships and attitudes began to be transformed in several Arab countries (though they persist in others). Military officers of peasant origins have been involved in revolutions and coups d'état in Syria, Egypt, Iraq, Sudan, and other countries. Supported by an educated emerging middle class, they managed to seize power, improve rural conditions, and dominate the cities.

Meanwhile old cleavages and biases continue to survive. During the Gulf War, in an article in the *Washington Post* (February 12, 1991) entitled "In Defense of Saudi Arabia: Why Has Such a Rich State Had Such a Weak Military?" the Saudi lawyer A. H. Fahad wrote:

> The Saudi state is the product of a historic struggle between the two major communities of Arabia: the Bedouins . . . and the Hadar . . . from time immemorial, the Bedouins . . . preyed on the Hadar . . . this "nomadic order" lasted for a long time, and all Hadari attempts to stem Bedouin hegemony failed until, under the leadership of King Abdulaziz, the Hadar were able to subdue the Bedouins . . . and the Saudi state was firmly established. . . . By serving the powerful Wahhabi ideology . . . King Abdulaziz . . . proceeded successfully to take on the Bedouins by ideological subversion. He . . . succeeded in essentially demilitarizing most of Saudi society, . . . and deliberately avoided building a strong or large army . . . the general attitude of Saudi Arabia today is that the country has been lucky this time to have a coalition of forces led by the United States willing to help in its defense.

In light of such contemporary developments as bedouin settlement and rural-urban migration, it is not clear to what extent old animosities and negative images continue to linger in the collective consciousness of these communities. On the one hand, the bedouin have traditionally shown great pride in their subculture and looked down on peasants, whom they consider weak and submissive to their masters. They also reject city life, which they see as a source of corruption, cowardice, deviance, and softness. Peasants in turn have shown great pride in village life and see land as the source of their dignity.

To them, bedouin are lazy parasites who survive only by raiding to steal the products created by others. City people are contemptuous of both bedouin and peasants, whom they consider primitive. Literature, folktales, and songs perpetuate such negative attitudes. Moreover, there is very little intermarriage between these communities to break down barriers brought on by social isolation, or to increase social contact and familiarity.

On the other hand, these negative images coexist with some highly positive ones. Several works of fiction by urban Arab writers celebrate bedouin courage, hospitality, and noble character. City people seem to yearn for the simplicity, quiet, ease, and natural beauty of village life. Bedouin and peasants, in turn, tend to be fascinated by the city and its conspicuous affluence and pleasures. These mixed feelings indicate ambivalence in the attitudes held by the three historic subcultures, an ambivalence that results from increasing closeness and overlapping value orientations. In the context of the Arab self-reflection that has been prompted by recurrent crises and the failure to confront contemporary challenges, it has been said that Arab society is hindered by tribalism and bedouin value orientations. The social geographer Fadil al-Insari has lamented the prevalence of bedouin customs and values in Arab villages and cities "as a result of constant bedouin migration. . . . The life of most rural people in the plains of Rafidayn [the region between the Euphrates and the Tigris], the Nile, Syria, and Maghrib is an extension of the life of bedouin societies. . . . The bedouin influence is not confined to agricultural communities of the Arab homeland, it has also extended to urban communities." [45] Ali al-Wardi classifies Arab countries by the prevalence of bedouin values and notes that Iraq is "one of the societies most influenced by bedouin values . . . for I found out that rural tribes, which constitute about 60 percent of the Iraqi population, continue to lead a way of life close to that of their ancestors, the bedouin of the desert. They share with them values of solidarity, patriarchy, hospitality, protection money, revenge, honor crimes, and so forth." [46] Similarly, Jacques Berque asserts that the bedouin model "forced itself on the city" and that the "patriarchal hierarchies and vendettas and the proud attitudes of the Arab riders have oddly and dangerously influenced these fellahs' [peasants of Egypt] mentality." [47] In times of national crises, some have expressed their hostility to the bedouin without reservation. Frank Stewart has noted that the Jordanian judge Faruq al-Kilani, "blames the continued official recognition of Bedouin law for the defeat suffered by the Arab states in the 1967 war." [48]

Reversing the attribution of common values, other observers have concluded that the city was the real source of values, which were diffused from it to the countryside. Ahmed Banani of Morocco calls the city of Fez "the mother of the country. . . . From it flow the good and the bad. . . . The rest of the country follows its model. . . . From it branched learning and customs."[49] Further support for this argument is the fact that Islam and the shari'a (Islamic law) are urban in origin, and that modernization began in the city. Political economy and economic history also tell us that it was the cities of the Arab world that began to be integrated into the world capitalist system, pulling the rest of the region after them. The subsistence economy was replaced with a cash-crop economy, leading to dependence on the city and the world market, as well as to the concomitant spread of urban norms and aspirations, and the emergence of new classes.

Both of these explanations are valid. Yet common values do not come about merely as a result of "diffusion," "integration," or "influence." They also emerge independently as a result of similar conditions and needs. The fact that the family serves as the basic unit of social organization, for instance, must have contributed to the emergence of similar or common value orientations.

Conclusion

The old tribal-rural-urban cleavages continue to play a disruptive role in the process of social and political integration. Many traditional barriers and misperceptions have begun disappearing, but several others have been able to survive or to take new forms. This may be attributed to the fact that certain basic contradictions continue to reinforce ancient disparities as well as to perpetuate modern dependencies. The present social divisions have overlapped with other vertical and horizontal ones to render them much more complex than they seem. In fact, an exploration of the dialectics of these overlapping divisions will show that new forces—such as political repression and uneven capitalist development—have added to the complexities of existing disparities and dependencies. Attempts at integration have tended to be coercive and haphazard. The challenge now is to move away from a hierarchical and imposed integration toward a more egalitarian national integration. So far governments have shifted between externally imposed schemes and neglect. What is needed is the transformation of prevailing structures and transcendence through comprehensive, sustained, even development.

PART TWO

Social Structures and Institutions: Out of One, Many

5 Social Classes

Beyond the Mosaic Model

Three major views debate the relevance of class analysis to the understanding of Arab society. One dismisses the relevance of class analysis, asserting that the key to understanding Arab and other Middle Eastern societies is the mosaic nature of a society constructed on communal cleavages. Another admits that class analysis may be of some relevance but suggests a redefinition of the concept of class in terms of power or status, in order to accommodate the peculiar social situation of Middle Eastern societies. The third asserts the need for class analysis and argues that communal cleavages mask class interests, and—by substituting a false consciousness focused on communal identity—undermine class consciousness and class struggle.

For Carlton Coon, who represents the first view, the key categories of analysis in Middle Eastern mosaic societies have been sect, tribe, ethnic group, village, and neighborhood.[1] Similarly, C. A. O. van Niewenhuijze has denied the existence of classes and argued that the way in which Middle Eastern societies achieve their distinctive articulation cannot be called social stratification. In his view, the nature of mosaic social organization—consisting as it does of roughly equivalent constituent parts—works at cross-purposes to stratification in the Islamic world.[2]

The second orientation has been represented by the works of James Bill, Manfred Halpern, and other Western or Western-trained social scientists. James Bill has noted a return to class as a central theoretical concept and complains that none of the prominent Orientalists have endeavored to examine the relevance of this concept within the Islamic setting. Hoping to develop a concept of class that would make it applicable to both the more-developed and the less-developed societies, Bill has proposed a stratification based on power or authority rather than economic interests, excessive reliance on which he considers a major inadequacy of Marxist class analysis. In the Middle East "where personalism reigns supreme," he argues, social and political systems are built upon informal and shifting relationships that involve "modes of maneuver rather than modes of production." Class struggle has been replaced by "a system-preserving balance of tension."[3]

Similarly, Manfred Halpern has asserted "that power has led to wealth far more often than wealth led to power." The political roles of the separate classes have thus been described without reference to their oppositional relationships. On the contrary, these roles are treated as potentially stabilizing forces. Of all the classes, only the new middle class has been "powerful and self-conscious enough to undertake the task of remolding society," to "take the leading role in modernizing the Middle East."[4]

The third orientation has been represented by Marxist social class analysis. Bryan Turner asserts that anyone "who wants to develop a Marxist analysis of North Africa and the Middle East must start with a critique of the mosaic theory and all of its related assumptions."[5] In the 1970s Nicholas S. Hopkins applied a certain notion of class derived from the Marxist tradition to developments in the social, economic, and political structure of the Tunisian town of Testour. He found a traditional precapitalist mode of production, in which the social organization of Testour was characterized by a ranking system associated with honor. Differential status correlated with extreme differences in wealth, with a few individual families at the top of the pyramid and the mass of people at the bottom. The dominant mode of production in Testour involved minimal development of the forces of production. The technology was simple and could be handled by one person working alone. The productive unit was the family or the household. The fact that families worked independently without supervision or external control contributed to the development and perpetuation of the illusion of equality among unequal families. Later developments—the mechanization of agriculture; improved communications, which facilitated a market orientation; wage labor; and the acquisition of land by foreigners—led to the emergence of a class system. In Hopkins's words, the town of Testour "shifted from a society based on ranking to one based on class," in which "vertical links [were created] between those who sense that they have interests in common."[6]

Other analysts benefited directly from the theoretical and methodological works of Nicos Poulantzas and Erik Olin Wright.[7] Poulantzas focuses on economic ownership in determining boundaries between classes and, in the process, distinguishes between real economic control of the means of production and actual possession of those means. To illustrate the subtle differences between these two capacities, he points out that in feudal society the peasant generally had possession of the means of production, which the feudal class owned. On the other hand, in capitalist society the bourgeoisie has both economic ownership and possession of the means of production.[8]

Based on the above premises and criteria, the political economist Mahmoud Abdel-Fadil has attempted to construct a schematic picture of the class composition of urban Egypt at the end of the Nasser era. Abdel-Fadil delineates four broad class categories in urban Egypt, while recognizing that the relevant data are "extremely patchy and incomplete." First, he identifies a bourgeoisie, which during the Nasser era consisted of the upper stratum of the bureaucratic and managerial elites, wholesale traders and capitalist entrepreneurs and contractors, and top members of liberal professions (for example, doctors and lawyers). The petite bourgeoisie, Abdel-Fadil's second class, covers self-employed artisans, small traders, and shopkeepers; line supervisors and foremen; and nonmanual workers such as technocrats, middle-ranking civil servants, school teachers, professional soldiers, and students. Wage laborers, or proletarian workers, fall into his third class, and the fourth and final class is a subproletariat or lumpenproletariat, including occasional laborers, street vendors and peddlers, domestic servants, porters, and the unemployed—the outcasts and the disinherited masses. [9]

In a comprehensive and systematic study of the old social classes and revolutionary movements of Iraq, Hanna Batatu has also raised the question of the applicability of class and the difficulties of class analysis. From a sociological standpoint, he defines a class as being essentially an economically based formation. The term *class* thus refers to the social position of the individuals or families that constitute such a formation and presupposes inequality with respect to property. It implies at least one other class (in opposition) and thus contains the seeds of an antagonistic relationship. However, Batatu adds, a class is a multiform and differentiated phenomenon. As such, and as Max Weber suggested, it may exist in a distinct form of its own, constituting an element within a status group (such as the landed stratum within a group of tribal sheikhs) or embody different status groups (such as the *sadah*, *'ulama*, agas, or sheikhs.) [10] Moreover, Batatu accepts the view that a class need not act as a unit at every point in its historical existence—it need not be self-conscious and organized. Here, Batatu is not dismissing class by defining it away, but merely emphasizing the Marxist distinction between a "class in itself" and a "class for itself"—that is, the objective and subjective aspects of class.

The studies in the third group make a very strong case for the significance of class analysis in understanding Arab society, but further exploration of its class structure is needed. This book constitutes an attempt in that direction.

The Emerging Arab Economic Order

Processes of status as well as class formation may be traced far back into Arab social history. Perhaps most important in shaping this emerging order was the spread of the Islamic empire. Notwithstanding the early revolutionary potential of Islam and its principle of equality of all believers, Islamic conquests contributed to the reinforcement or the reemergence of privileged status groups and classes. The second caliph, Omar Ibn al-Khattab, devised a formula for the distribution of the newly acquired wealth based on *nasab* (kinship ties to the Prophet Muhammad) and on Islamic precedence (based on the length of time since one's conversion to the new faith). Instead of eliminating inequalities, the new order thus maintained previous systems of stratification even as it contributed to the emergence of new status groups or classes. The Lebanese sociologist Zuhair Hatab observes that "Muslims began to be stratified into classes," and that the Hashemites (the Prophet's tribe) began to "enjoy affluence and the honor of *mulk* [power and ownership]. . . . Most of them immersed themselves in affluence inclining toward the easy life, building palaces and gardens, and owning a lot of concubines [*jawari*]. . . . Furthermore, the children of this aristocratic class . . . began to value land and seek to own it. . . . [The Hashemites were] thus transformed from an aristocracy based on *nasab* to an urban and landed aristocracy."[11] By the time the Umayyad dynasty was established, certain classes and status groups had been formed. At the top of the hierarchy were the Arabian tribes, followed by the *mawali* (non-Arab Muslims) and *ahl al-dhimma* ("People of the Book," mainly Christians and Jews), with slaves located at the bottom.[12]

Prior to the nineteenth century, then, the economic order and the social structure most prevalent in the Arab world were characterized by the dominance of the state or ruler and by land ownership. Subsequently, however, the *iqta'* (the *timar* or *iltizam* systems, defined earlier; see also discussion in the next section) began to acquire hereditary status, thus combining the forces of the landlords with those of other notables, such as the merchants, the affluent *'ulama*, the tribal sheikhs, and the military elite. Other features of the economic order were the simplicity of modes of production and the centrality of the extended family as a unit of social organization and socioeconomic activity. Society, in this economic context, was structured by patrimonial and client relations; an honor-ranking system; and the idea that society constituted an earned possession (*mulk*) of the ruler.

Dating from the nineteenth century, a gradual process began that integrated the Arab world into the European-dominated world. That is why the nineteenth century is considered to mark the beginning of the structural transformation of contemporary Arab society. In turn, economic integration of the Arab world into the capitalist world system resulted in the gradual emergence of new classes, particularly a local bourgeoisie directly linked to the West and serving as the mediator between the local consumer and the European producer.[13] This process of structural transformation has prompted a number of Arab researchers, among them Hannah Batatu, Afaf Lutfi al-Sayyid Marsot, and Philip Khoury, to conclude, in Khoury's words, that "it is only in the nineteenth century that we begin to witness the formation of classes on a significant scale."[14]

Social and economic historians disagree on the magnitude of the transformation resulting from European penetration of the region; they disagree as well on the claim that the region moved from a subsistence to an export-oriented economy. However, these disagreements do not preclude general consensus that the development of capitalism in the Arab world was owing to European penetration in the nineteenth century. To identify the roots of this transformation is, however, only the beginning of our effort. From this starting point we must answer a series of significant questions. What are the characteristics of the gradually emerging economic order in its present stage of development? What has the impact of integration into the world capitalist system been on old social structures? What are some of the new structural changes? How does the emerging economic order influence social class relations? Has the Arab world actually experienced a transition from a subsistence economy to a modern complex economy? These questions and others need to be raised here if we are to understand the social class structures and dynamics in contemporary Arab society. I would argue that we should begin with the observation that the contemporary Arab economic order is a peculiar cluster of different modes of production, all operating at once, which renders it simultaneously semifeudal, semicapitalist, and semisocialist.

The very different economic circumstances in different parts of the Arab world go far toward explaining this. As indicated by several social historians, certain economic changes involved in the incorporation of the Arab world into the modern world order predated the nineteenth century.[15] Moreover, Roger Owen has argued that the unevenness of the transformation has stemmed in part from the fact that the coastal regions were much more directly influenced by European trade than the cities of the interior and the countryside.[16] Thus, even in their precolonial social formations, Arab regions did not constitute a homogeneous whole. In the Arab world, Samir Amin has observed, one can distinguish three zones that differ widely from each other in social structure and in political and economic organization: the Arab east, the countries of the Nile, and the Arab west. Whereas Egyptian society was based on cultivation of the soil, the eastern and western parts of the Arab world were essentially urban and commercial—the east until World War I and the west until French colonization. In this "precolonial Arab world—a region characterized by its mercantile character, with Egypt the only peasant exception . . . the ruling class was urban, composed of courtiers, merchants and men of religion and around them the little world of craftsmen and clerics. . . . The ruling class cemented the whole together. . . . This is the class that created Arab civilization."[17]

The economic order now emerging therefore looks different in different parts of the Arab world. Depending on whether a region possessed a port city or other entry point for Western economic influence, the extent of urbanization and the degree to which a particular kind of urban elite was dominant, and the resulting economic base, the extent of Western penetration and the impact of the European-dominated world economy have differed. Recognizing these disparate beginnings, however, we may nonetheless also note certain similarities in the way contemporary social formations have emerged. There are four characteristic factors: relations of dependency; widening disparities between the rich and poor within each of the Arab countries; widening gaps among Arab countries themselves; and disequilibrium among the different economic sectors within the area as a whole. These four characteristic features, in turn, are inseparable from the structure of consumption and what it reveals about economic disparities in the Arab economic order. Let us look at each of these features in turn.

Dependency. Arab countries are separately and independently integrated into the world capitalist system. The links are comprehensive, involving economic, political, social, and cultural spheres of activity. The comprehensive but fragmented nature of linkage to the world capitalist system has rendered the Arab world peripheral and powerless. Interlocked in a network of dependent relations, the Arab world seems to have lost control over its own resources and destiny. The rich and more powerful countries conduct themselves as regional powers, imposing a system of local dependency on the poorer and weaker countries. Hence there exists a dual or even triple dependency system, which weighs heavily on the weak and impoverished countries. Having lost control over their resources (especially oil), the Arab countries, including the rich and more powerful ones, evidently lack the will to shape their own destiny. Instead, they drift, seemingly at the mercy of challenges and events such as those that led to the destruction of Kuwait and Iraq. It is this situation that explains why the relationship between the Arab world and the West is characterized more by conflict than cooperation and by consumption rather than production. It also explains the failure of development efforts.

Widening Disparities. Uneven development (that is, uneven development patterns biased in favor of cities, certain regions, and particular communities) has resulted in the exacerbation rather than the decline of class differences in all Arab countries, irrespective of the nature of the dominant order or the achievement of higher standards of living. The gradual emergence of a significant middle class may have blurred the boundaries and polarities of the nineteenth century, but disparities continue to grow.

As a market-oriented economy began to displace the subsistence economy in the nineteenth century, and as commercialization and communication networks developed, a landowning-bureaucratic class of notable families began to acquire more and more wealth and power. Philip Khoury has examined this pattern in the case of Syria and observes:

> All other classes witnessed a steady erosion of their positions, some completely dissolving in the face of intensifying European economic pressures and the forces of Ottoman centralization. In the country-side, small peasant proprietors were caught up in a mesh of capital . . . the small peasant family or village community found itself besieged by land and profit hungry city notables-cum-money lenders. Many peasants and, in some cases, whole villages lost their lands to the notables and turned to sharecropping; others, less fortunate, were completely dispossessed and either became wage laborers on the estates of big landowners or fled to small towns and cities.[18]

In urban centers, Khoury adds, many crafts were undermined or disappeared altogether. Furthermore, merchants suffered heavy losses in their competition with European trading houses and their local agents, who belonged to indigenous minorities.[19]

Raphael Patai notes that capitalist penetration resulted in "a vulgarizing and deterioration of the traditional arts and crafts," while at the same time widening "the distance between the top and bottom layers of society." The general decline in native arts and crafts, and consequently in the numbers of artisans and craftsmen themselves, was owing to the fact that local consumers became attracted to Western products and thus "ceased to be creators, inspirers, and consumers of native cultural products."[20]

This process of cultural alienation continues, accompanying the widening class differences that characterize present-day Arab society. The achievement of independence after prolonged struggles, and the coming to power of the emerging middle class in several Arab countries, challenged but never managed to arrest either cultural alienation or class differentiation. Even the various solutions proposed—the spread of education, land reform, nationalization, welfare programs, subsidies, economic growth, and the dominance of the public sector—have failed to stop these processes.

Disparities between Rich and Poor Arab Countries. Several Arab scholars have noted with regret the emergence of an intra-Arab stratification system resulting mainly from oil revenues. Comparisons have been made between rich and poor Arab countries. Based on the average GNP per capita, for instance, the Egyptian sociologist Saad Eddin Ibrahim classifies Arab countries into four main groups—the rich, the well-to-do, the struggling middle class, and the poor. At the top of the pyramid are such rich countries as Kuwait, the United Arab Emirates, Libya, Qatar, and Saudi Arabia, whose combined population was less than twenty million in 1987. Thus less than 10 percent of the Arab world's total population receives about 40 percent of the total Arab GNP. The well-to-do Arab states then included Oman, Bahrain, Iraq, Lebanon, and Algeria. In the struggling middle, Ibrahim included Syria, Tunisia, Jordan, and Morocco. The Arab states at the bottom of the pyramid included Yemen, Egypt, the Sudan, Mauritania, and Somalia. Together, this last group possessed about half of the Arab world's total population but received only about 15 percent of its GNP.[21]

This pattern has worsened over time. In 1970, the population of non-oil-producing countries was 88 million—that is, they held about 73 percent of the total Arab world population and received 51 percent of Arab GNP. This share decreased to 31 percent in 1975, and to 23 percent in 1980. Another set of data shows that the share of Saudi Arabia, 5 percent of the Arab world population, increased from 9 percent of the Arab GNP in 1970 to 25 percent in 1975 and 31 percent in 1980. In contrast, the share of Egypt (with 25 percent of the Arab world population) declined from 20 percent in 1970 to 9 percent in 1975, and to 8 percent in 1980.[22]

Other attempts at ranking Arab countries in terms of GNP and other socioeconomic indicators demonstrate increasing disequilibrium and disparities and explore some of their implications. One finding showed that by the mid 1970s, the ratio of the minimum to the maximum levels of the per capita share of the domestic product in Arab countries reached 1:123 (being then $94 in Somalia in comparison to $11,568 in Kuwait). The growing economic gap between the oil-producing countries and the rest of the Arab world has been increasingly divisive.

Lack of Balanced Development. These disparities result not just from the uneven distribution of natural resources. The Arab economy has suffered from varying degrees of disequilibrium in agricultural, commercial, industrial, service, oil, and other economic sectors. The contribution of the agricultural sector to total Arab GNP is very small in comparison to Arab needs and given the high percentage of the total population that agricultural workers comprise. Cultivable land constitutes no more than 5 percent of the area, and only 22 percent of that land is irrigated. Furthermore, the contribution of agriculture to GNP has declined in several Arab countries. Thus commerce has linked Arab economy to the world capitalist market at the expense of local industry and craftsmanship and intra-Arab trade.

Resource distribution does, in part, explain this disequilibrium. Industry is heavily oil-based, rudimentary in structure, and limited in scope and priorities. Even though no significant working class has formed, industrial revenue contributes to class inequalities, uneven consumption patterns, and the alienation of capital through investment abroad. According to Samir Amin, extreme Arab dependency is attributable to the weakness and disarticulation of the Arab mode of industrialization.[23]

Bases of Class Distinction and Formation

Taken together, these four interrelated conditions provide the basis for class distinctions and internal forms of domination. To understand how these economic conditions lead to social class formations, we need to look at the nature of dominance in the Arab world. That is, distinction between classes in Arab society requires some discussion of the economic and social criteria that separate the different classes and explain their antagonistic relationships. We might classify these criteria or social bases of class formation as having primary and secondary significance. The primary criteria are ownership or possession and control of land and wealth or capital. The secondary set of criteria are *nasab* or ascribed status, and occupational autonomy. Underlying both sets of criteria are explicit and implicit processes of exploitation and domination. Hence, inequalities as well as contradictions and conflicts of interest are significant in the analysis of class distinctions.

Landownership. The economic historian Charles Issawi has observed that in the Middle East "land has been for millennia—and except in the oil countries still is—the main form of wealth, and land tenure has been the principal determinant of income, political power, and social prestige."[24] Prior to the nineteenth century, land belonged to the state and the ruler. The notable families in the Fertile Crescent and Egypt derived their wealth mainly from the system of *iltizam* (an Ottoman tax-farming system) and from feudal estates held more directly under Ottoman rule (*timar*). The gradual rise of a system of private property over the past two centuries has led to the more advanced formation of social classes. In the Fertile Crescent, for instance, economically based classes of tenants, property owners, and hereditary feudal families began to develop. This division of society into a hierarchy of classes assumed a character of its own.

The landowning-bureaucratic class became one of the most stable and identifiable classes in Syria. Philip Khoury argues that its emergence coincided with the private appropriation of property, agrarian commercialization, and the development of modern means of communication and transport. Landownership combined with public office to produce this class. Land acquisition in Syria, in its turn, was stimulated by dislocations in the urban economy as a result of the penetration of European manufactured goods and the spread of cash cropping and commercialization during the first half of the nineteenth century. By the turn of the twentieth century, a powerful group of large landholding families had emerged and gained prominence on the Syrian social and political scene. The social elite of Damascus, for instance, consisted of about fifty families at the turn of the century. The cream of this elite included landowning religious scholars such as the Al-'Ajlani, Al-Ghazzi, Al-Kaylani, and Al-Hasibi families, as well as landowning bureaucrats such as the Al-'Azm, Al-Yusuf, Mardam-Bey, Al-Quwatli, and Al-Barudi families. [25]

In Palestine, too, certain families had become wealthy landlords by 1870 through land acquisition. By then, the Abdul-Hadi family owned 17 villages and 60 thousand dunums of land (4 dunums = 1 acre); the Jayyusis owned 24 villages; the Barghoutis, 39 villages; the Taji or Al-Faroukis, 50 thousand dunums; the Tayans of Jaffa, some 40,000 dunums; and the Shawwa family of Gaza, about 100,000 dunums. [26]

The abolition of the *iltizam* system by Muhammad Ali in Egypt in the early nineteenth century also encouraged the rise of private property. Afaf Lutfi al-Sayyid Marsot has pointed out that land was parceled and then distributed among the peasants for cultivation. Peasants had de facto rather than legal ownership but were able to pass land to their heirs as long they paid the taxes. Relatives and followers of Muhammed Ali became the owners of large estates. By the middle of the nineteenth century, Muhammed Ali and his family were the largest landowners, owning 18.8 percent of the land—"a pattern that continued and intensified until the revolution of 1952." [27] Indeed, in 1939, 1.3 percent of the total number of landowners possessed more than 50 percent of all land. [28] About 7 percent of the owners possessed 69 percent of the roughly six million cultivable feddan in Egypt in 1942.

Land reform in 1952 limited landownership to 200 feddan, but an additional 100 feddan could be retained by an owner who had two or more children. About 431,000 feddan were transferred to 163,000 families by the end of 1960. [29] In 1961, a new land-reform law reduced the ceiling on private landownership still further, to 100 feddan. The state claims to have redistributed 645,642 feddan, out of the 5,964,000 feddan of cultivable land in Egypt, to 226,000 families, expanding the ownership of private property, and more recent data on land distribution show that by 1975 large ownership (50 feddan or more) had been greatly reduced; small ownership (5 feddan or less) had increased immensely; and ownership of medium-sized plots held almost constant. [30] What has remained unchanged is the total area of cultivable land, the number of owners, and the landless status of the majority of Egyptian peasants.

The presence of smallholders with official title to the land has not appreciably changed the political landscape. A few families control the land and the political machinery, confirming the analysis regarding "the political character of social class struggle . . . for those who own aspire to authority in order to maintain their interests and ownership." [31] Field studies and official statistics since the 1970s show that landownership continues to play "the decisive role in the formation of social classes"[32] in rural Egypt, where it "constitutes the primary and probably the only mode of production."[33] Thus ownership and control over land is the primary point of entry to political power and high social status.

Similar findings exist for Iraq. We may see the connections between class status and landownership in the authoritative study of Iraqi social classes by Hanna Batatu. In 1958, Iraq, inhabited then by about six and a half million people, counted about a quarter of a million landholders (who held 32.1 million agricultural dunums, only 23.3 million of which were actually exploited). About four-fifths of Iraqi families owned no land at all, and 1 percent of all landholders controlled 55.1 percent of all privately held land. The majority of landholders were very small proprietors; 73 percent of them possessed less than 50 dunums apiece, or 6.2 percent of the total area.[34] The result of such an extreme concentration of private landownership, Batatu explains, was that

> the relations between Iraqis became less and less governed by kinship or religious standing or considerations of birth and more and more by material possessions. Property also assumed a greater significance as a basis of social stratification. . . . Thus the landed *shaikhs* and the landed *sadah* were now partly a tradition-based or religiously ratified status group, and partly a class, and their transformation from a status group into a class was slow and subtle; by the fifties of this century their property had clearly become a far greater determinant of their social position than their traditional status.[35]

The significance of landownership in the formation of social classes in contemporary Arab society may also be illustrated by similar trends in North African countries. The destruction of the precapitalist Maghribi society by French colonization led to the emergence of a dual system of inequalities. The region witnessed the extreme social contrasts and inequalities we might expect between European settlers and natives, but also the disguised inequalities between different classes of natives themselves. Most important for our analysis, since independence, the formerly disguised internal social class inequalities have begun to appear much more clearly. In the 1970s, statistics showed that 321,000 landowners in Tunisia possessed about 4.5 million hectares. Of these, less than 4 percent owned 34.3 percent of the land. In contrast, 63.4 percent of landowners possessed less than 18 percent of the land. Those in the middle, 32.7 percent of the owners, possessed 47.8 percent of the land.[36]

Wealth as Capital. Possession of wealth has been another significant determinant of class position throughout Arab history. Long-distance trade and a mercantile social formation characterized both the Mashriq (Arab east) and the Maghrib (Arab west) until the Arab world became integrated into the world capitalist system. Trade contributed directly to the emergence of the *tujjar* (merchants), who constituted the urban elites or notables. A factor shaping the development of the bourgeoisie as a whole was investment in commerce, trade, industry, and manufacturing. As with landownership, these fields of investment were dominated by a few notable families based in Arab cities. Consolidating the wealth in their own hands, they ruled their countries in alliance with big landowners, the *'ulama*, and the military elites. The ruler-capitalist-landlord triad of domination remained almost completely unchallenged until the middle of this century. What complicated the matter was the emergence of market-oriented agriculture and an export-oriented economy.

This precolonial pattern carried significant implications for Arab consciousness. Samir Amin argues that it was the mercantile character of the precolonial Arab world that led to the emergence of a ruling class interested in Arab unity. This was the class that

> cemented the whole together; everywhere it adopted the same
> language and the same orthodoxy, Sunni, Islamic culture. It was very
> mobile, able to travel from Tangiers to Damascus without feeling
> lost. This is the class that created Arab civilization. Its prosperity was
> linked to that of long-distance trade. This trade was the reason for
> the isolation of the agricultural zones which kept their own
> personalities—linguistic (Berbers) or religious (Shia)—but did not
> play an important role in the system. . . . This Arab world was thus
> at the same time diversified and deeply united—by its ruling class.[37]

The decline of this mercantile elite and the integration of the region into the world capitalist system thus simultaneously undermined this class and its ethos and weakened the Arab economy. The new economic and political situation led to the emergence of a new bourgeoisie of professionals, managers, bureaucrats, technocrats, agents, contractors, experts, and others interested in the reform of Arab society. Conflicts with the old bourgeoisie and colonialism made the new bourgeoisie regionally nationalist in character. The formation of nationalist parties indicates the transformation of the new bourgeoisie from a class-in-itself to a class-for-itself.

In the postcolonial period, access to new resources provided the necessary economic base for this regionally nationalistic bourgeoisie to attain and exercise power. Oil revenues, particularly in the 1970s, ushered in a new economic era. The unprecedented oil revenues created new prospects for economic development and capital formation. The assumption was that the newly acquired wealth could be utilized to achieve "self-sustained economic growth on the bases of a more diversified economic structure, the equitable distribution of the benefits of social and economic growth so as to enhance internal stability and create or maintain the social and political consensus, greater economic cooperation within the region, and an enhanced sense of economic, political, and technological independence."[38] Instead, it led to greater dependency on the West, enormous gaps between rich and poor Arab countries, an intensification of consumption rather than production patterns, and more internal disparities. Muhammed Rumayhi notes that the ruling classes of the oil-producing countries have been spending oil revenues on "essentially nonproductive consumption," in the process "transforming the merchant class from relatively wealthy to absolutely wealthy as a result of its monopoly of the import trade."[39]

Nasab, or Social Status. This is a secondary criterion for social class formation and distinction in Arab society. Serving more or less as an intervening variable, *nasab* is the ascriptive, special social status a person or family enjoys as a result of belonging to or claiming descent from a prominent family. It is both an outcome and a cause in the historical process of class formation.

Since an attempt will be made later to explore the relationship between social class and family more fully, it is sufficient here to point out that one of the historical peculiarities of social class formation in Arab society is the inheritance of social status based on religious and economic position. Economically, the legal system of inheritance secures the transmission of ownership of land and wealth within the family, hindering the process of vertical social mobility. Certain families in all Arab countries have thus managed to maintain their prominence over generations. Such families initially acquired status as a result of their economic standing in the community at a specific moment in history, but this status tended to be self-sustaining and to enable a family to acquire additional land or wealth. For example, the Quraish tribe of the Prophet Muhammad was the commercially and politically dominant tribe in Arabia. Following the rise of Islam, descent or asserted descent from this tribe guaranteed an unequal share of the wealth generated by Arab society. The result was the rise of the *ashraf* and *sadah* class.

Based on field research carried out in the early 1960s in the community of Hadramout in South Yemen, Abdalla Bujra has concluded that all Hadramis belonged

> to one of three social strata. The top one is that of the *sadah*, of
> people who claim to be the descendants of the Prophet Muhammed.
> The second is that of the Mashaikh-Gabail—literally the "scholars
> and the tribesmen." The third and lowest stratum is that of the
> Masakin—the "poor people." The system is based on descent; the
> strata are mutually exclusive, recruitment is by birth, and members of

each stratum have specific attributes and roles which differentiate them from members of other strata. [40]

Another illustration can be found in Batatu's study of Iraqi society. Several principles of stratification worked simultaneously there. In the case of the *sadah*, Batatu explains, their claim of descent from the House of Muhammad formed

> merely a supporting element, rather than the real underpinning of their social position. If they mattered in the society, they mattered essentially on some other ground—either on account of their wealth, or their holding of office, or their leadership of tribes or mystic orders, or a combination of two or more of these factors. Indeed, the trend appears to have been for the claim of sacred descent to be put forward after the claimants had risen in the world. [41]

Batatu has further explained that the *sadah* were not all of equal standing in society. The fact that there were *sadah* of limited means shows that the accident of birth did not by itself guarantee easy access to wealth; although it placed them "at a distinct advantage . . . a mere reputation as a sayyid could be turned into great material gain only in the more primitive parts of Iraq." [42]

Other illustrations of the significance of *nasab* in determining social class standing may be found in several works on other parts of the Arab world, such as Morocco. [43] This intervening variable, however, is losing its significance in the face of the increasing importance of wealth and landownership. Nevertheless, the accident of low birth may still serve as a barrier to the advancement of some impoverished segments of society, such as the *bedoon* of Kuwait and the *akhdam* (outcasts, or menial caste) of Yemen.

Occupational Autonomy. Another criterion at the base of social class distinction is what might be called career or occupational autonomy. The issue is one of direct control over the work process—that is, whether one works for oneself or for others. Traditionally, Arabs have considered working for oneself or for someone else, employing or being employed, serving or being served, and having full or little control over the production process to be matters of significance.

Occupational autonomy serves more as a mediating variable in that it influences or may even shape the extent to which the economic factor determines social standing in the community. A person who owns his business and works for himself would have a different social standing than a person with the same skills who works for and under the supervision of others. For example, a tailor who works for himself has a higher status than one who works for others, regardless of skill or earned income. Moreover, a tailor who owns his business and employs other tailors has an even higher status than the one who works for himself but works alone. *Khidma*, serving others, may in fact constitute a sort of stigma. A class of *akhdam* (singular, *khadim*) survives in Yemeni society. *Akhdam* carry out the menial tasks in Yemen and are poor, weak, subservient, insecure. They represent a historical link back to ancient institutions of slavery.

Basic Classes in Contemporary Arab Society

The interplay between the characteristics of the Arab economic order on the one hand and the grounds for social class distinctions on the other has created three major class groupings in Arab society: (1) the dominant class, or big bourgeoisie and notables; (2) the intermediate classes, or petite bourgeoisie, old and new; and (3) the working classes, made up of workers, peasants, and outcasts. Again, I must emphasize the dynamic nature of this process of class formation, and the extent to which it has been shaped by both external domination and internal social structures. Let us look at each of these groupings in turn to identify the processes that have created them.

The Dominant Class, or Big Bourgeoisie and Notables. This is the class that owns, possesses, and controls the dominant mode of production as well as the prevailing political system. Consequently, it enjoys wealth, power, and social prestige. Its relationship to others is one of exploitation and domination. It is composed of the large landowners, capitalists, big businessmen and contractors, big merchants, political and military elites, high-ranking managers and civil servants, prestigious professionals, prominent *sadah,* top religious *'ulama,* and important tribal chiefs.

Gamal Hamdan has described traditional Egyptian society as dominated by a repressive, autocratic landownership with three bases: rural feudalism, the theocratic *'ulama* elite, and the governing political bureaucracy—all dominating the worker-peasant proletariat. Egyptian society was thus traditionally divided into "a minority that owned and did not work, and a majority that worked and did not own."[44]

Another Egyptian scholar, Anouar Abdel-Malek, notes that prior to 1952, the Egyptian landed upper bourgeoisie and landed aristocracy, or feudalists, fell into two groups: the largest owners, who managed their property by leasing it to third parties, and rich cultivators who worked their land in order to produce raw materials, notably cotton, for sale to processing industries and agricultural produce intended for the domestic and world markets. This landed aristocracy was the basis of the Umma and the Liberal-Constitutional political parties before 1952.[45] The integration of Egypt into the world system, coupled with imperialism, enabled foreign capital to establish its grip on the finances and industries of the country. We may note two key moments in this process.

Prior to the turn of the twentieth century, the National Bank of Egypt was founded by the prominent Jewish financiers Ernest Cassel, Rafael Suares, and Constantino Salvago. Another development was the creation of the Committee for Commerce and Industry in 1917 by Ismail Sidky and Talaat Harb (who founded Bank Misr in 1920). It was from this point on, Abdel-Malek observes, that it became possible to speak of two wings of the Egyptian bourgeoisie: the national bourgeoisie and the upper bourgeoisie. The first consisted of wealthy rural intellectuals and the merchants associated with the Wafd party; the second consisted of the industrialists. What was notable about the Egyptian industrial economy was its "monopolistic character . . . in the sugar and cement industries, in distilleries, in chemical fertilizers, and above all within the group of industrial companies set up or brought together by the Bank Misr through a system of holding companies which became the main body of the whole economy." [46] The Egyptian revolution of 1952 removed this class and replaced it with another bourgeoisie composed, by the end of the Nasser era, of the upper stratum of the bureaucratic and managerial elites, wholesale traders, contractors, capitalist entrepreneurs, and top members of the liberal professions. [47] This class benefited later from the open-door economic policy of Anwar Sadat and Hosni Mubarak.

These same groups have constituted the bourgeoisie since the 1950s in Syria, Iraq, and Tunisia, replacing aristocratic notable families. In Algeria, these groups replaced the colonial settlers and constituted the national bourgeoisie. There were, of course, exceptions to this pattern. In Palestine aristocratic families gave way to Zionist settlers. In a few other Arab countries, such as Saudi Arabia, the Gulf states, Jordan, Lebanon, and Morocco, the aristocratic notable families managed to remain in power. Generally speaking, however, the pattern illustrated by the history of Egypt typifies the process by which the new dominant class emerged. Syria provides another case in point of this pattern.

In Syria, aristocratic notability was based on a combination either of landownership, wealth, and political power (for example, the families of Al-'Azm, Mardam-Bey, Al-Quwatli, Al-Jabri, Al-Barazi, Al-Atasi, and Al-Qudsi) or of landownership, the trades, and religious scholarship or *nasab* (for example, the Al-'Ajlani, Al-Kaylani, Al-Ghazzi, Al-Hasibi, and Al-Jaza'iri). [48] In Iraq, the old bourgeoisie was composed of the large landowners, top government officials, men of money and commerce (big merchants), the tribal sheikhs, and the prominent *sadah* families. The large landowners (*mallaks*) owned the greater part of and the best privately held land and constituted the nucleus of the ruling class until 1958. According to Batatu, in 1958, 49 families owned about 17 percent of all privately held land, about 5.5 million dunums. They included the royal family and those of tribal chiefs, *sadah*, sheikhs of mystic orders, merchants, and high state officials. The great majority of these 49 families produced deputies, high officials, ministers, or premiers: 27 produced deputies or senators; 4 produced premiers; 6 produced ministers of state; 1 was related by marriage to the royal family; 1 was related by marriage to the premier; 12 were *sadah*; 11 were merchants; and 22 were non-*sadah* tribal sheikhs. It was the Arab tribal sheikhs and Kurdish tribal beys and agas who formed the most important segment of the landed class during the monarchical period. To illustrate their great political power, it is worth mentioning that of the 99 members of the Iraqi Constituent Assembly of 1924, 34 were sheikhs and agas. The *sadah* (also known as *ashraf*) constituted a more or less closed group of families who did not enjoy the same standing. Only those who were *'ulama* or who possessed land and wealth enjoyed the high esteem of the important notable families. In fact, the term *sadah* began to lose its exclusive meaning before the revolution of 1958, when "birth had ceased to be a determinant of a person's worth. The relationships between Iraqis were more and more governed by money." [49]

The broad base of this new dominant class is, however, shrinking. The emphases on landowning, birth, and learning are retreating before the all-pervasive importance of wealth. Indeed, the current bourgeoisie in oil-producing countries is increasingly being redefined in terms of possession of wealth at the expense of other class distinctions. This is an extremely important development, since this wealth is mostly invested in Western industrial societies and geared toward consumption rather than production. The present Arab bourgeoisie, therefore, has become the most exposed to external control and fluctuations.

Intermediate Classes—the Old Petite Bourgeoisie and the New. The intermediate classes are so defined because of their position between the bougeoisie and the working class. They may also be defined as intermediate in terms of owning and possessing land or wealth, controlling to some extent the process of production, and/or practicing nonmanual or white-collar professions. The fact that members of these classes may occupy positions that render them closer to one of the two opposed or antagonistic classes tends to blur the boundaries, and to cast doubt on their own unity and the extent to which they form one class.

Before defining the boundaries between these intermediate classes and the bourgeoisie and the working classes, a distinction should be made between old and new petite bourgeoisie. Such a distinction may be at least as relevant in Arab society as in industrial societies and other Third World societies. In Arab society, the petite bourgeoisie is highly heterogeneous because it consists of all the groups who possess or control small amounts of land, capital, shops, or property, as well as those who have nonmanual specialized jobs. The old petite bourgeoisie in Arab society is composed of small traders and shopkeepers, self-employed artisans, and small and independent farmers. In the rural areas, such as in Egypt, this intermediate class is composed of those who work for themselves and have enough land to support themselves. According to Abdel-Malek, these medium landowners had 5–50 feddan apiece prior to the 1952 revolution. The upper level of them, owning 20–50 feddan apiece, aspired to become part of the class of large landowners and formed an integral part of the national liberal middle class that found its expression in the Wafd party.[50] In the urban centers, the old petite bourgeoisie included self-employed artisans, small retailers and shopkeepers, and the lower strata of independent professionals, such as the small traditional *'ulama*. Since the encounter with the West and the beginnings of integration into the world market, this subclass has been declining in importance relative to other subclasses.

The new petite bourgeoisie consists of civil servants or government employees, administrative staff, teachers, supervisors, technicians, white-collar employees, army officers, and middle- and lower-ranking professionals. The continuing growth of this new petite bourgeoisie is a product of the huge expansion of government administration, business and professional organizations, and private firms. Indeed, this growth measures the impact of new technology, education, urbanization, and mechanization. The increase in the size of the public sector and its bureaucracy is especially significant and may be credited for the substantial rural-urban migration. This subclass played a leading role in the development of national political parties and the power of the intelligentsia. In fact, it has managed to attain power and constitute an integral part of the ruling elites in a number of Arab countries, including Syria, Egypt, Iraq, Algeria, and the Sudan. The role played by the petite bourgeoisie in most Arab countries far exceeds in importance its estimated size of 5–25 percent of the population. It can be credited with removing the aristocratic ruling class from power in these Arab countries and taking up the tasks of governance and development.

Yet it is necessary to ask whether the petite bourgeoisie forms a single class. The heterogeneity of its members and the economic differences among them undermine its ability to cope collectively with old and new problems and to overcome conflicting ideological orientations. With regard to development and reform, it seems unable to change the conditions that lead to dependency on both the regional and world levels. This is what may have led Hisham Sharabi to call the Arab petite bourgeoisie a hybrid class characteristic of neopatriarchal society. As the most representative segment of neopatriarchal society and culture, the petite bourgeoisie has proved unable so far to carry out the tasks of comprehensive development. Nevertheless, in those countries in which the emerging petite bourgeoisie has not managed to become an integral part of the ruling class, it has served more or less as an insulating medium between the old ruling bourgeoisie and the working classes. In this role it has played a decisive part in preventing revolutionary change: instead of siding with the working classes even in times of crises, it has continued to dismiss class struggle and to call for limited reform from above.

The Working Classes—Workers, Peasants, and Outcasts. The mass of impoverished, repressed, disinherited, and weakened Arabs represents a class-in-itself by virtue of the alienating conditions under which it struggles to live. This class is divided into subclasses, including workers, peasants, soldiers, the lumpenproletariat, servants, street vendors and peddlers, porters, the unemployed, outcasts, and others. It is also divided communally. Although a class-in-itself, it has not yet been able to form a class-for-itself. The voices of the masses have been heard only through representatives of the petite bourgeoisie, who have taken power and monopolized the political process on their behalf. The disinherited masses, who live mostly in the slum areas of Arab cities and in isolated countryside communities, are the most alienated of alienated Arabs. Their alienation stems essentially from powerlessness and a preoccupation with securing their daily bread; they are vulnerable to exploitation, domination, humiliation, and sickness. Those in power who speak in their name are the main beneficiaries of their cause. Yet one might argue that workers and peasants (especially peasants) were treated no better previously.

Historically, the most ancient and deprived members of this impoverished class have been the landless peasants. Even unsympathetic and biased studies, such as those of Henry Ayrout on Egyptian peasants, have described them as producing much more than they consume. They have served their masters, who owned the land, as laborers, sharecroppers, and *tarahil* or *gharabwa* (migrant workers). They have been exposed to deep-rooted contempt and without the protection of social legislation. "The enormous economic and political pyramid of Egypt," Ayrout pointed out, "presses down upon the *fellah* (peasant) with all its weight . . . and it is this burden which shapes all his life." Knowing that the source of Egypt's wealth is the yield of the soil produced by the labor of the *fellahin,* Ayrout traced their wretchedness to ancient times and quoted the Muslim general 'Amr Ibn al-'As, who, after conquering Egypt for the Arabs, reported back to the caliph in Medina that "the inhabitants of Egypt are like bees, working continually, not for themselves but for others." The Egyptian peasants themselves are just as eloquent in describing their condition. One of their sayings depicts the peasant as a needle, which clothes others but remains itself unclad. Yet the writing of Ayrout reinforces the image of the *fellah* as passive, patient, obedient, cunning, suspicious, submissive, and lacking in understanding and originality. He also asserts that the peasant "does not feel the depth of this great misery. . . . The real evils, then, are the *fellah*'s lack of sensitivity."[51] In fact, the real evils are the alienating conditions that render peasants powerless and the images and attitudes the rest of the population have of them.

How accurate is this assessment of Egyptian peasants as passive and submissive? This negative image is represented in such works as Muhammed Hussein Haykel's novel *Zainab* (1913); the *Journal of a Prosecutor in the Countryside* (Youmiat Na'ib fi al-Aryaf); *'Awdat al-rouh* (The Return of the Spirit) by Tawfiq al-Hakim; and *Sindabad Misri* (Egyptian Sinbad) by Hussein Fawzi.[52] The opposite image is drawn, however, by the Israeli scholar Gabriel Baer, who documents peasant uprisings in Egypt between 1778 and 1951 to disprove Ayrout's statements that the peasant "puts up with any ill treatment from his superiors" and that peasants "are not the stuff of which rebels are made." Baer's study underscores, as well, the contradiction in Ayrout's statement that "occasionally it was necessary to put the ordinarily passive and obedient peasants down with police force."[53]

Accounts of the desperate condition of peasants in other parts of the Arab world are not as well documented. Brief and scattered assessments are found in the few works that address themselves to various aspects of peasant problems. Franz Fanon shows, for instance, how peasants were transformed into revolutionaries in the context of the Algerian revolution, which began in the countryside and filtered into the towns and cities through an uprooted mass of humanity that lived in shantytowns and formed a new lumpenproletariat constituting "one of the most spontaneous and the most radically revolutionary forces of colonized people."[54] A similar process of transformation among Palestinian peasants was studied by Rosemary Sayigh, who argues that they contributed more than other classes to the Palestinian resistance movement without ever coming close to leading it. Their lack of knowledge, and exclusion from decision-making, perpetuated their subordination. Following the establishment of Israel and the exile of the Palestinians, the new marginality attributed to refugee status was added to the marginality of the peasant. Similarly, the transformation from a class of small and landless peasants to a lumpenproletariat on the fringe of cities and towns in Jordan and Lebanon put them at the center of the revolution.[55] Peasants in other parts of the Arab world, such as Syria, have improved their conditions, but in some other countries they continue to be marginal and deprived either as agricultural laborers in villages or as a lumpenproletariat in the shantytowns surrounding Arab cities.

An emerging working class suffered similar deprivations and may be as marginal in status. Forming the next most significant class of the struggling poor, its members sell their manual and productive labor cheaply. They have little control over the process of production or the products of their labor. Notwithstanding that they put so much of their lives into their work, their products and their lives do not belong to them. Their work must thus be seen as coerced rather than voluntary; the net result is self-estrangement in addition to estranged labor.[56]

This is the condition of the working class in spite of the nonindustrial and semicapitalist nature of contemporary Arab society. The largest segment of workers are peasants who have escaped the misery of their villages to work in the cities as wage earners in construction, manufacturing, public utilities and services, shops, transportation, and maintenance facilities. Some of them are engaged more in providing services than in producing commodities, and cannot strictly speaking be included in the working class. According to an analysis of class in Syria by the French researcher Elisabeth Longuenesse, the working class there is composed mainly of those in traditional or modern manufacturing establishments and workshops—that is, in textiles, woodworking and furniture-making, food processing, metallurgy, and the like.[57]

Do these shared working conditions translate into a shared organizational base? Traditional artisans or craftsmen worked for themselves in family-owned shops and belonged to guilds, which provided some form of organization. The number of modern industrial workers has increased considerably in Arab countries; Batatu cites statistics, for instance, to show that Egypt's modern manufacturing sector more than doubled between 1952 and 1967. In Syria, the number of workers in all plants almost tripled between 1960 and 1979. Yet these increases have not been enough to render the workers important in a political sense.[58] Workers did organize themselves in labor unions, and they have actively participated in political parties and national movements in most Arab countries, but there are forces that undermine their achievements. For example, the Lebanese sociologist Sadir Younis concluded in 1980 that in spite of their revolutionary slogans, labor unions in Lebanon were no more than reformist because of the prevailing social reality, which they could not transcend, particularly the presence of sectarian kinship alliances. But this is also true of other Arab countries: they have not experienced bourgeois revolutions transforming the traditional structures and orientations of society, and thus have not paralleled the experience of industrial societies.[59]

The peculiar situation of the Maghrib, on the other hand, may have helped the union movement play a more important political role. The Moroccan scholar Abdullatif al-Mununi has argued that the union movement there was able to play an important political role because, from its inception in 1934, it had to struggle against foreign capitalism, with its dual impact of exploitation and colonization. A relationship thus developed between the labor and nationalist movements.[60]

These conditions, particularly the lack of a bourgeois revolution, have undermined the transformation of the working class from a class-in-itself to a class-for-itself. However, worse than this lack of political development is the economic condition of the lumpenproletariat and the underclass of servants, outcasts, street vendors, and casual laborers. Their wretchedness is comprehensive and dehumanizing. They are the most disinherited of the disinherited masses.

Class Relations: Class Consciousness and Class Struggle

Class relations in this partially formed society are essentially characterized by contradictions, conflicting interests, and antagonisms. These characteristics play a primary role in interclass relations, and a secondary role in the intra-strata relations that take place within the same class.

Differences in the relative locations of the first two groupings of classes within the social division of labor undermine the possibility of fair competition to acquire wealth, power, social status, and other scarce resources to which society assigns special value. The absence of equal opportunities and the obstacles inherent in Arab society have made vertical social mobility very difficult. Those who occupy positions of advantage acquire the more valued things and further privileges, which in turn leads to the reinforcement and perpetuation of positions of advantage. The greater the advantages, the greater the insistence of the dominant classes on maintaining their privileges at the expense of society, and the greater the difficulties of the oppressed classes in overcoming the conditions of alienation, except through class consciousness, mobilization, and class struggle.

In Arab society, then, social class relations are characterized by exploitation, domination, alienation of the oppressed, and antagonism (as reflected in hatred, jealousy, hypocrisy, and the like). Those with access to power and wealth have put a premium on conspicuous consumption and emphasize symbols of status. Their relationship to the other two classes is marked by condescendence, arrogance, and contempt for the less fortunate. Given this reality, to what extent do class consciousness and class struggle exist? As indicated at the beginning of this chapter, analysts respond to this question in very different ways, varying from complete denial to complete affirmation. Some analysts deny the existence of any class consciousness or class struggle. Others emphasize the political movements that have based their strategies on the assumption that the objective conditions of working-class life will motivate workers to rally to their support.

In order for a class to be transformed from a class-in-itself to a class-for-itself, it has to develop class consciousness, to mobilize, to organize into political movements, and to wage a struggle to replace the existing order with a new one. One would need to be extremely optimistic to believe that such a level of consciousness and activism has been reached in any part of the Arab world. Nevertheless, disguised and even clear forms of class consciousness and class struggle do exist in Arab society. Any serious examination of the development of political and social movements, the formal organizational structures of guilds and labor unions, voluntary associations, and the informal structures inherent in social and cultural organizations reveals aspects of class consciousness and class struggle. These aspects emerge, too, in studies of peasant uprisings, political opposition, wars of liberation, struggles for independence, military coups, civil wars, uprisings, labor strikes and demonstrations, and bread riots. They are implied, as well, in acts of political repression, and in the lack of stability characteristic of much of Arab society. They are also present in folktales and songs, popular sayings and poetry, literature, and intellectual discourse. Think of the class consciousness implied in such sayings as: "The one who has a piaster is worth a piaster"; "If you are not a wolf you will be eaten by wolves"; "The world stands by those who are in good standing"; and "The gate of misery is wide." Other implications of class consciousness may be read into "If you marry a poor man to a poor woman, you will have a lot of beggars"; "The dog of the prince is a prince"; "From your poverty increase our wealth" (said of the viewpoint of the rich); and "What you aspire to have, many others also aspire to have." Recognition of the unequal battle waged between the classes is suggested, too, in the saying that "The poor man sold his child out of need, and the rich bought him on credit." Also "Everybody sings for the rich"; "Money begets more money, and poverty begets more poverty"; "Only the weak need a witness"; "The rich can buy ice in hell"; "Onions are the meat of the poor"; and "Whoever becomes a lamb will be eaten by wolves."

Conclusion

Class consciousness and class struggle, however, are undermined and complicated by several features of Arab society. Among these, one of the most significant is the fact that a multiplicity of modes of production exists in Arab society—as noted earlier, it is simultaneously semifeudal, semicapitalist, semiagricultural, and semi-industrial. This has undermined the emergence of a clearly delineated bourgeoisie and proletariat and has blurred the boundaries separating the classes. Moreover, the survival of old structures and conditions and the emergence of corporations that sustain and promote communal solidarity continue to mask the real nature of the ongoing conflicts. In addition, political repression by authoritarian states controlled by the bourgeoisie or the petite bourgeoisie has frustrated all efforts to mobilize and organize the dominated and impoverished classes. This is exacerbated, as well, by the fact that the impoverished classes have been coerced into almost total preoccupation with securing their immediate daily needs. Finally, the dominant culture has contributed to masking and even legitimizing class differences, which are perpetuated, for example, by the application of the legal principle of *kafa'ah,* which calls for the equality and suitability of marriage partners. Ideological sanction for class differences is also sought in the Qur'an, as in the frequent citing of the verses "We have divided among them their livelihood in the present life and raised some of them above others in various degrees so that some may take others in subjection" (43:32) and "God gave preference to some of you over others in regard to property" (16:71).

These are only a few of the conditions and sanctions that undermine class consciousness and class struggle in Arab society. Yet the fact that the bourgeoisie and petite bourgeoisie are clearly conscious of their interests and have acted to maintain their privileges and domination will eventually lead to greater class consciousness on the part of the impoverished classes as well.

The Arab Family and the Challenge of Change

The family is the basic unit of social organization in traditional and contemporary Arab society. At the center of social and economic activities, it is a relatively cohesive social institution. Yet the family has been undergoing significant change and needs to be examined in the context of the transitional nature of Arab society. That is, the family becomes one of the crucial social units to respond to, as well as to be shaped by, the changing social structure, the ongoing confrontations with value systems, and the struggle for social transformation in response to formidable challenges. A comprehensive understanding of family cohesiveness and transformation requires an examination, in turn, of (1) the characteristic features of the Arab family; (2) patterns of marriage and divorce; and (3) placement of the family within society, and in relation to other social institutions.

The Basic Characteristics of the Arab Family

The Arab family may be described as the basic unit of production and the center of Arab social organization and socioeconomic activities. It evolved into a patriarchal, pyramidally hierarchical (particularly with respect to sex and age), and extended institution. Let us look at each of these characteristics in turn.

The Arab Family as a Central Socioeconomic Unit. The traditional Arab family constitutes an economic and social unit because all members cooperate to ensure its continuation and improve its standing in the community. Enterprises such as shops, factories, businesses, and fields are commonly owned and operated for the benefit of all. Until recently, when the state began to provide services for its citizens, the family undertook such diverse tasks and reponsibili-

---

A paper based on the material in this chapter appeared in E. W. Fernea, ed., *Women and the Family in the Middle East* (Austin: University of Texas Press, 1985).

ties as education, socialization, training, defense, welfare, employment, and religious upbringing.

The family is at the center of social organization in all three Arab patterns of living (bedouin, rural, and urban) and particularly among tribes, peasants, and the urban poor. The family constitutes the dominant social institution through which persons and groups inherit their religious, class, and cultural affiliations. It also provides security and support in times of individual and societal stress.

The success or failure of an individual member becomes that of the family as a whole. Every member of the family may be held responsible for the acts of every other member. The sexual misbehavior of a girl, for example, reflects not only upon herself but upon her father, her brother, and her family as a whole. Thus the "crime of honor," which sometimes still occurs in tightly knit communities, is an attempt to restore the family's honor and place in the community by killing a sister or daughter who has been detected in sexual misconduct.

One's commitment to the family may involve considerable self-denial. Parents, and particularly the mother, deny themselves for the sake of their children. The source of the mother's happiness is the happiness and prosperity of her children. Ideally, both children and parents are totally committed to the family itself.

The very concept of family in Arabic (*'aila* or *usra*) reflects such mutual commitments and relationships of interdependence and reciprocity. The root of the word *'aila* and also of *usra* means "to support." While the father's role is defined as that of provider (*janna*) and the mother's role as that of homemaker (*banna*), children change from being *'iyal* (dependents) to *sanad* (supporters) once their parents reach old age. This explains why parents in some parts of the Arab world may refer to a child as *sanadi* (my support). Another expression of the commitment and self-denial of parents is the tradition in the eastern Arab world of becoming known as "Abu," father of, or "Umm," mother of, one's eldest son. This symbolizes the dropping of one's individual identity and adoption instead of the identity or role of fatherhood or motherhood.

A tape sent by a young man from a Syrian village to his father and mother, who were on a two-month visit to their elder two sons studying in the United States, sheds considerable light on the internal dynamics of Arab peasant families. The Syrian youth addresses himself to his parents as follows:

> Hello, father, hello, mother . . . How is your health? How are my brothers Samir and Walid? . . . I can imagine how they met you at the airport. I am sure they were overwhelmed with joy at seeing you.

I hope you will keep in contact and if you plan to stay longer I wish you would write often and send us your pictures. I miss you very, very much. I miss seeing my father. I miss seeing you coming home smiling. . . . I don't know what to tell you, my father. I want you to rest assured. I remain an ideal model for the whole village. Don't worry at all. . . . My time is totally devoted to the fields. I am taking good care of them. Don't worry . . . I'm working the land more than if you were here. . . .

Now, mother, it's your turn, my mother. I don't know what to say to you. First, I kiss your hands and feet. . . . I always, always miss you. I miss the times when I say, "Mother, give me my allowance," when I embrace you, I kiss you, I cause you trouble and suffering. . . . My mother, I don't know my feelings toward you. When I say, "my mother," tears burn in my eyes. . . .

Now I come to my eldest brother, Walid. How are you, my brother? How are you, my eyes, my soul, the one we are proud of wherever we go? We raise our head [notice he does not say "heads" because the family is one head] among people. You are a model for everybody. May God protect you from the [evil] eyes of people. I'm sure you are very happy with my parents. . . .

Now you, the love of my heart, you, Samir. You, my brother. There is nothing more beautiful than the word "brother." May you finish your studies and come back, and I can call again to my brother. Samir, I don't know what to say. By God, by God, I miss you very, very, very much, my brother. . . . Please, tell me your feelings when your parents arrived at the airport, please. I miss my parents very much.

My grandfather misses you very much. He cried a lot after you left and sobbed, "Will my son come back before I die?"

Hello, father. How are you, father? There is one thing I forgot to tell you. I have sprayed the apple trees. . . . Do not forget to bring back the camera and film. And you, mother, don't forget to get me what I asked for. Whether you bring it or not, I am always grateful to you. My mother, my mother. My God, I'm right now sitting in the room by myself and recording on the bed. I don't know, mother, my mother, how much I miss you. God damn separation. I hope you return safely. I don't know how, when I pronounce the word "mother," my heart inside contracts. . . .

I conclude, my father, my mother and my brothers, by kissing your hands, father, and asking for your blessing. The son realizes all his dreams if he has the blessings of his parents. My mother, my eyes, my soul, you are my heart, you my mother. My mother, when I say the word "mother," it rises from deep inside me. My mother, when you hear this tape, please don't cry; don't worry. My brothers, my father, my eyes, I will conclude by asking for your blessings and particularly the blessing of my father. Father, you can't imagine how happy I am for you. I'm happy for you, you cannot imagine how. . . . You have worked hard, and we want you to rest, my father. . . . My mother, I asked you to bring me some underwear, to put it frankly. I like American underwear. My brother, don't forget the camera and the bottle of perfume. My brother, when I say the word "brother," I almost collapse. You are two, but I am alone. I'm alone. I'm alone in the world, I'm alone in the world. But God is generous, I hope to be with you. I conclude by kissing your hands and feet, my father, and you my mother. I kiss your hands and feet. . . . I ask for your blessing. With your blessings, my father, I can face anything. My brother Walid, I kiss you, I kiss your cheeks. You, Samir, how I miss your smile and your eyes. . . .

This tape illustrates many aspects of Arab family life, including its interdependence, sentimentality, commitment, and claims of self-denial. At the same time, the deep attachment to the family verges on morbidity (this is particularly true for mother-son relationships) and results in a shunning of society. The interests of both the individual and society are denied for the sake of the family.

Family loyalty is one reason why many parents still want to have large numbers of children. Children in peasant communities and among the urban poor start to work and earn money at a very early age. An extra child is seen usually not as another mouth to feed or another person to educate but as an extension of family power and prestige and an additional source of labor.

The centrality of the family as a basic socioeconomic unit is being increasingly challenged by the state and other social institutions. The state is gaining control of the economy and education and has already become the biggest employer in most Arab countries. Young men and women are seeking education and careers away from their parents in urban centers within and outside Arab countries. Expanding economies, industrialization, and urbanization have contributed to the emergence of bourgeois classes and cultures.

These structural changes have already begun to undermine traditional relationships, roles, and value orientations within the Arab family. Old patterns of marriage and divorce are being slowly replaced by new ones. Different sets of relationships are developing between family and society. However, young men and women show less alienation from the family than from any other social institution, be it religious, political, or social.

The Patriarchal Tradition of the Arab Family. In the traditional Arab family, the father has authority and the responsibility. The wife joins his kin group (patrilocal kinship) and the children take his surname (patrilineal descent). The father expects respect and unquestioning compliance with his instructions. His position at the top of the pyramid of authority is based on the traditional division of labor, which has assigned him the role of breadwinner or provider. Reinforced by socialization and rationalizations, this role makes him *rabb al-usra* (lord of the family). By contrast, the mother, assigned the role of the housewife, has become annexed to her husband as *'aqila* (tied), *qarina* (linked), and *hirma* (prohibited).

The image of the father is clearly reflected in contemporary Arabic literature. The famous novel *Zuqaq al-Midaqq* (Midaq Alley) by the Egyptian novelist Naguib Mahfouz, for instance, depicts Radwan al-Husseini as a highly positive and moral character who is well-known in the neighborhood for his goodness and piety. He is described as a "true believer, a true lover, and truly generous." Yet "it was remarkable that this gentleman was harsh and uncompromising in his own house. . . . Husseini imposed his influence on the only person who would submit to his will—his wife." He believed in the "necessity of treating a woman as a child for the sake of her own happiness before anything else." This belief was reinforced by his wife's lack of complaint and her acceptance of her role. She considered herself "a happy woman proud of her husband and her life."[1] A similar relationship is portrayed in Mahfouz's famous trilogy depicting life in Egypt of the family of Ahmed 'Abd al-Jawwad between the two world wars. When the father departed on a business trip, "a strange atmosphere of release and relaxation enveloped the household. . . . Each member began to think about how he or she might be able to spend this wonderful day, a day of freedom from the ever-present, ever-watchful eyes of the father."[2] The mother, Aminah (which means "faithful"), feels that the limits her husband has placed on her should be maintained, including his ban on her leaving home without his permission. Thus, she initially resists, but later accepts, a suggestion by one of her children that she visit the shrine of Hussein, a saint to whom she is greatly devoted. The husband learns of the visit and, upon his return, orders her to leave his house for challenging his pride and authority. Despite her twenty-five years of marriage, she returns to her mother and anxiously awaits her husband's forgiveness for her terrible mistake. Such an incident would be unusual even in a traditional household, but according to traditional norms, a woman commits a grave error in challenging her husband's authority. This culturally imposed powerlessness explains why women are depicted in Arab mythology as masters of trickery and wit.

In everyday life, the father is in fact off-stage, spending most of his time outside the home. After work, he comes home for a short while and then departs to the village square or neighborhood cafe. Although cultural norms assign family power to the father, it is the wife who actually exercises power over the children. She is, in effect, entrusted with raising and disciplining them, although she may often use the father to scare or threaten them. Both sons and daughters are consequently much closer to their mother than to their father. This may be interpreted by some to reveal the existence of a matriarchal system alongside the patriarchal system in the Arab family. However, this matriarchal system functions in support of patriarchy.

The father has traditionally maintained his authority and responsibility mainly because he has owned the family's property and provided the family's livelihood. However, recent changes in family structure have contributed to the democratization of husband-wife and father-children relationships. These changes have occurred in response to the emergence of competing socioeconomic units, the employment of women, and the migration of children to the city seeking education and work. In other words, the patriarchal tradition is in a transitional period. Increasingly, fathers are tending to relinquish their grip on family life and to share authority and responsibility with other family members. Yet the family remains patriarchal and hierarchical in structure.

This hierarchical structure of the traditional Arab family reflects the fact that families are stratified on the basis of sex and age. That the young are subordinate to the old and females to males leads Hisham Sharabi to conclude, in his study of the Arab family, that the most repressed elements of Arab society are the poor, the women, and their children.[3]

The Subordination of Women. Arab society has traditionally assigned women a subordinate status. Certain features of Arab society reflect this, varying by class. First, women are secluded and segregated. Veiling (a sign of separation) is still widespread in most of the Arab world, and although an increasing number of women are being educated and filling important roles and positions in the public domain, the majority continue to occupy the private domain of the household. Second, limited roles are available to women, notably those of daughter, sister, wife, mother, and mother-in-law. Few professional careers are available to women under the existing division of labor, and whatever is available tends to be an extension of their traditional roles. Social, economic, and political organizations relegate women to the margins. Third, personal status codes discriminate against women, particularly in such areas as marriage, divorce, and inheritance. Indeed, among certain classes, ownership of property is almost exclusively confined to men, in practice if not by norm. Fourth, buttressed by the prevailing religious ideology, which considers women to be a source of evil, anarchy and social disorder (*fitna*), and trickery or deception (*kaid*), the prevailing standard of morality stresses values and norms associated with traditional ideas of femininity, motherhood, wifehood, and sexuality. Fifth, in the resulting social climate, some women to this day suffer forced marriage, honor crimes, clitoridectomy, and other forms of abuse.

Arab writers tend to agree that society assigns women a subordinate status, but they strongly disagree on the extent of society's acceptance of this situa-

tion, its origin, and the reforms required. Arab analysts who concern themselves with women's issues tend to subscribe to one of three trends, ranging
from what we might call the traditionalist trend through the reformist trend to
a liberal or progressive trend. Followers of the traditionalist trend assert that
women are subordinate by nature or by God's will and design. 'Abbas Mahmoud al-'Aqqad, a prominent twentieth-century Egyptian writer, says in
Al-Mar'a fi al-Qur'an (Women in the Koran) that women are disposed to
shyness and receptivity both by nature and because they receive their character
(*'irf*) from men. That this traditional view has continued to dominate Islamic
establishments is evident from a 1975 special issue of *Majallat al-fikr al-islami*
(the Journal of Islamic Thought) published by Dar al-ifta' in Lebanon, in
which an editorial by the Mufti of the Lebanese Republic points out that Islam
decreed equality between woman and man "where equality was possible
. . . and preference was admissible where equality was impossible, for God said,
'Men are superior to women'; made it the duty of man to struggle . . . and to
provide for dependents, and relieved woman from such burdens on account
of her physical potential, personal circumstances, and financial responsibilities."[4] Another article in the same issue addresses itself to the question of
inheritance and explains that Islam gave the male twice the share of the female
because it "relieved the woman from financial responsibilities in the different
stages of her life. The father carries out this responsiblity before her marriage,
the husband after marriage, and the sons carry it out in case the husband dies
. . . consequently . . . the man is assigned twice the woman's share, for it is quite
clear that five bank notes without responsibilities are more valuable and last
longer than ten bank notes with immense responsibilities."[5]

The reformist trend attributes the subordination of women to misinterpre-
tation of Islam rather than to Islam itself. As we are told by the Egyptian author
Aminah al-Sa'id, Islam in its time

> appeared as a great social revolution in the history of women's
> position, not only for us in the Arab nations but also for the whole
> world. Just before the rise of Islam . . . woman was scarcely a human
> being; she had no rights . . . Islam restored to woman her total
> humanity; it . . . freed her from the domination of the male by
> giving her (a) the right to education, (b) the right to buy and sell
> property, and (c) the right to hold a job and go into business. . . .
> Islam did not differentiate between men and women except in giving
> the woman half the man's share of inheritance, in return for the fact
> that the man was to be responsible for the woman's material needs.
> At the time this was a gain, but it is now considered a curse. For
> with the decay of Arab civilization, reactionary forces gained
> ascendancy, and these forces used inheritance as an excuse to lower

the entire status of women to that of half the man or even, in some cases, less than half.[6]

More liberal or progressive writings reject both the traditional and reformist (reconciliatory, apologetic) trends. The subordination of women became a significant issue in the writings of Boutros al-Boustani (1819–1893), who wrote a book in 1849 entitled *Ta'lim al-nisa'* (The Education of Women). Qassem Amin (1863–1908), however, is often considered the pioneering voice on behalf of the emancipation of women. In *Tahrir al-mar'a* (The Liberation of Women), his first book (1899), Amin based his defense of women's rights on religious texts and drew upon modern ideas and views. In his second book, produced a year later, *Al-Mar'a al-jadida* (The New Woman), Amin based his arguments on the social sciences and was influenced by the liberal concepts of individual freedom and the rights of free expression and belief. He linked the decline of woman to the decline of society and saw her oppression as one of several other forms of oppression. In eastern countries, he pointed out, "You will find woman enslaved to man and man to the ruler. Man is an oppressor in his home, oppressed as soon as he leaves it."[7] Amin called for the removal of the veil, the granting to women of the right to divorce, banning of polygamy, specification of the conditions under which a man might be allowed to proclaim a divorce, the education of women as well as men, and women's participation in scientific, artistic, political, and social activities. Since then, other writers have contributed to a sophisticated and progressive understanding of the women's rights issue. These include Salama Moussa, the Algerian feminist Fadela Mrabet, the Lebanese novelist Layla Ba'albaki, the Syrian fiction writer Ghadah al-Samman, the literary critic Khalida Sa'id, the Egyptian physician-essayist-novelist Nawal al-Sa'dawi, Fatima Mernissi, and several others.[8]

I would argue that the third perspective is most convincing. We should look to socioeconomic conditions rather than a woman's nature to find explanations for woman's dependency on man (be it father, husband, or son). Without being able to work outside the home, women are evaluated in terms of their roles as mother, sister, or daughter. To the concern for controlling women in order to protect the family can be attributed the tendency to hold women responsible not only for their own sins but also for those of men, and for the expectation that they be totally faithful to their husbands (who, while expected to provide their wives with material support, are not held to the same strong moral commitment). Progressive elements in Arab society reject these limited views of women, building new roles for women in diverse domains ranging from education to work, politics, and social movements. In moving

outside these limitations, male-female relations have been significantly transformed within the context of revolutionary liberation movements such as
those of the Algerians and the Palestinians.[9]

Yet despite the achievements of women in many fields, they continue to
suffer from severe problems even on the most elementary level. The veil is still
omnipresent in several Arab countries and is widespread in others. Moreover,
as Khalida Sa'id has observed, the fact that women wear miniskirts in some
places (Beirut, for example) does not necessarily constitute a qualitative departure from the wearing of the veil. Both styles reinforce the image of the
woman "as being essentially a body to be covered or exposed." Furthermore,
Sa'id has argued that "the woman continues in most instances to be a persecuted follower and a private property . . . if we are asked about the identity
of a certain woman, we would say that this is the wife, the daughter, or the
sister of so-and-so. . . . What is the woman? She is the female of the man, the
mother, the wife. In brief, she is defined relative to the man, for she has no
independent existence. She is being defined in terms of the other and not a
being on her own."[10]

In a paper published in 1981, I suggested that the basic factors contributing
to the subordination of women are the prevailing general order and the nature
of its division of labor, property ownership, the degree and quality of involvement in social and economic activities, control over the production process
and products, and the overall position of women in the social structure.[11] If
we consider woman's subordination to be the dependent variable, we may
consider the prevailing socioeconomic conditions and structures as the basic
independent variables, while culture and psychological tendencies constitute
intervening variables. The relationships between these variables on the social,
cultural, and psychological levels are interactional. This model may help to
explain what is actually at issue in discussing and attempting to change the
status of women in contemporary Arab society. Change toward the emancipation of women must begin by transforming the prevailing socioeconomic
structures to eliminate all forms of exploitation and domination.

Subordination of Children. In an attempt to explain the inability of the Arab
world to cope with modern challenges following the 1967 defeat, Hisham
Sharabi has proposed that children in the feudal-bourgeois Arab family have
been socialized into dependence and escapism. The principal technique of
child-rearing in such families is shaming, while the learning process emphasizes
physical punishment and *talqin* (rote-learning) rather than persuasion and reward. The results are dependency, inequality, and the downplaying of challenges and difficulties.[12] Furthermore, children learn to link love and certain
expectations, and they consequently experience guilt feelings whenever they

annoy or fail to perform their duties toward their parents. Their main commitment in later life is usually to the family (sometimes at the expense of society or of their own personal interests).

My own data suggest that university students in Lebanon are least likely to be alienated from their families, while they are often alienated from religion, politics, and society. "Parents are usually overprotective and restrictive, and children grow up to feel secure only on familiar ground," I noted in *Lebanon in Strife*. "They avoid taking risks and trying new ways of doing things, for independence of mind, critical dissent, and adventure beyond the recognized limits are constantly and systematically discouraged by parents and other older members of the family."[13] By contrast, children in villages may become quite independent because village parents, unalarmed by their familiar environment, may allow their children to explore their surroundings freely. In general, however, the hierarchical structure of the Arab family based on sex and age traditionally requires the young to obey the old and adhere to their expectations. This hierarchy creates vertical rather than horizontal relationships between the young and the old. In such relationships, downward communication often takes the form of orders, instructions, warnings, threats, shaming, and the like. Furthermore, while downward communication may be accompanied by anger and punishment, upward communication may be accompanied by crying, self-censorship, obfuscation, and deception.

Extended Ties. The present-day Arab family is not usually extended in the strict sense. It is rare for three or more generations to live together in the same household. Recent studies show a continuing trend toward the nuclear family. Urbanization, industrialization, government employment, education, exposure to the developed world, and the emergence of a middle class have had some impact. According to data on the Arab Middle East collected by E. T. Prothro and L. N. Diab, the majority of wives interviewed who had married in the 1960s had never lived with their in-laws.[14] A more recent study of family and kinship ties in Iraq shows that the percentage of extended families changed from 82 percent in the 1940s to 34 percent in 1975.[15]

Yet despite the reduced prevalence of the extended family, relatives generally remain closely interlocked in a web of intimate relationships that leaves limited room for independence and privacy. They continue to live in the same neighborhood, to intermarry, to group together on a kinship basis, and to expect a great deal from one another. Such relationships and expectations are not severely damaged by emigration or by forced separation resulting from war or political upheavals. Palestinians are a case in point. Members of Palestinian families who have been dispersed as a result of the establishment of Israel and the subsequent wars continue to be interdependent and committed to one another. Special radio programs enable scattered Palestinian families to exchange greetings and information. A novel by Emile Habiby has described a striking encounter among dispersed Palestinian family members during the aftermath of the 1967 war. When a character who has lived under Israeli rule since 1949 meets his uncle and cousins, who have lived under Jordanian rule, he feels that "he is no longer a stranger without roots." [16]

The extended character of the Arab family is interrelated with its other characteristic features, and particularly with its functioning as a socioeconomic unit. This arrangement renders family members symbiotically interdependent. Thus, the tribe dominates among the bedouin in the desert, the extended family in villages and urban working neighborhoods, and the nuclear family in the city and among the bourgeoisie.

Marriage and Divorce Patterns

Marriage Patterns. Traditionally, marriage has been seen as a family and communal or societal affair more than an individual one. Officially, it has been perceived as a mechanism for reproduction, human survival, the reinforcement of family ties and interests, the preservation of private property through inheritance, socialization, and the achievement of other goals that transcend the happiness of the individual to guarantee communal interests. This principle is seen in most patterns related to marriage, including arranged marriage, endogamy, polygamy, age of marriage, the *mahr* (dowry), and the absence of civil marriage.

The system of arranged marriage, for example, has been directly related to the segregation of the sexes and the conception of marriage as a family or communal affair. Consequently, it has declined as a result of the mixing of the sexes in school and public life. Increasingly, marriage is seen as an individual choice that does not depend on parental approval. Love, which could serve as a reason for opposing a marriage in traditional communities, is increasingly becoming a prerequisite in the minds of young Arabs.

Custom requires parents to seek the consent of their daughter before they promise to give her in marriage, but that does not mean that they will abide by her expressed wishes. Traditionally, the daughter is expected to shy away from expressing her wishes, leaving them to decide for her. "As you wish" is the expected response from her. "You know what is best for me," she may add. According to the Egyptian religious scholar Ahmed Shalabi, "if the girl insists on her own choice without the consent of her father, Islam gives her this right as long as she makes a good choice and she is not deceived by false appearances. If she errs in her choice and marries a person who is not of her status [*kif*] . . . then the father has the right to object because of . . . the effect on the family and the future of the girl, who may be unaware owing to the immaturity of youth. In this case . . . the guardian . . . may object and prevent the marriage or nullify it if it has already taken place and the girl has abused her right."[17] This interpretation reinforces the parents' right to force a daughter into marriage (*haqq al-jabr*) to a man she does not like and to prevent her from marrying the man she loves.

The dilemma of Arab girls who must choose between abiding by their parents' will and making their own choices has been portrayed more than once in Arab fiction. The novel *Hunters in a Narrow Street* by Jabra I. Jabra, a Palestinian writer resident in Iraq, tells the story of Sulafa, who is to be forced by her father into marrying the son of a bedouin chief whom she has never met in order to reconcile the two families and halt her father's financial decline. She feels angry, terrified that sooner or later she may succumb to the harshness of a father whose "love can be as deadly as hate."[18] Similarly, *Season of Migration to the North*, a novel by the Sudanese writer Tayeb Salih, tells how a young widow is ordered by her father to marry an old man who "changes wives like he changes donkeys."[19] The woman threatens to kill herself, but the father is not swayed. He worries that he will become the joke of the community if she is allowed to disobey him. She is forced into the marriage, but she carries out her threat and kills her husband and herself.

A more recent novel by the Palestinian woman writer Sahar Khalifa, *As-Sabbar* (Wild Thorns), depicts the lives of Palestinians under Israeli occupation. Though radicalized by her involvement in her people's struggle for self-determination, a young woman, Nawwar, finds herself in an awkward situation. Her old father suddenly tells her that he intends to marry her to a doctor whose "material conditions are above the wind and whose clients gather in front of his clinic like flies." When Nawwar tells her father that she does not know this man, the father angrily answers, "For sure you don't know him. Did you assume the opposite?" Here again the girl cannot face the father. Her eyes avoid his, and her heart starts to pound with horror. She dare not argue with him lest he suffer a stroke that might end his life. It is a younger brother who faces the father and tells him that Nawwar loves an imprisoned fighter, Salih, and that she is too afraid to confess. Suddenly the girl explodes in defiance, "Yes, I will not marry anyone except Salih. I will not see another man. . . . I will not marry anyone except Salih even if I have to wait a hundred years." Shocked by such defiance, the father has a stroke and has to be taken to the hospital.[20]

Another possible outcome of a conflict with parents over marriage is elopement (*khatifa, shlifa*, or *nahiba*). In some communities, such an act results in the girl's ostracism for a long time, while in others it may cause great shame to the parents, especially those of the girl, who may find her and kill her.

Another aspect of traditional marriage that is undergoing change is the custom of endogamy—marriage within the same lineage, sect, community, group, village, or neighborhood. Like other customs, this one reflects the fact that the family rather than the individual constitutes the fundamental social unit. The advantage of endogamy lies not only in a lower *mahr* and the retention of family wealth and property within the clan, but also in the strengthening of kinship solidarity, in preventing the separation of the bride and her immediate kin. [21] The Lebanese sociologist Zuhair Hatab has observed that traditionally those Arab tribes who were economically more self-sufficient and concerned about their solidarity preferred endogamy, in contrast to trading tribes, which sought to improve their relationships and alliances with other tribes by intermarriage (exogamy). [22]

The most overstudied aspect of endogamy has been the *bint 'amm* (patrilineal parallel cousin) marriage—for example, marrying one's father's brother's daughter. It has been written that traditionally this type of marriage is the preferred form in tribes, villages, and closely knit communities. However, field studies conducted in diverse Arab communities during the present century reveal that the percentage of *bint 'amm* marriages usually ranges between 3 and 20 percent, although the percentage is considerably higher in more traditional and isolated communities. Of the 120 families that Shakir Salim interviewed in his 1953 study of an Iraqi marsh village, 38.4 percent of the marriages were to *bint 'amm,* another 12.8 percent to women of the same *fakhdh* (kinship group), another 11 percent to women of the same *hamula* (subtribe), and only 17.7 percent to strangers not of the villagewide clan. In other words, 51.2 percent of the marriages were within the same *fakhz*, 62.2 percent within the same *hamula*, and 82.3 percent within the village. [23]

A similar study in the 1970s found that half the marriages in the same marsh village and 42 percent in the Jamila neighborhood of Baghdad were endogamous. [24] At the other end of the Arab world, Dale Eickelman found in a field study conducted in 1968–70 that *bint 'amm* marriages among the Sherqawi family (descendants of the *marabout sidi* Mohammed Sherqi) of the town of Boujad, Morocco, totaled 30 percent, in comparison to 14 percent among town-born commoners and 22 percent among rural commoners. [25] In a study of two suburbs of Beirut in the late 1960s, Fuad Khuri found about 11 percent of Muslim marriages were *bint 'amm* marriages. [26] The *bint 'amm* marriage is customary among Muslims and Christians in bedouin tribes, rural villages, and traditional urban communities. The fact that this form of marriage was traditionally widespread is reflected in the common reference of the husband and the wife to one another as *bint* and *ibn 'amm*.

Endogamy is not limited to kinship ties. It extends to neighborhoods, villages, towns, cities, and sects. The Syrian sociologist Safouh al-Akhras found that in 232 of 400 families living in Damascus in the early 1970s, the husband

and wife had been born in the same neighborhood of the city. He also found that 88 percent of the husbands born in Damascus had wives who had also been born in Damascus.[27] The most lasting and exclusive form of endogamous marriage is within the sect. Marriage outside of one's sect is very rare and is the least condoned form of exogamy, both officially and unofficially. A Muslim woman is not allowed to marry a non-Muslim.

There is some disagreement about the meaning of the *mahr* (a dowry designated by the bridegroom for the bride on the date of the marriage). Some see it as a practice intended to protect women, particularly against divorce, and as money to be used for buying clothing and jewelry. Others see it as a bride price affirming male dominance. While the former view is mostly advanced by religious scholars, the latter is often put forward by Western observers. Still others see the *mahr* merely as a symbolic gift. The *mahr* is of two sorts: *muqaddam* (in advance) and *mu'akhkhar* (deferred). The *muqaddam* form is presented at the time of the signing of the marriage contract, and marriage is not considered lawful without it. This amount is supposed to be paid to the bride and not to her father or guardian. But the reality is often different. The amount and nature of the dowry are settled through a bargaining process between parents, usually the father of the bridegroom and the father of the bride.

In actuality, the *mahr* has been seriously misused. Complaints about its abuse and limitations include the fact that the *mahr* is presented to the father or guardian of the bride, enabling him to keep all or part of it instead of spending it on outfitting his daughter. The rising cost of the *mahr* is a target of constant condemnation. This is a custom that is intensifying, rather than atrophying, under the pressure of contemporary circumstances. Shakir Salim's field study of the marsh village in southern Iraq in the early 1950s showed that the amount of the *mahr* differed depending on whether the marriage was within or outside the kinship group. In the case of marriage within the *fakhdh* (kinship group), the *mahr* ranged between 3 and 20 dinars, but otherwise the *mahr* was much higher, ranging beween 50 and 100 dinars.[28] Richard Antoun found that the standard advance *mahr* in Jordanian villages was 200 dinars in 1960 and 250 dinars in 1966; the annual per capita income in the area at that time was about 30 dinars.[29] Muhammed Safouh al-Akhras also found that the higher the social status of the family, the higher the *mahr*.[30] In a more recent study of marriage crises in Syria, Buali Yassin says delayed marriage is connected with the high cost of the *mahr*. By Yassin's estimate, the average *mahr* in Syria was about U.S. $670 in the late 1970s, and he concludes that "the measure of a preferred girl over others . . . was the amount of paid *mahr*."[31]

A good case study of the changes in which we are interested is provided by Lebanon. An analysis of 3,398 marriage contracts in the court of the Druze sect in Beirut from 1931 through 1974 shows a consistent increase in the amount of *mahr* over the years. The average *mahr* has more than doubled each decade, and its level has generally been proportional to the prestige of the families involved. Other considerations that affected the amount of the *mahr* included the "physical status" of the bride (that is, whether she was a virgin or not, a widow, or a divorcee); her social class (whether she came from an elite or a common family); political affiliation within the Druze community; degree of endogamy (the closer the kin, the less the *mahr*); physical proximity and social distance (the further away and the higher in status, the more the *mahr*); and the bride's age. [32]

Besides affecting the amount of *mahr*, the age at which marriage takes place has an important effect on the status of women in Arab society. Traditionally, girls have married at a significantly earlier age than boys. Ottoman law required a girl to be at least nine years old to marry. Presently, the officially required age for marriage in Arab countries ranges from 15 to 17 for girls and from 18 to 20 for boys. However, actual records during this century show that the average age of marriage for girls in the eastern Arab world ranged from 14 to 18 up to the 1930s, and from 17 to 21 in the 1960s. For males, the average age at marriage ranged from 21 to 30. An examination of the records of the Sunni courts in Sidon and Tripoli shows that the average age at marriage for males ranged from 28 to 32 between 1920 and 1965, while for girls during the same period it ranged from 17 to 21. [33]

More significant, however, is the steady narrowing of the gap between marriage partners. While the average age of marriage for women has risen, for men it has remained almost constant. For instance, the average husband-wife age difference in Sidon was about 14 years in the 1920s but declined to 8 years in the 1960s. Safouh al-Akhras's study of the four hundred families of Damascus shows that the average age of husbands was about 44, while that of wives was about 37. The age gap differed according to generation, however, and the lower the age of the husband, the narrower the age gap was between the spouses. [34] Finally, it is worth mentioning that the trend toward a narrower age gap between husbands and wives represents a positive development in view of the problems inherent in the traditional large gap in age between marriage partners. In her book *Beyond the Veil,* Fatima Mernissi observes that boys quite often lost their girlfriends to older men. Folktales from contemporary Arabia tell of young wives married to old men who have secret boyfriends (*sahib*); the troubles the young woman has to go through to meet her *sahib*, the excuses she invents, the stupidity of the husband (who is invariably the last to know), and the often tragic and dramatic discovery of the wife's infidelity, which is always accompanied by violent and severe punishment, quite often death, are related in detail. The woman may be saved from death if the husband is afraid of scandal or the wife is the daughter of an important man. [35]

Another traditional Arab marriage pattern is polygamy, which is restricted by Islam to four wives, whom the husband is required to treat equally. Though polygamy is not encouraged, it has been justified or rationalized by conservative Muslims. Some argue that polygamy serves to prevent adultery: "We live in a society that allows for adultery . . . if a man does not marry another wife, what do you think of him if he commits adultery?"[36] Implicit here is the assumption that women are created for the convenience of men. The spoiled male is not willing to compromise his privileges; he insists on either adultery or polygamy.

The Qur'an says, "Marry women of your choice, two or three or four; but if ye fear that ye shall not be able to deal justly (with them), then only one" (4:3). This verse has been interpreted by some to mean that Islam allows unrestricted polygamy on the grounds that the verse is an example and not a limitation. Some claim that the allowed number of women is eighteen, interpreting the verse to mean 2 + 2, 3 + 3, and 4 + 4 = 18. Still others have claimed that the allowed number is nine, interpreting it to mean 2 + 3 + 4 = 9.[37] Other justifications invoked for polygamy include the sterility of the wife; lengthy absences of the husband from home; the impact of wars in shifting the ratio of appropriate males to females; the acceptance of the wife herself; and the fact that polygamy is practiced among non-Muslims.[38]

The prominent Egyptian writer 'Abbas Mahmoud al-'Aqqad insists that polygamy "is one of the means of emancipation of the woman, who on her own moves from a life replete with depression or humiliation to a dignified married life and decent motherhood."[39] The author of a book on polygamy, Abdul Nasser Tawfiq al-'Attar, explains that "God's decree . . . made woman unfit for polyandry while man is fit for polygamy, this is clearly demonstrated by the fact that woman possesses a womb . . . and man does not possess one. . . . Consequently, woman's nature contradicts polyandry out of fear that the embryo may come from diverse blood, making it impossible to determine who is socially and legally responsible for him."[40]

In reality, however, polygamy is now rare. It is limited to some tribal chiefs, feudal lords, childless husbands, and a few peasants in need of labor. Official statistics show that in the 1960s it was practiced by fewer than 2 percent of married Muslim men in Lebanon, 4 percent in Syria, 8 percent in Jordan, 8 percent in Egypt (1951), and 2 percent in Algeria (1955). Research conducted in the 1930s showed that 5 percent of married Muslim men in Syria had more than one wife and that this phenomenon was more widespread in rural than urban areas.[41] In the 1970s, a field study conducted by Safouh al-Akhras showed that only 2 percent of married men in Damascus had more than one wife. Similarly, studies of the family in Baghdad showed that of married men, 8 percent had more than one wife in the 1940s. This percentage was reduced to 2 percent in the 1970s.[42]

On the level of official policy in Arab countries, there are countries that approve of polygamy as a religious tradition, including Saudi Arabia, Kuwait, Libya, Jordan, Morocco, Lebanon, and Egypt. Those countries that make polygamy conditional include Iraq, Syria, and Algeria. Only Tunisia forbad polygamy in 1956. In 1953, a law was passed in Syria requiring a judge's approval for a polygamous marriage. Although forbidden in Iraq during the presidency of Abdul Karim Kassem (1958–1963), it was reinstated after his fall. Later, Article 4 of the Iraqi personal status law made polygamy conditional on the approval of a judge, who has to ensure that two conditions are met: the ability of the husband, as shown by a financial statement, to support more than one wife; and the existence of a public interest, such as the inability of the first wife to have children. [43]

The nature of the legitimizing authority for marriage is also important for the status of women. In this respect, it matters greatly whether marriage is regarded as a civil or religious ceremony—that is, whether the state or religious institutions sanction the marriage. Zuhair Hatab asserts that "marriage in Islam is a noncoercive contract between consenting [adults], and civil in that it does not submit to religious rituals and practices on the part of the clergy." [44] This claim is frequently heard, but it may be disputed if, as Abdalla Lahoud says, civil marriage is to be regarded as "a marriage contracted according to frameworks and conditions defined . . . by civil legislation . . . enacted for all citizens and [that] may be amended according to the evolution of public opinion trends and of the society. That is what distinguishes civil marriage from religious marriage, in which religious legislation regulates all aspects of its contracting, dissolving, prohibitions, and implications—an arrangement that applies to affiliates of a particular religion and rarely changes or changes slowly and with difficulty." [45] The fact of the matter is thus that marriage in all Arab countries continues to be religious.

The personal status codes governing marriage, divorce, custody, and inheritance differ in Arab countries according to religious sects. There are no common codes enacted and equally applied to all citizens by the civil authorities. This situation is of particular significance in religiously pluralistic societies. This matters because codes of personal status rarely change despite changes in circumstances and conditions. The existing religious codes are considered to be divine, and their source is God, not society. Laws and rules regulating marriage, divorce, custody, and inheritance are seen as absolute and eternal. Thus, a woman, no matter how mature, cannot marry without the permission of her guardian. Furthermore, Muslim women (unlike Muslim men) cannot marry non-Muslims.

Officially, all the sects in Arab countries, including Christian sects, reject civil marriage. At the same time, parents, particularly the father, fear that civil marriage may undermine their control over their children. Thus the lack of civil mechanisms for recognizing marriage have profound implications for women. Civil marriage allows for choice (that is, one may marry in religious, civil, or both courts), in contrast to religious marriage, which denies choice.

Divorce patterns are almost as significant as marriage in affecting the status of women. Where secularism has not yet had an impact, the rules and traditions regulating divorce are essentially determined by religious affiliation. Divorce is almost impossible among some religious sects (for example, Maronites and Catholics), but it is an accepted practice and *halal* (lawful) among others, although it has been described as *akrah al-halal* (the most hated of lawful practices).

Divorce was widespread in pre-Islamic Arabia, but it was not exclusively a man's prerogative. In certain communities, according to *Kitab al-Aghani* (an encyclopedic work by the literary historian Abu al-Faraj al-Isbahani [A.D. 897–967], replete with valuable information, anecdotes, stories, poems, and songs), a wife could easily divorce her husband. Islam ended this practice, but maintained the practice of divorce as falling almost entirely within the category of men's rights. Islam recognizes two major kinds of divorce. One is *al-talaq al-raj'i* (revocable), stipulating that married life may be resumed within three months (*al 'ida*) without a new contract or *mahr*. The second is *al-talaq al-ba'in* (clear divorce), which occurs when the divorce extends beyond the three-month *'ida* period, so that reunion would require a new contract and *mahr*. This second type of divorce can be minor or major. Both occur when divorce extends beyond the *'ida* period, but it is considered major or irrevocable if the husband says, "I divorce you" three times to his wife. Then remarriage is not allowed unless the divorced woman is first remarried to another man and again divorced.

The overall divorce rates have varied a good deal during the past century; they have climbed in response to the pressures of modernization, particularly in urban centers. Between 1958 and 1967, the number of divorces ranged from 66 to 105 per 1,000 marriages in Syria (170 to 210 in Damascus); from 119 to 149 in Jordan (166 to 236 in Amman); and from 61 to 74 in Lebanon (103 to 129 in Beirut). The study by Prothro and Diab of the religious court records in the Lebanese cities of Sidon and Tripoli shows that the rate between 1920 and 1924 was 463 for each 1,000 marriages in those cities. The rate declined in 1945–49 to 143 in Sidon and 169 in Tripoli. In the 1960–64 period, it declined in the latter city to 135, but reached 170 in the former. This phenomenon is also apparent in Algeria, where the rate was 410 in 1905, 133 in 1949, 35 in 1950, 84 in 1951, and 162 in 1955. This decline might be explained by such developments as the emergence of the nuclear family, the integration of the sexes, marriage by personal choice, or the narrower age gap between spouses. Yet it is also clear that the divorce rate has begun to increase again during the past few decades. In the Arab world, divorce is most common during the early years of marriage. Prothro and Diab found that about one-third of the divorces in Sidon and Tripoli took place before the actual marriage—that is, after the marriage contract was signed, but before the couple began to live together. From a Western point of view, this is closer to breaking an engagement than to a true divorce. Official statistics in Jordan and Syria show that in the early 1960s about 40 percent of all divorces took place during the first two years of marriage, especially when there was no pregnancy. According to Jordanian official statistics for 1973, about half of the cases of divorce occurred during the first two years of marriage. Furthermore, analysis shows that more than half of these divorced women (56 percent) were childless. The majority of the divorce cases in Amman (743 in 1968 and 909 in 1973) were of the minor sort (69 percent in 1968 and 71.5 percent in 1973), followed by the *al-raj'i* type (29 percent in 1968 and 27 percent in 1973). The percentage of major or irrevocable divorces was very small, 2 percent in 1968 and 1.5 percent in 1973. [46] The same trend was found in a similar study of the Egyptian family by Amira al-Bassiouni, who reports that 720 out of 1,000 divorces occurred among childless couples, and that minor divorce constituted the greatest proportion, about 75 percent, followed by *al-raj'i* divorce, about 20 percent. Major divorces were the least common. [47]

In many Arab countries the husband can easily divorce his wife, whereas it is impossible for a wife to divorce her husband against his will, except by consent of a court of law in extreme cases of neglect, maltreatment, nonsupport, indefinite absence of the husband, or impotence. The husband has the right to order his wife back to the home, known as *beit al-ta'ah* (the house of obedience). The wife is supposed to obey her husband or she is considered *nashiz* (disobedient); refusal to obey (*nishouz*) may constitute justification for the husband to stop payment of support. A husband may also divorce his wife without paying the deferred portion of her *mahr*, which occurs when he refuses to divorce her unless she forfeits her right to it. This is called *moukhala'a*, and Prothro and Diab report that the records of the Sunni courts of Sidon and Tripoli for 1930–65 show that the *moukhala'a* form of divorce constituted between 58 and 77 percent of all divorces in Sidon and between 65 and 86 percent in Tripoli in those years.

The feminist movement in Arab countries has been struggling to establish women's right to divorce and to prevent divorce outside a court of law. These demands were made by an Arab women's conference in Cairo as early as 1944. An increasing number of women insist that their marriage contracts include their right to a divorce. Certain reforms have been achieved. Since 1960, an Egyptian husband seeking a divorce must state his reason for doing so in court. Some other Arab countries, such as Algeria, Tunisia, Syria, and Iraq, also require that divorce proceedings take place in court. Tunisian law prohibits a judge from granting a divorce without looking into the reasons and counseling the husband and wife. By contrast, Articles 46 and 80 of the Moroccan personal status laws restrict the role of the judge to recording the husband's decision to seek a divorce.

The Family and Society

It has been a consistent theme of this discussion that the family has to be studied in relationship to all other social institutions, a relationship often simultaneously complementary and contradictory. This can be demonstrated through an examination of specific aspects of the complex network of interconnections between family and social class, family and religion, and family and politics.

It has been noted that the family is at the center of socioeconomic activities in Arab society. Persons and groups inherit their social class through the family in the same way they inherit their religion, sociopolitical affiliations, and language. Islam has further reinforced the connection between family and social class by making inheritance within the family circle compulsory. Individuals cannot dispose of more than one-third of their estates to anyone other than their legitimate heirs. Social class in turn regulates aspects of family life such as patterns of socialization, marriage, and divorce. Marriage across classes, for instance, is limited, a restriction reinforced by the religious principle of *kafa'ah*, equality of marriage partners. Persons and groups also receive their religious affiliations and orientations from the family. Religion reciprocates this continuity of support by stressing the holiness of a family and its ties, as well as the value of obedience to parents. Consider such proverbs as "A father's satisfaction is part of God's satisfaction" ("Ridha al-abb min ridha ar-rabb"), and "A father's anger is part of God's anger" ("Ghadhab al-abb min ghadhab al-rabb"). There are striking similarities between the religious concepts of the father and of God, indicating that God is an extension or abstraction of the father. *Rabb al-isra*, the lord of the family, became *rabb al-'amal*, the lord of work (a term that survives with reference to the employer), which in turn became *rabb al-kawn*, lord of the universe or of existence. Similarly, the mother's role of mediator between children and the father in the Arab family must have shaped believers' understanding of the role of Mary in Christianity and of 'A'isha, *umm al-mu'mineen*, the mother of believers, or Fatima or Zainab in Islam, who play the role of mediator (*shafi'*) between the believers and God.

Interrelationships between the family and politics may also be characterized as complementary-contradictory in several respects. While kinship loyalties may conflict with national loyalty and undermine national consciousness, much of the legitimacy of political orders and rulers derives from the family and its values. Political socialization takes place in the home, resulting in the congruency of political orientations among members of the family. Also, rulers and political leaders are cast in the image of the father, while citizens are cast in the image of children. God, the father, and the ruler thus have many characteristics in common. They are the shepherds, and the people are the sheep: citizens of Arab countries are often referred to as *ra'iyyah* (the shepherded). A central psychosocial feature of Arab neopatriarchal society, as Hisham Sharabi has pointed out, is "the dominance of the father (patriarch), the center around which the national as well as the natural family are organized. Thus between ruler and ruled, between father and child, there exist only vertical relations: in both settings the paternal will is the absolute will, mediated in both the society and the family by a forced consensus based on ritual and coercion." [48]

To consider the complexity of society and the variations introduced by social class, lifestyle (bedouin, rural, or urban), political order, and encounters with other societies, we must reexamine some previously accepted generalizations. One such generalization is that the Arab family socializes its children into dependency. The dependency present in Arab society is only partly a product of family; much of it is owing to political and economic repression, as the following example illustrates. After a three-week study of a Palestinian refugee camp in Jordan immediately after the June 1967 war, I concluded that a few well-armed and well-organized persons might be able to invade and control this camp of more than three thousand people because the camp lacked organization. Every family lived on its own, totally preoccupied with immediate and personal problems and interests. Less than a year later, in the spring of 1968, I visited the same camp and found it totally transformed. In the interim, Palestinian resistance organizations had mobilized the people, trained them, engaged them in political dialogue, and involved them in preparation for surprise attacks. People were talking about principles, arguing about ideological issues, learning about themselves and their enemies, and proudly narrating the stories of heroes and martyrs of the liberation struggle. The explanation for this sudden transformation from a condition of dependency to a condition of autonomy is located not in the realm of the constant (that is, early childhood upbringing) but in the realm of social variant.

Before 1967, Palestinians in Jordan and other Arab countries were not allowed to organize into political or even social movements. All significant organizations were dismantled and the people were watched, threatened, demoralized, and constantly pushed or bribed to remain in their own private and secure shells. Communities were atomized into separate families preoccupied with their daily needs and concerns. Since the family is the basic economic unit and no other forms of social organization were allowed, communities were exposed and accessible. In short, people were disarmed and forced into dependency.

In his early work, Sharabi analyzed the ways in which dependency resulted from socialization but did not say much about its relationship to political and economic repression. Nor did he address the fact that socialization is an ongoing process that is not restricted to childhood. People continue to be desocialized (unlearning what has been learned) and resocialized as a result of new experiences and involvement in new situations. National crises can transform consciousness. The emergence of radical parties and movements in Arab countries, for example, has served as an agency of desocialization and resocialization. However, the Arab family continues to be the most significant agency of socialization of the young as functioning members of society. Other such agencies include schools, the mass media, religious institutions, political systems, ideological movements and parties, and peers. While some of these agencies, such as religious institutions, tend to reinforce family socialization, others—such as ideological movements and peers—may conflict with it. The Arab family has served also as a mediator or link between the individual and community and society, by directly facilitating access by its members to positions, roles, and careers in public life, and by protecting them.

Conclusion

The Arab family has thus served as a society in miniature. As suggested earlier, similar sets of relationships prevail within both the family and the society as a whole, as well as in Arab economic, religious, political, and educational institutions. Stratified and patriarchal relations are common to all. The employer-employee relationship is another form of parent-child or father-son relationship. The educational system, even at the college level, is also patriarchal; students are constantly referred to as "my children" or treated in a paternalistic manner. Vertical relationships continue to prevail and are regulated and reinforced by a general, overall repressive ideology based on *at-tarhib* (scaring) or *at-targhib* (enticement) rather than on discussion aimed at persuasion. The dominance of those relations becomes even more comprehensive because of the extended nature of the Arab family (that is, being an integral part of a larger tribal structure). Claiming common patrilineal descent, the family belongs to broader groupings based on lineage (*hamula*), clan (*'ashira*) and tribe (*qabila*). In several parts of the Arab world, tribal loyalties continue to undermine social and political integration.

Arab society, then, is the family generalized or enlarged, and the family is society in miniature. Both act on and react to one another. The interconnection renders social institutions inseparable even for the purpose of abstract analysis. Within such a network of relationships, social phenomena develop and change in a manner dictated by their locations and affiliations with respect to the whole.

7   Religion in Society

Orientalists and Islamists alike seem to follow the same idealist or static approach to the study of Islam and therefore agree that religion constitutes the most significant force shaping Middle Eastern societies. Their exclusive emphasis on religious texts and the projected normative order implies an understanding of society as a product of religion—that is, as a dependent variable. Based on such static conceptions, "Muslim societies" have been presented as being permanently "arranged by the divine will." Hence the categorically conclusive propositions of the established scholarship on Islam and Muslims. To illustrate how this reasoning works, let us examine a few propositions advanced by an Orientalist and an Islamist. The static perspective of these propositions is derived from religious texts, thus asserting that Islam shapes society rather than being shaped by it.

In an attempt to describe the "essential structure of Muslim government," G. E. von Grunebaum lists a number of propositions derived from the classical works of Al-Mawardi (d. 1058) and Ibn Taimiyya (d. 1328):

> The purpose of man is the service of God, 'ibada.
>
> Complete 'ibada requires the existence of an organized community of believers.
>
> The existence of such a community requires government.
>
> The primary purpose of government is the rendering possible of 'ibada. [1]

By confining his analysis to the normative realm as revealed in religious texts, Manfred Halpern also was able to define Islamic history as the "history of a community in process of realizing a divinely ordained pattern of society." [2] From the same perspective, von Grunebaum asserts that "Islamic constitutional law never limited the power of the ruler" and that it was "only with Napoleon's expedition to Egypt (in 1798) that . . . Muslim civilization regained willingness to change."[3]

The traditional '*ulama* and militant fundamentalists start from this static viewpoint too. The renowned Muslim Brotherhood leader Sayyid Qutb has said, for instance, that the "divine path" is "represented in its final stages by Islam" whose "basic characteristic is this: that it never forgets for an instant, at any time or place, the nature of man and the limits of his capacities."[4]

Elements of a more dynamic approach to the study of Islam may be discovered in studies inclined toward social analysis of actual religious behavior and attitudes, in contrast to those that focus on the text. Jacques Berque, for instance, studied Arabs in history, emphasizing the Arab struggle to transcend accumulated contradictions, divisions, uncertainties, and incongruities. In other words, Berque examined religion in the context of a society undergoing formidable conflicts and transformation.[5] Wilfred Cantwell Smith made a similar attempt, concluding that "one cannot adequately understand the role of Islam in society until one has appreciated the role of society in Islam."[6]

Not unlike his pendulum-swing theory of Islam, Ernest Gellner has oscillated between Orientalist and sociological analysis. His sociological characterization treats Muslim religious life in terms of a rural-urban dichotomy. In Arab cities he sees strict monotheism, scriptural revelation, and the observance of traditions. In contrast, Muslims in rural areas emphasize hierarchical relationships and express belief through reliance on sainthood, symbolism, and mystical practices. In the same essay, however, Gellner shifts toward an Orientalist position by drawing comparisons between Islam, Christianity, Judaism, and other religions without taking into account that they exist in different societies. In contrast to other religions, he argues, Islam is more "a blueprint of a social order," "more total in a number of dimensions," and possesses "a kind of independent existence in scriptural record."[7]

The Sociology of Islam

Such sociological analysis suggests a need to reverse the notion held by mainstream Western scholarship that religion is the key to understanding Arab society. I would argue, from a sociological perspective, that society is the key to understanding religion. Mohammed Arkoun has been systematically trying to rediscover Islam in its intricate social and cultural space. He has managed to do so by favoring a historical, sociological, and anthropological approach that examines the concrete conditions in which Islam has been practiced. This method is described by Arkoun as one of deconstruction, a methodology that has only emerged with the modern critical epistemology used in the human and social sciences during the past two decades.[8]

Sociological analysis of religion derives many of its principles from the works of Max Weber, Emile Durkheim, Karl Marx, and a study of the sociology of knowledge in general. Of the prominent founders of the sociology of religion, only Max Weber addressed himself (with very little knowledge of the area) to the religion of one-fifth of the world's population. What he explored was mainly the socioeconomic origins of Islam, its traditional patriarchal authority or patrimonial domination, and the nature of the relationship between Islamic beliefs and the emergence and persistence of capitalist institutions.

With respect to the origins and rise of Islam, Weber overemphasizes the role of the powerful warrior groups in Arab society, who, we are told, managed to accommodate the new message to their group and class interests. As explained by Bryan S. Turner, Weber argued that the new message "became accepted and re-fashioned by bedouin tribesmen in line with their life-style and economic interests."[9] The major flaw in this view of Islam is Weber's uncritical acceptance of theories sharply contrasting Occidental and Oriental civilizations, which were common in Europe at that time. He may also be criticized for overstating the role of bedouin warriors, because, as we shall see, the city played a much more important role in shaping and sustaining the ethos of Islamic civilization than did the bedouin tribes.

This chapter attempts to present a sociological analysis of religion in contemporary Arab society. Rather than seeing religion as an independent force shaping Arab and other Middle Eastern societies, this chapter will focus on actual religious behavior and on the conflicting interpretations of Islam that emerge in specific situations and under certain conditions. Thus the starting point of analysis is society itself and not religious texts and traditions. Religion is therefore investigated as a social phenomenon. We can best understand such phenomena by focusing on the believers themselves: on their attitudes and conceptions; the roles and practices they assume; the rituals and symbols designed to express their beliefs and counterbeliefs. We should look, as well, at the religious institutions and movements that have emerged in the context of the ongoing confrontations in contemporary Arab society. When it is contextualized in this way, we also see that religion acts on society and becomes an integral part of the very definition of its identity and orientation. In this respect, Islam is not different from other religions, except to the degree that the prevailing social and economic conditions allow for such differences under certain historical circumstances. Furthermore, Islam is as dynamic as the other great religions and constantly changing, reflecting the interplay of many other forces.

Specifically, the present chapter attempts to provide a dynamic sociological approach to the study of religion in Arab society by discussing, in turn, the social origins of religion; the difference between a religion and a sect; the difference between official and popular religion; and the functions of religion (examining mechanisms of control, instigation, and reconciliation). I shall look, as well, at the interrelationships between religion, family, social class, politics, and other social institutions. Also important in this kind of analysis is an examination of the struggle between religious and secular movements, especially between fundamentalism and secularism. Finally, I shall want to look at two contemporary phenomena, the alienation many Arabs feel from, and within, religion; and the relationship to be identified between religion and change.

The Social Origins of Religion

The definition of religion and the analysis of its origins in society are central issues in the field of the sociology of religion. One approach used within this field is the emphasis placed on society, culture, and the human psyche, or a combination of all three. For Weber, religious behavior or thinking "must not be set apart from the range of the everyday purposive conduct, particularly since even the ends of religious . . . actions are predominantly economic." Hence, there ensues what he calls the rational manipulation of spirits in accordance with economic interests. This explains why the church has not succeeded in deterring "a south European peasant from spitting on the statue of a saint when he holds it responsible that a favor he sought did not material- ize, even though the customary procedures were performed."[10] There is an Arab proverb that expresses a similar sentiment: "Nobody burns incense in homage to God free." In Tunisia, the peasants pray for rain to Imm Tambo, the ancient goddess of rain. If their prayer is not met, the children gather and burn a toy representing Imm Tambo.[11] Based on his comparative analysis of what he calls world religions, Weber observed that religious movements carry the stamp of the classes and status groups that founded them. Their religious ethics and ways of life were "profoundly influenced by economic and political factors."[12]

The social origins of religion are also stressed by the French sociologist Emile Durkheim (1858–1917). For him, society itself is the real object of religious veneration. In other words, society reaffirms itself through religion, whose primary function is the achievement and preservation of social integra- tion. As such, religion expresses the totality of collective life, and religious representations constitute collective representations. Durkheim thus defines religion as "a unified system of beliefs and practices relative to sacred things . . . beliefs and practices which unite into one single moral community . . . all those who adhere to them." Here again religious conduct is seen as purposive;

relations between men and gods are interdependent, for "if it is true that man depends upon his gods, this dependence is reciprocal. The gods also have need of man; without offerings and sacrifices they would die."[13] Perhaps it is this very sense of reciprocity that has prompted the tribesmen of Beni Lam in Iraq to challenge God:

> Forgive, forgive
> You have to forgive
> If you refuse to forgive
> Your Paradise will be empty.

The relationship of believers to God is an expression of their relationship to the source of religious experience. In summing up, Durkheim says that "if religion has given birth to all that is essential in society, it is because the idea of society is the soul of religion." Religious forces, then, are social forces. Far from being external and above society, religion "is in its image; it reflects all its aspects."[14]

If Durkheim sees religion as the primary instrument of social integration, Marx sees it as a major source of alienation, although they seem to agree that it is society that produces religion. According to Marx, human beings project their own powers and values upon outside objects and superhuman beings— that is, upon reified abstractions. Hence, he concluded, the foundation of all criticism is the criticism of religion, which is considered an external power that organizes society, when it is in fact the structure of society that gives rise to religion. In his own words, the basis of the criticism of religion is this:

> Man makes religion; religion does not make man. Religion is indeed man's self-consciousness and self-awareness so long as he has not found himself or has lost himself again. But man is not an abstract being, squatting outside the world. Man is the world of men, the state, and society. This state, this society, produce religion which is an inverted world consciousness. . . . Religious suffering is at the same time an expression of real suffering and a protest against real suffering. Religion is the sigh of the oppressed creature, the sentiment of a heartless world, and the soul of soulless conditions. . . . The abolition of religion, as the illusionary happiness of men, is a demand for their real happiness. The call to abandon their illusions about their condition is a call to abandon a condition which requires illusions.[15]

Freud similarly views religion as an "illusion," originating in its early forms, he says, from feelings of guilt and remorse generated by the slaying of the tyrannical father by his sons. The totem, the first object of worship, served as a father substitute. The strength of religion is explained by Freud as one of several ways human beings seek to realize their repressed wishes and pleasures and avoid the pains of life. [16]

Whether sociological or psychological in nature, these interpretations seem to agree that religion is "an expression in one form or another of a sense of dependence on a power outside ourselves." [17] Underlining the interpretations, however, is the assumption that the power is nevertheless embedded in society, not outside it.

Religion and Sect

Distinguishing between religion and sect is essential to understanding the role and significance of religion in contemporary Arab society. *Religion* refers here to a system of beliefs, doctrines, rites, texts, and practices associated with sacred objects and the ultimate problems and values of human life. *Sect,* on the other hand, refers to the social organization of a community of affiliates. Examples might include the Druze, Shi'a, Sunni, Alawite sects and both the Orthodox and Catholic Christian communities. From this perspective, Abdul Karim Rafiq refers to sects as kinship groups, guilds, and occupational groups, as well as religious communities. [18] Kamal Salibi calls religious sects tribes in disguise. [19] Afaf Lutfi al-Sayyid Marsot views sectarianism as an integral part of the Ottoman feudal system and shows how society was built on "a series of intermediaries acting as buffers between the population and the administration. . . . The minorities relied on their religious leaders to act as intermediaries between them and the administration, while the populace had recourse to the ulama. The authority of the central government was gradually usurped by the intermediaries, especially in time of crisis." [20]

In a more recent Lebanese context, Nassif Nassar gives three definitions of a sect. In the first, a sect is defined as an organized community practicing its religious beliefs in particular ways; in time, such a community develops a certain social and political dimension, influenced by its understanding and application of religion, as well as by the historical circumstances it has experienced. The second definition puts greater emphasis on the social aspects of religion—that is, on sect as a social entity with members, institutions, buildings, endowments, slogans, customs, and so on. The third definition stresses the religious community's concern with practicing its beliefs and organizing its social and familial life. [21] The distinction between religion and sect is relevant in the eastern Arab world because—as we saw in Part I—the presence of a multitude of sectarian communities undermines social and political integration. The fact that so many sects have developed their separate subcommunities and subcultures requires that we reexamine the assumption that Islam, as the religion of the majority, represents a unifying force. The nature of the existing social organization renders sects more concrete; religion is comparatively abstract and remote from the daily life of believers. The unifying force of religion is therefore weak in the face of the divisive force of sects.

The social reality in the eastern Arab world, then, is one of sect rather than religion. Arabs must contend with more or less separate communities of Sunnis, Shi'as, Druze, Alawites, Syrian Orthodox, Maronites, Eastern Catholics, and the like. These sectarian affiliations are comparable to—indeed, inseparable from—tribalism or ethnicity. All three divisive subcategories of society relate in similar ways to systems of economic interdependence, political arrangements, and social movements.

Some aspects of sectarianism have roots deep in the Arab past. The development of *taqiyya* (denial of one's religious affiliation out of fear) among some sects, for instance, reveals the presence of sectarian persecution. Nevertheless, it is possible to trace current sectarianism to the conditions created or promoted by Ottoman rule and Western colonialism in deliberate efforts to maintain domination. Since independence, Arab rulers have continued to manipulate the same configurations for the same purposes. This pattern underscores the economic and political nature, rather than the spirituality, of sectarianism. The interconnection between sectarianism, tribalism, economic interests, and politics at the expense of religion is not confined to Lebanon. Examples of this emerge in a number of sociological works on Arabia and the Gulf states as well. Khaldoun al-Naqeeb notes that the rival tribes of Adnan in northern Arabia and Qahtan in southern Arabia coincided with the Wahabi and Abadi denominations respectively, as well as with the emergence of political movements and competition among the ruling families.[22] As in Lebanon, growing socioeconomic inequalities and gaps between social classes rejuvenated sectarian divisions in Bahrain and Kuwait, notwithstanding a previously common national struggle.

To conclude this section, sect rather than religion as such seems to prevail in the eastern Arab world, particularly in times of political and economic crises. Religion as a spiritual, moral, and integrative force has been in a state of decline.

Official versus Folk or Popular Religion

Another basic distinction from a sociological perspective needs to be made between official and popular religion. The former refers in the Arab context to the tradition of the religious establishment—which stresses religious texts, the shari'a (Islamic law), absolute monotheism, the literal interpretation of religious teachings, ritualism, the absence of intermediaries between believers and God, and the religious establishment's close connection with the ruling classes. Official religion is essentially located in cities and led by the *'ulama*, or that stratum in society composed of scholars learned in Islamic law and texts. Popular or folk religion, on the other hand, refers to a very different religious orientation. This pattern of religious life personifies sacred forces, emphasizes existential and spiritual inner experiences, seeks intermediaries between believers and God, and interprets texts symbolically. It flourishes in rural areas and appeals to peasants, women, and deprived classes and groups.

The mosque (or the church in the case of Christian minorities) is the center of activities for the official religion. Popular religion, however, features the shrine as a central institution for religious activities. Other contrasts are represented by the *'ulama* versus *awlia'* (clergy versus saints), the word versus the person, abstract teachings versus concrete experience, fundamentalism versus symbolism, ritualism versus charisma, extroversion versus introversion, and revelation versus direct experience.

These distinctions and others are clearly expounded by Gellner in what he calls the pendulum-swing theory of Islam. Benefiting from David Hume's doctrine of the tendency of society to oscillate endlessly from polytheism to monotheism and back again, Gellner finds this constant oscillation between the two poles to be the most interesting fact about Muslim religious life. He attempts a sociological characterization of the two opposing poles based primarily on his study of Moroccan society. One pole is distinguished by a set of characteristics that include strict monotheism, puritanism, a stress on scriptural revelation (and hence on literacy), egalitarianism between believers, the absence of special mediation, sobriety rather than mysticism, and a stress on the observance of rules rather than on emotional states. The other pole is distinguished by a tendency toward hierarchy, a multiplicity of spirits, the incarnation of religion in perceptual symbols or images rather than in the abstract recorded word, a tendency to mystical practices, and loyalty to personality rather than respect for rules. Gellner argues that the first set of characteristics is favored in an urban setting, while the second set is favored in rural communities. Cities are the center of trade, Muslim learning, and power. The rest of the society is composed of tribal lands that resist central authority. Such a paradigm of the traditional Muslim state tries to incorporate Ibn Khaldun's theory of the tribal circulation of elites and Hume's schema of religious life. The situation, however, is not entirely symmetrical.[23]

Another manifestation of popular religion in rural communities in the Levant is what the Syrian historian Hassan Haddad refers to as "georgic" cults. Underlying the apparent diversity of sectarian affiliations, he observes a common undercurrent of religiosity among peasants of all the religions and denominations of the area. They all flock to the same shrines to express their devotion and to present their offerings and sacrifices (*nidr*). Many shrines are shared by

Muslims (Shi'a, Sunni, Alawite, and Druze) and Christians (Orthodox and Catholic). One common popular cult is that of the fertility deity known as St. George, who is identified with the Khidr of the Muslims and with Saint Elias, the Elijah of the Bible. This common theme, Haddad tells us, "binds together the cults of these three saints in what one might call a rural religious system," which he proposes calling "georgic" to emphasize its agricultural aspects and the shared socioeconomic class status of the believers. Saint George, Khidr, and Elijah share a common identity, representing the popular deity of fertility and the cults of Baal of ancient Syria. Their penetration into all three monotheistic religions and survival and popularity to the present time in opposition to the systematized, canonized, and official religion may be seen as an indication of the basic social unity of peasant life and common agrarian religious attitudes.[24]

The role of shrines and saints (*awlia'*) is to provide mediation between ordinary believers and God, whom official religion has rendered too remote and abstract. Because of the elitist orientation of official religion, shrines have tended to constitute a highly personalized and concrete alternative for common people. An investigation of the role of shrines in Lebanon concludes that the relationship of ordinary believers to saints is more compatible with everyday life and its mundane, immediate, and concrete needs than is the relationship with a remote, abstract God. Thus, the mosque provides "spiritual contact with God through prayers," while the shrine constitutes a refuge from daily "agonies, problems, and crises in need of instant solutions and responses."[25]

This role must have escaped the Tunisian scholar Muhammed al-Marzuqi, who examines what he calls the question of belief in *al-awlia'* among the tribes of southern Tunisia from a biased urban perspective. He reports that "the land of the south is full of their domes [*qibab*], shrines [*adriha*], and orders [*zawaya*]. . . . Every village or tribe has a saintly grandfather to whom visits and offerings are made to earn his blessings. There stands a sheikh, grandson of that saint, receiving the offerings from all over the area." Al-Marzuqi notes that the believers tell many stories about the assistance they have received from their *awlia'*, such as helping a believer find his lost camel, revenging an oppressed person on his oppressor, liberating someone from prison, and the like. "Woe to him who doubts the blessings of the saints," Al-Marzuqi observes. "He will be accused of heresy or atheism . . . and if you try to convince them that such influence belongs only to God . . . they will tell you that the saint is accepted by God, that He will be angry because of his anger, that He will not refuse him a demand, and that there is no barrier between him and God. This blind belief has exposed the poor inhabitants to exploitation."[26]

The critical feature in determining the success of popular religion in meeting believers' needs is the extent to which it remains a dynamic and responsive system of belief, not whether it measures up to standards created in an urban environment influenced by the religious establishment or the reformist tradition. Alienation begins when symbols earn fixed meanings in a society undergoing change. The same principle applies both to official and popular religion. Official religion, regardless of the accuracy of its interpretation of, and adherence to, the original teachings as embodied in the sacred texts, is more likely to become institutionalized to benefit the elites and ruling classes, rather than the mass of believers. An anthropological study of the shrine of Sidi Lahcen (born in 1631 among the Berber tribes) in Morocco by Paul Rabinow shows that when "a culture stops moving, when its structures of belief no longer offer a means to integrate, create, and make meaningful new experiences, then a process of alienation begins."[27] Saint worship becomes an archaic institution when religious power is subordinated to the claims of genealogical transmission of *baraka* (divine grace) whose original source was personal charisma. The descendants of Sidi Lahcen in this instance claimed his *baraka* as something inherited and thus gained a superiority over others that led to social and economic rights. This process of exploitation is what needs to be contested as a source of alienation, rather than *baraka* as such (the focus of the reformist religious leadership).

Certain shrines may become highly institutionalized. This process is fully documented in several studies, such as the one conducted by Dale Eickelman on the Sherqawi Zawaya in the town of Boujad, Morocco. Some of these religious Zawaya centered in tribal areas began to propagate a "correct" understanding of Islam and to resist oppressive governments. They developed over time, however, into sites of pilgrimage and marketplaces controlled by the descendants of the saint; these descendants converted their religious status into social and economic power. This has led, of course, to visible incongruities between the religious ideals ostensibly represented by such leaders and "the way things are" in social and political reality, as the leaders use the offerings of the believers for personal benefit. Thus, official as well as popular Islam, like other religions, "constantly must face anew cycles of compromise and non-compromise with the social order."[28]

Many of the above principles apply, as well, to Sufi (mystical) orders and their role in modern Arab society. From the perspective of official Islam, Michael Gilsenan reports that the sheikhs of Al-Azhar University in Cairo assured him that those orders (or brotherhoods of mystics) "had nothing to do with Islam at all. . . . The brotherhood members in turn regarded many of the sheikhs as quite irrelevant to an experience of the inner truths of the ways to God and to the practice of Islam in general."[29] Brotherhoods must have spread, and they continue to flourish in periods of social crises. Since the beginning, Sufism has sought salvation through knowledge or discovery, creative imagination, and allegorical interpretation (*ta'wil*) of the revealed texts for their concealed meanings. The aim is to go beyond the visible world (*zahir*) to gain access to the inner reality (*batin*). Sufi orders have historically been organized around a pious founder or saint (*wali*), as indicated by the names of orders such as the Shadhiliyya, Qadiriyya, and Tijaniyya. The *baraka* of the founders reflects both vertical links between human beings and God and horizontal relations among believers as brothers in the same order. This demands a *sheikh-khalifa-murid* (sheikh–successor–pupil) hierarchy of authority on the twin bases of differential roles and egalitarian commitments through sharing the same beliefs. Both the process of seeking salvation through knowledge of God (*ma'rifa*) and internal organization are enhanced by the ritual of *dhikr* (a mystical practice designed for the remembrance of God that induces a trancelike state in the believer), which aims at transcending the separation of human beings from their Creator by way of mystical contemplation and reunion.[30]

The central point to be made here is that the Sufi orders may serve as a mechanism of adjustment to reality, particularly in times of social unrest, or as a mechanism for resisting repressive authorities. That Sufism serves as a refuge for the powerless and impoverished segments of society does not preclude the possibility of its manipulation by internal and external dominant powers. Impoverished classes seek out shrines and Sufi orders to find solutions to their everyday problems. An example is the believers' unusual practice of mailing letters to the shrine of Imam al-Shafi'i (d. 1150) in Egypt: deprived of any other channels, they present the imam with specific complaints and grievances and ask assistance in redressing wrongs and injustices against them.[31]

Religions as Mechanisms of Control, Instigation, and Reconciliation

Religion lends itself to contradictory interpretations and applications and serves different or even conflicting functions. States, ruling classes, religious establishments, movements, organizations, institutions, and believers all interpret and practice religion in accordance with their needs as defined by their places in the socioeconomic and political structures, by their ideologies, and their visions and conceptions of social reality. In the context of the transitional nature of Arab society and the ongoing confrontations and struggles, religion—as concrete behavior and defined in functional terms—seems to serve particularly as a mechanism of control, instigation, or reconciliation.

Religion as a Mechanism of Control. Religion has constantly been used to legitimize and maintain the prevailing order. In a positive sense, it has been a source of moral values and norms that regulate human relations and bind the believers together. Hence, Durkheim believed that the primary function of religion is the preservation of the unity of the community. In this positive sense, religion becomes a source of social integration. In a more political or functional sense, religion may be used by the ruling classes as a mechanism of preserving the social order that rewards them so lavishly at the expense of society and the dominated classes. In this way, religion is used as a coercive and repressive political force to enhance the control of the ruling classes over the masses. Although a historical study of the formative period and the origins of religion might emphasize the positive attributes, my analysis focuses particularly on the contemporary nature of the religious establishment, which plays a significant role in the making and maintenance of the dominant order.

Rulers throughout Arab history have used religion to discourage rebellion and dissent (*fitna*) on behalf of unity of the *umma* and the need to safeguard it against internal and external threats. In the twentieth century, religion has been used to undermine liberal and radical opposition and to justify repressive policies. Traditional governments and authoritarian rulers have attempted to establish their legitimacy and authority by the strict application of the shari'a in alliance with religious movements. Thus, dissent is considered disobedience to God's commandments and punishable by fixed *hidud* punishments.

Such a mechanism of control is not limited to politics. Perhaps even more effective is social and psychological repression in the name of religion. Essentially the privileged ruling classes and the fortunate segments of society need to justify their privileges and fortunes. Religion provides them with the necessary justifications. In this way, the privileged seem to deserve their privileges (that is, their privileges become rights), and the deprived seem to deserve their deprivation. Rules governing social relations come to be seen as laws of nature.

Religion as a Mechanism of Instigation. Perhaps in a countermove, religion has also been used by the colonized and the oppressed as a mechanism of instigation against their colonizers and oppressors. The stress on the Islamic-Arab character of Algeria served as a powerful countermeasure against the French insistence on total domination of political, economic, and cultural life. Similarly, the Iranian revolution managed to galvanize religious sentiments against one of the world's most repressive regimes and its allied global power, when that alliance showed total disregard for the nationalistic dignity and aspirations of the Iranians. In fact, one of the most significant reasons for what is called the Islamic resurgence is the active involvement of religious movements in opposition to colonization and dependent, repressive regimes. Domestically, the Muslim Brotherhood may be studied as representative of movements that use religion as a mechanism of instigation.

What needs to be noted here is that this dual capacity of religion—both to repress and to resist repression—can be harnessed by successful religious movements. That is, once in power, leaders of such movements may resort to the use of religion as a mechanism of control, even as they may continue to use it as an instrument to incite people against external forces, and to spread their influence to other countries.

Religion as a Mechanism of Reconciliation. One of the most basic functions of religion (whether intended or not) has been that of reconciliation of the deprived and oppressed to their harsh reality. Believers are expected to adjust and submit to their situations, accepting the norms that govern existing social relations. One element of such submissiveness is the portrayal of this world as insignificant, and the life hereafter as blissful, for the meek and docile.

For this reason, Marx considered that human beings lost themselves in religion and other sources of consolation, justification, and illusory happiness. It was this particular function of religion that Marx considered to be "the sigh of the oppressed creature, the sentiment of a heartless world, and the soul of soulless conditions. It is the opium of the people." [32] The Marxist call to revolution encouraged the oppressed classes to abandon "illusory happiness" and to demand "real happiness." In other words, Marx's basic concern was to change the conditions that required such illusions. No wonder, then, that his call found a response among the adherents of the theology of liberation in Latin America and of the Islamic left.

The Interrelationship between Religion and Other Social Institutions

To demonstrate this point, let us examine some concrete aspects of the links between religion and family, social class, and politics.

Religion and Family. Notwithstanding areas of conflict and tension between tribalism and the unity of the *umma*, religion and family tend to be mutually supportive and complementary. The origins of religion can be traced back to the family and ancestor veneration and worship. It also continues to be inherited in the family, not unlike class status, wealth, language, and even gender roles. Furthermore, one continues to be socialized into a secure religious identity in the family. In all these respects and others, religion may be considered as constitutive of the basis of family. Complementarily, the family is reinforced and rendered sacred by religion, which adopted many of its roles and values as its own and labeled these as dictated by God. Thus, patriarchy and norms governing marriage, divorce, and inheritance become expressions of God's will. Inasmuch as the family shaped religion in its own image, religion in turn reinforced and strengthened the family in its original forms. In this way, each serves as an instrument of the other.

One of the most interesting aspects of the process of mutual reinforcement is the great similarity between the image of the father and the image of God in the mind of believers. This process of abstraction may have passed through four basic stages. In the first stage, the father and ancestors were objects of veneration and worship, and religious rituals practiced in the family were led by the father, who played the role of priest (*kahin* or imam). In the second stage, the god of the family (*rabb al-usra*) became the god of the tribe (*rabb al-qabila*) or the god of the city as a result of the extension of the tribe's influence and control over others. In the third stage, the god of the tribe or the city became the god of the society as a result of the same processes of influence and domination. The unification of the society required such a transition from tribal gods and goddesses to a god of the society as a whole. (Mecca, for instance, represented this sort of pluralism in the pre-Islamic period. Venerated ancestors were gradually elevated to the rank of one god without being totally eclipsed.) In the fourth stage, the one God (Allah) became the ultimate divinity that created the universe and its creatures, totally eliminating earlier localized gods and goddesses originating in family or ancestor worship.[33]

Despite this pattern of increasing abstraction, the worship of ancestors continued to manifest itself in popular religion. The saints who served as intermediaries between the believers and God, for instance, passed on their *baraka* genealogically to their distant offspring. Another example is the *sadah* phenomenon, in which believers revere those who claim descent from the Prophet's family. These forms of popular religion make it clear that believers seek the assistance of saints (*awlia'*) because God has become too abstract and remote.

The great similarity between the image of the father and the image of God in the mind of the believers is also shown in the way both are characterized. Both the father and God are endowed by the believers with two contradictory sets of traits. On the one hand, both are characterized as *rahum* or *ra'uf* (merciful), *ghafur* (forgiving), *hanun* and *muhibb* (sympathetic and loving), *jalil* (dignified), *karim* (generous), and *'adel* (just). On the other hand, the father and God are also described by the believers as *jabbar* or *qawi* (forceful, strong), *sarim* or *qasi* (strict, severe), *mukhif* (fearful), *muhaymin* (hegemonic), *qahhar* (subduer, coercive), *muntaqim* (revengeful), *mutassalit* (domineering, authoritarian), *ghadub* (quick to anger), and *muta'li* (condescending). These seemingly contradictory characteristics were originally those of the father or family patriarch. The fact that they were extended to God suggests that He is an extension, abstraction, or symbol of the father. "Our Father which art in heaven" must be a magnified portrait of our father on earth.

Furthermore, there is a divine family in heaven corresponding to the not-so-divine family on earth. Besides our Father in heaven there are Mother Mary and son Jesus. Believers are seen as brothers and sisters of the same tribal sect. Quite often, the believers seek God through intermediaries (*shafi'*) such as Mary, not unlike children in an Arab family, who do not dare approach their father directly but seek his favors by asking their mother to mediate on their behalf.

Both the father and God in Arab culture are a promise and a threat (*wa'd wa wa'id*), grace and suffering (*rahma wa 'adhab*). In both cases, punishment is grace (*al-'iqab rahma*). Such depictions are not confined to popular culture. The concept of the father and the concept of God become one in Naguib Mahfouz's novel *Awlad haratina* (The Children of Geblawi), where each symbolizes the other to such an extent that it becomes difficult to discern which is the original and which the copy.

Eventually, God gained the upper hand. In pre-Islamic Arabia, human behavior used to be described as ignorance, *jahl*, or prudence, *hilm*. The first concept referred to human behavior resulting from loss of control over one's desires and emotions. *Hilm* referred to human will and the ability to control one's desires and emotions fully. In Islam, however, *hilm* became an exclusive characteristic of God, so that human beings lost one of their most significant attributes, and a person from then on could only be called "Abd al-Halim," the slave of the Halim—that is, of God. This is an example of alienation in religion.

Religion and Social Class. Four basic aspects of the relationship between religion and social class seem to be most relevant to this analysis. These include religious legitimization of the prevailing order and the privileges of the ruling classes; rationalization of poverty; justification of social inequalities; and variations in religious practices and beliefs by social class.

The emergence of an Islamic aristocratic class not surprisingly led to the legitimization of the prevailing order. The Moroccan scholar and political leader 'Allal al-Fassi notes that the conquests of Islam "resulted in the accumulation of a great deal of money in the hands of Muslims, so they lost the purity of the Prophet and his companions and there emerged wretched poor and affluent rich." [34] Clearly, believers view their religion and interpret its teachings from the perspective of their positions in the social class structure and in accordance with their relationship to the ruling classes. The Syrian scholar Sadiq al-'Azm observes that some Islamic intellectuals and *'ulama* "make great efforts to grant Islamic legitimacy to the order . . . they are linked to irrespective of its nature. . . . Every Arab order, irrespective of its coloration, possesses respected Islamic institutions prepared to issue a religious decree [*fatwa*] to the effect that its policy is in complete harmony with Islam." [35]

Theoretically, there is not supposed to be a clerical class in Islam, but who can deny that such a class in reality exists? Besides asserting their role as guardians and interpreters of the shari'a and sacred texts, the *'ulama* administer and control institutions such as mosques and schools, and the considerable wealth generated by the *awqaf* (religious endowments). As a result of holding such prominent positions in society, they began to constitute a privileged and powerful class in the early Abbasid period. In traditional Ottoman society, they were exempt from taxation and their "personal estates were not subject to confiscation by the state upon their deaths but could be passed on to their heirs."[36] They also enjoyed great prestige and status in their communities. They still constitute the core of the religious establishment and are the mediating agency between the ruling classes and the believers. They have been closely linked to governments and have attempted to explain away apparent contradictions between Islam and the actions of the ruling classes. In a paper on the 'ulama of Cairo, Afaf Lutfi al-Sayyid Marsot observed that the successive rulers of Egypt "realized the value of the 'ulama as a tool of government because of their influence on the population and on the manipulation and creation of public opinion."[37]

Here it should be noted that religion in its formative years may constitute a revolution of sorts against the established order, but sooner or later it begins to be transformed into an institution closely associated with the dominant order. This is what must have prompted Max Weber to distinguish the prophet from the priest, noting that it is "no accident that almost no prophets have emerged from the priestly class."[38]

An Egyptian legend says that ancient Egypt was divided into twenty-four shares. Four belonged to the ruler, ten to princes, and ten to the military. When somebody inquired, "What about the people?" the response was simple and clear, "The people own the twenty-fifth share, and its place is the kingdom of heaven." This is precisely the way in which religion serves to rationalize poverty.

In Islam, some Sufi orders contributed to the rationalization of poverty. A whole section of the classical book *Ihia' 'ulum ad-din* by Al-Ghazzali (d. 1111) is devoted to popular sayings and statements about poverty. Some of these sayings from Al-Ghazzali and the Sufis depict poverty as a virtue:

The poor of my *umma* enter heaven five hundred years prior to the rich.

Everything has a key, and the key to heaven is the love of the poor for their patience.

The closest to the heart of God is the poor [man] who is contented with his lot.

Hunger is stored by God in a closet, and He grants it only to those whom He loves.

The contented [man] is rich even when hungry.

Contentment is a limitless treasure.

Wisdom is in the empty stomach.

The essence of freedom is in complete enslavement.

I will be patient until patience is disgruntled with my patience.

This legacy is highly diffused in the Arab culture of poverty, which might to that extent be described as a culture of silence—the sort of culture that socializes people into passivity or submissiveness. A similar justification is applied by religion to social inequality. In the semi-autobiographical novel *'Usfour min ash-sharq* (Bird from the East) by the prominent Egyptian writer Tawfiq al-Hakim, the major character, Muhsin, representing the author, finds great comfort in whispering to himself:

> Slavery will never disappear from the world. . . . Each age has its slavery and its slaves, . . . the paradise of the poor will never be on this earth . . . the unsolvable problem in the world is the presence of the poor and the rich. . . . It is only because of this problem that messengers and prophets appeared . . . The prophets of the East understood that equality cannot be established on this earth and that it is beyond their ability to divide the kingdom of earth between the rich and the poor. That is why they introduced into the formula the kingdom of heaven. . . . The rights of those who are deprived of opportunity in the earthly paradise are preserved in the heavenly one.[39]

This is not simply a matter of religion being criticized by thoughtful observers for being part of the status quo. The Qur'an itself says: "God gave preference to some of you over others in regard to property" (16:71); "We have divided among them their livelihood in the present life and raised some of them above others in subjection" (43:32).

For some, the meaning of these verses is that social inequalities are natural and God-made. When asked to interpret them, the prominent Lebanese Islamic scholar Sheikh Faysal Mulawi said that they "refer to one of God's fixed laws. . . . That is why there have been inequalities among people since the beginning. . . . Subjection is mutual and reciprocal among all, and there is no subjector and subjected. For the worker is subjected to the employer and the employer is subjected to the worker."[40]

Yet there have been others who have reached different conclusions in their search of Islamic texts and practices for any signs of identification with the "oppressed of the earth" (*al-mustad'afin fi al-ard*). For example, some left-leaning writers see one of the companions of the prophet, Abu Dharr al-Ghifari, as a pioneer socialist.

As indicated earlier, believers view their religion and interpret its teachings from the perspective of their respective social classes. Religious beliefs, practices, and emotions vary from class to class; different classes pursue different religious tendencies. The ruling and privileged classes tend to use religion as a mechanism of control and a justification of their fortunes. This is clearly shown by Ayman al-Yassini's study of the relationship between religion and the state in the kingdom of Saudi Arabia—a kingdom the author sees as more identified with traditional Islam than any other country in the world.[41] The middle classes tend toward a self-promotional practice of religion, pursuing their worldly interests and identifying more with their sect and the religious establishment than with religion as such. For the poor, religion is an expression of their repressed feelings. The oppressed social classes in Arab society have been religiously disposed toward what was referred to earlier as popular religion. Thus peasants and women have been inclined to seek refuge in shrines and saints.

Religion and Politics. The rise of militant Islamic movements following the dramatic success of the 1979 Iranian revolution has constituted an issue of great interest in the media and centers of scholarship throughout the world. Wave after wave of articles, books, conferences, and documentary films addressed to this issue have sought to assert preconceived notions and express deep-rooted biases.

A number of works have described how Islam has become such a visible force in Arab and Middle Eastern politics, but they often avoid analysis and overlook the contributory conditions. When analysis is attempted, the focus is diverted from these conditions to events and individual personalities. *Voices of Resurgent Islam*, a collection of essays edited by John L. Esposito, promises to explore the origins of this resurgence through an examination of the relationship of religion to politics and society. Unfortunately, the main approach continues to be an emphasis on normative analysis of the sacred texts and beliefs rather than on actual behavior by members of society. The essence of this idealist approach is clearly reflected in Esposito's introduction, which reiterates the old notions that Islam is "distinguished from Christianity by the unity and totality of the Islamic view of reality" and that the "Islamic state is a community of believers. Allah is the ultimate sovereign of the state and, indeed, of all creation."[42] Again, as in Orientalism, the starting point is the sacred text rather than society. There is a reference now and then to a few psychological and political explanations such as identity crisis, loss of self-esteem, disillusionment, and the failure of governments to respond to the needs of their societies. But this tells us very little about the dynamics of the processes in which social forces operate.

The Islamic perspectives explicated in Esposito's collection tend to follow the same idealist approach. In an article on the Islamic state, Hassan Turabi of

Sudan asserts that "all public life in Islam is religious, being permeated by the experience of the divine. Its function is to pursue the service of God as expressed in a concrete way in the shariah, the religious law . . . an Islamic state is not a nationalistic state because ultimate allegiance is owed to God . . . an Islamic state is not an absolute or sovereign entity. It is subject to the higher norms of the shariah that represent the will of God." [43]

Both of the above perspectives assume that Islamic norms and values determine political behavior. That shared assumption has prompted Eric Davis to observe that "Western and non-Western scholars alike have presented a reified, reductionist, and ultimately ideological understanding of the relationship between Islam and politics." [44] As an alternative, Davis proposes a "sociohistorical perspective," which he attempts to apply to analysis of the relationship between Islam and politics in modern Egypt. In this approach he emphasizes the significance of the social context from which the advocates of Islamic reform emerged and the need to historicize the study of Islam and politics.

Undertaking a similar task, the social historian Philip Khoury has attempted to construct a framework for explaining Islamic revivalism in its historical context. Focusing on Egypt and Syria, he concludes that the phenomenon can best be understood as a reaction to a crisis in the modern secular state. Revivalism must thus be seen as "the vehicle for political and economic demands, rather than being itself the 'impulse' behind these demands." The crisis to which Khoury refers is the inability of the state to modernize the whole society—that is, to assimilate certain classes to a new socioeconomic order. Instead, the classes that have been most closely attached to the traditional Islamic social and moral system have been disfigured and disoriented. To further support his argument, Khoury supplies four additional reasons for the crisis: international pressures on the state to accept its role and fate as a weak and dependent economic and political entity; the inability of the ruling classes and elite to close the gap in wealth and opportunity between themselves and the rest of the society; the state's inability to solve several long-term problems; and the suitability of revivalist Islam as the most convenient and readily available ideological vehicle for the political and economic demands of the classes sponsoring the Islamic resurgence. [45] As to the nature of the classes sponsoring revivalism, several studies have agreed that they form a marginalized "class caught in-between," that is, uprooted peasants led by an urban lower-middle class.

Religion and the State—Secularism versus Theocracy

The complicated relationship between religion and politics may be further clarified by addressing the issue of secularism as an alternative to the claim of ruling by divine authority. Earlier I examined the notion of secularism in the

context of social and political integration and suggested that it has to become
a genuine and integral part of Arab nationalist ideology because of the urgent
need to achieve national unity and to secure equality for all citizens before the
law regardless of religious affiliation or other differences. The promotion of
rationality and scientific thinking, the liberation of women from discriminatory traditions, the enhancement of modernity, the liberation of religion itself
from government control, and the democratization of the state and other
institutions should also result from the adoption of secularism.

To the extent that Arab secularism resembles Western secularism, it is
because both are related to processes of urbanization, industrialization, democratization, modernization, and nation-building. What the process of secularization involves is the separation of religion from the state. The abolition of
political sectarianism, the encouragement of rationalism, and the scientific
interpretation of reality all follow from this. These alterations in the relationship of the state to its citizens in turn strengthen basic civil rights and ensure
the universal application of laws.

Unfortunately, however, secularism continues to be one of the most controversial and sensitive notions in the Arab world, particularly in times of
Islamic resurgence. Hence, serious discussions of secularism are avoided for
fear of a possible clash with religious institutions and movements. At the root
of the controversy over secularism is its ambiguity regarding several related
issues and questions: Does Islam allow for secularism? Is secularism an alien
concept imported from the West and externally imposed on the Arabs? Is
secularism necessarily anti-religious and atheistic?

Opinion is almost unanimous that Islam is opposed to secularism by its very
nature. Muslim traditionalists and reformers agree that a Muslim state must in
theory be administered in accordance with the principles of the shari'a. Sayyid
Qutb claims that Islamic government is opposed to "human positive laws" and
is obligated to carry on the "total revolution" of Islam, and the Muslim scholar
Fazlur Rahman goes even further, saying: "Secularism destroys the sanctity
and universality (transcendence) of all moral values . . . secularism is necessarily
atheistic." [46]

Such views have also typically been expressed by the religious establishment. The Lebanese Council of 'Ulama, for instance, declared in 1976:
"Secularism is a system of principles and practices rejecting every form of
religious faith and worship. Secularism has no place in the life of a Muslim;
either Islam is to exist without secularism, or secularism is to exist without
Islam." [47] Orientalists seem to agree that Islam, unlike Christianity and Judaism, is necessarily opposed to secularism. Von Grunebaum observes that "the
Arab most fully realized the integration of religion and what we now call
nationality. To him, state and religion became co-extensive to such a degree

that . . . he . . . became immune to that movement of complete secularization
. . . even where he took the side of progress and reform." [48]

Constant struggle has been taking place in Arab society between secular and
fundamentalist religious and sectarian forces at least since the beginning of the
nahda in the middle of the nineteenth century. This struggle is clearly reflected
in the ensuing intellectual and ideological debate, in action-oriented activities,
in social and political movements, and in state-building. On the level of states,
there is evidence in the changes that have taken place in Turkey, Egypt,
Tunisia, Syria, Iraq, and Algeria. New civil codes were introduced and advocated for a number of these countries and other Arab nations by such
well-known jurists as 'Abd al-Razzak al-Sanhuri, who advocated secularism
based on the assumption that "the Islamic system could not be applied . . .
without prior adaptations to the needs of modern civilization. . . . We believe
that the point of departure . . . should be a separation of the religious from the
temporal portion of Islamic law." [49] These changes have not been confined to
criminal, commercial, and constitutional law, but have also involved personal
status laws governing marriage, divorce, inheritance, support, and guardian-
ship. The Turkish government abolished shari'a law, even in personal status
matters, in 1924. The explanatory note attached to the civil code adopted by
the Turkish Republic includes the following observation:

> The state whose law is based on religion becomes incapable, after
> a short time, of satisfying the needs of the country and the nation.
> . . . Otherwise the laws will support an intolerable tyranny over
> citizens who profess a religion other than that adopted by the state.
> . . . For countries whose citizens belong to different religions, it is
> even more necessary to break with religion . . . if laws are enacted
> for each religious minority, the political and social unity of the nation
> will be broken. [50]

The personal status code adopted in Tunisia in 1956 made fundamental
changes including outlawing polygamy, allowing Muslim women to marry
non-Muslims, and making recognition of divorce a prerogative of the
courts. [51]

Arab national and progressive movements have increasingly sought to secularize society, confronting the religious forces until the 1980s, when they
began to retreat into the safety of compromise. The tide of nationalism,
particularly during the third quarter of the twentieth century, brought secular
forces to unprecedented prominence. Religion and the state seemed to be
going their separate ways. However, the defeat of nationalist movements and
the success of the Iranian revolution in 1979 reversed the tide. Until then, the
need for modernity and national strength seemed to hinge on secularization

and liberation from the legacies of the traditional past. Now, the potential for resistance through religion seems to have won the day.

Nevertheless, we should not abandon hope entirely. A strong literature urging secularism now exists, on which Arabs may continue to draw. Indeed, secularism achieved great prominence in the ongoing intellectual discourse initiated at the beginning of the *nahda*. In its earliest forms, it was featured in the works of a number of Arab intellectuals, such as Rifa'at al-Tahtawi (1801–73), Butrus al-Bustani (1819–93), 'Abd al-Rahman al-Kawakibi (1854–1902), Shibli Shummayil (1850–1917), and several others.

Al-Tahtawi promoted the concept of love of country (*hubb al-watan*), asserting that "there is a national brotherhood among [members of the same *watan*] over and above the brotherhood in religion. There is a moral obligation on those who share the same *watan* to work together to improve it and perfect its organization in all that concerns its honor and greatness and wealth."[52] These same emphases appear prominently in the works of Butrus al-Bustani, who dedicated eleven issues of his journal *Nafir Suriyya* to the analysis of the 1860 civil war in Lebanon. He began his articles by addressing all sects, not as sects, but as "children of the country" (*ya abna' al-watan*) and ended them "from the lover of the homeland" (*min muhibb al-watan*). The causes of that civil war, he pointed out, were the "lack of religion and civility . . . it should not be permissible for religion, and it is not in the interest of religion itself, to interfere in political affairs and get mixed up with worldly affairs . . . as long as our people do not make a distinction between religion which is a relationship between the created and the creator and civility which is a relationship between them and their government . . . it is not expected that they will succeed in either of them."[53]

'Abd al-Rahman al-Kawakibi, who strongly opposed the Ottoman caliphate, called on all Arabs to manage their "worldly affairs and to make religion rule only in the next world. Let us unite under one motto: Long live the nation, long live the homeland."[54] Since then there have been generations of Arab secularists, including 'Ali 'Abd al-Raziq, Qasem Amin, Taha Hussein, Lutfi al-Sayyid, Amin Rihani, Antun Sa'ada, Ma'ruf al-Rusafi, Sidqi al-Zahawi, Khalid Muhammed Khalid, 'Abdallah al-'Alayli, Muhammed al-Nuwayhi, Muhammed A. Khalafalla, Fuad Zakariyya, Mohammed Arkoun, Zaki Naguib Mahmud, Farouq Fooda, and Sadiq al-'Azm.[55]

In 1925, in the context of the intense debate between the supporters of the Ottoman caliphate and liberal nationalists following World War I, 'Ali 'Abd al-Raziq published a controversial book, *Al-Islam wa usul al-hukm* (Islam: The Bases of Authority), in which he argued that Islam did not determine or impose on Muslims any special form of government but rather granted them full freedom to organize the state as required by prevailing conditions.

Twenty-five years later, in *Min hunna nabda'* (We Start Here), Khalid Muhammed Khalid chastised the clergy in the strongest terms; this was despite the fact that he himself was a clergyman, trained in Cairo at Al-Azhar. He described religious governments as instruments of repression that bring much suffering to humanity. Thus, "without limiting the authority of the clergy and separating civil and religious authorities, there can be no awakening for society nor survival for religion itself. Only by doing that can religion achieve its sublime goals."[56]

In 1970, another prominent Egyptian scholar, Muhammad al-Nuwayhi, published several articles that were later combined in a book entitled *Nahwa thawra fi al-fikr al-dini* (Toward a Revolution in Religious Thought). In it he makes the following assertions:

1.   Islam does not grant any special group the right to monopolize interpretation of its teachings or the representation of the community of Muslims.

2.   Islam does not offer a final, complete order for human society that is not subject to change.

3.   Most Islamic worldly laws and rules enacted by early legislators were derived from the codes of conquered countries and not from the Qur'an or the Traditions.

4.   Qur'anic laws are not all equally binding.

5.   Some binding Qur'anic laws at the time of the Prophet were eliminated in later periods, even as early as the period of the second caliph, 'Omar Ibn al-Khattab. Thus, legislation concerning worldly affairs was not meant to be eternal, literal, or unchangeable. The principle of "community interests" is at the root of all legislation.[57]

The prominence that secularism has gained in the ongoing intellectual discourse since the beginning of the *nahda* reflects real indigenous needs rather than the thwarted tendency to import Western concepts. An explanation for this prominence must be sought in the present condition of Arab society and other countries inhabited by Muslims. What we know for a fact is that these countries differ in regard to their social diversity and the need for integration. As pointed out by Egyptian historian Gamal Hamdan, there were, in the 1970s, more than sixty-seven states in which Muslims constituted from 1 to 99 percent of the population (five in Europe, twenty-three in Asia, and thirty-nine in Africa). Of these, twenty-nine states had non-Muslim minorities; others were divided evenly between Muslims and non-Muslims; and in some Muslims constituted minorities. The Muslims in this latter group made up more than half the Muslim world. More than half of all Muslims thus live in minority status.[58] If the status of the religious community is the most likely factor in determining its attitudes toward secularism, then one can hypothesize that, other things being equal, Muslims in countries where non-Muslims are the majority will have a more positive attitude toward secularism than Muslims who make up a majority in their own countries.

An eloquent defense of secularism was made by one of the leaders of the Muslim community in Burma, a nation characterized by religious pluralism. In Burma, it is the Muslim community that has carried the banner of secularism and opposed government attempts to specify a state religion. U Rashid, a respected member of the Burmese cabinet in the early 1960s and a leader of Muslims, opposed the prime minister's attempt to make Buddhism the state religion. He questioned whether, in view of the religious pluralism that characterized contemporary Burmese society, a state religion could serve to integrate and unite the nation:

> As a Muslim, I believe there should be no compulsion in religion.
> Everyone should be free to adopt and practice the religion he likes.
> As a Muslim, I do not and indeed cannot object to or oppose
> anything that Buddhists and persons professing other religions may do
> for their own religion. All I can and do ask for is that as Muslims, we
> should have the same freedom. . . . I am apprehensive that the
> adoption of a state religion will have a deep psychological effect
> upon the Buddhists in the country. They will begin to imagine that
> they have a special role in the administrative, economic, social and
> educational life of the country. The adoption of a State Religion will
> open the door to extremists to make more and more demands based
> on religion. We have already received some indications of these.
> Suggestions have already been made that . . . the President of the
> union of Burma, Cabinet Ministers, The Chief Justice of the Union,
> the Speakers of Parliament and the Commander-in-Chief should be
> Buddhists. It will not be easy for succeeding Governments to resist
> such demands. Such a situation will lead to unnecessary conflicts
> between the various religious groups in the country. A situation of
> that type will not be good for the country. All religious communities
> will not then pull together. The country and the people as a whole
> will suffer . . . any attempt by the religious majority to secure
> administrative, economic, social or educational advantages based on
> religion will be resisted by the religious minorities.[59]

U Rashid is quoted at length here because his views are applicable to Lebanon and other Arab countries, especially those characterized by religious pluralism. Lebanon must recognize that the sectarian system has encouraged extremist Christians to believe that they have a special right or role in running the country and to make or oppose demands based on sectarian affiliation to secure their privileges. Other Arab countries must also recognize that insisting on a state religion will encourage religious extremism and lead to unnecessary conflicts.

Muslim traditionalists and most Orientalists agree that secularism is foreign to Islam, and that this contrasts with the historical position of Christianity, which declares, "Render . . . unto Caesar the things which are Caesar's; and unto God the things that are God's" (Matt. 22:21). Nevertheless, based on historical facts, it is easy to challenge these characterizations of both Islam and Christianity, and to demonstrate that under certain conditions Muslim, Judaic, and Christian traditionalists have rejected secularism on the same grounds, considering it alien to their dogmas. Notwithstanding urbanization, industrialization, and democratization in Western societies, the battle between fundamentalists and secularists is not completely over there either. In the Arab world, the patriarchs of two major Christian sects recently expressed their opposition to secularism. The patriarch of the Maronite Church, Bulos-Butros al-Ma'oushi, has declared, "Part of the respect for God and man is respect for authority, which represents God."[60] Similarly, the patriarch of Antioch and all the East of the Syrian Greek Orthodox Patriarchate, which has been most flexible on the question of secularism, dismissed the notion as an "unrealistic demand at the time being" and as "unacceptable to Muslims, so why should we impose it on them." He added, "I am personally convinced that family in our society is a divine thing. Frankly, I am opposed to secularism and hope that family will always be subject to divine grace [*al-ni'ma al-ilahiyya*]. . . . What family system in this Orient is not controlled by divine law [*al-Shari'a al-ilahiyya*]? That is why I am against secularism. I do not believe it is part of our eastern heritage."[61] Secularism was not borrowed from the West out of imitation. As a matter of historical fact, the concept has genuinely emerged out of and in response to urgent needs in Arab countries, particularly in pluralistic ones. Secularism is not necessarily atheistic or anti-religious. On the contrary, it may contribute to the creation of a better climate for the development of greater spiritual purity when religion is outside the arena of power politics. Instead of being used as a tool of control and instigation or reconciliation, religion could pursue the more enriching enterprise of achieving its central, sublime goals.

Alienation from and in Religion

Religious resurgence, so important a marker of contemporary Arab society, may be traced to several interrelated conditions. The inability of nationalist and socialist regimes or movements to provide either a satisfactory ideology or concrete solutions to contemporary problems has left a vacuum, and the distortions introduced by the peculiar nature of modernization in the area call out for redress through the contributions to society that religion can make. We have noticed, too, the pervasive state of anomie generated by the transitional nature of Arab society and culture, and the overall need for coherence in an acute period of turmoil. It is the condition of anomie that concerns us here. Essentially, the Arab struggle to create new strength and to achieve the *nahda* has been frustrated by fragmentation, repression, the breakdown of traditional norms, and uncertainties about the future. The disjuncture between articulated goals and the capacities and means needed to achieve them has created a number of unfortunate characteristics or reactions to contemporary life, including ambivalence, hesitation, greed and an insatiable need to consume, corruption, and rivalries for wealth and power by any means and at the expense of others and the society.

The return of individuals and society at large to religion and authenticity seems to provide a compelling alternative sense of coherence, unity, certainty, and inner strength. By choosing the sacred and universal, believers insert themselves into a predictable divine order and develop a sense of oneness. Yet this reorientation to overcome anomie has actually intensified the already-prevailing condition of alienation. As noted by Peter Berger, a prominent authority in the sociology of religion:

> The essence of all alienation is the imposition of a fictitious inexorability upon the humanly constructed world . . . the innumerable contingencies of human existence are transformed into inevitable manifestations of universal law. Activity becomes process. Choices become destiny. Men then live in the world they themselves have made as if they were fated to do so by powers that are quite independent of their own world-constructing enterprises. . . . The projected meanings of human activity congeal into a gigantic and mysterious "other world," hovering over the world of men as an alien reality.[62]

The net result, in other words, is confirmation of total dependence on an external force. Human beings lose control over their creations and activities, entering a relationship in which they deny rather than assert themselves. The result is alienation in religion and what Berger calls "alienating power" or the "alienating propensity of religion."[63]

The Moroccan historian Abdallah Laroui has described a form of alienation perpetuated by the religious *salafiyya* movement through a "quasi-magical" evocation of apparently authentic and indigenous classical Arab-Islamic culture. This example not only illustrates a perpetuation of the alienated state, it also ensures that society can make no progress in addressing the conditions that induce alienation. The movement, identified with what was called pure religion, traced its origins to the early formative years of Islam. In effect, it became a kind of sanctification of society in an archaic mode, an exaggerated medievalization, and a fossilization rather than a renewal of culture.[64]

Alienation resulted from more than new restorative movements. The blocking of change by the religious establishment has also been a continuing source of alienation. This alienation is expressed through the rejection of prevailing religious conceptions and principles and of the religious establishment promoting them. Such alienation has manifested itself in a widespread phenomenon with several aspects. First, a paradoxical contrast emerges between the affluent religious establishment and the impoverished believers. A common sight throughout Arab cities and towns is impoverished neighborhoods surrounding monumental religious edifices. More striking and ironic are the scale and generosity of gift-giving by poor believers to rich shrines; this generosity is linked to their requests for relief from their distress. Second, the believers derive their reality from God by announcing their inferiority, insignificance, and enslavement. This is seen in the large number of Arab names beginning with *'abd* (slave), affirming complete resignation and surrender. Third, worship has become mostly ritualistic, separated from the subjective experiences of the believers and from their unique responses or personal religiousness. Fourth, a process of alienation renders the believers into objective states: they become products and objects, rather than creative actors engaged in meaningful activities. Thus, they apprehend reality as external and opposed to themselves. The best of their nature is projected onto external beings or forces alien to humanity. Hence their self-estrangement. All human creations become nonhuman. Creativity itself becomes a nonhuman characteristic. Fifth, as we have noted, religion is often misused as a mechanism of control, instigation, and reconciliation. Sixth, a unique phenomenon grows out of this misuse. Two contrasting societies are implicitly created: a highly visible public society and an invisible private society. The latter I call an underground society because of its oppositional and clandestine nature. The taboos and prohibitions of the public society are kept outside the closed doors of the underground society. This should not be described as hypocrisy but as a reaction to a very restrictive order.

Taken together, these phenomena alienate believers, who experience themselves as powerless objects rather than creative actors. Even when they enthusiastically support activist religious movements, the ultimate product of their engagement is impoverishment rather than enrichment, and repression rather than the transformation of reality.

Religion and Change: Transformation or Conformity?

A perennial sociological question has been the extent to which religion is a product of, a barrier to, or a prime agent of change. One point of view

(Marxist) sees religion as a manifestation or a function of interests of certain groups or classes. From this perspective, C. Wright Mills has told us that if religious ideas do not gain an affinity with the interests of certain members of a special stratum, they are abandoned. [65] The mainstream literature, however, says that "religion appears in history both as a world-maintaining and as a world-shaking force." [66]

In its formative stage, religion may be revolutionary in destroying an old order and replacing it with a new one. Islam in its formative period constituted such a revolution by transforming Arabia from a tribal society into a unified *umma*. But once the caliphate was established some thirty years later, the new state began to manipulate religion and tribe to further its goals. It is then that what Adonis has called the culture of stability (*thabit*) began to gain prominence at the expense of the culture of change (*mutahawwil*). [67] Political and religious thought strove to legitimize the prevailing order and to reconcile religion and philosophy. The ascendancy of this culture accompanying the establishment of the caliphate is responsible for dismissing creativity as a *bid'a* (departure from orthodox custom), and dissent and opposition as *fitna* (social disorder). Yet it would be wrong to conclude that creativity and opposition to government are alien to Islamic thought. The battle between the forces of stability and the forces of change has continued unabated throughout Arab medieval and modern history, taking many forms and orientations. This is a natural outcome of the continued presence of unresolved contradictions and conflicting interests. What is referred to in contemporary Arab discourse as cultural and intellectual struggle and the battle between the old and the new, or between tradition and modernity, has gained momentum as a result of several developments, but we must see these developments as continuous, rather than discontinuous, with the past.

Conclusion

Religious reformers have always thought that they had to battle the religious establishment if they hoped to overcome the sickness that afflicted the Muslim world. They sought to reconcile tradition and modernity through the adaptation of religion to new challenges, including scientific and technological challenges. They sought to return to the original sources of Islam. Such an orientation, however, creates a viewpoint shaped by the perspective of the past rather than that of the future. It denies the historical context that initially gave meaning to these original aspects of Islam. Because of their ahistorical approach, reformers took it for granted that old notions could be applied to new problems, regardless of the immense differences between present and past social and political realities. Consequently, religious movements, whether or not they managed to achieve power (such as the Wahabiyya in Arabia, Mahdiyya in Sudan, and Sanusiyya in Libya), or continued to play the role of instigator (such as the Muslim Brotherhood), envisioned a strict application of the shari'a. They proved to be narrowly restrictive and conformist (requiring strict conformity to traditions including those acquired during periods of decline) rather than transcendental and transformative (transforming the existing structures and building a new order).

Thus, the question arises: Can religious movements be revolutionary? We define revolutionary to mean constituting a salvationist movement that can in theory and practice transform the society, replacing the dominant order with a new one. In the context of Arab society, this entails a comprehensive transformation to end underdevelopment, dependency, class differences, authoritarianism, and alienation. To put it in positive terms, it means building a new and just society on the basis of democratic principles and mastering its own destiny. That Islam might provide the framework for such a revolutionary movement seemed most likely following the success of the 1979 Iranian revolution. Indeed, the prospects seemed so great that even some well-known secular nationalists and critics shared the sweeping euphoria.

Now, however, I would argue that historical developments suggest that religion does not constitute a revolutionary or transformative movement. The major constraint on its potential in this regard is the alienating propensity of religion. In addition to rendering believers powerless and insignificant, religion becomes an establishment inseparable from the prevailing system of power holders. Details and rituals gain significance over essence and prophethood. As such, religion stands in opposition to the spirit of the age in which we now live. Every age has it particular philosophy, vision, and reality. The present reality is one of nation-states rather than a community of believers dispersed in different and distant societies. The lack of congruence between these two modes of social and political organization makes religion an alienating power, rather than a liberating force. What religion lacks in the contemporary context are a vision and a program for the future.

8   Arab Politics
Its Social Context

A fundamental premise of this study has been that the focus should be on society rather than on the meanings implied by the existence of artificial nation-states created by external powers for their own purposes. This premise is rooted in political sociology, which sees human nature as essentially social and traces the roots of political formations to social formations—an approach that differs significantly from traditional idealist political science, which starts with an Aristotelian notion of man as a political animal. I have thus attempted to examine political behavior and culture in their social and historical contexts. This chapter serves to sum up the first two parts of this book by relating political configurations and movements to the socioeconomic conditions examined in the preceding chapters.

Prominent in political sociology have been a number of attempts to analyze Arab politics in social terms. These analyses have isolated what they have seen as the most salient characteristics of Arab political processes; the most compelling of these we might identify in shorthand as the segmentary, the patrimonial, the patriarchal, the social mobilizational, the social structural, and Oriental despotism. A brief reference to each of these perspectives is needed to clarify aspects of the present analytical framework, and to prepare for a comprehensive and detailed overview of Arab politics.

Segmentation theory conceives of Arab politics primarily in terms of communal (tribal, ethnic, sectarian) relations and loyalties. This approach traces the emergence of a mosaic structure composed of relatively autonomous communities and sees the results as political fragmentation that undermines the process of state formation.[1] The challenge, in this view, is for the state in the Arab world to assert itself in a diversified or pluralistic society against the communal cohesion that has controlled politics.[2]

From Max Weber's emphasis on patrimonial rule has come another view of what have been categorized as "Oriental societies." This analysis poses, in sharp contrast to the rational and institutionalized politics of Occidental societies, a very different relationship of the ruler and the ruled in Arab countries— one characterized as patrimonial and considered an arbitrary form of political domination. Elbaki Hermassi, for instance, has described the political legacy of the Maghrib as one which has evolved from Ibn Khaldun's theory of the state; based on tribal cohesion in the patrimonial state, the bureaucracy and the army are separated from society and loyal to the person of the ruler.[3]

This form of patrimonialism is not very different from the Marxist notion of Oriental despotism, a state form seen as rooted in the Asiatic mode of production. Ahmed Sadiq Saad, an Egyptian political economist, has concluded that in spite of the recent dominance of the capitalist mode of production in Egypt, several characteristics of the Asiatic mode and consequently of Asiatic despotism have continued to exist there up to the present time.[4]

The patriarchal and the more recent neopatriarchal character of Arab politics has been systematically explored by Hisham Sharabi. By *patriarchy,* he means "a universal form of traditional society" in contrast to modernity, which "occurred in its original form in Western Europe." A basic assumption of Sharabi's work has been that the Arab renaissance deformed rather than displaced the patriarchal structure of Arab society. In other words, modernization provided the basis for a hybrid society and culture. Neopatriarchy, which is neither traditional nor modern, is incapable of performing as an integrated social or political system. One of its central features is "the dominance of the father (patriarch), the center around which [the] national as well as the natural family are organized. Thus between ruler and ruled, between father and child, there exist only vertical relations: in both settings the paternal will is the absolute will, mediated in both society and the family by a forced consensus based on ritual and coercion."[5]

The concept of modernization has also been used by Michael Hudson as a tool to interpret the volatile nature of Arab political behavior. He has argued that the central problem of government in the Arab world is political legitimacy. Lacking the necessary legitimacy, Arab political systems "cope with the pressures in two basic ways. One formula, in which traditional autocratic authority combined with diffuse nationalism and the ethos of development, is followed by the modernizing monarchies. The other, in which autocracy [is] clothed in modern democratic norms and buttressed with more militant nationalism and a commitment to social equality as well as development, is practiced in the Arab republics."[6]

Another alternative approach has been the social structural theory, postulating a relationship between the economy, Arab politics, and the development of the Arab state system. Attempts by Hanna Batatu, Samir Amin, and Khaldoun al-Naqeeb illustrate this theory. Batatu has used class analysis in his study of the revolutionary movements of Iraq prior to 1958, arguing that in addition to economic hierarchy, there was also a hierarchy of status. He identifies "a great degree of coincidence between all these hierarchies; that is those who stood, say, at the top in the scale of power tended also to stand at the top with respect to wealth or in terms of religious, sectarian, ethnic, or status affiliation."[7] That is also what I found in my investigation of the stratified communal structure of Lebanese society in *Lebanon in Strife*. Similarly, Samir Amin characterizes Arab society (with the exception of Egypt, which he identifies as the only peasant society) as mercantile, and its ruling class as urban. The collapse of long-distance trade as a result of European imperialism and the subsequent gradual integration of the Arab world into the capitalist world system undermined the urban ruling class and the economic base of Arab unity. As the urban commercial class that dominated the central state lost control over long-distance trade, the nation began to "regress into a formless conglomeration of more or less related ethnicities" and "to lose its previous unity."[8]

A similar interpretation has been provided by Khaldoun al-Naqeeb in his book on society and state in Arabia and the Gulf. His thesis is based on three interrelated arguments. First, Arabian and Gulf society was originally mercantile in nature and characterized by the constant circulation of tribal elites. The center of political control lay in the commercial coastal cities. The collapse of this natural state under British imperialism (1839–1920) shifted the center of political control to the tribal interior, thus causing the emergence of a ruling-family system based on sectarian-tribal alliances and protected by foreign powers. Second, rentier states (*rai'yyah*) developed as a result of oil revenues. These authoritarian states achieved a monopoly over the sources of power and wealth and used them for the benefit of the ruling elites. Third, this state of affairs has prevented real development and will eventually lead to a critical impasse.[9]

The Starting Point of Analysis

The above attempts at a social analysis of Arab politics and others like them cannot easily be integrated into a more comprehensive framework of analysis because they focus on different aspects of the same phenomena, without identifying the linkages among those aspects. Such a framework can be developed by focusing on the dynamics of the relationships in society and state and by systematically incorporating four broad principles of analysis, detailed below.

The first principle is that political behavior needs to be examined in its social and historical contexts. The significance of this principle is perhaps most vividly illustrated by the great difference in politics and state-building between

Egypt, which is relatively socially homogeneous, and more heterogeneous societies such as Lebanon and Sudan. It is not accidental that a highly centralized state and a strong political consensus on national identity have developed in Egypt and not in the other countries (see Chapter 2).

Second, the starting point of analysis is society—organizational structures and the behavior of constituent groups—rather than the institutions of the state. I have discussed this principle in other contexts, but it is important to reiterate it as we begin to analyze the political sociology of Arab society. Politics and state development can only be explained by reference to their social context, and in terms of the positions that groups and classes occupy in the socioeconomic structure. In the course of history, society and the state became intertwined beyond separation. For Marx, however, civil society was "the true source and theater of all history"; he considered it absurd to describe as history that "which neglects the real relationships and confines itself to high sounding dramas of princes and states." [10]

A third principle guiding this analysis is to examine the way the state influences society through a process of political reification that occurs when the state acquires independent powers over civil society. These powers are then treated as natural attributes and used to curtail the vital functions of society. Instead of the state serving the people, the people have to serve the state; the state begins to be perceived as needing citizens to govern, rather than as needed by citizens to regulate their affairs. Instead of being protected by the state, citizens are called upon to protect it and have to be protected from it. The subjects become objects, and the objects of governing become subjects. The human quality of thought is attributed to bureaucracy, which is given the task of thinking on behalf of the citizens; in this process, it dominates their lives, exercises power over them, and interferes in their private affairs, while proclaiming its own independent existence. Consequently, the people stop recognizing the state as their own, and political activity becomes a matter of refraining from political activity. The power of the people becomes the power of the state, thus rendering them powerless. The state exercises this power because it is controlled by a class whose interests are antagonistic to the interests of the mass of people. The Arab states fit this model and have thus imposed themselves on civil society—excluding their citizens from the political process.

Fourth, the emphasis on political alienation reflects a desire to be issue-oriented. Arab politics can be clearly understood only in the context of the issues that have been at the center of political activity for the past century and a half. Among the most important are national liberation and unity, the achievement of social justice, institution- and state-building, democratization, and the cessation of dependency. This is the essence of the *nahda* Arabs have been seeking.

A fifth principle is predicated on the assumption that an analysis of Arab politics is valid and reliable to the extent that it recognizes rather than dismisses both internal and external contradictions. Politics is not the art of governing or capturing power but, rather, involvement in an ongoing struggle between opposing forces on the local, national, regional, and international levels. By focusing on contradictions and conflicts, particularly in this transitional period of Arab history, it should be possible to achieve a greater understanding of Arab political life. These contradictions are interrelated, deeply embedded in the prevailing order and system of relationships. That is, conceptions of conflict are embedded in more comprehensive ideologies that emanate from the positions that groups, classes, and individuals occupy in the prevailing socioeconomic and political structures. For instance, the basic alternative perspectives on change—the evolutionary, reformist, and revolutionary—tend to correspond to three opposing political ideologies—the right, the center, and the left. These, in turn, tend to correspond to existing class divisions: the traditional big bourgeoisie (merchants, large landowners, and tribal chiefs), the intermediate classes (old and new petite bourgeoisie), and the lower classes (workers, peasants, the underclasses). Of course, these corresponding relationships are not mechanical and absolute. There are many exceptions to this schema, many instances of false consciousness, and many cases of betrayal of class origins and affiliations.

Historically, the dominant class and the dominant political culture have been mercantile and urban. The urban mercantile elites who constituted the core of the ruling classes in the Arab world subscribed to a conservative or rightist ideology and preferred an evolutionary model of development. But the turbulent postindependence period following World War II and the establishment of Israel on the ruins of Palestinian society following World War II brought about unforeseen challenges. The emerging intermediate classes had already begun to mobilize into ideological political parties and managed to capture power through military coups in Syria, Egypt, Iraq, Sudan, and Yemen. In Saudi Arabia, the Gulf emirates, Jordan, and Morocco, however, the traditional big bourgeoisie continued to form the core of the ruling class. The lower classes continued to be only tacitly and indirectly represented by the intermediate national bourgeoisie—a group that derived its legitimacy from identifying with the causes of the lower classes, but that insisted on treating them as uninvolved and passively loyal masses.

This is the broad outline of the transformation the Arab ruling-class structure has undergone. Essentially, the present political configuration has been in the making since the collapse of the Ottoman Empire and the onslaught of Western imperialism. The political struggle has since then taken many forms and has evolved around several core issues. What follows is an examination of Arab political formations, focusing on the actual and professed roles of the competing ruling classes, as well as the source of their power and failures.

The Politics of the Traditional Urban Big Bourgeoisie

The traditional urban big bourgeoisie (merchants, absentee landowners, and city-dwelling tribal chiefs) constituted the ruling classes and dominated Arab politics until the middle of the twentieth century; they continue to do so today in several Arab countries. Their control over commerce and subordination of the agricultural hinterland historically enabled them to monopolize the government bureaucracy and hence guaranteed their political dominance. The armies of states served as mechanisms of repression; legitimacy was sought in religion and tribalism. Networks of powerful urban families were also established through ambivalent cooperation with the Ottoman rulers and later with agents of European imperialism. The tempered struggle of the big bourgeoisie for independence aimed simply at substitution of themselves for foreign rulers, rather than the building of a new society and the establishment of a nationalist order, but it obliged them to expand the army and remove some of the barriers to recruitment of officers from the emerging intermediate classes. It also forced them occasionally to overlook the establishment of ideologically based political parties.

In the Fertile Crescent, Damascus served as the regional capital and "the nexus of political life between the province and the imperial capital" during the approximately four centuries of Ottoman rule. Notable urban families, the *a'yan wa zawat al-balad,* combined commerce and landownership with control of public offices, acting as intermediaries between the imperial authority and their local clienteles. Although they could not jeopardize the interests of the latter, they "openly identified with and defended the interests of the Ottoman state and more clearly defined its relationship with local society as one of outright control and domination." [11] Following the collapse of the Ottoman Empire, these urban notable families continued to dominate. However, nationalist movements began to emerge, thriving on confrontation with the French and British mandatory powers. These movements posed a new challenge to the traditional ruling families, who maintained their power through patron-client relationships. Things were beginning to change. Khoury observes that the years between the two world wars were

> an important pivotal period for political life in Syria. Many new
> features were introduced into politics which had their origins in the
> changes that had swept Syria since the second half of the nineteenth
> century—in administration and law, in commerce, industry, and
> agriculture, in the movement of goods, peoples, and ideas, and above

all, in her relations with Europe. Such changes encouraged the
development of new, more broadly-based, and better organized
movements of protest and resistance than previously known in
Syria. [12]

Eventually, the emerging ideological political parties—angered by the partition of the region and the monopoly of power—began to threaten the old
political order. The first stage of resistance in the 1920s was followed by
imposed accommodation in the 1930s, and agitation for the replacement of
foreign rule in the 1940s. The military coup of 1949 in Syria ushered in a new
period, in which the national bourgeoisie began to dominate political life in
the eastern Arab world. The postindependence period thus created the arena
for a fierce struggle for power.

In Arabia and the Gulf, according to Al-Naqeeb, an authoritarian state
emerged in the mid 1960s, monopolizing the sources of power and wealth for
the benefit of ruling elites. These regimes have survived because of the partition of the Arabian peninsula into separate states, to which foreign protection
was extended. These states were organized around ruling families, to whom
political loyalty is tendered, precluding a shared sense of a national homeland
larger than particular elite families. [13] Yet as it makes economic gains, a new
class is becoming the nucleus of nationalist resistance. This process in turn
unleashes greater concern for the security of the state, however, which leads
to increased repression. The result is the dismantling of the institutions that
have provided for at least minimal popular participation in the political process.
Observers like Al-Naqeeb thus believe the political process has reached an
impasse, in which the masses can play no role and elites seek only to aggrandize
their own power.

The old precapitalist Maghribi society has been characterized as divided
into different spheres of power, depending on the degree of control achieved
by the urban central authority. According to Hermassi, the model of the
traditional Maghribi state did not exert equal control over all its territory.
Rather, it controlled three concentric circles: the central power based in the
cities, which relied upon privileged, tax-exempt tribes; the subject tribes,
which paid the heaviest taxes and suffered the greatest exploitation; and the
peripheral dissident and semidissident tribes. [14] Historically, however, this
tribal structure did not prevent the emergence of strong ruling dynasties. As
demonstrated by Ibn Khaldun, tribal cohesion (*'asabiyya*) formed the basis for
empires and states in the centuries of Arab ascendancy. Religion was a complementary force in such cases, as illustrated by the history of the Almoravid and
Almohad dynasties. Tribe and sect were the foundations of the ruling dynasties.

With time, the boundaries separating the concentric circles began to disappear, being replaced among inhabitants of the Maghrib by an increasing emphasis on a shared Islamic-Arab cultural identity. This led to greater social integration and control by the urban central authority. The Moroccan monarchy imposed unification on the country and built its legitimacy on strong religious foundations. One form of legitimacy has been the Islamic tradition of loyalty to the descendants of the Prophet. The other tradition is *mubai'a* (community approval), particularly among the notables and *'ulama*. Emir 'Abdul-Kader managed to build an army and provide the basis for Algerian national unification and the centralization of authority in a way similar to the Moroccan monarchy. Tunisia, which was less fragmented, became one of the most centralized and integrated states.

Colonial domination, which lasted 132 years in Algeria, 75 years in Tunisia, and 44 in Morocco, overwhelmingly benefited the Europeans and, secondarily, the local notables. In contrast to developments in Morocco, the Tunisian and Algerian national movements struggled to end both colonial domination and the rule of the notables. The competing elites in these circumstances included (1) the nationalist-scripturalist groups formed from scholarly urban families, such as the 'Allal al-Fassi of Morocco, Ben Badis of Algeria, and Tha'albi of Tunisia; (2) the modern intelligentsia exposed to European influence, such as the young Ben Barka, Messali, and Bourguiba; and the more radical intelligentsia including the later Ben Barka, Mohammed Harbi, and Ahmed Ben Salah. In all cases, the ruling families came from the commercial and learned urban bourgeoisie. [15]

Political authority in Egypt is often characterized as extremely centralized and overwhelmingly hegemonic. A river state has existed in Egypt for over six thousand years as a result of the interaction between people and the Nile in a desert environment. The need for control and management of an elaborate irrigation system resulted in the emergence of an ancient civilization based on the belief that Egypt was owned and ruled by a "god" who guaranteed the country's welfare and prosperity. [16] This legacy has been continuous under pharaonic, Arab-Islamic, and more recent rulers. A monopoly over power and wealth has been maintained in a rigidly hierarchical and bureaucratic system. At the center of the ruling classes until 1952 were the big landowners, who lived in Cairo to ensure their full control over the state. The ruling families, army officers, and civil servants, as well as merchants, constituted the bureaucratic elites before, during, and after Muhammad Ali's rule. With the support of the native elites—merchants, *'ulama*, and bureaucrats—Muhammad Ali hoped to turn Egypt into an industrial society. He conceived of the country "as a mulk, a possession he had won by the sword." By 1845, his family became the largest landowners (owning 18.8 percent of the land), followed by civil servants, at the expense of the intermediate classes and peasants.[17] This landed aristocracy continued to dominate political life until 1952.

The traditional big urban bourgeoisie in the different regions of the Arab world dominated Arab politics until the middle of the twentieth century. It continues to do so in several countries. In all these instances, the state represents the privileged class rather than the people as a whole. To maintain themselves in power, the ruling classes have promoted political fragmentation, practiced repression, relied on foreign protection, and monopolized all sources of power and wealth. They also established their own modern armies and political parties, and sought legitimacy in religious and tribal values and affiliations.

These processes may be said to have resulted directly from the dismemberment of Arab society into several artificial states, a process that served the interests of some privileged groups and brought into being new ruling classes and dynasties. Iraq, for instance, was established in 1918 by a series of British acts, which included bringing Faysal on a British ship from Jeddah to Basra to serve as king. He arrived on June 23, 1921, and was crowned king of Iraq two months later. His brother, Abdalla, was brought to Amman in the fall of 1920 to become the ruler of the emirate of Trans-Jordan (today the Hashemite kingdom of Jordan). During the same period, France issued its 1920 decision to form the state of greater Lebanon. The kingdom of Saudi Arabia became an independent state in 1932, followed by Kuwait in 1961, South Yemen in 1967, and the United Arab Emirates in 1971. Sudan achieved statehood in 1957, and the Mahgribi countries gained their independence in the 1950s and early 1960s. Since then, separate ruling classes and families have begun to assert the sovereignty, separateness, uniqueness, and legitimacy of their countries, supported by both internal and external interests that benefited from the new arrangements. The disgruntled masses, who would have preferred unity, began to adjust slowly to the new realities and to become socialized into accepting a dual national identity.

Like their artificial nation-states, modern state armies are the product of fragmentation designed to serve the big bourgeoisie. Such armies, which have existed in the Arab world since the reign of Muhammad Ali, are designed essentially to provide internal security and defend the dominant order and the ruling classes. This is almost always done under the guise of defending the country against foreign threats. To ensure that these modern armies adhere to their assigned role, officers, especially those destined to occupy leadership positions, have traditionally been recruited from the notable and ruling families, which continues to be done today in some countries. At times, however, modern armies have ended up playing different roles. In some Arab countries, the armies seized power in military coups and then implemented new social programs. The army has emerged as a viable alternative out of the struggles for independence and Arab defeats in Palestine and elsewhere. The emergence of new intermediate classes, the surge of nationalist feelings, greater popular involvement in politics, the development of ideologically committed parties, and the broadening of the base of officer recruitment have all served to reinforce the appeal of the army over local elites. Indeed, instead of protecting the big traditional bourgeoisie, modern armies became the instrument of its elimination in several Arab countries.

The traditional big urban bourgeoisie resorted to another modern instrument in consolidating its rule—the institution of political parties. Attempts by this group to control the formation of political parties have meant that such parties are primarily composed of blocs and alliances of notables. Such parties have been formed to compete in elections; to defend and implement certain policies; to bolster the power of the urban bourgeoisie; and to counter oppositional forces.

In Egypt, for instance, the parties formed by the ruling elites included the Hizb al-umma (National party), formed in 1907 under the leadership of Hassan Abdul Raziq and other aristocratic notables at the instigation of the British and in cooperation with them. The Hizb al-ahrar al-dusturiyyin (Liberal Constitutional party) was formed in 1923 to represent the aristocracy and the big landowners and to compete with the Wafd party. These and similar parties published their own newspapers, which called for cooperation with the British or justified British rule and even contributed on some occasions to sectarian strife.

Similarly, in Syria under the French mandate, urban notables and influential landowners formed several political parties to lead or participate in caretaker governments. These parties opposed or accommodated the French mandate as circumstances or competition for power required. Some of these political parties were more inclined toward opposition, such as the Jam'iat al-qabda al-hadidiyya (Iron Hand Society), led by Dr. Abdurahman Shahbander. Shahbander, a physician and the son of a prosperous merchant in Damascus, was also the prime mover behind the first legal nationalist party, the Hizb al-shaab (People's party), which received popular support in spite of being an elitist organization. Other political parties combining opposition and accommodation included Al-Kutla al-wataniyya (the National Bloc), established and headed by such Syrian and Lebanese notables as Ibrahim Hananu, Hashim al-Atassi, Sa'ad Alla al-Jabri, and others. These leaders came mainly from the urban Sunni landowning and bureaucratic class; they accommodated the French in anticipation of replacing them after their eventual departure. Another political party that acquiesced to French rule was the Hizb al-wahda al-Suriyya (Syrian Union party), which was led by the president of Syria, Subhi Barakat, and secretly supported by the French high commissioner.[18]

In Iraq during the period of the monarchy, several political parties emerged that aimed at consolidating the rule of the traditional bourgeoisie (the land-owners, the tribal sheikhs, the merchants, the old aristocracy of administrative families, and the ex-Sharifian officers). [19] These parties included progovern-ment and in some cases pro-British organizations such as the Al-Hizb al-hurr al-Iraqi (Iraqi Liberal party), which embraced pro-British notables, and the Hizb al-taqdum (Progressive party), led by Abdul-Muhsin as-Sa'dun, who came from a tribal, *sadah* landowning family and served as premier in the years 1922–23, 1925–26, and 1928–29. As-Sa'dun was accused of implementing the goals of the British and in effect upholding Iraqi subordination to British power. Other parties included the Hizb al-ittihad al-dusturi (Constitutional Union party), established by Nuri al-Said in 1949, and the Hizb al-shaab (People's party), led by Yassin al-Hashimi, an ex-Sharifian officer and premier in 1924–25 and 1935–36, who protested the extension of the 1926 British-Iraqi treaty but eventually threw in his lot with the government. Later in the 1930s, however, he tried to regain the confidence of the popular opposition and headed the powerful Al-Ikhwa' al-watani (National Brotherhood) front, which opposed the new treaty regulating Iraqi-British relations signed by Nuri al-Said. [20]

In the greater Maghrib, loyal parties, mostly in the form of alliances or blocs of notables, were formed and reformed in order to counter the opposition parties that had emerged. Prior to the Algerian revolution, the Ittihad al-Muntakhbeen al-Muslimeen (Union of the Muslim Electorate) was formed; this party called for integration into France and for French citizenship, and was led by Farhat Abbas, Mahmoud Ben Jalloul, Rabi' al-Zanati, and others with French higher educations. Multiparty systems and political pluralism in Morocco encompassed loyal as well as oppositional parties. Indeed, loyal blocs and alliances have always been mobilized to support the policies of the monarchy and to counter those of the opposition. For example, the front of notables formed to defend constitutional institutions was led by Ahmed Rida Ghadira, director general of the royal office. Another wing of the loyal forces has attempted to represent the rural Berbers. Fronts of this sort lacked programs of action. Their existence therefore complicated the processes by which political actors could implement substantive change. In the 1984 elections, the loyalists of the Constitutional Union party (Hizb al-Ittihad al-dusturi), founded in 1983 by Premier Al-Mu'ti Bu'ibaid and Al-Tajmo' al-Watani and led by Ahmed Osman, won 144 of 306 seats in the Moroccan parliament. Several opposition parties, mainly the Hizb al-istiqlal (Independence party) and Al-Ittihad al-ishtiraki (Socialist Union) shared the remaining seats. [21]

The traditional bourgeoisie has not relied completely on foreign protection and supportive privileged groups and communities to consolidate its power, or even on the formation of modern state armies and political parties or blocs. It has also continued to seek legitimacy from the value systems of tribal society and religious belief.

Tribalism as a Source of Legitimacy. Traditional Arab rule may be described as tribal in form and essence. Theorizing about tribal cohesion as a necessary condition for building empires, Ibn Khaldun demonstrated the process by which tribes provided dynastic lines for centuries. On another level, tribalism as a system of roles and values is embodied in the dominant patriarchal and neopatriarchal relationships. Also, as both a structure and a system of values and roles, tribalism is inseparable from religion, traditional rule's other basic source of legitimacy, a subject to which we shall return.

Ruling families or dynasties continue to control at least eight of the twenty-one Arab countries, not including those in which a network of tribally related political leaders monopolizes power. Most of Arabia is called Saudi after a family belonging to the Masalikh, a subtribe of the Rwala, who are in turn a subtribe of the 'Aneza of the Najd and parts of Iraq and Syria. In the Gulf, Al-Sabbah have ruled Kuwait since the beginning of the eighteenth century; Al-Khalifa rule in Bahrain; Al-Thani in Qatar; Al-Abu Said in Oman; Al-Nihian in Abu Dhabi; Al-Maktum in Dubai; and Al-Qassimi in Shariqah. Iraq and Jordan were created for the Hashemites, and the latter country is named after and still ruled by them. Morocco has been ruled by dynasties as far back as historians have traced; the present Alawite dynasty has ruled since 1664. Modern Egypt was ruled by a royal family for over a century and a half.

Other ruling families controlled Tunisia until 1956 and Libya until 1969. Prior to 1949, Syria was ruled by a network of notable families. A similar network ruled Lebanon and led it into the anarchy of the 1975–76 civil war. The intense rivalries among notable families, each of which had its own political parties and internal and external alliances, were a significant factor undermining Palestinian resistance to Zionism in 1948. One of the most serious challenges to the sovereignty of the Yemeni state is tribalism. Tribalism may also have been at the root of the former South Yemen's bloody confrontation, a conflict that undermined the first serious Marxist experiment in the Arab world. In Sudan, the two dominant tribal-sectarian parties are the Umma party, which is based on the tribal-religious order of Al-Mahdiyya, and the Democratic Unionist party, which is based on the tribal-religious order of Al-Khatmiyya. Their struggle for political dominance has been interrupted by several coups since 1958, but these two parties have recently (1985–) resumed their rivalry.

Religion as a Source of Legitimacy. I argued in an earlier chapter that rulers throughout Arab history have used religion as a mechanism of social and political control. One phenomenon in this process is the Wahabiyya movement, which has served as a major underpinning of the House of Saud since

1744, while satisfying deep-seated reformist impulses within Arab society. The same role was played by the Mahdiyya in the Sudan and the Sanusiyya in Libya.

Another phenomenon has been the development of a unique class or status group in Islam, the *sadah* (those who claim to be descendants of the Prophet), which was examined earlier. People in traditional Yemen sought their supernatural powers (*baraka*) and feared their curse (*hatf*), so old and young alike kissed their hands and called them *habib* (beloved).[22] However, Hanna Batatu concludes in his study of the old social classes and the revolutionary movements of Iraq that the claim of descent from the Prophet made by the *sadah* was merely a supporting element rather than the real underpinning of their social and political position. Nonetheless, combined with wealth, it often led to prominence. Similar roles were also played by mystic orders, which were often guided by the *sadah*.[23]

The sectarian-tribal alliance in Arabia, which is deeply rooted in ancient divisions between Qahtan and 'Adnan, has proven very durable and has been instrumental in securing internal stability for the House of Saud through its dominant political position in the region. The alliance has been especially successful in countering nationalist forces in the rest of the Arab world and has enabled this religious-tribal elite to expand even into sub-Saharan Africa and Asian countries like Pakistan, Afghanistan, and Indonesia. Indeed, as part of an American-Saudi strategy to use Islam as a counterforce against nationalist and progressive forces, several publications have even launched attacks on Arab nationalism itself.[24] This battle against nationalist and progressive forces has been conducted by what the Egyptian intellectual Fuad Zakariyya calls petro-Islam.[25]

The political legitimacy lent by Islam has also contributed to the development of ideas such as loyalty to the ruler, and has provided dynasties with an encompassing ideology that legitimized political institutions. This enabled countries like Morocco to unify tribes into a larger *umma* and may also partly explain why certain dynasties successfully established empires even in tribally segmented societies.[26]

In summary, then, the urban mercantile elites at the center of the big bourgeoisie traditionally constituted the Arab ruling classes. Under their rule, which began to be challenged by the middle of the twentieth century, the state was hardly distinguishable from the class interests of this urban bourgeoisie. This elite monopolized power and wealth, rendering the people powerless and impoverished. The society was clearly divided into *a'yan wa zawat* and *'amma* (notables and commoners) and *ra'i wa ra'iyya* (rulers and subjects). The system that supported the big urban bourgeoisie in power proved to be an effective repressive system that will only be challenged by basic transformations in the world order and in regional and local socioeconomic structures. This kind of challenge is what has been in the making for almost two centuries; the beginning of the actual collapse occurred in the middle of the twentieth century, after decades of struggle for independence.

The Politics of the Intermediate National Bourgeoisie: Western Liberalism, Nationalism, Arab Socialism, and Religious Fundamentalism

As a result of the socioeconomic changes and other developments examined in earlier chapters, the twentieth century has witnessed the expansion and increasing prominence of an intermediate class of merchants, tradesmen, landowners, artisans, civil servants, army officers, professionals, employees of private companies, and students, which rapidly began to pose a political threat to the traditional ruling class.[27] What these various strata have in common is their position between the big bourgeoisie on the one hand and the working and peasant classes on the other. Despite these shared conditions, however, the intermediate class is marked by a heterogeneous amorphousness resembling that of Arab society itself, and closely linked to the capitalist structure that began to take shape in the Arab world in the late nineteenth and early twentieth centuries.[28]

The rise of the intermediate class resulted in the development of several political orientations in its ranks. The most significant and identifiable of these orientations are Western liberalism, nationalism, socialism, and religious fundamentalism. Some of the movements expressing these orientations have managed to capture power through military coups and wars of liberation, while others have failed to do so and continue to struggle as besieged and marginal efforts. Before examining these developments, however, some other observations need to be made regarding the dominance and comprehensiveness exercised by nationalism, and hence the emergence of the national bourgeoisie in opposition to the traditional big bourgeoisie.

Nationalism developed as a strong force in response to structural changes as well as to the need of Arab countries to free themselves from repressive Ottoman rule and to counter the onslaught of an aggressive European imperialism and colonization. For the eastern Arab world, particularly the Fertile Crescent, nationalism provided an alternative to divisive communal arrangements. Since the middle of the nineteenth century, the call for nationalism has been central to the process of social, political, and cultural renewal—that is, the achievement of the *nahda*. In the beginning, some conceived of nationalism as a movement to redress Arab grievances through decentralization and the creation of a new balance of power in the area. Others conceived of it as a secular alternative to the caliphate and a way to achieve full independence. Since the end of World War I, the latter view has become a strong, and ultimately dominant, political force. There have, however, been divergent orientations: nationalism is defined by local versus regional versus pan-Arab referents. It has been given either secular or apologetically religious overtones. It carries socialist versus capitalist or leftist versus rightist or progressive versus conservative implications. Nationalist goals can be reactionary or reformist or revolutionary.

A major split that has endured to the present time has been that between the comprador bourgeoisie and the more nationalist bourgeoisie. The former has been inclined toward preservation of the status quo, expressed through a local nationalism that coincides with the existing artificial nation-states. It has also tended to be pro-Western and to favor free enterprise and conservative ideologies. The latter has been inclined toward a greater political unity that transcends the more recent, artificial barriers, such as the calls for the creation of a greater Syria or greater Maghrib and pan-Arabism. The nationalist bourgeoisie has also tended to be more anti-Western and somewhat secular and leftist. Originally, the nationalist forces were led by the big bourgeoisie. This group sought freedom from foreign domination and succeeded in replacing the foreigners, but it failed to establish a new order. The national bourgeoisie, which is based in the intermediate class, began seriously to challenge the big traditional bourgeoisie by seeking popular support and social mobilization through ideological political parties. This is where the two clusters of the bourgeoisie began to diverge politically, following different courses and distinctive articulations. Gradually, as the national bourgeoisie began to expand and gain more prominence, the nationalist movement evolved into a liberation movement seeking to dominate externally as well as internally. These developments and others disprove the notion that nationalism was borrowed from the West. They demonstrate, instead, the emergence of nationalism as a genuine result of the internal and external dynamics of Arab society.

Western Liberalism. A more direct result of the encounter with the West has been the infusion into Arab political culture of a range of values we associate with broad-based popular participation in governance. These values include the notions of constitutionalism, pluralism, parliamentary democracy, rationalism, secularism, representation, personal freedoms, and open-mindedness. Such notions, however, have had a greater impact on political discourse than on actual behavior. In other words, debate swirled around such abstract issues as the applicability of secularism or the significance of pluralism, but rarely were such concepts embodied in movements or implemented in enduring structures and institutions. Nonetheless, serious debate in intellectual and political circles led them to be considered prerequisites for political modernity and the achievement of the *nahda*. Given this shared recognition, we need to examine the appearance of constitutionalism, parliamentary democracy, and so on in the philosophies of Arab political movements and associations, as well as their actual application.

Liberalism seemed most likely to endure in Egypt, Lebanon, and Tunisia. The ideas of Rifa'at al-Tahtawi, Lutfi al-Sayyid, Taha Hussein, and others provided the guidelines that influenced political modernization and the ideologies of political parties like the Wafd. But the Egyptian experiment with some aspects of liberalism, such as parliamentary elections, proved ineffective and temporary. The Tunisian experiment, starting with the implementation of some of the ideas of Khair al-Dain during the second half of the nineteenth century, survived under the rule of the Neo-Destur party and the leadership of Habib Bourguiba for some time. However, personal authoritarianism proved to be stronger than the institutions of the party and the state in Tunisia. The ill-founded experiment in Lebanon proved fatal. Democratic in form rather than substance, the semifeudal confessional system collapsed under the weight of complex internal and regional problems. The freedoms the Lebanese enjoyed for a few decades in contrast to other Arabs eventually led to anarchy and civil war rather than to the establishment of a truly democratic society.

Survival of some of the basic principles of liberalism only on the level of political discourse may be attributable to a basic flaw in the perspective of Arab liberalism itself. Arab liberals have hoped to change the prevailing mentality without emphasizing the need for drastic change in the socioeconomic structure. Although it was social and economic conditions that initially prompted the call for a democratic society, liberals have often dismissed the significance of the relationship, arguing that there is little connection. For example, Constantine Zurayk, one of the most prominent Arab liberal intellectuals, says it is "highly mistaken, and dangerously so, to attribute all that underdeveloped peoples are presently suffering . . . to their prevailing [socioeconomic] orders."[29] From such a perspective, liberals in or outside power never systematically concerned themselves with the structural changes needed to overcome growing socioeconomic disparities. They never attempted to remove material barriers to the participation and representation of the deprived and lower middle classes or to end, or even check, deepening dependency.

Nationalism and the Arabization of Socialism. This failure on the part of Western-style liberalism may be related in part to the fact that the expanding intermediate class and Arab masses showed much more interest in nationalism and a hybrid Arab socialism, an inclination explicable in terms of the dual oppression that characterized the Arab world—national oppression by Western imperialism and colonization and class oppression imposed by the big traditional urban bourgeoisie, whose goal was to replace foreign rulers with themselves rather than to build a new nation–state and a new social order. Thus, the intermediate class and masses needed to fight a dual battle, one against foreign domination and the other against internal class exploitation.

Essentially, nationalism means a people's consciousness of their distinctive identity. From this sense of identity comes a loyalty to the country, a belief in self–determination and liberation, and an assertion of national rights and interests above all. Such a political trend began to take shape in the Arab east during the second half of the nineteenth century. Ibrahim Yaziji's call, "Tanabbahu wa istafiqu ayouha al-Arabu" ("Arise, ye Arabs, and awake"), was one of the first articulations of nationalist sentiment. In the early twentieth century, according to Philip Khoury, Syria became a hotbed of Arabism; the Syrian brand of Arabism evolved through literary and cultural organizations led by prominent intellectuals like Tahir al-Jaza'iri (b. 1851), Rafiq al-Azm, Abdul Rahman Shahbandar, Muhammed Kurd Ali, and Fakhri al-Barudi. In the 1930s, however, ideologically committed parties began to present a more systematic view of nationalism. The leaders and ideologues of the new movements belonged mostly to the emerging professional stratum. These more radical and ideological movements sought, as Khoury has noted, to bridge "the widening gap between the nationalism of the upper classes and the nationalism of popular sentiment." [30] In so doing, they left a lasting mark on the politics of nationalism, revealing "a strong middle class component. In their front ranks stood men from merchant backgrounds or from the middle levels of the state bureaucracy. They were composed of members of the liberal professions and of a nascent industrial bourgeoisie, and were armed with European educations and new, sophisticated methods of political organization acquired abroad." The League of National Action (Isbat al-'amal al-qawmi) emerged in Syria in the 1930s. Although it did not survive for long, it challenged the National Bloc (Al-Kutla al-wataniyya) and proved to be the ideological parent of the Ba'th party some of whose founders—such as Zaki al-Arsuzi and Jalal al-Sayyid— were former members of the League. [31]

Some remarkably similar trends and forms of organization appeared in the rest of greater Syria and in the Fertile Crescent, evolving from cultural societies such as the Pan–Arab Muthanna Club in Iraq. Founded in 1935, this cultural club committed itself to "disseminating the spirit of Arab nationalism . . . preserving Arab traditions . . . strengthening the sense of Arab manhood in youth, and creating a new Arab culture which would unite to the Arab heritage what is worthy in the civilization of the West." As pointed out by Batatu, this club was led by men from mercantile backgrounds or from the professional middle class and derived its strength from its links to army officers. The club reached the height of its development in 1938–41, but British military intervention led to its breakup. It reemerged in 1946 within the ranks of the Independence party, which called for the eventual establishment of a federated Arab state.[32]

Besides the pan-Arab movements formed in the 1930s, other nationalist, ideological movements appeared, calling for what their founders believed to be a more realistic unity—that is, a unity focused on regional identity. One of the most ideological and systematic of these parties is the Syrian Social Nationalist party, which was founded in 1932 by 28-year-old Antun Sa'ada, the son of a physician-writer from Shuwair, Mount Lebanon. Calling for the unification of greater Syria based on the oneness of its geography and society, the party opposed both what it considered the narrow, Lebanese-based nationalism of the Maronite Christians and expansionist, Sunni-based Arab nationalism. In perhaps the first book in the Arab language on the meaning and evolution of nations, *Nushu' al-umam* (1936), Sa'ada defined a nation in geographical and social rather than cultural and religious terms. A nation, he argued, was a completely constituted society, one that emerged through a lengthy historical process of interaction between a people and their distinctively defined geography. Consequently, each nation developed common economic interests and a social character of its own. Based on this definition, he identified four Arab nations: Syria or the Fertile Crescent, Arabia, Egypt and the Nile Valley, and the Maghrib. Once united, these four nations would form an Arab front.

Ideologically, Sa'ada's party also claimed to have a new outlook or vision for achieving the *nahda*, transforming society, and creating a new human being (*insan jadid*). As analyzed by Beshara Doumani, several significant facts about the party stand out: (1) it was the first disciplined, modern nationalist party to form in the region, as well as the first with rural roots; (2) Antun Sa'ada was its sole, uncontested founder, ideologue, and lifelong leader (*za'im*); (3) the French mandatory authorities and traditional leaders were hostile to the party; and (4) the social background of the leadership was mixed in terms of religious sect, while all were well-educated and drawn from a village or small-town background.[33]

Another major ideological party in the Arab East is the Hizb al-ba'th al-'arabi al-ishtiraki (Arab Socialist Renaissance, or Ba'th, party). As documented by Hanna Batatu, the Ba'th of the 1950s emanated from three groups organized around the particular, personal leadership of three members of the intermediate class. The merger of these three groups was completed in 1952 and called the Arab Socialist Ba'th party. Ideologically, the party subscribed to Arab nationalism, defining it mostly in cultural terms, with Michel 'Aflaq as its authoritative ideologue. As observed by Batatu, " 'Aflaq's ideas are nowhere systematically developed. They are scattered through his public speeches . . . and very short essays composed, for the most part, under the pressure of events. When drawn together, they do not add up to an entirely consistent

point of view. This is not unrelated to 'Aflaq's tendency to rely more on feeling
. . . than on analysis."[34]

The values the Ba'th party embraced were Arab unity, freedom, and socialism, but it has so far failed to achieve any of these goals, and future prospects
of doing so look dim, in part at least because of the makeup of the Ba'th cadre.
A summary analysis of the biographical data relating to the national command
of the Ba'th party from 1954 to 1970 shows that it was drawn predominantly
from members of the professions and the middle and lower-middle classes. By
nationality, 30 percent were Syrian, 26 percent Iraqi, and 24 percent Lebanese.
By sect, 49 percent were Sunni, 21 percent Shi'a, 16 percent Orthodox
Christian, 7 percent Druze, and 6 percent Alawi. By occupation, 62 percent
were members of professions, such as lawyers, teachers, engineers, and physi-
cians; 13 percent were army officers, and 25 percent were party workers. The
data also show that 18 percent of the national command came from the lower
class, 29 percent from the lower-middle class, and 44 percent from the middle
class.[35]

Two other versions of Arab nationalism are the Movement of Arab Nationalists and Nasserism. The first (Harakat al-qawmiyyin al-'arab) distinguished
itself not by its conception of nationalism but by its preoccupation with the
Palestinian struggle, which made it dynamic and genuinely open to the socialist
movement. Until 1967, it survived in the shadow of Nasserism, and it subsequently reemerged as the radicalized Popular Front for the Liberation of
Palestine.

The Nasserite view may represent a shift from the nationalist legacy of
Mustafa Kamel, Sa'ad Zaghloul, Lutfi al-Sayyid, Taha Hussein, and others who
adhered to an Egyptian rather than an Arab nationalism. Yet one can also argue
that the Egyptian concept of what constitutes the *umma* was much more
flexible than that of the Arab East. The fact that Egypt has existed as a unified
nation-state for so long resulted in greater agreement among Egyptians concerning their national identity. Nasserism was also distinguished by its appeal
to the masses, both in addressing the people in their own language "from heart
to heart" and in credibly challenging the imperialist forces. The fact that Nasser
posed a challenge to Western imperialism made him a hero to the Arab people
and also a target of attack by the Western powers; his stance against the West
both led to his prominence and explains his tragic defeat. Indeed, Nasser's rise
to power represented Arab pride and his downfall Arab submission. The six
goals of the Nasser-led political and social revolution launched on September
23, 1952, included the elimination of feudalism, the elimination of monopolization and the dominance of capital over government, the elimination of
imperialism, the achievement of social justice, the establishment of a strong
national army, and the building of a sound democracy. However, it was

neither these goals nor the futile, bureaucratic land reforms of 1954 and 1962 that gave meaning to Nasserism. At its heart was the revival of national pride. Nasserism failed not because of its ambition but because it was dominated by the national bourgeoisie, who excluded the mass of Egyptians from the political process.

The Maghrib, too, tended to see no conflict between local, regional, and pan-Arab brands of nationalism. Not unlike Nasser during the first period of the revolution, the prominent Moroccan leader and intellectual 'Allal al-Fassi used the concept of the *umma* in reference to Morocco, to the larger Maghrib, and to the Arab or even the Muslim world as a whole, sometimes in the same speech. What has distinguished the political Maghrib from the political Mashriq, Elbaki Hermassi notes, is the existence of a relatively strong political center, whose focal point is a strong, shared sense of collective identity, not unlike that in Egypt. The establishment of the regional or local nation-state cannot be separated from a national struggle against imperialism and colonization. Thus all the Maghribi parties and groups providing leadership to the nationalist movement mobilized people in the name of the homeland rather than in the name of Arabism and Arab unity. This emphasis on the Maghrib leads Hermassi to conclude that the state occupies different positions in the Maghrib and the Mashriq: it is considered an artificial entity in the Mashriq and "in opposition to nationalist goals," but in the Maghrib it is regarded as a positive achievement, something for which generations have struggled. [36]

The intermediate classes, in attempting to replace the big traditional bourgeoisie and to achieve new sources of legitimacy, had to identify with the masses and try to understand their problems. Eventually, they realized that they could not overlook class contradictions even in the name of national unity. The increasing dependency following independence also revealed that contradictions between nations are inseparable from contradictions between classes. Gradually, vague notions of what later came to be called Arab socialism began to infiltrate Ba'thist and Nasserite ideologies. In 1936, 'Aflaq defined socialism in totally nationalistic and utilitarian terms, saying: "I do not view socialism . . . as a means to feed the hungry and dress the naked only. I am not so much concerned about the hungry because they are hungry as because of the potentialities . . . that hunger prevents from developing." This utilitarian view of socialism continued to be rearticulated in many forms in 'Aflaq's later writings. In the postindependence period, he clearly reasserted his view: "The Arab nationalist realizes that socialism is the most successful means for the awakening of his nationalism and nation, because he knows that the present Arab struggle cannot be carried out without the cooperation of all Arabs for they cannot participate in this struggle as long as they are exploited and divided into masters and slaves. The necessities of nationalist struggle require the socialist outlook, that is, that we believe that Arabs cannot awaken unless they felt and trusted that this nationalism will secure justice, equality, and a decent living for all."[37]

The Arab socialism of the Ba'th and the Egyptian revolution also rejected the underpinnings of Marxist analysis. Ba'thism and Nasserism were uninterested in a materialist interpretation or class analysis; they regarded private ownership of property as a natural right; and they appealed to religion and religious sentiments. After almost two decades of hazardous trial and error, Arab socialism failed to challenge poverty and the sharp class differences that existed. Experiments with bureaucratic land reform, nationalization, and state capitalism were all unsuccessful. The result, says Mahmoud Abdel-Fadil, was "the emergence of a 'new class' composed of administrative and military elites and senior civil servants whose consumption patterns have larger components of services and manufactured goods than those of the rest of the population. . . . The temptation to copy western consumption patterns was particularly strong among the rising urban middle class."[38]

The case of Algeria is qualitatively different. The Algerian revolution was an epic confrontation between insurgent violence and brutal colonization, leading to a very different political pattern after independence in 1962. The Algerian nationalists soon rid themselves of the old ex-assimilationists and ex-centralists. They nationalized agricultural and industrial enterprises and experimented with workers' self-management. However, the nationalists were by no means a homogeneous group. They belonged to different classes and had divergent interests. The military and the Boumediene group succeeded in deposing Ahmed Ben Bella's radical government and replaced self-management with national corporations directly under the control of the central authority. Marnia Lazreg notes that a "balance appears to have been struck between a skilled bourgeoisie and a nationalist petty bourgeoisie. The former cooperates with the latter within certain understood boundaries. Thus, measures taken in favor of the peasantry are counterbalanced with decisions in favor of the bourgeoisie."[39]

Elbaki Hermassi notes that Houari Boumediene's regime eliminated most of the members of the traditional political class and united what he calls the symbolic elites, those with guerrilla experience, and the instrumental elites who actually managed the economy by virtue of their special training at French universities. In addition, he argues, "the regime itself came to power as a result of what many considered to be a coup d'état. . . . It is at this point that one can locate the bifurcation between Ben Bella's and Boumediene's regimes. . . . The first regime held basically a Fanonian view of the national liberation movement, as predominantly a 'peasant' revolution. Once in power, this regime sought to validate the agricultural workers' occupation of the settlers' lands, organize the whole operation according to the ideals and principles of self-management, and seek . . . an increasingly peasant and working class political base. The second regime . . . departed from its predecessor in almost every respect: the Mujahidin (guerrilla fighters and their dependents) replaced the peasant base, self-management . . . has been succeeded by state management." [40] These same leanings were clearly reflected in the Algerian National Charter of 1976. On the one hand, it borrowed directly from Marxist socialism, emphasizing the "elimination of private ownership of the means of production," and declared "that socialism in Algeria expresses the deep ambitions of the working class." On the other hand, the National Charter emphasized the Islamic Arab character of Algeria in articles stating that "socialism in Algeria does not emanate from any materialist philosophy . . . the building of socialism goes in accordance with the prosperity of Islamic values which constitute one of the basic components of the personality of the Algerian people." [41] This orientation, coupled with a monopoly of power and the destruction of civil society, as well as a failure to achieve stated goals, has contributed significantly to the emergence of Islamic fundamentalism in Algeria.

Palestinian society has also been transformed through armed struggle. But Palestinian nationalists are not a homogeneous group either. The Arab nationalist movement has become Marxist-Leninist, but the mainstream within the Palestine Liberation Organization have already renounced the PLO's past and made concessions (including the recognition of Israel and acceptance of UN resolutions 242 and 338) in exchange for the mere willingness of the United States to talk to them and facilitate a peaceful process of negotiation.

Arab nationalism and Arab socialism as conceived and practiced by the intermediate classes have clearly failed to achieve unity and social justice. What the nationalists have managed to do so far is to maintain themselves in power in spite of their loss of legitimacy (which they originally earned through identification with the aspirations of the masses). What they rely on now is naked oppression and the destruction of civil society. As a consequence, a desperate vacuum has emerged that other segments of the intermediate classes are trying to fill by appealing to religious sentiments.

Religious Fundamentalism. The vacuum created by the failure of Arab nationalism and Arab socialism seems to have encouraged certain segments of the middle class and the lower middle classes to resort to an old political weapon. Other conditions have contributed to the revival of Arab religious fundamentalism as a political movement: enduring economic crises, social anomie, distorted modernization, deliberate manipulation and even sponsorship of religious movements by some governments, and tyranny of the state over civil society. Two results of these conditions have been the 1979 Iranian revolution and the success of religious fundamentalism in Israel.

The rise of militant Islamic movements is an issue of great interest in the media and centers of scholarship all over the world. Wave after wave of articles, commentaries, books, conferences, and documentary films have addressed this issue, reiterating preconceived notions and deep-rooted biases. Very few scholarly works seem capable of transcending pervasive Orientalist notions in order to examine the new phenomenon in its social and historical contexts.

Enduring economic crises clearly reflect the growing gap between rich and poor in Arab states, which relates both to increasing dependency on, and integration into, the capitalist world system and to uneven development. This gap is expressed, for example, in conspicuous consumption by the bourgeois classes in the midst of widespread poverty, and in the failure to solve long-term problems.

As a contributing factor to religious revivalism, social anomie manifests itself in the destruction of primary group relations, and in the breakdown of traditional values, which are not replaced by new ones. The transitional nature of the contemporary scene has been exacerbated by rapid rural-urban migration. Society is marked by frustrated aspirations, and by the insatiable desire for achievement by any means (that is, by a dissociation between means and goals), resulting in unrestrained opportunism and corruption.

Distorted modernization is closely connected with this conspicuous consumption, Westernization, and anomie. Society is neither modern nor traditional. As a consequence, society becomes preoccupied with authenticity (*asala*) and rejects alien notions regardless of their usefulness and relevance.

Some governments have deliberately manipulated religion to undermine internal and external enemies. The Islamic Republic of Iran uses religion as a means of disseminating its revolution, particularly in Iraq, the Gulf, and Lebanon. The Saudi government uses religion as a mechanism of control, promoting pan-Islamism as an alternative to Arab nationalism in order to combat both communism and national liberation movements. The Saudis have also sponsored religious movements and institutions all over the Arab world and in Third World societies. One subtle Saudi initiative is the sponsoring of Islamic education, even at the risk of divisiveness, as in Yemen, the Sudan, the West Bank, Egypt, Lebanon, and Afghanistan. Many opportunistic Arab intellectuals have joined the Saudi bandwagon for personal gain.

Objective social, economic, and political conditions have led to the participation by certain strata and groups more than others in Islamic movements. The main source of support for such movements comes from intermediate merchants, artisans, university students from lower-middle-class and rural origins, semi-employed or unemployed graduates, and depressed and marginalized workers, who are constantly reminded of their deprivation relative to the affluence of the elites. It was not accidental that the Muslim Brotherhood society formed in 1928 by Hassan al-Banna was located in Isma'iliyya—the center of foreign influence and affluence in Egypt at that time.

This is not to say that Islamic movements have been seeking social justice. Sayyid Qutb has clearly pointed out that Islam gives greater priority to spiritual values, such as purity and fear of God (*al-taqwa wal-wara'*), than to economic equality. In his view, Islam "does not impose . . . literal equality in wealth because achievement of wealth follows from unequal capacities. Absolute justice requires economic inequalities and that some be preferred over others." Thus, for the Muslim Brotherhood, inequalities are primarily a question of differentiation rather than discrimination. [42] Ultimately, this view is most typical of emerging middle and lower middle classes, who tend to explain their relative success in terms of their special capacities and hard work; they see these characteristics as distinguishing them from the impoverished masses.

In spite of the apparently strong animosity to the West exhibited by Islamic movements, they are quite capable of reconciling themselves to Western influence, given their static view of reality. Just as the lack of equality is part of the natural order, so is the West; in this they resemble floods, earthquakes, rivers, and rain. No matter how strongly the believer may feel about this natural order, he or she has to accept and adjust to it as long as it does not present a direct threat.

To summarize this analysis of the politics of the intermediate national bourgeoisie, the heterogeneous and amorphous nature of the intermediate classes has resulted in three major political orientations: Western liberalism, nationalism and socialism, and religious fundamentalism. The infusion of Arab political culture with the values and notions of Western liberalism (including the ideas of constitutionalism, pluralism, parliamentary democracy, rationalism, personal freedom, and a free economy) has had some impact on political discourse. Egypt, Lebanon, and Tunisia experimented with aspects of liberalism, but the experiments failed to take root and endure. Arab nationalist regimes have been largely responsible for the destruction of civil society in the Arab world. Within less than a quarter of a century (1949–70), more than thirty-five coups brought new regimes to power in Arab countries. These nationalist coups put the majority of Arabs at the mercy of authoritarian rule without achieving social justice and without ending economic dependence on the West. The way Arab nationalist regimes have imposed their version of nationalism on their people and on neighboring countries has proved counterproductive, contributing to greater divisiveness and direct Western intervention. As the dominant political force in the 1950s and 1960s, socialistically inclined Arab nationalism may resume its role as the most central current in Arab politics, but only to the extent that it is capable of formulating a more progressive and realistic program for unity. I believe Arab nationalism should incorporate secularism, class analysis, pluralism, and the promotion of civil society into its ideology. This would lead to a very different exercise of power.

Religious fundamentalism has tended to share or augment power in the Arab world. It seems only capable of serving as a mechanism of control or incitement, and not as a salvation movement. Thus the crisis goes on unchallenged, in spite of the desperate struggle of Arab people, who seem to be "waiting for Godot." This is the cause of the widespread sense of deep despair and political alienation in the Arab world.

The Working Classes and the Left

The politics of the working classes have been mostly those of survival. Dominated and rendered powerless by all, they have been overwhelmed by the pressure of securing their daily bread. The mass of impoverished, oppressed, disinherited, and weakened Arabs represents a class-in-itself by virtue of the alienating conditions under which all struggle to make a living. Fragmented into subclasses (workers, peasants, soldiers, lumpenproletariat, underclasses, servants, street vendors, peddlers, and the unemployed), they have not been able to form a class-for-itself. Their voices have generally been heard filtered through the national bourgeoisie, who claim to identify with them and represent their interests, and consequently monopolize the political process on their behalf.

Among these subclasses, workers and peasants are the most significant forces of the oppressed. Their involvement in both national and class struggles can be traced far back in Arab history. Yet it was the progressive intelligentsia of the intermediate classes who initiated and led organized struggle. In this respect, the workers and peasants have rarely been represented in the leadership of the nationalist and leftist movements and hardly at all in government institutions. Although they have supposedly formed the basis for leftist revolutionary movements, the tasks of raising class consciousness, unionization, organization into political parties, and formulation of strategies have all required the active participation of the progressive intelligentsia. It was the intelligentsia who articulated nationalism and socialism, the two basic tenets of Arab revolutionary culture.

Nationalism and socialism were originally quite distinct, but the nature of the struggle has rendered the two aspects of liberation inseparable and perhaps one and the same. We have already examined the development of nationalism. Here, we shall explore the development of scientific socialism and the radical left. On the level of intellectual discourse, contemporary notions of scientific socialism were introduced in the Arab world by such prominent thinkers as

Abd al-Rahman al-Kawakibi (1848–1902), Shibli Shumayyil (1850–1917), Farah Antun (1874–1922), and Salama Musa (1887–1958). Chapter 11 presents their views; in this chapter we shall focus on the development of leftist revolutionary movements.

The development of socialist parties can be traced to early attempts at organizing trade unions and strikes waged in Egypt around the last decades of the nineteenth century. Foreign socialists (Russians, Greeks, and Armenians) participated in these developments. Batatu found that it was a Russian Jew, Joseph Rosenthal (a jeweler in Alexandria), who set communism on its course in Egypt. Rosenthal organized strikes by the employees of tailors and barbers and a protest by shopkeepers against high shop rents. In 1920 he formed a communist club, and a year later he launched the Egyptian Socialist party,[43] whose participating Arab founders included writers, lawyers, doctors, and other members of the professions, such as Ali al-'Anani, Mahmud Hussni al-'Arabi, Salama Musa, Safwan Abu al-Falih, Ahmed al-Madani, Antun Marun, Hussein Namiq, Mustafa Hassanein al-Mansuri, Abdul Rahman Fadl, and Sheikh Abdul Latif Bakhit.[44]

According to Batatu, the early efforts of these activists were unwittingly assisted by British intelligence. The British succeeded in obtaining a formal religious opinion (*fatwa*) from the Egyptian Grand Mufti against Bolshevism. Contrary to British expectations, however, the *fatwa* proved to be counterproductive. Some newspapers attacked the *fatwa* and defended the activists, and the movement became a general topic in Egyptian circles. But as soon as the movement began to mobilize workers and gain confidence, it found itself in direct confrontation with the popular leader Sa'ad Zaghloul, who had become premier following the triumph of the Wafd party in national elections. The Socialist party instructed workers at Alexandria to go on strike, seize factories, and eject owners and managers. Perturbed by the challenge, Zaghloul sent in a battalion of infantry and managed to end the strike. The top socialist leaders were arrested and imprisoned. The movement disintegrated.[45] Meanwhile, socialist and communist parties were being formed in other countries (Palestine in 1919, Tunisia in 1920, Syria and Lebanon in 1924, Iraq in 1924).

The founding of these parties was preceded by the slow formation of a working class. The process had begun with industrialization of Egypt under the rule of Muhammad Ali and Ismail Pasha. Their efforts were strengthened by the cotton boom resulting from the Civil War in the United States (1861–65). The first Egyptian labor union was formed in 1899. By 1920, there were 44 unions in Egypt and the number increased to 491 in 1950, with over 33,000 members.[46]

The first Lebanese-Syrian Communist party was formed by Fuad Shimali and Yousif Yazbek. Shimali was a worker, the son of a peasant from a village in the Kisrwan district of Lebanon. Earlier he had been a member of the Alexandrian socialist group. Yazbek, a Maronite intellectual, hailed from the Beirut suburb of Hadath. Their first activities included agitation among and the organization of tobacco workers in 1925. Shortly afterward, Shimali was arrested. Upon his release from prison in 1928, he was elected secretary general of the Communist party of Lebanon and Syria; he was succeeded by Khalid Bakdash in 1936.

The early beginnings of the Communist party in Iraq have been meticulously analyzed by Hanna Batatu. Husain al-Rahhal formed the first Marxist study circle in Iraq in 1924. Al-Rahhal, a student at the Baghdad School of Law, had been born into a family of officials and merchants. Other members of the circle included Muhammad Salim Fattah (a law student, son of an ex-official of the Ottoman government, and Al-Rahhal's brother-in-law), Mustafa Ali (a schoolteacher and the son of a carpenter), 'Awni Bakr Sidqi (a teacher-journalist and son of a petty official), and Mahmud Ahmad as-Sayyid (a novelist who was born into a family of *'ulama* and *sayyids*). The circle published an unusual paper called *As-Sahifah*, which focused on social problems, promoted rebellion against traditions, and challenged the very foundations of religion and the family. This circle and other groups formed the nucleus of the Communist party of Iraq. Of the seventeen leading communists in 1935, nine were of lower-middle-class origins, six of middle-class origin, one was a slave, and one was from a well-to-do landowning family. With regard to sect, eight were Sunni, five Christian, and four Shi'ite. According to Batatu, other relevant factors shared by those espousing Communist party membership included support from an extended family, location in the same city quarter of Bab ash-shaikh in old Baghdad, and a college education (which ten had had). Batatu concludes that "[all except two of the] leading communists shared neither the wretchedness and anguish of the mass of Iraqis nor the ease and abundance of the privileged few, but led the grayish life characteristic of the middle and lower middle class families to which they belonged."[47]

This overview of the development of communist parties, while not comprehensive, illustrates the nature of their early experiences. The nationalist and communist movements were very closely associated because of the congruity of political and social domination. At the same time, the movements forced one another to redefine their conceptions and to reorganize. This process is illustrated by the experience of the Moroccan National Union of Popular Forces. This party branched off from the Independence party and later renamed itself the Socialist Union of Popular Forces (Al-Ittihad al-ishtiraki lil-quwat al-sha'biyya). The growing gaps between classes led Al-Mahdi Ben Baraka to split from the Independence party. Al-Ittihad al-watani decided at its second congress in 1962 that the "socialism of modes of production" was the only force that allowed for "liberation from dependency and under-development," and that "there can be no natural unity under a feudal and reactionary system."[48] The convergence of nationalist and socialist forces is also illustrated by the evolution of the Palestinian resistance and the Lebanese National Movement during the civil war that began in Lebanon in 1975. However, the convergence has yet to achieve the aspirations of the deprived Arab masses. To discover the reasons for this failure, we must look at the following characteristics, which have been investigated by a number of analysts.

The Authoritarian Nature of the Arab Systems

Authoritarianism is not merely an attribute of the political system. Interpersonal and social relationships are also characterized by authoritarian tendencies. These tendencies can be traced back to the dominant patriarchal system and related practices. Absolutist religious conceptions of reality and the socioeconomic interdependency reflected in kinship ties and the patron–client system also contributed to the continuation of authoritarianism at the expense of institutional and professional relationships.

What concerns us here is the political manifestations of authoritarianism and the resulting crisis of civil society. Arab society is increasingly becoming a "government society" rather than a civil society. That is, Arab governments tyrannize over society and deny the Arab people their basic human rights. Arab citizens have been rendered powerless by their exclusion from the processes of conducting their own affairs and by deprivation of their right to active and free participation in political movements. The Arab left is excluded, marginalized, deprived, and oppressed. Without exception, the Arab left is routinely exposed to persecution, imprisonment, torture, and assassination in all Arab countries, regardless of the forms of rule.

Weak Social Base. The working class is intrinsically weak because of the underdeveloped nature of the economic systems (which I have described as semi-agricultural, semicapitalist, semifeudal, and semi-industrial). No full-fledged working class can emerge and be sustained in such systems. Workers have been divided into the industrial, agricultural, and service sectors. Consequently it has been very difficult to mobilize workers into unified unions and political parties.

Conflicts between and within Nationalist and Socialist Movements. The inherent conflicts between and within nationalist and socialist movements have had damaging effects on the ability of Arabs to confront serious historical challenges. All parties have failed to distinguish between the primary issues of class dependence and secondary contradictions of religion, regional nationalism, and the like. The fact that true liberation requires activists to address both national and class needs simultaneously has confused issues and priorities. The process of achieving national and class liberation must be the same, but preoccupation with secondary contradictions continues to distract activists from the primary goals. One might assume that by now no movement could claim to be nationalist and ignore the impoverishment of the majority of Arabs or dismiss class struggle, yet that continues to be the case. Similarly, no movement ought to claim to be socialist while ignoring the national oppression to which Arabs are exposed everywhere. A truly progressive movement would have to be nationalist, and vice versa. The national and social revolutions should become one.

Dominance of Traditional Loyalties. Nationalism and social class consciousness have been significantly undermined by persisting traditional loyalties. This fact has been dramatically demonstrated in Lebanon, the Sudan, Yemen, and Iraq. In Iraq, Batatu has shown how the progressive movement had to contend with the power of traditions "not only in the society at large but also within their own ranks." [49]

Military Coups as an Alternative to People's Revolution. As noted above, in less than a quarter of a century (1949–70), thirty-five coups d'état have taken place in Syria, Egypt, Iraq, the Sudan, Yemen, Algeria, Libya, Mauritania, and Somalia. The coups have led to the elimination of political parties, deprivation of basic human rights, and exercise of control over all communication networks (mass media, education, publication, and the distribution of information sources). The phrase "in the name of the revolution" has been applied in Arabic to struggles for independence, military coups d'état, wars of liberation, the replacement of one regime by another or even of one political leader with another, and even mere strikes and demonstrations. The problem is not merely one of misrepresentation. What is most misleading is the role that military coups have played as an alternative to comprehensive popular revolutions.

Crisis of Leadership. Leftist movements have been led by the intelligentsia, who have shown a greater inclination to engage in political and cultural debates than to mobilize workers and peasants or prepare them for leadership positions. Many of the intelligentsia are motivated to serve as custodians of the working classes based on ideological and theoretical conclusions rather than on direct experience of the reality workers know. This lack of knowledge means that the leadership of progressive parties has failed to redefine and reinterpret acquired concepts in light of Arab reality and the actual experiences of the working classes. They have also failed to translate their thoughts into concrete projects. Their very political language reveals a growing distance between themselves and the masses. Socialist parties have failed to maintain their independence, to take the initiative in the Arab context, and to rely on their own internal resources. Batatu has pointed out that many of these parties represented "little more than an expression . . . of the Soviet state, a power which has long ago lost its revolutionary ethos."[50]

These are some of the factors that explain the crisis of the Arab left. Conditions that call for revolutionary change continue to prevail in Arab political life. The dominant social orders have lost their legitimacy, and they increasingly rely on means of oppression and enticement to maintain regimes in power. Yet the search for a better social order continues, undeterred by previous failures.

Conclusion: The Crisis of Civil Society

Arabs need to transcend prevailing conditions to achieve the *nahda* for which they have struggled so long and so desperately. The main obstacle to achieving the *nahda* is the condition of alienation that renders Arabs powerless, excluded from the political process, and marginalized. The tyranny of the state and the ruler over civil society is a central cause of the condition of alienation felt by so many Arabs. Civil society requires people who are actively involved in conducting their own affairs and those of society at large.

Ultimately, the *nahda* can be achieved by overcoming political alienation and freeing civil society from the grip of the state. Arabs have to reassert themselves to achieve the goals they have set for themselves over a century and a half: national unity, state-building, establishment of democratic institutions, elimination of socioeconomic disparities, the ending of dependency, achievement of comprehensive development, and the regaining of control over their destiny.

PART THREE

The Dynamics of Arab Culture

9　National Character and Value Orientations

Learning about Arab culture is a dual process of unlearning the static, oversimplified views that have guided Western thought, then relearning by following a dynamic, analytical approach to a highly complex and contradictory reality. While both Western and Arab scholarship may express similar criticisms of Arab culture and Arab national character, their points of departure represent totally different perspectives. Unlike mainstream Western scholarship, Arab critical approaches are deeply embedded in a sense of Arab belonging and a commitment to the transcendence of the prevailing order. By identifying with forces of change, the Arab critical perspective insists on recognizing the existing contradictions. Such a critical analysis of Arab cultural identity begins by discarding notions of mere similarity or variation, and explores instead the realm of oppositional relationships; it is these oppositions that constitute the ongoing struggle to achieve the *nahda* (the awakening and remaking of Arab society). There would not have been any need to reassert this fact, were it not for the misrepresentation of Arab culture in a Western Orientalist scholarship that emphasizes the constancy of Arab culture and the "oneness" of what is referred to as "the Arab mind."

Societies have their own particular and unique cultures (see Chapter 3). By culture, we mean the whole way of life of a society, consisting of three basic constituent elements: values, self-expression, and knowledge. These three form the subjects of the penultimate three chapters in this study. Values—the symbols, ethics, norms, traditions, concepts, beliefs, customs, means, and skills of people in their interactions with their total environment—are discussed in this chapter. Artistic self-expression, including literature, music, drawing, and

A paper based on the material in this chapter appeared in Hisham Sharabi, ed., *Theory, Politics and the Arab World* (London: Routledge & Kegan Paul, 1990).

the arts in general, provides the focus of Chapter 10. Knowledge and thought, or science and philosophy, are discussed in Chapter 11. These interrelated elements constitute the general culture of a people. Regardless of the stage of development, at any point in time, each society has its own culture—diverse and even contradictory, perpetuated by learned behavior, and constantly changing. At the center of culture is language, which is thought to distinguish human beings from other creatures.

Beyond these generalities, culture is interpreted and classified in many different ways depending on the dimensions and levels of concern of researchers. From a nationalist perspective, culture may consist of universal, seminationalist, or more exclusively nationalist elements. Based on class differences, culture may be characterized as high, mass, bourgeois, elitist, peasant, working-class, official, popular, and so on. With respect to field of study, scholars refer to scientific, literary, political, materialist, and spiritual cultures. Within society, one may speak of bedouin, rural, or urban cultures, of traditional or modern cultures, and of authentic or borrowed cultures. Comparative studies of regions and civilizations may deal in terms of contrasting Western and Oriental cultures. These are only a few examples of a limitless number of potential ways of classifying and characterizing culture.

From the perspective of this study, I would argue that culture should be viewed as an intervening variable between the general order and social structures on the one hand and actual human behavior in everyday life on the other. That is, culture is seen here as emerging out of a certain social reality. It is intended to regulate human relationships and actions, particularly with respect to maintaining or changing the prevailing order of things. In assessing the role of culture in defining Arab identity (Chapter 3), it was noted that culture is a distinctive way of life of a society but is rarely characterized by complete uniformity.

Like other societies, the Arabs have their own dominant culture (that is, what is most common and diffused among Arabs), its subcultures (those peculiar to some communities and classes), and its countercultures (those of alienated and radicalized segments of society). As a result of such diversity among constituent cultures, and as a product of new inventions and resources, culture changes constantly. Thus, one of the most significant characteristic features of contemporary Arab culture is its transitional nature.

The Question of National Character

Notwithstanding reservations about the validity of the concept of national personality (or other concepts one encounters in social psychology, such as basic personality, national mind, national character, modal personality, and the like), some Western and Arab scholars have engaged in such abstractions in an attempt to discern common Arab value orientations and attitudes. Writers such as Raphael Patai follow a static approach emanating from antagonistic attitudes toward the Arabs in the context of power relations and Western domination,[1] or what Fanon and Memmi called colonizer-colonized relations. Others with a Westernized viewpoint, such as Sonia Hamady, engage in oversimplifications taken out of context.[2] Among Arab writings in this area, there are those that tend to be rather defensive, such as Fuad Moughrabi's critical survey of the literature on the Arab "basic personality."[3] Other Arab writings, such as El-Sayyid Yassin's book on Arab personality, have an Arab nationalistic framework and follow a dialectical approach.[4]

Patai has legitimized his stereotyping by calling it an abstraction reached by processes of generalization about Arab mentality, the Arab mind, or the mental characteristics of Arabs as a population and human group. By national character, he means "the sum total of the motives, traits, beliefs, and values shared by the plurality in a national population."[5] Thus he assumes that Arabs are fairly homogeneous and that the Middle East, although inhabited by a mosaic of peoples "speaking many different tongues and exhibiting many different physical features," is nevertheless "the domain of one basically identical culture." Based on a conception of Arab culture as characterized by "coherence, balance and inner consistency,"[6] Patai abandons any restraints that might qualify his statements about Arabs and Islam. His approach, and its attendant distortions, are revealed in these samples of oversimplified generalizations: "To the Arab mind, eloquence is related to exaggeration" (p. 49); "Several Western scholars have been struck by the pronounced Arab tendency to take a polarized view of man and the world, to see everywhere stark contrasts rather than gradations . . . to perceive extremes." (p. 156); "For the tradition-bound Arab mind, there is even something sinful in engaging in long-range planning, because it seems to imply that one does not put one's trust in divine providence" (p. 150); "In general the Arab mind, dominated by Islam, has been bent more on preserving rather than innovating, or maintaining than improving, or continuing than initiating" (p. 154); "The Arabs were always a poetic nation" (p. 211); "Eloquence is to the Arab an achievement akin to the attainment of masculinity" (p. 49). How does Patai reach these definitive conclusions? To do so, he must overlook plurality of culture, cultural variations, and cultural struggle. He dismisses the effects of social diversity and social class differences (though he discusses these matters in different contexts). Moreover, he perceives Islam as an external force shaping society rather than being shaped by it. So a statement attributed by the Mamluk historian Al-Maqrizi (1364–1442) to Ka'b al-Ahbar, one of the companions of the Prophet Muhammad, may be applied to contemporary Muslims. One wonders, as well, about Patai's familiarity with Arab sources: whenever he refers to an Arab source, it turns out to be taken from a Western source. For instance, he quotes Bernard Lewis, who quoted Abdel Aziz al-Duri, who quoted Al-Tha'alibi (d. 1038) to prove that "throughout the vast Arabic language area, people hold with relative uniformity that Arabic is superior to other languages" (p. 44). Patai also quotes Taha Hussein as summarized by von Grunebaum in reference to the unchangeable character of Egypt and its lack of fear of Westernization. Similarly, Patai quoted my novel *'Awdat al-ta'ir ila al-bahr* as analyzed by Trevor Le Gassick in an article published in the *Middle East Journal* to demonstrate Arab ambivalence (see pp. 199, 203, and 350–51). Several of his oversimplified generalizations are based on selected proverbs, which he contends "yield a fascinating folk view of the Arab character" (p. 22). He fails to realize that proverbs convey only specific meanings in specific situations under certain circumstances. He does not seem to realize that there are conflicting proverbs as well as conflicting implications. Based on the frequently quoted proverb "I and my brothers against my cousin; I and my cousins against the stranger," for instance, Patai theorizes about Arab "in-group loyalty and out-group enmity."[7] He jokes about the absence of a female counterpart proverb that would say "I and my sister against my female cousin; I against my sister," (p. 36) and views the "Arab nation as an Arab family" (p. 42). What Patai fails to realize is that Arabs quite often repeat this particular proverb in criticizing tribalism. He also fails to realize that Arabs frequently employ proverbs to the opposite effect, such as "Al-jar qabl ad-dar" ("The neighbor before the homefolk") and "Jarak al-qareeb wala akhouk al-ba'id" ("Your close neighbor and not your distant brother"). Furthermore, these alternative proverbs are considered by Arabs to be more normatively positive than is the first one Patai cites.

Several stereotypes and counterstereotypes in Arab culture have been taken by Patai at face value and treated as accurate descriptions instead of signs of tensions and conflicts. He tells us that astute Arab observers remarked on the differences in national character between one Arab country and another many centuries before the concept of national character was formulated in the West. After quoting Al-Maqrizi to this effect, Patai concludes that "educated Arabs in the fourteenth and fifteenth century were well aware, not only of the existence of an Arab national character, but also of character differences between the Arab peoples inhabiting various countries" (p. 23). If such character differences between Arab countries are so great, what becomes of Patai's notion of the Arab mind?

The same sort of enmity underlying Arab stereotyping is reflected in Morroe Berger's book *The Arab World Today*, written at much the same time. Not one positive value is mentioned. Berger does not grapple with the implication that human society can function and survive without any positive

values. For him, there is no need for explanation beyond merely naming what
he believes to be the sources responsible for formation of the Arab personality,
including "the nomadic bedouin values that permeated Arab society and Islam,
the claims of the religious system itself, the long history of subordination,
crushing poverty, and patterns of child rearing which stem in part from these
sources and reinforce them in generation after generation."[8]

Fanon tells us that colonial domination requires that the colonized be
painted "as a sort of quintessence of evil. Native society is not simply described
as a society lacking in values. . . . The native is declared insensible to ethics;
he represents not only the absence of values, but also the negation of values."[9]
Albert Memmi further explains that such an image of the colonized is required
because these "images become excuses without which the presence and conduct of a colonizer . . . would seem shocking."[10] Berger's generalizations
should not, then, surprise us. "The Arabs display the double effect of wounded
pride—self-exaltation and self-condemnation," he says (p. 136); "The whole
tenor of Arab society is to encourage self-esteem and egotistical claims" (p.
143); "Though secretive about facts, the Arab is quick to express his feelings.
He knows few bounds in revealing his emotional state" (p. 152); "Fatalism is
a way of defeating the fear of the unknown. . . . Political quietism has been
another facet of behavior through which Arab society has expressed its tenacious refusal to confront the unknown, to challenge fate for the predetermined
order of things. Nowadays we call this tendency authoritarianism. . . . There
is a high degree of authoritarianism in the personal make-up of Arabs" (p. 157);
and "One aspect of the cultural outlook . . . is the Arab's infatuation with ideal
forms; he clings to them emotionally even while he knows they are contra-
dicted by reality" (p. 160).

On what basis could writers like Patai or Berger reach such conclusions?
One would think that sociologists and anthropologists would want to base
their views on field research and empirical data. Instead, they rely on carefully
selected sayings, anecdotes, proverbs, quotations, readings, and Orientalist
scholarship. Janet Abu-Lughod has remarked of the methodology of Western
historiography with respect to what has been called "the Islamic city" that in
some ways this historiography "takes the same form as the tradition of the
Prophet. The authenticity of any proposition is judged by the isnad or 'chain'
by which it descended from the past. Certain claims are deemed more trust-
worthy than others. . . . The idea of the Islamic city was constructed by a series
of Western authorities who drew upon a small and eccentric sample of premodern Arab cities, . . . but more than that, drew upon one another in an isnad
of authority."[11] Accordingly, Raphael Patai draws on Morroe Berger or
Bernard Lewis or Sir Hamilton Gibb or von Grunebaum, who may have
quoted Hassan al-Basri (d. 728) or Ibn Taimiyya (d. 1328) or Al-Maqrizi to

make a strong generalization about contemporary Arab value systems. This sort of *isnad* may at least partly account for what Edward Said has described as "the internal consistency of Orientalism and its ideas about the Orient . . . despite or beyond any correspondence, or lack thereof, with a 'real Orient.' "[12] Orientalism has served as a system of citing works and authors out of social and historical context, hence the dominant view of Arab society as being unchanging and uniquely uniform, or uniformly unique.

In order to confirm the texts, in a few instances reference is made to some field or empirical studies such as those conducted by E. Terry Prothro, Levon Melikian, and Hamed Ammar. In an attempt to discover whether "residence in an authoritarian culture" leads to greater acceptance of some items of the California Public Opinion Scale, Prothro and Melikian administered a 33-item questionnaire to 130 Arab freshman students at the American University of Beirut. The results tended to confirm claims for the validity of the F scale but did not show a positive correlation between authoritarianism and politico-economic conservatism. This questionnaire was administered (we are not told how the sample was chosen) in the early 1950s. The students were mostly Lebanese (77 out of 130) and Christian (70 out of 130). The authors based their study "upon the assumption that the culture of 'Greater Syria' . . . is authoritarian, and that authoritarianism is in general somewhat stronger in the Moslem than in the Christian communities." This authoritarianism, they point out, "begins in Syrian family life where the father is the absolute head of the household, and both wife and children obey him." Upon comparison of Near Eastern and U.S. students, it turned out that the mean score of AUB students on the 33-item abbreviated F scale was 5.03 in comparison to 3.56 for a sample of California and Oregon students and 4.1 for Oklahoma students. These results were deemed significant by the authors in spite of the fact that the F scale items are culturally loaded and that they made no attempt to control for variables such as social class, social background (for example, rural-urban background) and prevailing conditions at the time of conducting the research. The researchers admit that the F scale was constructed in such a way that in "some instances the 'everyday phrases' of American life are unfamiliar to Arabs." Furthermore, more detailed comparison between Christian and Muslim students showed some inconsistencies in regard to scores on certain specific items. The mean score of Muslims on items connected with "insult to honor," punishment of "sex crimes," and attitudes toward homosexuals was much higher than the mean score of Christians. On the other hand the "Muslims were as liberal as or even more liberal than Christians" on those items connected with the responsibility of society to guarantee everyone with adequate social services, increasing taxes on large companies, and solving social problems.[13]

In a similar paper, Levon Melikian examines the correlations of authoritarianism with exposure to modernization in what he describes as "the relatively authoritarian culture of the Arab Middle East and . . . the relatively non-authoritarian culture of the United States." He does so even though he admits that "no measure of cultural authoritarianism is available," based on the wrong assumption that "there is enough anthropological evidence to substantiate the claim made about the two [Arab Middle Eastern and U.S.] cultures." [14] Exactly in the same fashion, anthropologists themselves (particularly Raphael Patai) have tended to base their generalizations about the authoritarian character of Arab culture on the assumption that there is enough social and psychological evidence to substantiate this claim.

Another source of speculation about problems of Arab national personality and culture is Hamed Ammar's book *Growing Up in an Egyptian Village*. Some of Ammar's observations are overgeneralized to the Arab world or the Middle East as a whole, even though he himself clearly warns us that he cannot claim that the village of Silwa in which he conducted his field research is typical of rural Egypt, saying unequivocally, "it is extremely difficult to show the extent to which Silwa is a typical Egyptian village." [15]

A later book by Ammar develops the concept of the Egyptian "Fahlawi personality," which has also proved useful to several other scholars in their attempts to portray Arab national character and culture. For Ammar himself, the attributes of the Fahlawi model character are rooted in the prevailing socioeconomic conditions in Egypt and the organization of Egyptian society. These basically negative attributes of "the present social mode of Egyptian personality," or typical responses that occur in certain specific situations, include: (1) quick adaptability to various new situations, reflecting both genuine flexibility and insincere agreement to avoid punishment; (2) quick wit (*nukta*), giving vent to anger and resentment in confronting misfortune; (3) self-assertion, or a tendency to exaggerate in demonstrating one's superior power out of lack of confidence; (4) a romantic view of equality, as a result of the prevailing inequality and discrimination (hence the tendency to reject authority and leadership, as well as to decline responsibility in embarrassing situations); (5) the psychological security derived from a preference for individual as opposed to group activities; and (6) a desire to reach one's goals by the shortest and quickest route. In presenting these attributes of the Fahlawi personality, Ammar insists on examining them in their social context and argues that they alter with changing conditions. He also explains that he has focused on "the weak points rather than the strong ones" in the Egyptian character out of a strong belief in self-criticism as "an indispensable necessity and a basic step in the building of the society." [16]

It is within this process of self-criticism—but much more highly intensified by the defeat of 1967—that Sadiq al-'Azm has restated the attributes of the Fahlawi personality. This mode of behavior, Al-'Azm points out, was an integral part of the structure of traditional Arab society and inseparable from the characteristics of the social personality into which Arabs have been socialized to a lesser or greater degree under specific circumstances and situations. In confronting and responding to the June war of 1967, Arabs exhibited many of the above inclinations, including the use of short-cuts to achieve their goals, impression-making, covering up failures out of fear of disgrace, disclaiming responsibilities, and blaming external forces for the disaster. [17]

Another critical Arab view in this regard is expressed by the Tunisian historian Hichem Djait, who bases his analysis of Tunisian national character on the Kardnerian concept of basic personality. By the middle of the twentieth century, Djait observes, the Tunisian personality was characterized by stress on manliness (and hence identification with the father, veneration of authority and power, contempt for the weak, and both fear of and contempt for women), aggressiveness, fatalism, magic-making (*sihr*), and weakness of the superego. Socioeconomic and political changes in the 1960s, such as reforms in the field of personal status and the movement in the direction of Western liberal rationalism, altered this basic character to some degree, but Djait argues that the Tunisian personality remained essentially the same. Noting that the complexity and diversity of Arab society are obstacles to investigation of the broader "Arab personality" and to generalizing from Tunisia to the Arab world as a whole, he nevertheless concludes that "it is possible to speak of a Maghribi basic personality and a Mashriqi basic personality that are distinct in only detail but similar in essence," notwithstanding differences such as those between bedouin and urban Arabs, and between Egyptian narcissism and Iraqi aggressiveness. [18]

Fuad Moughrabi has argued against the validity of psychological studies dealing with such constructs as the "Arab basic personality" or the "Arab mind." Methodologically, the problem is one of representation or generalization based on anecdotal reports and research studies of either village populations or highly educated subjects. He points out that such generalizations tend to ignore the richness and diversity of Arab society. This criticism is very accurate. These studies do fail to take account of the diversity and transitional nature of Arab society. Moughrabi is also correct in commenting on the psychological reductionism and the ahistorical nature of the majority of such studies. Where Moughrabi fails miserably is in his lack of differentiation and distinction between Western and Arab scholarship in this area. Though he recognizes that Arab intellectuals are "irritated by the weaknesses that plague their respective societies," he nevertheless dismisses the process of self-criticism by Arab social scientists by suggesting that they see themselves from a

Western perspective and "mistakenly accept this pattern of analysis and the model of development."[19] The inadequacy of the social-psychological literature on the Arab basic personality should not preclude Arab reflection on the dominant systems of thought and value orientations.

El-Sayyid Yassin, rather than Moughrabi, has offered the most effective and comprehensive critique of Western social psychological studies of the Arab national character. He sees the above characterization of Arabs by Orientalist and antagonistic Israeli scholarship as a distortion of the Arab image in what amounts to psychological warfare. His task is thus twofold: to trace the roots of "the historical antagonism to Arabs in Western thought" and to explore the true nature of the "Arab national personality." In addressing himself to the first part of his task, Yassin concludes that Western thought on Arab national characteristics has focused on the negative aspects and neglected the positive ones. To demonstrate this, he examines Orientalist literature, the mass media, and Israeli research studies. In his attempt to explore the true nature of "Arab national personality," Yassin notes that it is normal for nations to raise questions about their identities during decisive historical moments. In the case of Arabs, that is exactly what happened after the 1967 defeat and the war of October 1973. Many questions were raised then, and continue to be raised, about the Arab ability to confront historical challenges. Yassin defines the concept of national personality as the distinctive and relatively enduring psychological, social, and civilizational characteristic features of a nation. He dismisses both the concept of basic personality associated with Abram Kardner and that of model personality used by Ralph Linton, preferring Erich Fromm's scientific socialist framework, which conceives of personality dialectically and in constant interaction with the economic and social situations of a specific society and historical context.[20]

Yassin concludes that one may talk of "an Arab personality" to the extent that the dominant mode of production in the Arab world is consistent across Arab territory. Nevertheless, he also recognizes that there are a multiplicity of social formations in the Arab world. The validity of describing the characteristic features of an Arab personality should not lead us to overlook the fact "that the social history of every Arab country is likely to result in distinctive national features that do not exist in other Arab societies." Admitting this obliges Yassin to reconcile what he calls the primary and secondary characteristic features of the Arab society. "The true challenge confronting the Arab nation," he concludes, "is how to establish lively and creative harmony between the primary and secondary patterns—that is, between the various subpersonalities and the Arab personality."[21]

Convincing though Yassin's presentation may be, questions still remain: How valid is the concept of national personality itself? Is it possible for highly complex modern societies, composed of a dominant culture, subcultures, and countercultures, to have one national personality? The problem relates not just to the social diversity that we know exists but to the dual impact of internal and external contradictions. I remain doubtful about the validity of the concept of national personality.

Arab Value Orientations

In my view, a more valid approach to the study of distinctive Arab culture is to examine Arab value orientations in their social and historical contexts. In fact, the very distinctiveness of national character is often assessed in terms of the prevailing value orientations. But what makes studies of national character problematic is their tendency to oversimplify, ignoring diversity and complexity; to invoke abstractions at the expense of concreteness; and to rely on textual sources of knowledge at the expense of in-depth study of everyday behavior. It may be hoped that in undertaking to study value orientations in their social and historical contexts, we are more likely to avoid such theoretical and methodological problems.

Values are defined here as beliefs about desired or preferred objects, goals, and forms of human behavior. Specifically, *instrumental values* consist of certain forms of behavior considered preferable to others (as courage, for instance, is preferable to timidity); *terminal values* define ideal goals (such as happiness, national unity, and social justice). Both sets of values are intended to guide, to regulate social relations, and to define the meaning of human existence. In many instances, values tend either to justify human actions and facilitate adjustment to a given reality or to expose problems and instigate changes to rectify them.

Values, then, are relative (multifarious in their sources and functions), conflicting, in a state of constant becoming. They emerge out of a specific reality and gain ascendancy to the extent that religious interpretations present them as imposed externally through a process of *tanzil* (descent). Value orientations in Arab society differ according to social class, patterns of living, social affiliations, isolation or exposure to the outside world, their sources and functions, and the prevailing order. Struggle and contradictions exist within the dominant culture, subcultures, and countercultures. Comprehensive examination reveals conflicting value orientations in contemporary Arab culture: fatalism versus free will, shame versus guilt, creativity versus conformity, past versus future orientations, culture of the mind versus culture of the heart, form versus content, collectivity versus individuality, open- versus closed-mindedness, obedience versus rebellion, charity versus justice, and vertical versus horizontal values.

Fatalism versus Free Will. Western scholarship has reached an almost unanimous conclusion that the Arab world, in contrast to the West, views the universe (including human life) as having a predestined course. Morroe Berger draws on Ammar, the Finnish anthropologist Hilma Granqvist, and H. A. R. Gibb to support the argument that Arabs accept their fate or lot in life. Ammar observed, he says, that "the villager's apparent happiness comes from his sense of resignation regarding things as they are. This contentment (perhaps a more appropriate word than happiness) derives from his acquiescence in what has been ordained by God and cemented by tradition." Granqvist, writing in 1947, said that many expressions current among Palestinians indicate that heredity determines human character "in such a way as to make it useless to try to change it." Surprisingly in a period of high turmoil, Berger wrote: "Political quietism has been another fact of behavior through which Arab society has expressed its tenacious refusal to confront the unknown, to challenge fate or the predetermined order of things." Berger also cites Gibb's belief that "Islam looked upon knowledge as a mechanical process of gathering in the known, the given and eternal, rather than a creative reaching out for the unknown."[22]

G. E. von Grunebaum seeks elements of fatalism in Islam's claim to the totality of the believer's life and thought, and in its comprehensiveness, for "there is nothing too slight, too personal, too intimate not to stand in need of being arranged by the divine will. This approach, while completely ritualizing life, imparts meaning to the most insignificant act and hallows it as a necessary affirmation of the eternal order. . . . Such a system is bound to prize stability. God is above change and so is His order, revealed once and for all by His Messenger." At one point, von Grunebaum starts to question the fondness of the West for viewing "the Oriental as a fatalist . . . who resigns himself in all vicissitudes to the whims of destiny," but then he adds that Islam in its answer to the problem of free will "inclines to a deterministic solution; it is equally true that it cherishes the concept of predestination. . . . All this is to say that the Muslim deeply feels man's insignificance, the uncertainty of his fate, and the omnipotence of the uncontrollable power above him. Therefore, perhaps, he is more readily prepared than the Westerner to accept the accomplished fact."[23]

No other scholar has surpassed Raphael Patai in making sweeping generalizations about Arab fatalism, seeking evidence in Islamic concepts, proverbs, and supporting quotations from other works. Allah, he says, "not only guides the world at large, but also predestines the fate of each and every man individually." To demonstrate this view he quotes a number of verses from the Qur'an, such as "Lo! We have created everything by measure" (54:49), " . . . createth, then measureth, then guideth" (87:2–3), and "Allah verily sendeth who He will astray, and guideth whom He will" (35:8). Such a deterministic view, Patai argues "had become an ancient Judeo-Christian heritage by the time Muhammad lived. However, in the course of their development, both Judaism and Christianity in the West have considerably modified their original determinism, allowing human will to play a more and more decisive role. Not so Islam, where absolute will is still considered as one of God's attributes operating in the manner of an inexorable law."[24]

Patai also finds evidence of fatalism in the occasional invocation of God's name in Arab culture, as in the exclamations "Bismi Allah" ("In the name of God"), "In sha'a Allah" ("If God wills"), and "Allah kareem" ("God is generous"). He also cites concepts like *kismet wa nasib* (one's lot and luck), *bakht* (lot), and *maktub* (predestined) as reflecting belief in predestination. Finally, as previously noted, Patai quotes others to this effect, such as Edward W. Lane, Sonia Hamady, and Al-Maqrizi.

Patai also describes other character traits closely related to fatalism, such as improvidence. "For the tradition-bound Arab mind," he concludes, "there is even something sinful in engaging in long-range planning, because it seems to imply that one does not place one's trust in divine providence. . . . The improvidence of the fellah has been for centuries a contributing factor to their impoverishment."[25] To counter these oversimplifications, I wish to make several arguments. First, quite opposite orientations are easily detected in Arab culture. One can just as easily demonstrate that Arabs emphasize free will by referring to other verses in the Qur'an and other religious traditions, and by utilizing other secondary sources, as well as indigenous proverbs, anecdotes, expressions, and the like. Some of the most popular slogans of the Algerian revolution were from the Qur'an: "God does not change what is in a people unless they change themselves" (13:11); "Thus does God make clear His signs to you in order that you may understand" (2:242); "And know that God is strict in punishment" (2:196), implying individual responsibility for one's acts; and "Let there be no compulsion in religion" (2:256). Equally important is the fact that there are different interpretations of Islam. "Destiny and fate are strife and work" ("Inna al-qada' wal-qadar huma as-sa'i wal-'amal"), Abd al-Rahman al-Kawakibi observed.[26] Not unlike other religions, and in spite of its specificity, Islam has lent itself to different interpretations according to the needs and situation of believers.

In the realm of proverbs and common sayings, diverse views and interpretations are even easier to find. An Arab possesses a repertoire of proverbs asserting human free will and responsibility. By way of illustration, consider: "Whoever toils will achieve"; "Livelihood is management"; "The one who does not sow does not harvest"; "Hope without effort is a tree without fruit"; "Only he who goes to the market will buy and sell"; "Don't blame [anyone] except yourself"; "Think things out first and then rely on God."

These are but a few of many popular sayings. Others treat those with fatalistic attitudes sarcastically: "Sit on a beehive and call it fate." Arab poetry is also an extraordinarily rich source of expressions of both fatalism and free will. Two of the most popular lines of Arab poetry referring to the power of fate are:

> —We walked our predestined course
> And whoever's course is written
> Will have to walk it.

> —Not every human wish is fulfilled
> The wind may blow contrary to sailors' desire.

Equally popular lines of poetry express free human will:

> —The greater the strife, the greater the achievement,
> And whoever aspires to high aims
> Will have to toil day and night
> And whoever demands glory without effort
> Wasted will be his life in asking for the impossible.

> —If the people ever want life
> Fate will inevitably have to respond;
> Inevitably, night will have to clear
> And the chain will have to break.

Moreover, explicit expressions of fatalism do not always imply submission, resignation, or refusal to take personal responsibility. For both early and present-day revolutionary Muslims, fate is understood to mean having to struggle to change reality. Many Arabs at the present time consider it their fate to fight until they achieve liberation and build a new order. Upon hearing of the assassination of his comrade Ghassan Kanafani, a renowned Palestinian writer, George Habash is reported to have said, "That is our fate." In other words, by engaging in struggle to liberate the country, one knows beforehand that the risks include death.

In this respect, statements indicating fatalism need to be interpreted in their social context or in reference to the particular occasions on which they are repeated. In his novel *Zuqaq al-Midaqq* (Midaq Alley), Naguib Mahfouz tells us that when confronted by her fiancé, who finds her with a British soldier in a tavern, Hamida is able to escape certain death by saying that although she wished to be faithful to him, God must have chosen a different destiny for her. Given the context, we must understand this statement simply as an effort to avoid death; we should not interpret it at face value to mean she refuses to accept personal responsibility for her actions. In another novel by the same author, a young woman character defies a powerful man who threatens to destroy her unless she surrenders to him. Although she badly needs his support,

she counters by saying, "My future is not in your hand; it is in God's hands."
Here, by contrast, fatalism means self-assertion.

Thus proverbs or expressions indicating fatalism serve as mechanisms of adjustment to specific situations and should not be interpreted in absolute terms or at face value. They may have the opposite meaning. In order to grasp their real rather than their ostensible meaning, we must explain them in terms of the actual functions they serve in particular circumstances. They need to be examined as psychological mechanisms for dealing with human reality.

Shame versus Guilt. Western scholarship has often claimed that one of the distinguishing differences between Arab and Western value orientations is the greater emphasis in Arab culture on shame and in Western culture on guilt. The emphasis is so pronounced that Arab society has been referred to as a "shame society."[27] Patai says that "what pressures the Arab to behave in an honorable manner is not guilt but shame, or, more precisely, the psychological drive to escape or prevent negative judgment by others."[28] "What will people say?" is one of the main reasons Arabs fear nonconformity according to Sonia Hamady. Support for this thesis has also been sought in the child-rearing techniques of shaming in the areas of sexual conduct: the honor-shame syndrome generates acute feelings of shame about all aspects of sexuality. Another area where this syndrome is said to play an important role is in conflict resolution and mediation, the goal of which is to encourage opposing parties to cease their fighting without dishonor and shame. Harold W. Glidden (an ex-employee of the Bureau of Intelligence of the U.S. Department of State) has tried to explain what he calls "the hostility of the Arab collectivity toward Israel" by pointing out that this Arab attitude "is governed by two key emotions inherent in the Arab culture. Their defeat by Israel brought them shame, which can only be eliminated by revenge." To further simplify the issue for experts in the State Department and his American readers, Glidden engages in the following generalizations:

> Conformity brings honor and social prestige. . . . Failure to conform,
> however, brings shame. Shame is intensely feared among Arabs, and
> this fear is so pervasive that Arab society has been labeled a
> shame-oriented one. This contrasts sharply with Judaism and with
> Western Christian societies, which are guilt-oriented. . . . Shame is
> eliminated by revenge. It is difficult to describe the depth of the
> Arabs' emotional need for revenge, but suffice it to say that Islam
> itself found it necessary to sanction revenge. . . . Therefore all
> members of the Arab collectivity are bound to support the cause of
> their kinsmen, the Palestine Arabs. . . . This is the vengeance that the
> Arabs feel must be taken not only to restore to the Palestine Arabs
> what was wrongfully taken from them, but to eliminate the shame

that had been visited on them and the other Arabs by their defeats by Israel.

Many Westerners and Israelis think that since Israel has more than once demonstrated that it is objectively stronger than the Arabs, the only rational thing for the Arabs to do is to make peace. But for the Arabs the situation is not governed by this kind of logic, for objectivity is not a value in the Arab system. For the Arabs, defeat does not generate a desire for peace; instead, it produces an emotional need for revenge.[29]

Worse than the insults to Arabs embedded in this comment is the fact that the policy of the U.S. State Department is based on such distorted analysis. Glidden seems to have totally forgotten President Franklin D. Roosevelt's characterization of the surprise attack at Pearl Harbor—which was not entirely dissimilar to the Israeli surprise attack on Egypt, Jordan, and Syria in June 1967—as "a date which will live in infamy," leading directly to a declaration of war against Japan. He also seems to have forgotten that the concept of other-directedness, which he considers to be "characteristic of both the Arab tradition and of the outlook of Islam" (p. 98), was first coined by David Riesman in *The Lonely Crowd* to describe the most dominant cultural trend in American society (in contrast to the tradition-oriented and the inner-oriented trends).

Perhaps we should not award so much importance to such self-explanatory oversimplifications and distortions, given that they have been used to justify a foreign policy undoubtedly shaped by other concerns. Nevertheless, they seem to resonate with a need in the United States and Israel to believe them. Besides being repeated so often in scholarly works, they have forcefully invaded the media and popular literature. Erica Jong's uninhibited novel *Fear of Flying* joins the band:

> Arabs, I thought, goddamned Arabs. What a disproportionate
> sense of guilt I had over all my petty sexual transgressions! Yet there
> were people in the world, plenty of them, who did what they felt
> like and never had a moment's guilt over it—as long as they didn't
> get caught. Why had I been cursed with such a hypertrophied
> superego? Was it just being Jewish? . . . Is it any wonder that
> everyone hates the Jews for giving the world guilt?"[30]

An examination of the assumption that the societies of the United States and Israel are dominated by feelings of guilt shows it to be an exaggeration at best. While one may detect guilt-feelings over sexual transgressions, it seems that gradually Americans and Israelis have increasingly overcome this problem. In the political and economic arenas, it is very doubtful they felt much guilt to begin with. How much guilt do Israelis feel over causing the uprootedness, dispersal, and suffering of the Palestinians? Amos Elon has told us that the Israelis cannot totally close their eyes to "the bruises of continuous war, and the scars of another people's agony"; he describes "an undercurrent of guilt feelings toward the Palestinian Arabs, caught as they are under the wheels of history. Indeed, a certain sense of guilt toward individual Arabs runs like a red thread through a great number of novels, plays and poems."[31] On the other hand, a letter to the editor of *Ha'aretz* (December 1, 1983) from Dr. Shlomo Ariel reported that his interviews with several groups of young people randomly representative of Israel's Jewish population indicated a high incidence of racist attitudes toward Arabs. In every discussion group he held, "there were several boys who argued that the Arabs of Israel should be physically eliminated including the old women and children. When I drew comparisons with Sabra and Shatila and the Nazi extermination campaign, they voiced their approval and declared in all honesty that they were willing to do the extermination with their own hands, without guilt feelings or hang-ups."[32]

Objective analysis suggests that Arabs exhibit both shame and guilt-oriented behavior. Arabs do not necessarily experience guilt feelings about the same issues that prompt guilt in Westerners (for instance, in sexual conduct). They experience great guilt where they violate internalized values and expectations—such as disappointing their parents (especially their mothers). They also feel guilty if they have neglected their friends, or harmed innocent people, or promoted themselves at the expense of others and their country. Many Arabs living abroad (for example, in the United States) experience extreme feelings of guilt about forsaking their countries, particularly in times of distress.

Conformity and Creativity. Von Grunebaum argues that originality is not as highly prized in the Muslim world as in the West. "The Arab's unimaginative mind," he says, "and his sober realism, his powers of accurate observation, his exactitude . . . are all accommodated by the pattern of Islamic civilization. The formalism of the religious approach is repeated in literature, even in science. Throughout the great age of Arabic literature the critics placed verbal perfection above poetical originality. . . . Inherited forms were faithfully preserved."[33] Similarly, Morroe Berger observes that conventional speech, by "providing ready-made phrases, . . . obviates the need for thought and originality, and encourages the treatment of every situation in a traditional, familiar manner."[34]

Muslim fundamentalists themselves have argued that creativity (*ibda'*, *khalq*) is a characteristic of God rather than of human beings, who are considered unable to make something out of nothing. So every innovative idea (*bid'a*) is a kind of misguidance (*dalal*) that deserves severe punishment. Such views reflect what I have called "alienation in religion."

In Chapter 10, which deals with creative life, we shall see, however, that there has in reality been constant struggle in Arab culture between creativity and conformity, modernity and tradition—what Taha Hussein has called the battle of the old and the new. These two opposed currents manifest themselves in much of Arab life, from the religious to the political, from the ideological to the literary aspects of Arab culture. In every period of Arab history, there has been a modernist trend that rejected prevailing traditions and static values. This creative trend aspired to change the world and to create a new mode of thinking as well as new forms of literary expression.

This struggle has been ignored by mainstream Western scholarship. Western scholars see only the conventional side of Arab society, with its emphasis on conformity rather than creativity and on *naql* (traditional-authoritative transmission) rather than *'aql* (reasoning). The one-dimensionality of the Western treatment thus ignores what is most essential about Arab culture, particularly in transitional periods—namely, cultural struggle, or the battle between the old and the new. This cultural struggle is an integral part of a larger struggle between the dominant order, which represents the interests and values of affluent classes and groups, and countercultural or revolutionary movements motivated by alternative visions. One trend or other may prevail in any given period, but the cultural struggle itself is constant. Some Arabs judge the present and the future in terms of the past; others condemn or reassess traditions in the name of uniqueness, originality, and creativity. General Arab culture is a product of these contradictions and battles. In this way the general culture constantly changes; the most permanent thing is struggle itself.

Past-Oriented versus Future-Oriented Values. A similar debate pertains to the differences between those who call for the revival of early Islamic values and those who call for liberation from traditional values and a search for a new model based on the dynamics of the present reality and shaped by aspirations for the future. Four distinctive orientations seem to have emerged out of this debate. Besides the *salafiyya* movement (the past-oriented traditionalists) and the future-oriented modernists, there are those who try to reconcile the old and the new, as well as the eclecticists who willingly adopt Western values and styles of living. The Moroccan historian Abdallah Laroui has classified Arab intellectuals according to only two of these categories. Most of them, he observes, profess a traditionalist rationale; the rest profess eclecticism. Both trends fail to see reality and fall victim to ahistorical thinking.[35] Similarly, the poet Adonis notes that the principle of modernity is the struggle between the *salafiyya*-based order and the desire to change that order. In other words, Arab modernity was born historically out of the interactions between these two mentalities.[36]

The movement to reconcile *salafiyya* and modernism is often overlooked, despite the fact that it has always represented a significant trend in contemporary Arab culture. This movement has attempted to combine authenticity with modernity by reviving sound elements of Arab heritage and maintaining an open mind about the future and other cultures. Constantine Zurayk tells us that cultural transformation "should strive to realize a positive integration of four main values: rationality in the broadest sense of the word . . . ; a genuine sense of identity springing from the discovery and the incorporation of the abiding contributions of the Arab heritage; the diffusion of intellectual and cultural values among the masses of the population; and a yearning to contribute creatively to the enrichment of human life as a whole."[37] Similarly, the Moroccan intellectual and political leader 'Allal al-Fassi says "we strive to change our customs and gradually to begin to think about events before they occur." He warns against the splitting of "the society into two groups: one that considers that everything that the old did or thought was correct . . . and the others who are so overwhelmed by their desire for innovation and creativity that they begin to believe that everything transmitted from the past should disappear . . . the fact of the matter is that both groups commit a great mistake."[38] Renewed interest in cultural authenticity has emerged in the wake of the Islamic revival of the 1980s. As a consequence, revivalist trends continue to insist on combining old and new values without telling us what the terms actually mean or how reconciliation can be achieved.[39]

Adonis wrote the three volumes of *Al-Thabit wal-mutahawwil* on the changing and the permanent in Arab culture as an advocate of creativity and modernity. His future orientation is perhaps most vividly portrayed in his poetry. Of his pioneering spirit, he writes:

—Before the time of day—I am.
Before the wonder of the sun—I burn.
Trees run behind me.
Blossoms walk in my shadow.

—From roots and ashes I create
a country for the night
and watch it grow.
Fields fountain into song.
Flaring out of thunder, lightning burns the mummies of the centuries.
O my thunderbolt,
Change everything,
Change all the maps.
Be in a flash
My likeness in the sun,
My turn in madness.[40]

Arab ideas of time are reflected in poetry, proverbs, and a variety of forms of collective consciousness. Essentially, the Arab view is that a relationship of constant struggle exists between human beings and time. One such proverb says, "Time is a sword; if you do not cut it, it will cut you." A person may retreat from the present and seek refuge in the past or dream of the future. Whatever the choice, the dominant outlook seems to say that the present does not breed sanity and is to be rejected.

Culture of the Mind versus Culture of the Heart. Another oversimplified analysis offers a dualistic view of culture that draws pronounced contrasts between mind and heart, reason and faith, spirit and matter. From this dualistic perspective, Arab culture is variously characterized as a culture of the heart, the spirit, or the faith. In sharp contrast, Western culture is characterized as being one of mind, matter, and reason.

Rather than refuting this assertion of two separate patterns, some prominent Arab intellectuals have tried instead to claim the superiority of the heart over the mind. A recurring argument in the works of the prominent Egyptian writer Tawfiq al-Hakim is that Egyptians "know a great deal, but they know it in their heart and not their mind" and that "the only power of Europe is in the mind . . . whereas the power of Egypt is in the bottomless heart."[41] Similar contrasts are drawn in the novel *Qindil umm Hashem* (The Lamp of umm Hashem) by another Egyptian writer, Yahya Haqqi, who says that the West represents the civilization of science, whereas Egypt represents the civilization of faith.[42] Based on such premises, the renowned Iraqi poetess Nazik al-Mala'ika refuses to define Arab nationalism, pointing out that "the search for definitions came to us from . . . Europe where thought is built on doubt. . . . As for us in this Arab east, we possess such an abundance of spirituality and emotion as well as of pure faith . . . that we have always passively accepted great facts without discussion or attempt at definition. This is at the base of our eastern wisdom. No, we have not attempted to define things like 'God,' 'Arabism,' 'beauty,' 'spirit,' 'supernatural,' [and] 'emotion.' We have not attempted to do so until the coming of modern times, which delivered the guidance of our thinking to doubting Europe."[43]

Other Arab intellectuals perceive this very attitude to be at the root of our underdevelopment and failure. They see rationalism as a prerequisite for achieving the Arab renaissance. This trend has been represented by several generations of intellectuals since the middle of the nineteenth century.

Whether held by Western or Arab analysts, this dualistic view lacks accuracy in its assessment of both the West and the East. Neither culture is exclusively rational or emotional, spiritual or materialist. The fact that under certain conditions one trend may prevail over the other does not preclude the fact that the two tendencies must coexist or struggle in opposition in all cultures. In the case of Arab culture, a subtle combination of coexistence and struggle between the mind and the heart takes place on all levels in everyday situations.

Form versus Content. Arab culture is often characterized as emphasizing form or word at the expense of content and meaning. This orientation is supposedly apparent in Arab attitudes to language. Assessments of these relationships have been made by such scholars as Albert Hourani and Jacques Berque. Berque observes that "the East is the home of the word," that "the Arab language scarcely belongs to the world of men; rather, it seems to be lent to them," and that Arabic writing is "more suggestive than informative." [44] Hourani begins his *Arab Thought in the Liberal Age* with the statement that Arabs are "more conscious of their language than any people in the world." [45] Patai's oversimplified generalizations include the assertions that "[to the] Arab mind, eloquence is related to exaggeration," "The Arabs were always a poetic nation," and "Rhetoricism is a very important feature in the Arab model personality." [46]

Exaggerated or not, such statements and many others to the same effect have depicted a peculiar relationship between Arabs and their language. As with any other relationship, it may have its negative or positive consequences under certain specific conditions. In times of national crises, Arabs themselves have been most critical of the emphasis on language. A character in my novel *'Awdat at-ta'ir ila al-bahr* (translated as *Days of Dust*) says in a reflective angry mood, following the defeat of the June 1967 war:

> Words are the only weapon we know how to use. Our houses are of words, our castles are of dreams, our dreams are of words. Words are what we export. And we have an odd relationship with them: We invent them, but in the long run they gain control over us and recreate us as they wish. The created becomes the creator, the creator the created. . . . We eat words, we drink words. We live in words. We kill ourselves with words. [47]

Such a relationship to language is not constant. It is not to be explained as indicative of the nature of the Arab language, or of the nature of the Arab. What it truly reflects is impoverishment of Arab culture in a specific historical period. That is exactly what Western scholarship fails to see.

E. Shouby, a psychologist with training in both clinical and social psychology, has explored the influence exerted by the Arabic language upon the psychology of Arabs; unfortunately, his analysis entirely fails to specify the period or the historical conditions. Shouby indulges in oversimplified generalizations about the influence of language on "the psychology of the literate Arab: general vagueness of thought, overemphasis on the psychological significance of the linguistic symbols at the expense of their meanings; stereo-typed emotional responses, over-assertion and exaggeration; and two levels of life." Indeed, in addressing himself to each of these aspects, he makes wild statements like: "Naturally, Arabic that deals with simple or familiar questions creates no difficulties; but the more novel or abstract the content, the more difficult it is to understand Arabic with accuracy. Words and even sentences may be transmitted, not as units but as whole structures, from one context to an entirely different one without sufficient modification (or even without modification at all)." Elsewhere he argues: "The tendency to fit the thought to the word . . . rather than the word to the thought, is a result of the psychological replacement of the thoughts by words, the words becoming the substitutes for thoughts, and not their representative."[48]

Such statements seem to reflect Shouby's biases; they may even reflect personal frustrations in learning Arabic. A more appropriate point is that the Arab language lends itself to all sorts of styles of writing. The more successful Arab writers accept the classical definition of eloquence to mean "what is brief and denotative" (*al-balagha hiya ma qalla wa dalla*).

Collectivity versus Individuality. Throughout this book it has been pointed out in different contexts that the collectivity rather than individuality serves as the basic unit of, and the source of the dominant value orientations in, Arab society. Early on, I stated that a highly distinctive feature of Arab society is the continuing dominance of primary group relations. Entering into these relations means that individuals engage in unlimited commitments to the group. Instead of asserting their separateness and privacy as independent individuals, they behave as committed members of a group—hence the significance of family, tribe, neighborhood, community, village, sect, and so forth. Generally speaking, one may claim that the need for affiliation is nurtured at the expense of needs for power and achievement. In fact, however, the latter two needs are often met through affiliation.

Solidarity with the group may require the individual to identify with other members by sharing their joys and sorrows, achievements and failures, victories and defeats. Members of the same group expect a great deal from one another. Failure to live up to these expectations may result in deep bitterness. This explains the extreme expressions of such conflicting emotions and tendencies as love and animosity, cohesiveness and divisiveness, self-denial and jealousy, cooperation and competition, friendliness and hostility, or amity and hatred. No matter what, Arabs assert, "People are for people" ("An-nass lil-nass"); paradise without others, they say, is unlivable ("al-janneh bidoon nass ma bitindass"). Even in the present transitional period, Arabs, whether rural or urban, continue to maintain intimate affiliations from which they derive a great deal of intrinsic satisfaction and a strong sense of belonging. Nevertheless, they are exposed to immense family and community pressures, and to constant interference in the most private aspects of their personal lives. Demands for conformity undermine individuality, the formation of independent views, and free self-expression. So profound a gap results between the private and the public in Saudi Arabia that two completely separate behavioral realms are created: what we might call "above-ground" behavior takes place in the realm of public life, while "underground behavior" occurs in the privacy of one's home. Stringent demands for strict conformity to religious traditions are responsible for this dichotomy.

Open- versus Closed-Mindedness. Arab culture at present is a product of its interaction both with its own environment and with other cultures. In the past, it represented a delicate fusion of Arab-Islamic culture with ancient civilizations. Modern history has witnessed a dialectical interaction with Western cultures. One mental outcome of these kinds of interaction has been the emulation of the advanced culture of conquerors. An opposite mental response has been to reject the invading culture and to seek refuge in a revival of the past. In between these two opposed alternatives, there have been some significant processes of acculturation and transformation emanating from new realities and changing needs.

In a previous study on Arab-Western polarities, I found that the dualities fostered by this process have been too strong to be overcome by modernization. On the one hand, openness to the West has resulted in the creation of some islands of *tamaghrub* (Westernization). On the other hand, escape into the past and mere reaction to Western dominance produced fundamentalism rather than genuine transcendence. This is illustrated by the attempts of the Tunisian ruling class under Bourguiba to create a "new Tunisia" by way of combining openness to the West, creation of a nation with an Arab-Islamic character, and "Tunisianization." Rather than achieving a real integration of tradition and modernization, these efforts have tended to serve the cause of legitimizing the dominant order.[49] A similar process in Lebanon has resulted in a relentless civil war. Based on the Tunisian experience, Hichem Djait has concluded that, "there is an implicit dogmatism that moves the conflicting horizons of the Arab mind. . . . Arabs tend to accept what they have most recently discovered warmly and enthusiastically. If they opt for modernity, then everything else becomes the target of their disdain. If they become revolutionaries, then there is no place for anything but revolution. If they became critical, every constructive suggestion with regard to the future is dismissed as irrelevant. . . . This intellectual enslavement coupled with lack of tolerance constitutes a tiring burden for the one who has a genuine will."[50]

This burden suggests the presence of conflicting trends on a deeper level. The present value orientations, not unlike previous ones, are inseparable from the circumstances in which their holders find themselves; these circumstances are shaped by the nature of Arab-Western relationships.

Obedience versus Rebellion. When examining the nature of the relationships of Arabs to their institutions and organizations, analysts have often stated that these relationships are regulated by obedience and respect, rather than by rebellion and individual freedom. This contrast has long shaped Western perceptions of Arab culture; when asked why he preferred to teach in Syria rather than in the United States, for instance, the first president of the American University in Beirut, Daniel Bliss, noted: "I am inclined to think that students in the East are more easily kept in order than are those of the same class of students in the West. . . . The East has greater reverence than the West for parents, teachers, the aged, and religious leaders, and hence, when they come in contact with teachers in schools, they are more easily governed."[51] Records of student revolts at AUB, however, disprove this generalization (particularly when compared to such records for Bliss's alma mater, the University of Massachusetts at Amherst).

Some analysts have traced the origins of obedience and respect for authority to family socialization. Here again, one may selectively cite all sorts of evidence in support of either this position or its alternative. More to the point is the rich tradition of struggle between the opposing orientations. Under certain conditions, obedience and related values may seem to prevail, but they will never completely overwhelm the appeal of individual freedom. Furthermore, compliance may be given grudgingly or forced by external pressures even when obedience and reverence are not valued. In contrast, reasonable rebellion for the sake of asserting one's freedom and dignity is almost always seen as a highly admirable virtue. Indeed, to the extent that Arabs are forced into compliance, they tend to value rebellion. That may explain why, for instance, the most respected Egyptian leaders in modern history have been Ahmad 'Arabi, Sa'ad Zaghloul, and Nasser, all three of whom were known for their spirit of defiance.

Charity versus Justice. The existing social class structure and predominance of religious virtues have promoted the values affiliated with charity. These values may be juxtaposed to those connected with a concern for justice. Promotion of charity implicitly recognizes class inequalities as a natural phenomenon and chooses to minimize their effects rather than to provide an effective solution. In fact, charity may unintentionally reinforce class inequalities and undermine the development of social class consciousness. Charitable giving overcomes feelings of guilt, develops a sense of righteousness, and leads to the expectation that God will compensate the giver in this and the next world. The giver may also develop a feeling that the privileged life that makes charity possible is an earned right and—concomitantly—that the misfortunes of the poor are attributable to their lack of talents and ambition. By contrast, the receiver of charity is likely to internalize perceptions and beliefs that promote appreciation, gratitude, dependency, and humiliation. Such attitudes on the part of both the givers and receivers of charity complement one another; together they perpetuate the dehumanizing class system and the rationalizations put forward for the prevailing order.

A countercultural emphasis on justice rather than charity has been slowly and gradually developing in Arab society since the decline of the Ottomans. Increasingly, Arabs are becoming convinced that justice is a basic human rights issue, and that societies are judged by their readiness and ability to secure the well-being of all their people. Societies must provide for equal opportunities in developing the capabilities of all their people, and in improving the conditions under which all citizens live.

Vertical versus Horizontal Values. Arab culture is also characterized by the struggle between vertical values, which regulate human relations on the bases of status differences, and horizontal values, which relate individuals and groups to one another on the bases of egalitarian principles.

Value orientations stemming from family organization and social class structure are vertical or hierarchical in nature. Vertical value orientations engender discrimination (based on sex, age, tribe, sect, social affiliations, and the like), as well as subordination and authoritarianism in everyday relations. The positions that individuals and groups occupy in the hierarchical structure determine their life chances and opportunities.

The ability of Arab society to grow and prosper, however, requires conditions in which horizontal values dominate. These values are mostly lacking in present Arab society. Yet a counter-orientation is in the making—hence the desperate struggle for equal rights and opportunities, for freedom of expression, and for the universal application of legal norms.

Conclusion

Conflict between sets of value orientations is the greatest indicator of the complexity and contradictory nature of Arab culture at present. The task of understanding such a culture is rendered even more difficult by its transitional state; an intense internal struggle of becoming is under way.

For the purpose of analysis, I have focused on each of these value orientations separately. It is clear, however, that they are closely interrelated, overlapping, and complementary. They merely represent different aspects of the ongoing struggle of Arabs to transcend their present reality. The complementary nature of these interrelationships may be revealed more clearly if we reiterate the distinctions made earlier between dominant culture, subcultures, and counterculture. The dominant culture, on one hand, tends to put greater emphasis under certain conditions on fatalism, conformity, shame, obedience, charity, collectivity, form, vertical values, and so forth. On the other hand, the counterculture is more inclined to attach greater significance to free will, creativity, guilt, open-mindedness, rebellion, justice, and horizontal values. In the midst of this struggle, subcultures may insist on their distinctiveness but in the last analysis they can hardly be neutral and will have to emphasize one set of values or the other.

Traditional values continue to prevail. But that is not what distinguishes Arab culture. What most distinctively characterizes Arab cultural identity in this transitional period is the ongoing struggle between opposing value orientations. It is no surprise, then, to find this same struggle applying to creative life and to intellectual discourse, the subjects to which we turn in the following chapters.

10   Creative Expression
Society and Literary Orientations

Arab society has been characterized in this study as being inclined to spontaneity and expressiveness, reflecting deep-rooted sensitivity and a special fascination with poetry, imagery, metaphor, and symbolism. These inclinations are easily detected in expressions of both high culture and folk culture. Indeed, throughout folk culture, the functional and the artistic are scarcely separable.

At the center of Arab artistic expression is language. The word constitutes the most celebrated element not only of literature but also of music, painting, architecture, and even sculpture in certain instances. Numerous scholars have been prompted to draw attention to the special influence that the Arabic language has on Arabs. For example, Philip Hitti has asserted that, "no people in the world, perhaps, manifest such enthusiastic admiration for literary expression and are so moved by the word spoken or written, as the Arabs."[1] Similarly, the Palestinian artist Kamal Boullata writes that traditionally, "Arab creativity revolved around the word: the word as spoken revelation and as visible image. Poetry, being the elixir of language, was the natural art form in which Arabs excelled. On the visual plane, the arabesque became the spiral product of Arabic."[2]

This distinctive relationship to language is not often appreciated. In the struggle for modernity, many critics decry such literary inclinations at the expense of science. It is in this spirit that Amin Rihani said he would willingly barter the poetry of the East for the airplanes of the West.[3] In a novel I wrote on the Arab defeat of June 5, 1967, the major protagonist complains about an odd relationship we have with words: "We invent them, but in the long run they gain control over us and recreate us as they wish. . . . We become soldiers whose leaders are words."[4]

Such critical statements expressed in times of national crises should not bias us against the symbolic expressive aspects of Arab culture. By exploring these aspects, we are likely to develop a deeper understanding of Arabs' subjective meanings, of their shared conceptions, and of the social reality they construct (and reconstruct or deconstruct) in the process of their struggle to achieve the *nahda*. Our understanding must be rooted in the assumption that subjective meanings emerge from social reality and are then reabsorbed into the collective consciousness of the people. In this sense, culture is understood here to be "at base an all-embracing socially constructed world of subjectivity and inter-subjectively experienced meanings."[5] On a more objective level, culture is the totality of human creations.

The present analysis views culture both as being shaped by social structures and social activities and, at the same time, gaining some importance in its own right in the process, inasmuch as it influences our perceptions and interpretations of social reality. (This is in no way an attempt to combine or reconcile two conflicting views of culture—the view that culture is a mere reflection of social structure and social activity, and the view that culture stands in its own right. These two views cannot be simply combined without dismissing their inherent contradictions.) Based on this understanding of culture, the focus here is on contemporary Arab literary orientations rather than merely a survey of the evolution of all forms of Arab arts in modern times. For clarity, the focus will be on the novel, which seems to be more infused with social reality than other literary forms.

A brief reference must be made, however, to some of the current diversified forms of artistic expression. When all else is in transition in the Arab world, what may we say about literary production? Up until very recently, Arabic literature meant poetry. Being most central to the Arabic artistic heritage, poetry was the art form through which the most intense battles were fought between the old and the new. The Syrian poet Adonis defines modern poetry as a vision representing a leap outside the realm of the dominant conceptions: a prophecy, a transformation of the old poetic forms and ways, an expression of human anxiety, a distinctive and unique creation, an ambiguous exploration transcending the closed systemized world.[6] On another level, Khalida Sa'id has traced Arab cultural modernity to what she describes as the beginning of the exit from the divine age and the entrance into the human historical age. This beginning she ascribes to the occurrence of disequilibrium in the dominant patriarchal, sacred, and absolutist view of the world, and the resultant beginning of the search for a more human identity.[7]

Emerging new literary genres (novel, drama, short story, sketch) jointly contributed to a shift in the nature of the battle between the old and the new. This shift moves us beyond the question of standardized forms of expression to that of the nature of our vision of reality. The new genres, unlike poetry, had to be judged in terms, not of their imitation of classical models, but of their new visions and experimentation. Classical narration (particularly as embodied in the Arabian Nights and Maqamat stories) is essentially inspirational rather than restrictive. The novel and the short story have been seen as new literary forms originating in the emergence of the printing press and rise of an educated middle class in the second half of the nineteenth century. Similarly, although elementary forms of drama have been traced to ancient times in the Middle East (such as the puppet show called Khayal al-Zill), the first modern Arab plays had their origins in the second half of the nineteenth century. [8] From the 1930s on, drama began to be incorporated into the literary tradition through the serious works of Said Taki el-Din, Tawfiq al-Hakim, Yusuf Idriss, Alfred Farag, Nimaan Ashour, Saadalla Wannus, and a few others.

Finally, in the sphere of pictorial arts, modern Arab painters began by imitating Western works, ignoring the splendor of the arts of the ancient civilizations in the region. This break with the past is often explained by saying that, because Islam prohibits representation of living figures, the tradition did not provide a basis to build on. That is, to explain the direction taken by the Arabs' artistic tradition, analysts have argued that artists sought legitimate outlet in nonrepresentational forms of a geometrical character (such as the arabesque style and decorative Arabic calligraphy). Abdelkebir Khatibi and Mohammed Sijelmassi have challenged this contention, stating that it is "a common mistake to suppose that Arabic graphic art is characterized by its strongly abstract quality, in contrast to the representational and figurative nature of Western art." [9] Linked to this argument is Kamal Boullata's analysis of modern Arab art, which is seen as unfolding in three transitional phases. In the first phase, the Arab artist imitated Western art. The second phase did not differ radically from the first, but stylistically the borrowing by artists shifted to more modern schools. The end of World War II marked the start of the third phase; at this time certain European artists, themselves inspired by Arab culture, became the main source of inspiration for a large number of Arab artists. [10]

Much of this analysis applies to high culture. Folk culture is neglected, often being dismissed as lying outside the realm of the artistic and creative. Popular narration (including even *One Thousand and One Nights*), folk poetry (such as Zajal or Malhoun), singing, weaving, jewelry-making, and the like may be much enjoyed even by the elites, but they are rarely recognized as art forms. Instead, they are associated with entertainment and defined in functional terms.

For the masses (*sha'b, jamahir*), the artistic and the functional blend together uniquely. This understanding of cultural activity transcends the separation between the useful and the beautiful. Consequently, folk art is quite independent of urban elitist culture. It emerges genuinely from popular everyday life and the social environment. Many of its forms and themes are valued precisely because they derive from ancient traditions and collective experiences.[11] Folk art is characterized by a rich diversity, revealing both the uniqueness of the individual artist and the particular environment of the community; as a result, this kind of art reasserts the individual as well as the social identity of its creators. Folk art vividly depicts the relationships of human beings to themselves, to nature, and to the larger universe. Women, children, plants, mountains, planets (stars, sun, moon), birds, deer, lions, fish, and other domestic and wild animals are featured prominently in these popular works. Dominant themes include fertility, growth, and human adventure.

Beyond these similarities are the specifics of the community from which these cultural expressions emerge. The arts of villages and of the bedouin of the desert are each distinctive and different from those in the city. Urban art forms reflect the presence of a central authority and a stable socioeconomic life; they express these through an inward-looking focus, standardized structures, definitive frameworks. In contrast, open and limitless lines, rather than closed forms, constitute the basic elements of artistic creations in the non–urban setting. Movement, rather than a central focus, characterizes village and bedouin works of art. A cooperative relationship to nature is often pictured, rather than one of conquest. Perhaps cooperation becomes such a dominant theme because women are the main creators of such art. Women folk artists overcome the duality between reality and art, work and creativity, tools and pieces of work, people and their creations.

Arabic music is inseparable from the word and the human voice. Musical instruments are compatible with vocal expression of human feelings and reflections. According to Edmond Mousally, the distinctive quality of Arab music is derived from five different characteristics. First is the use of the microtone (intervals that are smaller than those employed in Western music, such as third and quarter tones, which create more tonal and melodic possibilities). Also distinctive is a modal system called *maqamat* (Arab music uses twelve essential *maqamat*, or modes, whereas Western music employs only two modes). Rhythmic cycles or *iqa'at* (patterns of strong and weak beats) are also numerous. *Lahn* is another important characteristic; the term refers to the style or feeling with which one performs. Finally, Arab music relies on a number of traditional instruments, including the *oud* (lute), the *durbake* (drum), the *kanoun* (zither), the *nay* (flute), the *duff* (tambourine), and the *kemancheh* (fiddle).[12]

The form and content of artistic expression are intimately related to changing Arab social reality. It is this very intricate relationship between the creator (or the created product) and society that I intend to explore in the remaining sections of this chapter. This exploration is based on the assumption that poems, stories, novels, plays, paintings, graphics, and songs constitute historical sources of knowledge about society as well as aesthetic objects to be appreciated in their own right. Besides being an artist, the creator is also a historian, a philosopher, a psychologist, and a sociologist. A second assumption underlying my inquiry is the belief that a work of art both reflects and shapes reality at the same time.

Orientations in Arabic Literature

From a sociological perspective, literature (and particularly the novel) may be analyzed in terms of at least four interrelated phenomena: an alternative field of exploration into human behavior; a social product or manifestation; a subliminal and cathartic expression; and a system of communication influencing human consciousness. Literature is a way of exploring human behavior like science and philosophy. Great novels depict reality in its innermost essence and in its totality. The novels of Naguib Mahfouz, for instance, portray Egyptian life and society more comprehensively and accurately than the works of all the social scientists put together. The same may be said of Abdelrahman Munif's novel *Cities of Salt*, which depicts the impact of oil on the evolution of Arabian society.

Literature lends itself to analysis and reflects changing social reality. The rise of the Arab novel is connected with social and political transformations, such as the emergence of the middle class, the spread of mass media, and the struggle for the establishment of a new national order. As such, artistic creations are deeply rooted in collective life and embody common experiences. Artistic expression represents a process of self-consciousness and self-fulfillment for the creator, while evoking the same process in others.

Moreover, literary works have their own impact on reality and are not just a reflection or a product. Great works of art (poems, novels, paintings, pieces of music) may transform consciousness. By examining the Arab novel in terms of these phenomena, this chapter aims to probe the extent to which contemporary Arab novels have reflected Arab aspirations and the desperate search for liberation. We want to see the ways in which novels have depicted the Arab plight in confronting overwhelming historical conditions. Finally, we want to see how novels have contributed to the transformation of consciousness.

Yet the literary works of a society differ widely in their representation of reality, as well as in their goals for society. The different orientations may be identified in terms of various criteria derived from (1) the writer's vision of social reality—that is, in terms of whether he or she perceives reality as a state of harmony or conflict, degree of alienation, class origins and identifications, extent of concern with major societal problems, and the nature of involvement in changing or maintaining the prevailing conditions; (2) conceptions of issues such as justice, equality, freedom, love, women and their place in society, revolution, death, and time; and (3) artistic styles in terms of being traditional or modern, creative or imitative, broad or narrow in scope.

Three major literary orientations have competed for dominance in contemporary Arab novels: novels of reconciliation, novels of exposure, and novels of revolutionary change. I shall examine each of these orientations in some detail through discussion of specific works and authors. But we should first note that novels are complex wholes. Consequently, they may have contradictory aims owing to their genuine, uncompromising, and comprehensive treatment of reality. Writers are often able to detach themselves from their own social class interests and biases. In this sense, novels are likely to reflect conflicting trends and views. Yet consistent differences and particular patterns may be identified through systematic analysis.

Novels of Reconciliation

Visions depicting social reality in a state of harmony are combined with concern about threatening changes in novels of reconciliation. Identification with the aristocracy, efforts at integration into traditional culture, and the romanticization of reality are additional characteristics of a number of Arab novels. This orientation is eminently reflected in two novels by Tawfiq al-Hakim: *'Awdat ar-ruh* (The Return of the Spirit), originally published in 1933, and *'Usfour min ash-sharq* (Bird from the East), which appeared in 1938. In both, Al-Hakim deals with the East-West encounter and indulges in a reductionist argument that the East represents the spiritual, or "heart," while the West represents materialism, or "mind." By vehemently accepting the former as typical of Egyptian culture and rejecting the latter as typical of European culture, the novels implicitly expound a nationalistic argument that has had a great influence on Egyptian intellectuals. This nationalistic interpretation has been enhanced by the fact that the last twenty pages of *'Awdat ar-ruh* make reference to the 1919 revolution.

The two novels lend themselves to class analysis. The type of nationalist spirit manifested in them springs from a vision that romanticizes peasant life, portrays the Egyptian village as a harmonious entity, and depicts the peasant as a submissive, peace-loving, and contented person. Upon his return to the village owned by his feudal parents, young Muhsin (Al-Hakim's protagonist in both novels) happily contemplates the unity of the peasants with nature, with other creatures, and even with their masters. While in the village, he feels deeply "the beauty of life," "the balanced rhythm," and the sensation that "everything around him was strong, sane and vivid."[13] He describes the peasants as "one person"; they are "delighted to be able to make the Junior Bey [Muhsin] laugh joyfully" (*'Awdat ar-ruh,* vol. 2, p. 10). Muhsin continues to be fascinated by the "inherent good-heartedness of the peasant" and "the feelings of solidarity and mutuality among the people of Egypt" (ibid., p. 5). Here, a distinction needs to be made between nationalistic solidarity in opposing British rule and rejecting Western culture, on the one hand, and the solidarity of conflicting classes in the service of the ruling elites, on the other. So far, Arab critics and readers have conceived of *'Awdat ar-ruh* and *'Usfour min ash-sharq* as promoting the first rather than the second form of solidarity. Their neglect of the second form (which is in fact more dominant and fundamental to Al-Hakim's vision in the two novels discussed here) constitutes an interesting phenomenon for future study. For the present, however, it will suffice to consider how solidarity of conflicting classes in the service of the established order is promoted in these two literary works, written at a time characterized by apprehension among the Egyptian aristocracy about the gathering storm of social change.

Muhsin experiences a profound sense of pride on hearing a French archaeologist assert that

> feelings of solidarity . . . have converted all these people into one
> single individual that could transfer huge stones for twenty years (in
> order to build the pyramids) smiling, rejoicing, and accepting pain for
> the sake of the worshipped. It is my strong conviction that these
> harmonious thousands were not coerced to construct the pyramids as
> claimed by the Greek historians. . . . On the contrary, they freely
> walked to work in groups chanting the anthem of the worshipped, as
> is still done by their descendants on days of harvest. Certainly, their
> bodies bled, but that was a source of hidden pleasure for them, and
> they used to look joyfully at their own blood dripping from their
> bodies. This sentiment—the sentiment of enjoying pain as a group,
> the sentiment of beautiful patience and smiling endurance . . . the
> sentiment of faith in the worshipped and in sacrifice, and of unity in
> pain without complaint . . . is the secret of their power. [*'Awdat
> ar-ruh,* vol. 2, p. 60]

Muhsin listens with exultation to this pronouncement, and the peasants are overheard singing as they harvest the fields. The archaeologist observes:

> Have you ever witnessed in another country more miserable people
> than these *masakin?* . . . Have you ever found anybody poorer than
> this Egyptian peasant? . . . constant sacrifice and lasting patience, and
> yet listen to them sing. . . . I assure you these people feel great
> pleasure in this common hard labor. That is also the difference
> between us and them. Whenever our workers suffer from pain in

common, they become infected with the germs of revolution,
mutiny, and dissatisfaction with their conditions. But whenever their
peasants suffer pain in common, they experience hidden joy and
pleasure of unity in pain. What a marvelous industrial people in the
future. ['*Awdat ar-ruh,* vol. 2, p. 61]

In this view, the secret of the Egyptian peasants lies in their self-sacrifice,
cheerful acceptance of misery, and deprivation in order to satisfy their master.
Their goal, therefore, is not to improve their conditions but to construct
pyramids for kings, to harvest fields for the benefit of feudal families, and, it
is hoped, to labor hard for the capitalists in a future industrial Egyptian society.

One may argue that these were not necessarily the views of the author but
of one of his characters. But the author's protagonist Muhsin expresses exultation and pride in these views. There is no hint of opposing ideas. The same
attitudes are repeated in other works by Al-Hakim.

In '*Usfour min ash-sharq,* Muhsin whispers to himself with comfort or at least
without remorse: "Slavery will never disappear from the world. . . . Each age
has its slavery and its slaves."[14] The French archaeologist is replaced by a
Russian worker, Ivanovich, who lives in France. The same arguments about
the "East" and the "West" are restated, and Muhsin is once again delighted
to hear them. With the same kind of zeal, Ivanovich says that he has thought
about the problem of "the existence on earth of the rich and the poor, and of
the happy and the miserable" and has reached the conclusion that "the paradise
of the poor will never be on this earth" and that it was

> only because of this very problem that prophets appeared . . . and
> brought about from heaven the best solution. . . . The prophets of
> the East realized that equality is impossible on this earth, and that it
> was not within their power to divide the kingdom of earth between
> the rich and poor. Consequently, they introduced the kingdom of
> heaven into the distribution. . . . Whoever is deprived of good luck
> in the earthly paradise, has his place reserved in the heavenly
> paradise. . . . Then our prophet Karl Marx came onto the scene with
> his earthly gospel, *Das Kapital,* who wanted to achieve justice on this
> earth. . . . What happened was that people grabbed one another by
> the neck, and massacre befell the classes. . . . He planted the bomb of
> materialism and hatred, whereas the prophets of the East planted the
> flowers of patience and hope in the souls of people. . . . They even
> deprived us of that delicious illusion . . . with which the true
> prophets of the East engulfed us. ['*Usfour min ash-sharq,* pp. 78–81]

The ideology propagated in these two novels is conservative as much as
reactionary. The distinction made between the two types of ideologies by the

British novelist and scholar David Caute can be neatly applied here: "The conservative wishes to preserve the fabric of the existing social order, whereas the reactionary aspires to turn the clock back to reclaim a noble but forgotten age."[15] Al-Hakim's characters strongly condemn the notion of public education or literacy, because these are held responsible for the decline in taste and loss of spirit in the East. When Ivanovich expresses his desire to return to the East—the source of light and purity—and drink from its springs and rivers, Muhsin discourages him, saying, "the springs and rivers . . . are all poisoned now. . . . The noble and beautiful clothes of the East are replaced by a strange mixture of European clothes. . . . Similarly, public education or learning to read and write, and even parliamentary elections—all of these European ideas have become lasting principles in the East. . . . Yes, today there is no more East" (p. 170). His rationale for rejecting the idea of the public learning to read and write is that "the masses are the masses, and nothing refines their hearts and minds better than the natural Eastern means of refinement, namely, enriching their hearts by religion and their minds by holy books" (p. 157).

An anti-peasant bias can also be found in Al-Hakim's most famous novel, *Yaumiat na'ib fi al-ariaf* (Maze of Justice), written in 1937.[16] In this work the author endeavors to expose the malfunctioning of the courts and the inapplicability of a modern legal system to the peasants' situation. Al-Hakim repeatedly criticizes both laws and judges as foreign to village life. But the novel reveals a strong bias against peasants. Seeing his assignment to serve in a village as an intolerable banishment, the author's protagonist develops an animosity toward peasants. He doubts their capacity to bear witness in court, calls them "flies," "cattle," "worms," and "monkeys," and expresses his exasperation at having to listen to their complaints: "I see no reason for such complaints. Is it really oppression or the disease of complaining that has inhabited the blood of the peasant with time? Why should I—a slim, sensitive person who longs to devote half an hour to reading a beautiful book—bother to review the files of insignificant events?" (pp. 157–58).

The image of women in Al-Hakim's novels is quite consistent with his traditional and reconciliatory vision. Female characters are sex objects, fully integrated into their traditional roles. They seek salvation in marriage and household life. They conform to their repressive and prohibitive world. They restrict themselves to the narrow confines delimited and enforced by men. They are expected to be loyal, devoted, unselfish, and contented. They want to gratify the desires of their parents, brothers, husbands, and children. In all situations, women are seen as easily tempted, for they are "pushed by drives beyond their will . . . maybe the sexual instinct" (*'Awdat ar-ruh,* vol. 1, p. 210).

A brief description of Al-Hakim's style of writing illustrates how form spontaneously emerges out of the author's vision of reality. Conventional views reflect themselves in conventional styles of expression. If form is content itself spontaneously taking its own shape in accordance with its own internal logic and principles, then Al-Hakim's reactionary vision would be most likely to take a static conventional form. Change in form only occurs as a result of developing a new consciousness and having a new vision. Since reality for Al-Hakim is harmonious and more or less static, his major characters tend to be rounded, finished, and almost complete in themselves. His European characters are used as instruments to convey his ideas and views. Not surprisingly, Al-Hakim's metaphysical views are expressed in inherited imagery, with much repetition of words and meanings. His style of writing is characterized by simplification, exaggeration, and unpoetic prose. He exhibits a lack of originality and relies on detailed descriptions of amusing incidents that could be totally discarded without undermining the flow of narration or the inner unity of the novel.

The author's simplification and exaggeration do not emanate from any concern for the masses or ordinary readers. Al-Hakim clearly points out in his introduction to *Yaumiat na'ib fi al-ariaf* that he writes out of a need to maintain his own freedom in times of difficulty. He confesses that his writing is his open window on himself and that it serves to release his own tensions. This is what is usually claimed by conservative and reactionary authors. Their insistence on art for art's sake and on the notion that art is primarily a form rather than content is meant to mask their conservative ideology. We are told by Alain Robbe-Grillet that "literature is not a means which the writer puts at the service of some cause. . . . I write to understand why I feel the desire to write," and he adds that the true writer "has nothing to say, only a manner of saying it." [17]

All writing serves some social cause. In this sense, all writing is committed. The literature of reconciliation is explicitly or implicitly intended to divert attention from the predicament of the deprived, to preserve the existing social order, to pacify the dissatisfied and accommodate them to their conditions, and to abort the process of liberation. The literature of reconciliation portrays the desperate as reconciled to their preconceived social reality.

The whole Egyptian national uprising of 1919 is also explained by Al-Hakim in psychological terms. He suggests that his characters participated in the uprising in order to forget their failure in love. He concludes *'Awdat ar-ruh* with the remark: "I wonder whether this revolt was inevitably intended to channel the feelings of those afflicted in their emotions" (vol. 2, p. 246). National and socioeconomic problems are thus reduced to the level of personal emotional difficulties. In this way, attention is diverted from the social conditions of deprivation and oppression. Instead of contributing to the transformation of consciousness, such writing avoids the issue and reinforces the dominant culture.[18]

Novels of Exposure

This type of novel exposes the weaknesses of society and its institutions without exhibiting real commitment to the restructuring of the existing order. The major characters, and particularly the protagonists among them, are bourgeois in social origin, identification, longings, and aspirations. In essence, their visions criticize the social reality, but they seek individual salvation from conditions of alienation. The characters do suffer from problems resulting from social pressures to conform and from lack of control over their destinies, but they do not link their tormenting predicaments to existing social contradictions. Aligning these novels on the bases of the responses they propose to alienating conditions, and the particular forms of individual salvation they portray, novels of exposure may be further subdivided into novels of (a) compliance, (b) nonconfrontation, and (c) rebellion.

Novels of Compliance. These novels portray human beings divided by social intolerance, censorship, and repression. The inner and outer worlds of the individual are incongruent and dissociated, for people face immense pressures to conform to the existing order. They are preoccupied with making adjustments to their harsh situation; they must mask their real feelings from others, particularly from those with the power to reward or punish them. Outwardly, they pretend to accept the system, but deep inside they abhor its very essence.

The works of Naguib Mahfouz (1912–) expose the repressive nature of the established order by lucidly portraying the pressures for submission. The great majority of his characters (mostly middle-class or aspiring to be) desperately try to transcend their conditions through conformity. Their destinies are shaped by events and changes beyond their reach. The masked intention of the author is to expose society's restrictions on free expression.

The theme of compliance is repeated in one form or another in all of Mahfouz's works. The poor inhabitants of Midaq Alley in the novel *Zuqaq al-Midaqq* submissively attribute their misfortune to "the evil in ourselves." They desperately try to adjust to new conditions created by the circumstances of World War II. Motivated by a new dream of success, they are tempted into playing the game. Their struggle to improve their conditions is in vain, and the consequences are always catastrophic. Because they lack legitimate opportunities, they resort to opportunism and illegitimate means. The lively and proud Hamida is tempted to run away with the bourgeois gentleman Farag Ibrahim, thinking that he loves her. As a soft-spoken pimp catering to English soldiers,

Farag instead manipulates her into prostitution. Similarly, Abbas al-Hilou ventures beyond the alley to enlist in the British army, hoping to earn enough money to marry Hamida; instead he is killed in a tavern by British soldiers. Another character, Hussein, also lured by the same dream of middle-class success, ends as an alcoholic. Trapped in these desperate conditions, the characters seek solace in the speeches of Radwan al-Husseini, who calls on them to accept their conditions in terms reminiscent of those of Al-Hakim and his novels of reconciliation: "Don't say I am bored . . . or rebel against God's will. Every condition has its own beauty. . . . Believe me pain has its joy and pleasure." In response to this call, the community returns to "its eternal virtue of silence and indifference."[19]

The theme of compliance is also portrayed in a novel that Mahfouz wrote almost ten years later, in 1959—*Awlad haratina* (The Children of Geblawi). Again, we are told that "the people got used to buying . . . security with compliance and humiliation. They have been haunted with severe punishments for the least slip of tongue or deed, and even a flash of thought that the face may disclose." At certain rare moments of self-reflection, they realize that "surrender is the worst sin." Stormy moments in history threaten this world; sooner or later the rebels find themselves trapped into silence, and the "future looks dark with no choice but compliance." This novel ends, like the previous one, with the characters engulfed by heavy and desperate silence. Again, "the people patiently endured oppression," hoping to witness "the defeat of despotism and the dawning of light and miracles."[20]

Two years later, in 1961, Mahfouz published *Al-Liss wal-kilab* (The Thief and the Dogs), a novel in which the main character, Sa'id Mahran, finds himself an outlaw after serving a four-year prison sentence. He tries in vain to avoid conflict with the system, consciously experimenting with all sorts of compliant behavior. He pours "cold water on his burning interiority so as to appear peaceful and domesticated"; suppresses his anger by convincing himself that "nothing comes out of words except a headache" and that "it is bad luck to attack a man of prestige." He tries to keep alert, patiently awaiting the right moment when the stroke of the people "will be as heavy as their long patience."[21]

The theme of compliance recurs (1962) in Mahfouz's novel *As-Samman wal-kharif* (The Quail and Autumn). The aristocrat 'Isa (who was affiliated with the Wafd party and was a high-ranking civil servant in the old royal regime) tries vainly to adjust to the new situation created by the 1952 revolution. He loses his job. His fiancée, Salwa, breaks her engagement to him and marries the bourgeois Hassan (symbolizing the transfer of Egypt from the aristocracy to the bourgeoisie). The poor classes continue to struggle in vain. They are Egypt, but Egypt is not theirs. In the end, exactly like exhausted flocks of quail, they all fall "into their inevitable destiny after a tiring journey full of fancifulness and heroism." Neither the aristocrat, the bourgeois, the peasant, nor the worker "dares to disclose his political views . . . and since politics is an unavoidable part of any meeting, they could not avoid hypocrisy." Meanwhile, in order to endure, they need tranquilizers, "for whoever is inflicted with pain would welcome tranquilizers even if poisonous."[22]

In *Ash-Shahhadh* (The Beggar), written in 1965, Uthman asserts, "I have become fully convinced that if we were to be thrown into hell, we would eventually get used to it."[23] The same idea is repeated in *Hubb taht al-matar* (Love in the Rain) where the army draftee Ibrahim says, "I became convinced that one could live in hell itself and eventually get used to it."[24]

Mahfouz continues to reiterate the theme of compliance, discomfiting the diligent reader. His characters insist on tolerating or even accepting conditions that render them "as insignificant as a mosquito . . . without rights, dignity and protection." They fear the secret police and practice self-censorship. Speaking for the author, the narrator of *Al-Karnak* confesses, "We avoided talking politics as much as possible, and I told them, 'If we have to discuss a national topic, let us talk imagining Mr. Khalid Safwan [director of the bureau of secret police] to be seated in our midst.' "[25] Those who do not heed this advice are killed (Hilmi Hamada); others are recruited into the secret police (such as Zainab, who also becomes a prostitute) or forced to adjust to marginality and hardship (like the narrator, who lacks the courage to expose himself, although he is bent on exposing society and others). The consequences are the same for all. Playing the game of the system is equally catastrophic, for "the roads are closed to the point of suffocation."[26]

In the late 1970s, Mahfouz published a novel entitled *Al-Harafish* (The Despondent Ones), perhaps meant to be a sequel to and substitute for *Awlad haratina,* which has never been permitted to be published in Egypt. Religious prophets are here replaced by tribal patriarchs, who identify with the poor only to be converted into powerful notables later on. Sooner or later, the poor discover that salvation is poor protection; they resort to old ways of seeking safety in compliance. Conflicts in this version are depicted in terms of good versus evil rather than as class struggle. In the final analysis, people have to conform or fall victim to the most brutal attacks. The question becomes one, not of why rebellions fail, but why it is that God allows them to happen. As developments evolve contrary to human will, the individual person "moves within a circle of fear . . . playing his role as expected." So people "surrendered to their fate and admitted their powerlessness."[27]

Mahfouz's Cairo trilogy, *Al-Thulthiyya,* the most famous of his works, published 1956–57, expands on the theme of compliance within a family whose members (children and wife) submit completely to the authority of the father. The wife, Aminah (whose name, meaning "faithful," reflects her character), has denied herself all rights and "obeyed him [her authoritarian husband] to the extent that she hated to blame him . . . even in private . . . and never questioned her desire for safety and submissiveness."[28]

Mahfouz's conceptions of love, women, death, religion, family, and inequality complement this vision. Love, for instance, is seen as a cure (or more accurately as a tranquilizer) that helps people withstand hardships and disasters but never enriches them. This may also explain why love is portrayed as a form of struggle or battle between man and woman, for each is trying to solve his or her own problems through the other. The aspects of love explicitly mentioned by Mahfouz include anger, bitterness, threat, making an impression, deception, fear of scandal, beastly desire, sexual fantasies, daydreaming, persistence, torment, repression, tragedy, and game playing. With or without the benefit of love, women continue to be victims of oppression.

Radwan al-Husseini in *Zuqaq al-Midaqq* is well known in the community for his goodness and piety and is described as "a true believer, a true lover, and truly generous." Yet this man is "very strict and cruel at home. He imposes his authority on his wife who . . . submits to his will"; one way he rationalizes his behavior is by asserting a strong belief in "the necessity of treating a woman as a child for the sake of her own happiness before anything else," and his behavior is unchallenged by anyone, including his wife, who accepts her role and "considers herself a happy woman, proud of her husband and her life." In her opinion, a woman is a woman and she is virtuous inasmuch as she does her best to please her husband, and a "man is a man and nothing would really smear him" except, to be sure, "being a woman in the clothes of a man." Authoritarianism is a measure of his manhood, and dedication or loyalty is a measure of her womanhood.[29]

In short, Mahfouz's novels portray women as submissive creatures who faithfully conform to their traditional role. Specifically, women diligently seek marriage as "an inevitable natural ending," and see as God's will the "verdict that women worship men."[30] Women also are constantly pressured to live up to a complex set of demands and expectations surrounding femininity, motherhood, housekeeping, wifehood, and sisterhood. They are talkative, highly dependent on the sharpness of their tongues, their sole weapon of defense, aside from cunning and trickery. Indeed, women are noted for their oral aggression, for being "an encyclopedia of ill-deeds" (*mu'jam al-munkarat*). At the same time, women are seen (and sometimes see themselves) as a source of evil and temptation. Consequently, they are held responsible for men's deviations. Moreover, women who fail in love or marriage most often become prostitutes in Mahfouz's novels. His novels *Hubb taht al-matar* and *Al-Karnak* do not spare even university graduates from this fate.

These characteristics underscore the fact that the conception of women is part of a more comprehensive ideology that reflects a lack of social emancipation. Traditional values prevail in Mahfouz's works. His positive characters are distinguished by their piety, decency, faith, mercy, hospitality, manliness, loyalty, patience, serenity, charity, and piety. This ideology is also reflected in Mahfouz's style of writing. Here again, the form emerges freely out of the author's vision of man in a state of compliance. Georg Lukács's brilliant observation that "resignation plays a very important part in the bourgeois literature"[31] applies almost perfectly to Mahfouz. His style reveals a tendency toward submissiveness, self-censorship, and conformity. In order to "have his cake and eat it too," Mahfouz resorts to techniques that allow him to criticize society and get away with it. He constantly plays it safe by criticizing from a distance.

Mahfouz effectively establishes this aloof neutrality through seemingly objective treatment of a wide variety of characters and themes. By representing all sorts of conflicting groups and ideologies, he conveys an image of himself as a realistic writer who stands above divisions and partisanship as a father figure. Mahfouz is the most accomplished Arab realist, but one should not be tempted into characterizing him the way Lukács characterizes Balzac—namely, as a realist able to depict "reality even if that reality ran counter to his own personal opinions, hopes and wishes."[32] The narrator in *Al-Karnak*, for instance, maintains his aloof and paternal role while investigating the other characters and disclosing their innermost secrets. We come to know the views, secrets, and political affiliations of Zainab, Ismail, Hilmi, and others, but never of the narrator, who represents the author. He questions everybody, and, whenever pressured to express his own feelings, he deliberately "speaks hiding behind generalities."[33]

The realism of Mahfouz is constrained in important ways. His ability to show the workings of social forces on the Egyptian scene and to present a balanced picture of the existing ideologies and groups is compelling. Yet he falls short by ignoring the revolutionary forces working underneath the visible layers of the society. Although *Zuqaq al-Midaqq* describes a stormy period in Egyptian history, it fails to include a single positive revolutionary character. Mahfouz also fails miserably to describe the condition of the poor in Egypt; his attempts to do so (as in *Awlad haratina*) are abstract, and his descriptions of poor people and neighborhoods in Cairo tend to be vague. Mahfouz rarely explores the inner worlds of his characters. He is insensitive to their inner torments—his structuralism is not really intended to reveal their private and existential dilemmas. This disjuncture between the inner and outer worlds explains why Mahfouz's writing is highly prosaic and traditional, lacking in poetry and imagery.

Some of these shortcomings may be ascribed to political timidity. Mahfouz's novels deal with past periods rather than the controversial present when it comes to sensitive issues. During Nasser's rule, he wrote mostly about the prerevolutionary period, and it was only after 1970 (when the Sadat regime came to power) that he started dealing with the Nasser period. His characters avoid confrontation by addressing themselves to ancient pharaohs, when they really intend to speak to the contemporary ones. The character Anis Zaki practices self-censorship even unconsciously, as if in a state of hallucination. "Your aides lied to you," he tells an ancient pharaoh. "You possess wisdom, insight and a sense of justice but you allow corruption to devour the country. Look how your orders are violated."[34] In fact, there is double evasiveness in this statement: addressing an ancient pharaoh and putting the blame on his aides. One may even argue that there is a third form of evasiveness in his praise of the ruler, for in case the first two tricks do not work, he attributes wisdom, insight, and a sense of justice to the pharoah.

The impact of Mahfouz's works is further undermined by his use of mystifying allegories and riddles in the place of artistic symbolism. The aim of allegory is to insulate or mask the critical message. Artistic symbolism aims not to hide but to inspire, enrich, create a poetic climate, transcend the limited and particular, and embrace universal human experience without loss of concreteness and uniqueness. Mystifying techniques (as reflected in Mahfouz's allegories and riddles) are often used by writers in repressive societies to avoid danger and censorship. In this sense, however, they become a form of self-censorship.

Novels of Nonconfrontation. These novels portray society as a brute force crushing the individual. Human beings are defeated creatures, trying to resolve their alienation through escape from reality. Humans retreat into a world of their own making as their only remaining alternative. Lukács describes this tendency as a strategy "to avoid outside conflicts and struggles rather than engage in them . . . all the relationships have ceased to exist. . . . This self-sufficiency of the subjective soul is its most desperate self-defense; it is the abandonment of any struggle to realize the soul in the outside world."[35]

This trend of nonconfrontation is vividly depicted in two Arab novels: *Tharthara fawq an-Nil* (Chattering on the Nile) by Mahfouz (1966), and *As-Safina* (The Ship) by Jabra I. Jabra (1970). The two novels diverge in their points of departure and their interpretations of human experience. They also treat the workings of social forces differently, using very different forms of artistic expression. The two novels converge, however, in their attempts to expose the existing social system as being responsible for the crushing of the individual ego, for imposing constant pressure on human beings to conform or seek help from without. The two novels are also similar in terms of setting, and of what we might call the creation of a mechanism of nonconfrontation.

A floating cabin on the Nile in the former novel and a ship on the Mediterranean in the latter tale provide calm refuges for a number of desperate characters. They have retreated, giving up the hope of transcending their alienation through struggle. Their mechanisms of escape from themselves in these calm resorts include gossip, sexual fantasies, alcoholism, arguments, art, myth-making, and the verbalization of their bitterness and aggression against society and themselves. The characters of *As-Safina* are more flexible in sublimating their desperation and, consequently, waver between exasperation and euphoria.

Mahfouz portrays the characters in *Tharthara fawq an-Nil* as escapees who consciously and willingly isolate themselves from society and show the minimum possible concern with it, except as a source of their jokes. As time passes, however, they lose even their ability to enjoy humor, since life itself "became a boring joke."[36] They ritualistically smoke hashish every evening to escape reality. Their behavior becomes almost totally predictable, not only in terms of their fixed daily schedule, but also in what they say and do. That the author succeeds in sustaining the reader's interest and curiosity when the situation reaches this state is a noteworthy accomplishment.

Except for the servant who guards the cabin and attends to the needs of his masters, all the characters in this novel are bourgeois. They include a civil servant, a movie actor, a storyteller, a lawyer, an art critic, a woman playwright, a college girl, and a divorced housewife. The unfolding events reveal that these characters are profoundly alienated from their work, life, and society. They work during the first half of the day merely to earn a living. At work, they are constantly aware of the triviality of what they are doing, and they become active only after work, when they gather in the cabin—the kingdom of their drug addiction—where they try to relax and forget. They realize that they are leading absurd lives, and their only value is absurdity itself. Even their talk about absurdity is not taken seriously, and the only solution they would consider seeking is non-solution. They are indifferent to what goes on in their society and care less about politics. "We do not care about the world, and the world in turn does not care about us," one of them says. Another character proclaims their total dissociation: "In fact we are not Egyptian or Arab or even human." Now and then they make sarcastic remarks about the world, but they want to avoid doing even that, so as not to sound concerned. Their rationale for avoiding analysis lies in their strict belief in nonbelief and in their perception that "the ship moves without any need of our opinion or cooperation. Thinking, thus, becomes fruitless and may bring about pain and high blood pressure," for "nothing spoiled fun more than thinking." In this particular novel of nonconfrontation, people lose the capacity to love. In their futile attempts to exchange love, the men and women characters instead inflict pain on each other. They contribute to each other's deterioration rather than growth and enrichment. Love seems least evident in married life. The fact that the married men are totally detached from their families does not undermine their traditional conception of women. A woman is seen as a mere sex object and as an appendage to man's existence. For a while, we are enticed by an attractive idea that the woman playwright, Samara, may be able to transform the group. As the only serious character in the lot, she tries to change them by preaching faith in humanity and science as opposed to faith in absurdity. Eventually, however, she, too, deteriorates. A woman's alienation lies at the root of her problem as well, for under the pressure of the prevailing conditions she continues to look at herself from the male point of view. When Samara is described by one of the men as having a strong personality, it is one of the girls who objects, "This is a repulsive description of a woman." [37]

Mahfouz's style in this novel provides another piece of evidence supporting the premise that style emerges out of content and the author's vision of reality. Clearly Mahfouz's style here differs from that in his novels of compliance. The shift in his focus from the working of social conditions to their impact on individual characters requires a substantial change in style. The fact that he resorts to poetic free association can be accounted for by the situation of nonconfrontation. Individuals are now on their own, living separated from significant others in a world of their own making, which is reinforced by drug addiction and resulting hallucination. Mahfouz therefore has to focus on their inner lives, which explains why his prose in *Tharthara fawq an-Nil* is much more poetic than in his novels of compliance. Yet Mahfouz again fails to use symbols to embrace human experience in both its universality and particularity.

As-Safina (The Ship) by Jabra I. Jabra, a Palestinian writer who lives in Iraq, is another important novel of nonconfrontation. It offers a dark perspective on society and humanity in the Arab east. Several bourgeois characters from Iraq, Kuwait, Syria, Lebanon, Egypt, and other countries meet on a tourist ship. As events unfold, we discover that the journey over the Mediterranean is another improvised means of escaping reality. Unlike the characters of *Tharthara fawq an-Nil,* Jabra's voyagers show some willingness to reflect intelligently on their respective conditions and possible means of escape. Constantly involved in soul-searching and intellectual dialogue about their lives, they resort to illusions in their desperate attempts to transcend their alienation. Yet sublimation through reflection, dialogue, and art leads nowhere. It is just another form of escape or tranquilization, for they fail to satisfy themselves and transcend their reality. The poet and the painter as well as the physician, the architect, and the student of philosophy continue to perceive time as a terrible thing that robs human life of its novelty and freshness. As one of these characters puts it: "If I were a painter, I would have painted it [life] as a black blotch interrupted in two or three places by red spots. Time is the enemy." [38] We are told further that the few scattered red spots stand for rare moments of joy, women, art, battles, and politics.

In fact, the voyagers are escaping from repressive systems, traditions, routines, other people, and even themselves. These characters are greatly tormented by society and its contradictions: big money, ownership, marriage, children, and above all the pressures to conform and keep silent in an age of injustice, domination, hypocrisy, and opportunism. One has constantly to swallow the lies of reporters, writers, and politicians: "How can I . . . read a paper, hear a speech. . . . The word means its opposite, and the opposite means nothing. I lie to you, and you lie to me, and the cleverest guy among us is the one who makes his lies sound most plausible. . . . I am fed up, bored, disgusted. . . . Let the liars marry one another; let the liars bury one another" (p. 130).

Those who are unable to withdraw physically or to reestablish adequate relationships with other people and reality itself tend to develop their own forms of denial and escape. Being bound to a repressive and impoverished world, they escape into unique illusions of their own. One of the characters in *As-Safina* reflects, "No doubt whoever invented the flying carpet . . . never departed from his overcrowded, poor, dirty, smelly neighborhood in Baghdad or Cairo." These conditions require illusions. Hence, the saying "destroy illusions . . . and pleasure will vanish, with nothing remaining except salt." [39]

Yet no matter what kind of illusions a person may resort to, the conditions generating them will continue to press hard for resolution. Real emancipation requires the development of a new consciousness that calls for transformation of these inhuman conditions. The characters of *As-Safina* never draw any real satisfaction from their illusions. On the contrary, illusions become a source of further torment. Yet they never develop a new consciousness. While they continue to suffer from the torment of being condemned to marginality and insignificance, the prevailing inhumane conditions persist. Consequently, as pointed out by Lukács in *The Theory of the Novel*, these characters will "fade away because of their precipitous and unconditional surrender in the face of reality." [40] By the end of their illusory journey, those who have not committed suicide are more desperate than when they began the journey. The illusion itself is converted into a new prison, and nonconfrontation becomes another hopeless entanglement. As a result, the whole experience intensifies deep bitterness against society and the self.

In its own way, this novel of nonconfrontation illustrates human incapacity for love in spite of the great need to belong. Even during moments of lovemaking, the thirst for love remains unquenched. It is clearly seen as a form of escape based on doubt, selfishness, deception, and misuse of the other person. There are no real encounters between lovers, for each is a star moving along its own orbit with almost total disregard for others. Here again, a woman is a sex object: Lama, a beautiful woman who has studied philosophy at Oxford, believes that men do not love intelligent women, and that her tragedy lies in her sophistication.

Stylistically, *As-Safina* is well-planned and neatly integrated. Characters, events, ideas, and plots evolve slowly and spontaneously. The inner world and intimate secrets of the major characters are unraveled more through what each tells us about others than through what they say about themselves. The multidimensional nature of human experience and behavior is effectively revealed through symbols, poetic imagery, free association, and legends.

The characters of novels of nonconfrontation do not realize that the issue of life lies in the deep-seated contradictions of social reality. Human beings most adequately transcend alienation by transforming reality. The question is not one of imposing solutions, but of developing a new consciousness. The answer lies not in nonreflection (*Tharthara fawq an-Nil*) or in sublimation (*As-Safina*), but in transformation.

Novels of Individual Rebellion. These novels also expose society, but in a more defiant way, by focusing on individuals fighting their own separate battles. Self-centered individuals who seek to resolve their alienation on their own without the benefit of contextualizing this struggle in an explicitly articulated point of view regarding society and reality are the point of departure in these works. Basically, they are preoccupied with their egos and the problems posed by social limitations on their individual freedom. Unable to transcend their individuality, the heroes confine their attempts to aggressive social criticism, defiantly rejecting prevailing value orientations, or launching relentless attacks on others. Some heroes disdain politics and dissociate themselves from ideological political movements. Others practice some sort of self-styled political involvement, in which their rebellion is confined to mere oral aggression or desperate attacks on immediate individual targets. This orientation is most typically portrayed in some of the works of Layla Ba'albaki, Jabra I. Jabra, and Tayyib Salih, among others.

The defiant mood of Lina—the protagonist of Layla Ba'albaki's 1958 novel *Ana ahiya* (I Live)—is deeply rooted in her egotistic assertion of her individual freedom. Her strong feelings and ideas spring from her own ego, to the almost total exclusion of social reality. What is at issue for her are her personal problems. Lukács's characterization of modernist literature applies here; he points out that the process of negation of history takes "two different forms in modernist literature. First, the hero is strictly confined within the limits of his own experiences. There is not for him . . . any preexisting reality beyond his own self. . . . Second, the hero himself is without personal history. He is thrown into the world: meaninglessly, unfathomably."[41]

Lina proudly proclaims her separation and self-sufficiency by contemplating the following analogy: "I am a luxurious palace. . . . It has everything necessary for the sustenance and reproduction of life; it needs no help from the outside world. . . . The wall around it is high and separated from the road by a moat. I am an autonomous world whose life course is not influenced a bit by any outside event that does not spring from my ego." Being preoccupied with herself to the point of narcissism, almost totally engaged in the nurturing of her ego, Lina pays little attention to others, "to those strange creatures who slide on the outer surface of my life." It is consistent with this view that she has no interest in politics: "I simply confess that I do not have the mind to find a solution to the problem of Palestine, Kashmir, or Algeria. What worries me . . . is how to walk for the first time with my shoes that raise me seven centimeters above the ground. Will they break as I rush into the streets?" [42] Let no one be tempted into believing that the author's intention here is simply to expose Lina's trivialities. The intent is to shock and defy society. The defiance is most intense when directed against the family. Lina despises her father and his wealth and shows ambivalence (reflected in feelings of pity and disgust) toward her mother.

The individual ego also constitutes the focus of concern in the works of Jabra I. Jabra. In his first novel, *Surakh fi laylin tawil* (Cry in a Long Night), which appeared in 1955, Jabra sees writing as being motivated by a psychological need for relief and for coming to terms with oneself and the world. The writer is in search of catharsis through creative self-expression. Unlike Ba'albaki, Jabra has shown increasing concern with social reality and historical events. His focus on the individual does not preclude taking account of the social and political forces shaping human life. Yet his characters cannot free themselves from their subjectivity. In this novel, they seek self-salvation from despair, anxiety, boredom, meaninglessness, and oppression without identifying with others in the ongoing struggle to transform reality. This explains why they never come to terms with themselves, since the conditions making for alienation continue unchallenged.

Jabra's novel *Hunters in a Narrow Street* (1960) exposes the corruption, degeneracy, brutality, sensuality, and triviality of the Iraqi aristocracy before the 1958 revolution. The novel's exposure of the Iraqi aristocracy is coupled with a portrayal of the Iraqi people as powerless: relegated to marginality, deprived, haunted by repressive police, and pushed into compliance. The response of Jabra's characters to these challenges turns out to be highly individualistic. The pivotal characters in the novel—Adnan and Jameel—object to the idea that literature should be guided by political principles or even committed to the liberation of the people. This task, they say, should be left to prophets, teachers, political leaders, and learned economists. In their opinion, "the only literature that will survive is the work of obstinate minds that don't care two hoots for . . . masses." This novel by Jabra does not move beyond the portrayal of self-centered rebellion to revolutionary involvement. Bourgeois rebels like Adnan confess their basic flaws: "What else is politics for us? You don't suppose we can do anything . . . some talk, some organize piddling little cells, some fill acres of paper with sh—y articles. That's about all we can do."[43]

Riddled with their own contradictions, Jabra's defiant characters end up fighting lonely battles, attempting suicide, or assassinating a political leader. In a desperate and defeatist attempt, Adnan (the most politically sophisticated of these characters) concludes his mission by assassinating his old retired uncle. The net result is devastating. Jabra's characters fail even to surmount themselves, and the system continues to prevail, unchallenged, in spite of its degeneracy.

Because of the conditions making for individualism in Arab society, individual rebellion and defiance prevail even among those characters who belong to revolutionary political movements. This tendency is portrayed in the works of the Iraqi novelist Gha'ib Tou'ma Faraman. Although the characters of Faraman's novels *Khamsat aswat* (Five Voices) and *Qurban* (Holy Offering) are politically committed, they continue to be preoccupied with nurturing their own egos. They proclaim their rejection of the established order, but are too powerless to fight. Instead, they resort to verbal aggression against others and themselves, boasting about their imaginary sexual adventures, exaggerating the virtues of societies they have never visited, and seeking recognition and security in dreams, fantasies, poetry, and childhood.[44]

The problem of individual marginality, uprootedness, banishment from community, and suicidal defiance are reflected accurately in the works of the Sudanese novelist Tayyib Salih. The first page of Salih's *Mawsim al-hijra ila ash-shamal* (Season of Migration to the North) announces the rejoicing of a major character at leaving the coldness of Europe and returning to the warmth of his tribe in a small village at the bend of the Nile. His tongue almost slips to say "warmth of womb," revealing a great desire to seek roots in the past and childhood. Back in the net of intimate relations, it is not long before he feels "as though a piece of ice were melting inside" him.[45] In the last analysis, Mustafa Sa'eed is a highly sophisticated and unusual character, whose relationship to the West is one of defiance. He has a need to avenge the colonization of the East. He purposefully establishes sexual relationships with European women, kills one of them, and possibly causes the suicide of three others.

Tayyib Salih's major characters still resort to individual rebellion and defiance rather than revolution. When they fail in Europe, they seek personal rather than societal salvation in the warm relationships of the village. In the long run, they fail to adjust to village life and traditional culture. Mustafa Sa'eed dies or commits suicide, it is not clear which. In such moments of truth, Sa'eed continues to feel uprooted, tormented, and marginal. His search for personal salvation ends in despair. He finds himself half-conscious in the midst of the river not knowing whether he is alive or dead. He does realize that his goal is in front of him, not below him, and that he must move forward and not backward. Like a comic actor, he screams for help. Yet there is no indication that Sa'eed develops a new consciousness and redefines his goals. He is too preoccupied with himself to be transformed.

Novels of rebellion and defiance reject traditional values governing male-female relations as an integral part of the culture of repression, which sees love as shame and disgrace. The major female characters in all of these works suffer from total lack of freedom, reveal great anger against their parents, and desperately seek love as a way out of their traps. Both Sulafa in *Hunters in a Narrow Street* and Hasna in *Mawsim al-hijra ila ash-shamal* were to be forced into marriage by their parents to promote family interests. This explains why their anger is directed solely against their fathers, whose "love can be as deadly as hate." Since they are totally exposed and powerless, they try to escape through romantic and silent love. In seeking such an exit, they are constantly terrified and sooner or later they succumb under great pressure, either to run away or to kill themselves.

For both men and women, love is dominated by uncertainty and risk. They find themselves in the grip of great forces beyond their control. Yet the means of escape are much more available to men than to women. Sometimes men are portrayed in novels of individual rebellion as lacking the genuine capacity to love, as in *Ana ahiya* by Ba'albaki and in *Mawsim al-hijra ila ash-shamal*. In the latter work, we are explicitly told that Mustafa Sa'eed lacks the capacity for love and that he conceives of his relationship to women as a battle, which he wages with "arrows, swords and spears."

Novels of individual rebellion tend to focus on the protagonist's inner world, which is made manifest in free association, inventive imagery and language, short sentences, poetic descriptions and personification of the external world. The artistic forms of expression characteristic of these novels are intimately connected with a multidimensional vision of the human interiority in constant search for meaning and identity. What is most appealing about these novels is their vividness, originality, and liberation from traditional forms of expression. The imagery and language in these novels are strikingly new in modern Arab writing. They provide colorful bridges to islands that have hitherto been beyond reach. Above all, they portray human emotions undergoing new experiences in a changing world through highly vivid, poetic, and concise imagery. It is these features that make *Mawsim al-hijra ila ash-shamal* one of the most successful novels in Arabic.

Compliance, nonconfrontation, and individual rebellion may allow for temporary solace but never serve to transcend the conditions of alienation. All sorts of contradictions and limitations are exposed in these works, but little happens to transform consciousness. The search for salvation ends in tragedy and without heroism. Social systems continue to be as repressive and exploitative as ever. This obstinate preoccupation with individual salvation (as opposed to societal salvation) is deeply rooted in the identification of the authors with the bourgeoisie and in their liberal perspective on change. As a consequence, they persist in feelings of defeat. These authors lack revolutionary vision.

Novels of Revolutionary Change

Arabic novels of revolutionary vision are still in a state of becoming. What we have, in fact, is prerevolutionary writing committed to radical change. A number of pioneering novelists have tried to depict Arab struggle and the longing for transformation of the existing order. The content and form of their writings engender an encompassing vision of society as a whole, in a state of conflict rather than harmony. Society is depicted as a complex and vital whole in which individual or psychological issues cannot be isolated from social issues. The inner struggle that constitutes the main preoccupation of novels of rebellion is explicitly portrayed as a manifestation of external struggle in novels of revolutionary change. This holistic view, which presents human activity within the totality of life in a society, is of the utmost significance. The point of view shifts as well; these novels regard society from the perspective of the exploited, degraded, and oppressed classes. The focus shifts from individual struggle to struggle for social salvation and human liberation. The aim of writing is not to experience catharsis, to idealize reality, or to reproduce it as it is. Rather, the writer seeks at one and the same time to reflect reality and to transform consciousness. The stress in these novels on description, and on an interpretation of the world, emerges out of a genuine effort to change the existing order by developing a new consciousness. The process of liberation is seen as multidimensional—involving political, economic, social, cultural, and personal transformation. The author relates economic and political oppression to social oppression. For example, women's liberation is not a problem that can be viewed in isolation. Changing the conditions of women is connected with changing an existing order that promotes other forms of domination as well. Consequently, emancipation from one form of subjugation has to be accompanied by emancipation from the others.

In order for literature to transform consciousness, it has to aspire to much more than mere political commitment. In fact, the impact of literature on society is diminished by narrow-minded commitment to a party or a regime. There is a great qualitative difference between revolutionary and propagandistic writing. The latter is a mere tool, while the former is an expression of man's struggle and longing for emancipation from all sorts of bondage. The issue is often blurred when seen solely as an artistic question. Robbe-Grillet's assertions that "literature is not a means which the writer puts at the service of some cause. . . . The writer by definition does not know where he is going," and that he "writes to understand why he feels the desire to write,"[46] merely proclaim the author's self-centeredness. Robbe-Grillet also confuses two basic issues. The question of what message literature should transmit has to be preceded by a more basic one connected with the sensitivity of the author to human aspirations and ordeals. Although this sensitivity is a necessary precondition for great writing, it never constitutes a sufficient condition.

Revolutionary literature gains its significance from genuine, realistic treatment of peoples' inner lives, with all their contradictions, predicaments, aspirations, and ordeals. Literature's power to evoke change in our consciousness and to generate dissonance lies in its critical vision of prevailing conditions. Yet in order for it to succeed in moving us, literature has to free itself from abstraction, slogans, and strict partisanship. Originality, skill, genuineness, specificity, concreteness, realism, and justice to every party: these are not just a list of demands. Each component is an integral part of the creative process. The failure of many committed literary works to be both creative and genuine does not condemn commitment as the necessary starting point for great literature. It just means that committed writers must take on greater challenges.

Prerevolutionary Arab novels emerge from the class with which the writer identifies, rather than from the author's class of origin. Although the two are related, what becomes crucial is where the writer stands. Most often those who distrust commitment are ideologically committed in their own explicit or implicit ways to the cause of the ruling class or the bourgeoisie. If all literature is committed to some cause, the question becomes: Are we committed to basic change or to maintenance of the established order?

Prerevolutionary Arab novels evolved from a critical perspective reflected in the works of Khalil Gibran, Jabra, Abdelrahman Munif, Hani ar-Rahib, Jamal al-Gitani, Sinalla Ibrahim, Rashid Boudjedra, Muhammed Bourrada, Elias Khuri, Sahar Khalifa, Haydar Haydar, and myself. The works of such novelists as Abdel Rahman al-Sharqawi, Ghassan Kanafani, Emile Habiby, Hannah Minah, Yusuf Al-Qa'eed, and Tahar Ouettar have a more pronounced political ideology. Another relevant distinction may be made between the prerevolutionary writings of novelists whose societies have undergone revolutions or wars of liberation (Palestine, Algeria) and those of novelists whose societies have not yet been through such an earthshaking historical experience. Writers like Hannah Minah of Syria tend to be revolutionary in an abstract political or ideological sense, failing to address themselves strongly to deeper social issues. The works of Emile Habiby, Ghassan Kanafani, Mohammed Dib, Kateb Yacine, Rashid Boudjedra, Assia Djebar, and Tahar Ouettar depict a more comprehensive revolutionary ethos.

In 1954 the Egyptian writer Abdel Rahman al-Sharqawi published a novel entitled *Al-Ard* (The Earth), which presents a realistic picture of village life in the 1930s. In sharp contrast to *'Awdat ar-ruh* by Al-Hakim, the Egyptian village is portrayed here amidst conflict and struggle. Without the benefit of an ideology, the peasants gradually become aware through combative involvement that their local enemies—the security guards, the *'umda* (mayor), and the *ma'mour* (district magistrate)—represent the feudal lords and the central government; the peasants' profound problems reflect the alliance of local elites with the government and British imperialism. Laws, such as the rules regulating the use of irrigation water in the area, are enacted and enforced not to protect the actual cultivators but to promote the interests of the feudal lords. Government forces attack the peasants, ruin their farms, confiscate their harvests and lands, and imprison them. State representatives humiliate rebels in front of their children, force them to drink the urine of horses, and whip them regularly. The peasants' very source of life is not theirs but belongs to the state. "We are thirsty and the Nile is in our country," they shout desperately.[47] The peasants also discover to their utter dismay that their sheikhs, effendis, and educated relatives are willing to compromise on issues or even sell them out.

In its commitment to realism, *Al-Ard* makes no case for heroism and shows no unwarranted infatuation with its characters. The peasants do try to elevate their conditions and confront their enemies, for "man must always raise his head and believe that it is never impossible to start anew." Yet they are still overwhelmed by their traditional culture, which undermines revolutionary spirit and enhances compliance, nonconfrontation, and divisiveness. They search for solace in jokes and stories of endurance. Even the most rebellious and educated characters in the novel are portrayed as immersed in this traditional culture. For instance, the rebel Suwailim is humiliated when security men shave his moustache, call him a woman, and give him a beating in front of his daughter. By contrast, experience proves to him that "the government could be moved by fear, never by shame."[48] The novel portrays the peasants as highly religious, but hints are given that the clergy are often linked to the centers of power, and that the prevailing religious culture constitutes a counterrevolutionary force.

The realistic approach of the novel demands such a presentation of life in an Egyptian village of that time. This is also the dilemma of another novel of the 1960s about Egyptian village life. In Abdel Hakim Qassem's *Ayyam al-insan as-sab'a* (Man's Seven Days), the persecuted and impoverished peasants are again portrayed as totally immersed in religion, family, and local community.

There is no hint of involvement in the struggle through which people might slowly liberate themselves from tradition.[49]

Another articulate revolutionary vision is depicted in some works by Yusuf Idriss. His village characters of both sexes exhibit nationalist and socialist consciousness, which is gradually raised to higher levels as a result of their involvement in the ongoing struggle. *Al-Haram* (The Sin), first published in 1965, mirrors the complexity of social contradictions inherent in the social class structure of an Egyptian village. His realistic presentation of these social contradictions is accurate, multidimensional, comprehensive. Idriss's vision penetrates far beyond the range of Mahfouz, Al-Hakim, and other prolific Egyptian writers. The struggling groups in the novel include migrant peasants (*al-gharabwa* or *tarahil*), who barely survive at the base of the social pyramid; just above them are the native peasants of the village, who live in poverty but consider themselves a higher order of people. They dissociate themselves from the *gharabwa* and regard them "as human discards, hungry, and forced into migratory labor."[50] The characters of the novel also include the fat middlemen who exploit the peasants and the middle-class representatives of the absentee feudal lords and the government. The pivotal character in *Al-Haram* is a *gharabwa* peasant woman—that is, the lowest of the lowest in this rigidly stratified society. Since she is a weak victim of society, her illegitimate new-born baby will also face scorn and further victimization. She is faced with the reality that there is no escape for people in her position, and her life becomes a brutally slow death. What she does is not her individual responsibility, but a result of the workings of overwhelming social forces.

Peasant women do not escape victimization by moving into the city. The fact that they continue to suffer exposure to rape is revealed most clearly in Idriss's other works, such as *An-Naddaha* (The Clarion) and *Qaʿ al-medina* (The Dregs of the City), one of the most concrete accounts of poverty in Arab literature.[51] The journey of the judge Abdallah from the wealthiest section of Cairo into its poorest neighborhood in search of his servant, a peasant woman whom he accuses of stealing his watch, is not a horizontal journey. Rather, it is an excavation in depth of human torment in the abyss of the city.

Female characters in these works by Idriss are portrayed as passive victims. The image changes in his novel *Qissat hubb* (Love Story), in which Fawzia, a young schoolteacher, is depicted as actively involved in armed struggle. She is able through persistence to change some of the attitudes of her male comrades, who giggle when she first arrives at their training camp. Hamza, her boyfriend, is also transformed. Upon their first encounter, he discovers that deep inside he does not have much confidence in women's fitness to engage in armed struggle in spite of his constant assertion that there is no difference between the sexes. Confronting his inner contradictions is the first step in an agonizing process of self-transformation. He has first to overcome his view of women as sex objects. That is not easy to do in a repressive society. For him, true love cannot occur at first sight; rather, it has to be an enriching existential experience that grows gradually as a result of intimate interaction. Through constant exploration of each other's worlds, Hamza and Fawzia are drawn together into a lasting and compatible relationship.

Fawzia herself has been raised in a liberal family climate. Her father has encouraged her to work, and when people criticize him for this, he responds, "There is no shame in work. In fact, those who work are more decent than those who don't." When he is blamed in addition for allowing her to move to another city and live by herself, he says, "If she cannot protect herself, nobody else can." When relatives object that they have seen Fawzia carried on male shoulders in a student demonstration, he replies, "Go talk to her, I am her father not her master."[52]

The consciousness of some of these characters is raised to higher levels in several other areas as a result of involvement with armed struggle. Through actual experimental encounters, Hamza comes to realize that he can count on the miserable and deprived classes but not on his bourgeois friends for protection from the police. He learns that the poor have withstood fierce battles against British soldiers. Struggle should be sustained out of love for the people and not out of hatred for their enemies. Time is significant and every minute should count.

The novel depicts the peasants and workers in a state of desperate search and struggle for salvation. Young rebels pledge themselves to the cause. Hamza speaks for them when he proclaims: "My private ambitions are precisely the public demands of the people." In spite of bitter failures, he remains optimistic deep inside because of a strong conviction that "it is impossible for millions of Egyptians to remain dispersed in a society closed against its people . . . where poverty is impartially distributed among all."[53]

It is most difficult to discuss one's own works. I have avoided doing so in lectures and class discussions based on drafts of the present chapter, but in each instance students have inquired about the place of my novels in this model of analysis. My evasiveness may be attributable to the difficulty of self-confrontation. Yet I wish to admit that my intentions for Arab society are revolutionary. The basic rationale for my emphasis on radical change and liberation from the myths of the existing order lies in my assumption that the dominant systems, structures, institutions, and cultural orientation of Arab society are essentially opposed to human well-being, that they prevent growth, self-realization, the transcendence of misery, and creative involvement. Instead of being at the center of their own concerns, human beings survive on the fringes of the universe, always calculating the risks of failing. While everything around them is seen as being constantly enlarged, they feel like shrinking into insignificance. Arab society exists in a state of dependency because of the great gap that separates it from the developed world. There is widespread misery owing to a similar gap between the privileged and deprived. The people are powerless because they lack a functioning civil society, and because repressive sociopolitical systems dominate everywhere.

An awareness of these conditions and a commitment to revolutionary change are the main features to be detected in my novels *Sittat ayyam* (translated into English as *Six Days*), *'Awdat at-ta'ir ila al-bahr* (translated into English as *Days of Dust*), *Ar-Rahil baina as-sahm wal-water* (The Voyage), and *Ta'ir al-hawm* (The Ibis). Another distinguishing feature of my novels is an attempt to depict the plight of the disinherited and uprooted (such as the Palestinians).

The main characters in *Sittat ayyam* are given a choice between surrender or struggle in the face of certain destruction and death. They opt for struggle, realizing that they are like a pioneering sailor who must voyage over rough, unfamiliar seas without benefit of a rudder or even a chart. The major characters refuse to accept the prevailing reality and remain committed to struggle until death in hope of profoundly changing the nature of their existence.

The emphasis on the inner torment of individual characters is intended to expose the impact of a repressive society on the human psyche. Personal struggle is a reflection of external struggle and can only be understood as embedded in its social context and in its relationship to the totality of human life. The link between the social and the personal is reflected in my style of writing, which seeks to eliminate the distance between poetry and prose. The depiction of the inner world as a reflection of social reality animates and enriches the treatment as well as contributing to a broader understanding of the problems being depicted. This explains why the hero of *Sittat ayyam* is society itself, symbolized by Dayr al-Bahr (the name of an imaginary town) and embodied in individual characters. The problems of these characters are intricately connected with the plight of their threatened society. In this respect, an attempt is made to eliminate the distinction between symbols and reality. This task may be accomplished by allowing for the spontaneous emergence of symbols from concrete reality, and by freeing reality from temporality and immediate locality. The concrete experience under exploration becomes humanly universal and symbols overcome abstraction. The aim is not to hide feelings and ideas, but to generate new ones beyond even the intentions of the author. This method allows for the creative involvement of the reader in processes of reflection and exploration.[54]

In my novel *Days of Dust*, the major protagonist, Ramzi (which translates as "my symbol"), "wanted to merge with his country, for the two somehow to become one, so that the aspirations throbbing within his country would beat in him as well." [55] Herein lies the reason for my attempts to eliminate space-time obstructions. Experiences become shared. What happens to Abdel-Qadder in Jerusalem is felt by Ramzi in Beirut. The occupation of Palestine is his own occupation, and its destruction becomes his own inner shattering. Distances and temporalities are eliminated or blurred through the sharing of the same existential experiences. Different individual characters experience the same tragic consequences although separated in place and time. Time, space, and inner predicament are blended together to convey total identification with a society facing crisis.

A revolutionary orientation is also reflected in the works of the Palestinian writer Ghassan Kanafani, who never separated his roles as writer and as citizen of a stateless community. By integrating the two roles, he changed the quality of his writing. His destiny was to meet death like a flower about to bloom. Kanafani dedicated his life and writings to the revolutionary task of changing the fate of the Palestinians; he regarded his own personal fate as inseparable from theirs. It was through their plight that he eventually championed the cause of all "underdogs" regardless of sex, nationality, race or ethnicity. His 1963 novella *Rijal fi ash-shams* (*Men in the Sun*) portrays the Palestinians as trapped and threatened with death. Three characters try to wend their way through Kuwait in the belly of a tanker truck. At the border, the driver is delayed and the three Palestinians suffocate to death. [56] As brilliantly pointed out by Edward Said in his introduction to my novel *Days of Dust*, the Palestinian as portrayed in *Rijal fi ash-shams* is impelled by exile and dislocation to "carve a path for himself in existence," uncertain of both his immediate and ultimate fate.

After 1967, a new Palestinian situation emerged, and death took on a different meaning. The Palestinians were no longer resigned to die without struggle or merely to exist in a state of waiting. Instead of passively suffocating to death, they stand on their own feet and die fighting in Jordan, Israel, Lebanon, and Palestine. Now death marks the beginning of the future. One of Kanafani's protagonists, Umm Saad, a poor Palestinian refugee woman, proclaims a fresh start when the resistance movement springs up. "Don't you realize we live in prison?" she asks. "What are we doing in the camp? Prisons are of different sorts. . . . The camp is a prison, your house is a prison, the newspaper is a prison, and the radio is a prison. . . . Our life is a prison and the past twenty years have been a prison." Suddenly it dawns on the Palestinian refugees that instead of shoveling mud in their camps, they should stop the rain. Shoveling the mud is compliance and accommodation to their miserable situation, but stopping the rain is a radical transformation of reality. In sharp contrast to Abdel Jawwad who (in Mahfouz's trilogy) is disturbed to learn that his son has participated in a demonstration in support of Egyptian independence, Umm Saad is very proud that her son joins the resistance movement. Because becoming a commando is the way out of prison, she is delighted to "give births and Palestine takes them away."[57] Thus Umm Saad is socially transformed. Her husband, Abou Saad, is similarly transformed through the involvement of his children in the fight for liberation. He begins to overcome his tendency to lose his temper easily, and improves his relationships with others and consequently with himself. Before the emergence of the resistance movement, he felt crushed under the multiple burdens of poverty, gambling, the ration card, the tin roof, and the government boot. The departure of his children to join the resistance movement means the return of his spirit, and life begins to have taste again. This transformation of the individual and society is at the root of the emergence of Palestinian resistance (1967) and the *intifada* (1987).

The same kind of social transformation is reflected in *Sudasyyiat al-ayyam as-sittat*, a novella by Emile Habiby, who has lived under the Israeli occupation since 1948. Written after 1967, it explores the impact of the reunion of Arabs living under Israeli rule with their relatives and friends who come to visit them from the West Bank, Jordan, Lebanon, and other Arab countries. When Mas'oud encounters his uncle and cousins for the first time in his life, he suddenly feels that he has not been without roots and is not a stranger in this world any more. Similarly, an old woman is changed upon the return of her daughter, and her "smile became so different . . . closest to the traces of waves on a sandy beach in moments of ebb tide." Even the past is redefined in this novel. One of its characters says: "I realize now that the reason for retreating into my shell was to sever relationships with my past. What is the past? It is not time. The past is you, him, her, and all friends . . . our past, which I wish would return like spring after every winter." "Whenever I think of the future I envision the past. . . . The future I think of is the past," another character also says in a different context.[58] The past as envisioned by Palestinians under occupation means the return of their freedom and sense of belonging. The implications are revolutionary. This is a reunion for the purpose of reconstructing reality. That is the essence of revolutionary writing.

This revolutionary essence is depicted most vividly in another novel by Habiby, *The Secret Life of Saeed, the Ill-Fated Pessoptimist*, a sardonic account of a comic anti-hero. The protagonist Saeed represents those powerless and frightened Palestinians who, since 1948, had stayed behind in the state of Israel. Living under alienating and discriminatory conditions, Saeed collaborated with the enemy and named his son Walaa ("loyalty," but also a term for a meowing cat). It takes the events of the war of June 1967 to transform the Palestinian community. Walaa becomes a defiant freedom fighter (*fida'i*) and is joined later by his mother.[59]

This transformation is also reflected in the works of other Palestinian writers, including Mahmoud Darwish, Samih al-Qassim, Sahar Khalifa, and Yhia Yakhlif. Their revolutionary spirit has evolved from the experiences of a whole society undergoing revolutionary change. This is at the root of what distinguishes Palestinian and Algerian literature from that being written in other Arab countries.

The fact that literature is shaped by the experiences of the society in which it is produced prompted Abdelkebir Khatibi to probe the impact of the Algerian revolution on literature, rather than the other way around.[60] To conclude that this is the more important angle to investigate does not minimize the importance of the role of writers as witnesses to the suffering of their own people or of their ability to shape a new consciousness. Some Algerian writers involved themselves in the revolution and produced committed literature. That explains why the year 1956 represents a point of departure in the history of Algerian literature.

Mohammed Dib (1920–) focused on the transformation of the Algerian people from a state of stagnation to one of national awareness through the revolution. His trilogy (The Great Mansion, The Fire, The Looms) depicts the impoverishment of the people prior to the revolution (1954–62).[61] Mother Algeria had to be freed in order for Algerians to regain their humanity.

Another prominent Algerian writer, Kateb Yacine (1929–89), dedicated his writings to revolutionary change and perceived the writer as a fighter. He used the word as a weapon. His novel *Nedjma* (1956), titled after the protagonist, a woman symbolizing Algeria, represents an intense search for a country. Like Algeria, Nedjma is both illegitimate and has had marriage imposed on her, and both defiantly resist fierce attempts at their domestication.

The impact of the Algerian war of independence on social life (particularly on women and female-male relations) is intimately reflected in the novels of Rachid Boudjedra and Assia Djebar (1936–). Djebar's first two novels (*La Soif,* 1957, and *Les Impatients*) deal with romanticized love relationships rather than the war of liberation; the latter gains major prominence in *Les Enfants du nouveau monde* (1962) and *Les Alouettes naïves* (1967). Boudjedra's novels embody themes of social liberation, as exemplified in his novel *La Repudiation.*

Among the first prominent Algerian novelists to write in Arabic was Tahar Ouettar (At-Tahir Wattar). One of his most important works, *Al-Laz (L'As),* depicts class struggle within the ranks of the revolution between the nationalists, representing the national bourgeoisie, and the communists, representing the disinherited. The eventual confrontation results in the defeat of the communists, who suffer the fate of a "burning candle" and of "a fish thrown by a flooding river onto the bank where it struggled and struggled, and then yielded to eventual death."[62]

The revolutionary ethos in the works of Palestinian and Algerian writers tends to be more comprehensive and genuine than in the works of progressive writers whose societies have not actually undergone revolutions or wars of liberation. A case in point is the work of the Syrian novelist Hannah Minah. His progressive political views do not seem to reflect total liberation from traditional outlooks in the realm of social life. Despite exposing social class inequalities and contradictions, the author seems amazingly able to retain some of the most traditional views on women. His traditional social views are matched by a traditional style, as reflected in his ready-made images and highly structured language.

In general, prerevolutionary novels are new in both their political and social conceptions, reflecting a constant struggle to transcend and restructure existing arrangements. Such novels affirm the view that commitment to a message is convincingly compatible with experimentation and creativity. Revolutionary writers are concerned about form, but never for its own sake. In their view, literary form emerges most naturally from a more general vision of social reality. This sort of literature is able to subordinate politics to creative and reflective thinking and can thus undertake the task of promoting new consciousness.

Conclusion

Great literary works resist strict categorization. Because they depict reality in its totality and explore the innermost secrets of human existence, they never completely fit into preconceived models of analysis. They inspire readers, mean different things to different people, encourage reflective thinking, and call for self-confrontation. Yet great writers do have their own unique visions of reality and intend to communicate specific messages to us in their own ways. The complexity and intricacy of their writings cannot be taken as evidence against the existence of definite patterns and orientations in great literary works. It is the job of analysts to unravel such patterns in the light of comprehensive and flexible perspectives.

11   Arab Thought

Problems of Renewal, Modernity, and Transformation

For purposes of discussion we need to place the diverse currents and sources of contemporary Arab thought within a coherent analytical framework. Much more can be discerned through such an analysis than the mere product of the encounter between East and West, or the simple emulation or rejection of European paradigms. We shall see, instead, the results of conflicting intellectual trends as these emerge from the Arab search for an alternative order in the context of Western domination, exploitation, and confrontation.

A brief reference to some of the basic sources of knowledge about contemporary Arab thought may clarify the need for a critical approach. Albert Hourani says contemporary Arab thought began when educated Arabs became aware of the ideas and institutions of modern Europe and felt its power in the nineteenth century. The problem was presented as one of borrowing: what should these intellectuals take from the West to revive their society? And, if they borrowed from the West, how would they maintain their identity? Hourani tries to show how such questions were articulated and answered in the works of seemingly disparate intellectuals.[1] Thus began the debate that is still raging about traditionalism versus modernity, and authenticity (*asala*) and specificity (*khususiyya*) versus Westernization.

Hisham Sharabi has studied Arab intellectuals during the formative years 1875–1914 in the context of Arab society struggling to find its way into the modern world. Not unlike Hourani, Sharabi argues that the rise of intellectuals must be seen as "a manifestation of the process of education and enlightenment brought about by increasing contact with Europe," but he goes beyond Hourani in pointing out that this rise was "associated with [the] transformation of the political power of the aristocratic families and urbanized feudal chiefs, the rise of [a] mercantile class, and the disintegration of Ottoman hegemony with [the] corresponding extension of European domination."[2] Instead of focusing on the works of particular individual intellectuals as Hourani does, Sharabi identifies existing groups and trends, using a typology based mainly on religious affiliation and secular orientations in the context of the division between ruling and dominant social strata and masses. Generally speaking, Sharabi treats Arab intellectuals "as witnesses of the process of change and as participants in the awakening."[3] Sharabi also tries to map the development of what he calls the neopatriarchal discourse from its early stages in the late nineteenth century to the more recent stage in the 1970s and 1980s.[4]

Several other works have examined Arab thought as mainly inspired by Western paradigms and as shaped by a need for modernization. In a 1943 book contributed to by twenty-nine Arab writers, the Lebanese literary critic Ra'if Khuri (1913–67) made a systematic attempt to demonstrate the great liberating impact of European ideas, especially those of the French revolution, on Arab thought.[5] Another set of selections from Arab writings has been put together by Anouar Abdel-Malek; this collection departs somewhat from the approach that treats Arab intellectual developments as derivative. Abdel-Malek points out that Arab thought has its own content and themes and shows two main tendencies. The first of these is Islamic fundamentalism, whose essence is the call for a return to the origin of the faith for the purpose of restoring past glory. The second tendency is liberal modernism, which aims to create a modern society similar to those in the West; this group of thinkers encompasses a whole range of orientations, from conservative liberalism to Marxism.[6] Many analysts have, however, focused on the influence of the West. Issa Boullata has argued that the introspection of Arab intellectuals during the 1970s and 1980s had three pronounced trends. The first was represented by those Arab intellectuals who called for a cultural revolution. The second consisted of those who stressed the need to interpret traditional Arab culture in the light of modern needs and experiences. Their aim has been to seek renewal and reform rather than transformation and radical change. Third, there was the vocal group of Arab intellectuals committed to the religious aspect of Arab culture.[7]

Finally, there is the Moroccan historian Abdallah Laroui, who has consistently called for a historical approach to the study of Arab intellectual life. Laroui's thesis is that the concept of history is peripheral to the major trends in Arab thought in modern times, and particularly to its two main rationales: the *salafi*, or traditional, and the eclectic. Both are ahistorical and signify alienation—through medievalization in case of the former, and through westernization in the case of the latter. The only way out of this crisis is to do away with these two ways of thought and adopt the discipline of historical thought.[8]

This chapter will move beyond the emphases explored in these other analyses. Intellectuals and their ideas will be presented as representatives of conflicting movements and ideologies rather than as separate individuals or affiliates of certain groups. Ideas are not mere commodities to be exchanged or borrowed in encounters between civilizations. As presented here, they are inseparable from social and political movements representing conflicting social forces and interests and aiming at the reconstruction or transformation of the prevailing order. As pointed out by Alaine Touraine, social movements are not merely groups of actors with specific views of their own. Instead, they must be seen as part of the historical context in which they are situated and treated within a coherent analytical framework. [9]

Knowledge is a society's attempt to construct images and models of and for itself. Certainly, it involves individuals who think, but they do so as partners of social and political movements and within society. They do so as participants in movements seeking to maintain, restructure, or transform society through their images of it. Knowledge is always—whether consciously or unconsciously—ideological in essence. In the Arab world, which has been undergoing an intense transition for at least a century and a half, debates have raged about how events and concepts function, evolve, and act on society.

As an ideological debate, Arab thought is marked by an intense awareness of the calamities of the present and the coming of a new era. The decline of the Ottoman Empire and subsequent European domination required that Arab society be activated to regain control of its destiny. Educated Arabs believed they served as crucial actors in a historical movement in which the society had to defend and define itself. Hence, there is the tendency in Arab thought for individuals and ideas to be considered inseparable from social and political action. In this embeddedness lies the promise that Arabs will be able to reacquire their capacity to shape their history. Representing social and political life and seeking to reactivate society, Arab thought has been preoccupied with problems of awakening, renewal, and the establishment of an alternative order.

I therefore argue here that Arab thought can best be understood in the context of ongoing external and internal contradictions and challenges in a highly transitional era. The historical tasks of forging a nation out of conflicting communities, of achieving independence, and of establishing social justice have been central to the ongoing Arab debates. In these debates, the West has been viewed as a challenge, and in most instances as an exploitative and repressive force. So the need to confront the West has coexisted with the emulation of Western models and paradigms.

Analyzing Arab thought as a series of intense debates among intellectuals representing opposing movements makes it clear that there were specific periods during which these intellectuals were aware of one another's views and argued with them from their own perspectives. [10] Observers and historians of the development of Arab thought have attempted to delineate the phases, periods, and stages of this development. In this section, Arab thought will be examined in three periods since the modern Arab awakening: the formative phase from the 1850s to World War I; the period of nationalist struggle for independence between the two world wars; and the independence and postindependence periods.

Arab Thought in the Formative Period (1850–1914)

Contemporary Arab thought emerged in a transitional period shaped by the gradual decline of the Ottoman Empire and the invasion and domination of Arab countries by European powers. The ensuing debate between intellectuals representing different segments and classes of society focused on issues of national identity and renewal in response to these new challenges. Some concerned the reasons for the weakness or "sickness" of the East and the required remedy; the sources of European strength and prosperity; the nature of the conflict between the East and the West; and the grievances of people under oppression. Other issues involved national identity and the redefinition of the concept of the *umma*; reform through science or religion; the awakening and struggle for achievement of the *nahda* (renaissance); new directions for the future; the inhibiting nature of tradition; and which Western innovations could be adopted without compromising religion and value orientations. Gradually, distinctive voices began to emerge. These voices reflected deep divisions, contributing to the development of three major contending movements: the religious, or *salafiyya*, movement; the modernizing liberal movement; and the progressive, or radical, movement. Representatives of these opposing movements continued to debate issues throughout the three periods outlined above. It is necessary to focus on each period separately to capture the nuances of the debates and the variations in questions and competing forces.

Religious Trends: Traditionalists versus Reformists. The dominant voice in the debate during the formative period was that of the religious thinkers who continued to adhere to the notions of an Islamic caliphate. Early on, however, there were intense divisions between traditionalists and reformers within the circle of Islamic thinkers. The former group consisted mostly of the *'ulama* serving as officials and advisors to the sultan and feudal families. They had their own privileges, functioning within the framework of the bureaucracy in accordance with the instructions of Ottoman authorities. They were the establishment thinkers and had their own sect-based courts and school systems. In terms of the sociology of religion, these traditionalists used Islam as a mechanism of control, expressing their views in assertive rather than analytical terms as political weapons of repression. We might see Abul-Huda al-Sayyadi (d. 1900?) as representative of traditionalists during this period. An Arab from Aleppo province, Al-Sayyadi served as chief advisor to Sultan Abdul Hamid.

In this capacity, he denounced and persecuted such prominent reformers as Al-Afghani, Abdu, and Al-Kawakibi.

Muslim reformers took a different approach. Together, these intellectuals pioneered the *salafiyya* movement for the rejuvenation of the Islamic caliphate through a return to the original sources and the purity of early Islam. They opposed the Western invasion but expressed their appreciation of Western scientific and cultural achievements. The most prominent representatives of this reform movement were Jamal Eddin al-Afghani, Muhammad Abdu, and Rashid Rida. They were preceded, however, by pioneering liberal intellectuals, whose writings and activism prepared the way for the rise of both the Muslim reform and liberal movements.

The first of these pioneering intellectuals and activists was Rif't al-Tahtawi (1801–73), whose affinity with Islamic thought did not prevent him from articulating nationalist ideas and propagating many of the notions of the Enlightenment. In fact, he was inclined to welcome rather than to oppose the West and to emphasize Egyptian nationalism rather than the Islamic caliphate. Another pioneering intellectual and statesman was Khayr Eddin al-Tunisi (1810–99), who balanced his loyalty to the Islamic caliphate and opposition to the West with his realization of the need for Western-inspired reform. Casting himself as a modern Ibn Khaldun, he published a book entitled *Aqwam al-masalik fi-ma'rifat ahwal al-mamalik* (The Straightest Road to Knowing the Conditions of States) in 1867, in which he tried to impress on contemporary Muslim rulers and elites the urgent need for modernization. Based on the principle of *maslaha*, or self-interest, he argued that whatever was conducive to the welfare and strength of the Islamic *umma*—such as the expansion of science and learning—should be adopted from Europe. He warned Muslims against their tendency to close their eyes to what is praiseworthy in other civilizations. As a statesman who served as minister and prime minister in Tunis and Istanbul, he argued that the power of the ruler should be limited by revealed or rational law (*shari'a* and *qanum 'aqli*) and by consultation (*mushawara*) with the *'ulama* and notables (*a'yan*).

Perhaps the most prominent and controversial of the Islamic reformers was Jamal Eddin al-Afghani (1839–97), who appealed to Muslims to unite and reform Islam both as a religion and as a civilization in order to confront the common danger posed by Europe. An activist and eloquent orator, he was forced into exile and attacked by his enemy, Sheikh Abul-Huda al-Sayyadi, who called him "Al-Mutaafghin"—accusing Al-Afghani of claiming to be an Afghan when he was in reality a Persian, the implication being that he was a Shi'ite. Based on his premise that the Muslim community was sick and needed a remedy, Al-Afghani proposed two seemingly contradictory courses of action: a return to the original sources of Islam and the adoption of liberal European ideas and institutions, including Western sciences, constitutional rule, communal unity, elections, and national representation. His agitation in support of these courses of action is considered to be more significant than his few writings. Indeed, he staged confrontations with the khedive (viceroy) of Egypt, Tawfiq, with the czar of Russia, and with Shah Nasir al-Din of Iran. "I want all that is good for the Egyptians," Tawfiq is said to have told him. "But, unfortunately, most of the people are lazy and ignorant." Al-Afghani replied: "Allow me, Your Highness, to say with freedom and sincerity that the Egyptian nation, like all other nations, has among its members the lazy and the ignorant, but it is not totally destitute of the learned and the wise. As you consider the Egyptian nation and individuals, so do they consider your Highness. If you accept the advice of a sincere man like myself and hasten to let the nation . . . partake in ruling the country . . . by arranging for the election of national representatives . . . this procedure will add more stability to your throne."[11] His approach was not always combative, however. Al-Afghani served as an advisor to many rulers, mediated between the Sudanese Mahdi and the British, and died an esteemed man at the court of Sultan Abdul Hamid.

In 1894, with Muhammad Abdu, Al-Afghani edited the journal *Al-'Urwah al-wuthqah* in Paris (eighteen issues in all appeared) and published a work entitled *Al-Radd 'ala al-dahriyyin* (Refutation of the Materialists) in response to Ernest Renan's Sorbonne lecture "L'Islamisme et la science" (1883). In this work Al-Afghani attacked materialists like Darwin for endangering the truth, human society, and its well-being. Controversy continues to surround Al-Afghani and much of it has been generated by the obscurity of his origins.[12] Nevertheless, the controversy has never seemed to diminish his immense influence.

Another influential reformer in Egypt and the rest of the Arab world was the Egyptian Muhammad Abdu (1849–1905), who began as a rebel and ended as a partner in authority before the age of forty. Exiled for most of the 1880s because of his support for the 1882 Arab revolt, he became an associate and student of Al-Afghani's. The khedive allowed his return to Egypt in 1888, and in 1889, he became the Grand Mufti of Egypt and assumed control of the religious establishment. He also established good relations with Lord Cromer, the British consul general, and dedicated himself to the task of formulating an enlighted interpretation of Islam. His call for a return to the original sources of Islam was matched only by his ardent insistence on the need to adapt to the requirements of modern life. The tasks he set himself included liberating Islamic thought from the shackles of tradition by returning to the sources of Islam, reforming the system of Islamic law, and modernizing religious education. His emphasis on education rather than politics led him to criticize Al-Afghani; instead "of meddling in the intrigues of the palace at Constantinople, he [Al-Afghani] should have tried to persuade the sultan to reform the system of education," Abdu said. [13]

From the same perspective, Abdu attacked radical and progressive thought. A controversial exchange of views resulted between him and Farah Antun concerning the latter's progressive interpretation of the classical Arab philosopher Ibn Rushd. In this exchange, Abdu insisted that religious authority derived its rule from God and that "civil authority in Islam is linked to religious authority in accordance with the shari'a because the general ruler is both a ruler and a caliph." [14]

The third member of this trio of Muslim reformers was Muhammed Rashid Rida (1865–1935). Arriving in Egypt in 1898 as a refugee from "Bilad al-Sham" (Tripoli, Syria) in the company of Farah Antun, Rida founded the magazine *Al-Manar* (Lighthouse) as the mouthpiece of the Islamic reform movement. He called for Islamic and Arab unity within the framework of a restored caliphate that would incorporate a constitution to restrict the authority of rulers and end tyranny. Following the restoration of the Turkish constitution in 1908, Rida preached Arab unity with the Turks and "religious brotherhood." He warned that encouraging Arab discord and dissension would be harmful to the Arabs because "we are in utmost need for unity with Turks and loyalty to them because of common interests. But we need them more than they need us, and whoever seeks to separate us is an enemy of us and them." [15] Rida's enthusiasm was rooted in his strong belief that Islam, if correctly interpreted, would provide the only adequate solution to modern social, political, and religious problems. [16] This appeal expressed a central argument of Muslim reformers; it has continued beyond the formative period up to the present. It attempts to reconcile the old and the new rather than to transcend the old and achieve an alternative liberal or progressive order.

The Liberal Trend. While an Islamic reform perspective was being articulated in defense of the vanishing Ottoman religious system, an alternative idea was being formulated based on a new vision of society and new sources of values and authority. During the second half of the nineteenth century, a distinctive liberal and nationalist movement emerged. In contrast to the religious movement, it opted, hesitantly in certain instances, to replace the Islamic *umma* with a nationalist *umma*, and hence to replace theocracy with secularism, and a backward-looking orientation with a future-looking one. The rise of this movement cannot be totally explained in terms of the encounter with the West and the adoption of European ideas. Some internal developments and transformations within the Ottoman Empire contributed to the emergence of this new movement. These included decentralization, the appearance of local and regional autonomous ruling families (such as that of Muhammad Ali in Egypt), the spread of education, the revival of ethnicity and classical Arab culture, the intensification of the region's integration into the European economic system, and the rise of the middle class.

The liberal trend was represented during this formative period by a group of pioneers of modernity in direct or indirect opposition to the *salafiyya* movement. These included Rif't al-Tahtawi, Ahmed Faris al-Shidiaq (1804–87), Butrus al-Bustani (1819–83), Yacoub Sarrouf (1852–1927), Qassem Amin (1863–1908), Sudqi al-Zahawi (1863–1936), Ahmed Lutfi al-Sayyid (1872–1936), and several others. Al-Tahtawi was closer overall to the liberal trend than to the religious one, as indicated by his systematic attempt to articulate new allegiances based on Egyptian nationalism and Enlightenment ideas. He certainly resorted to explanations of his modern views cast in the terms of Islamic thought, but the European ideas he had learned during his visit to France between 1826 and 1831 left a permanent mark on his thinking. This is clearly evident in his most famous work, *Takhlis al-ibriz fi talkhis Bariz* (The Purification of Gold and the Summary of Paris), in which he reveals his special interest in the French constitution and political system, including the concept of equality before the law regardless of creed and rank. For Al-Tahtawi, "the contrast between Muslim decline and Europe's ascendancy lacked the menacing aspect it would later have for Afghani," Sharabi observes. "To Tahtawi, Europe appeared as less of a threat than a promise." [17] This positive attitude is explained by Albert Hourani as being because Al-Tahtawi "lived and worked in a happy interlude of history, when the religious tension between Islam and Christendom was being relaxed and had not yet been replaced by the new political tension of East and West." [18] Still, Al-Tahtawi lived in France at the time of the occupation of Algiers and wrote about it in his book on Paris.

Al-Tahtawi's liberalism is also revealed in his call for Egyptan nationalism as an alternative to the religious *umma*. He came to believe that national brotherhood is most binding on members of the same *watan* (homeland), "for there is a national brotherhood between them over and above the brotherhood in religion. There is a moral obligation on those who share the same *watan* to work together to improve it and to perfect its organization in all that concerns its honour and greatness and wealth." [19]

Butrus al-Bustani, writing after the Lebanese civil war of 1860, went beyond this concept of *watan* to call for replacement of sectarianism with nationalism. In support of this idea, he dedicated himself to the revival of knowledge and the Arabic language. He was the author of an Arabic dictionary, *Al-Muhit*, and an Arabic encyclopedia, *Da'irat al-ma'arif*. He founded his own school on national, not religious, principles. Al-Madrassa al-wataniyya (the National School) withstood the pressures of the Syrian Protestant College, known later as the American University of Beirut, and published *Nafir Surriyya* and other periodicals. [20] In each of the eleven numbers of *Nafir Surriyya*, there was an address to his "fellow countrymen" (*abna' al-watan*) signed by "him who loves the homeland" (*muhibb al-watan*). The stress on nationalism in each of these eleven issues earned this broadsheet a reputation as "the first important document of nationalist thought in the history of the modern Near East." In one of those issues, Al-Bustani pleaded the cause of secularism, stating, "As long as our people do not distinguish between religion, which ought to be a relationship between the believer and his creator, and civilizations, which represent relationships between fellow citizens and government . . . and do not draw a dividing line between these two contrasting principles . . . it is not [to be] expected they will succeed in either or both of them together." Al-Bustani was also noted for his appeals for the education of women, the incorporation of the sciences into education, and the use of the Arabic language as a medium of instruction, so that "Syria would not become the Babel of languages as it is the Babel of religions." [21]

It is possible to criticize the tendency of liberal intellectuals like Al-Bustani, Yacoub Sarrouf, Nimr Faris, and Jurji Zaydan to borrow liberal ideas from Europe, but it should be pointed out that they were not eclectic and indiscriminate in what they borrowed. On the contrary, they accepted some concepts and principles on their merits and forged them together, shaped by a nationalist point of view opposed to the West. Their stress on nationalism, secularism, and scientific thinking should be seen as indigenous, rooted in the desire of the eastern Arab world, especially Syria, to free itself from oppressive Ottoman rule and overcome social and political fragmentation. They contributed to the revival of the Arabic language and literature and worked for unity while the West worked at fragmentation of the Arab world.

Yacoub Sarrouf and Nimr Faris started their intellectual careers at the Syrian Protestant College (American University of Beirut). Their appointments were terminated by the board of managers of the college; according to a subsequent president of the AUB, "Although they were young men of outstanding ability they were dropped for some mysterious reason, probably because of being connected with one of the secret societies which were beginning to ferment Arab nationalism." [22] After their termination, Sarrouf and Faris published two fighting articles in their magazine *Al-Muqtataf*. The first of these, published in the May 1885 issue, was entitled "Learning and Universities" and argued that knowledge could not be achieved by any university unless it "rids itself of religious fanaticism." They expressed their disappointment that their college had turned away from the purpose of spreading learning and sought to impose a particular creed on its pupils. They also expressed their disappointment that the university had abandoned the goal of teaching in Arabic. [23] The second article was critical of the AUB for teaching in English rather than Arabic and for limiting the number and advancement of Arab teachers in order to keep the college "American root and branch."[24] Similarly, Jurji Zaydan accused the AUB board of managers of "racial prejudice and disrespect for Arabs as they considered it too much for Arabs to complain against American professors."[25] Al-Bustani ended an arrangement whereby the AUB used his private school, Al-Madrassa al-wataniyya, for college preparation work because he insisted on keeping the school openly nonsectarian and arranged for his students to attend the religious services of their parents.[26]

These few references to early conflicts with Western educators are intended to illustrate the point that these liberal intellectuals did not adopt nationalism and secularism imitatively but as a result of their desire to meet Arab needs. They identified with Arab culture and sought to contribute to its revival. By seeking refuge in Egypt, many of these Syrian liberal nationalists contributed to the spread of the Arab enlightenment movement and the intellectual convergence of Syria and Egypt. This left its permanent imprint on Arab culture and enabled it to continue to confront the traditional and reformist as well as the conciliatory and apologetic religious movements.

In opposition to the various religious movements, Qassem Amin (1863–1908) championed the cause of women's liberation. He wrote two books on the subject: *Tahrir al-mar'a* (The Liberation of Women) in 1899, and *Al-Mar'a al-jadida* (The New Woman) two years later. In his first book, Amin based his defense of women's rights on the reconciliation of religious and modern ideas. In his second book, however, Amin based his arguments on ideas derived from the modern social sciences, including the liberal concepts of individual freedom and the rights of free expression and belief. He also went a step further to link the decline of the status of woman to the decline of the society as a whole, and to see the oppression of women as one of several oppressive forms. In Eastern societies, he pointed out, "You will find woman enslaved to man, and man to the ruler. Man is an oppressor in his home, oppressed as soon as he leaves it."[27] In reaching this conclusion, Qassem Amin reflected the influences of radical intellectuals like Shibli Shumayyil, thus extending his thinking beyond the realm of the liberal into the realm of the radical.

The Progressive Radical Trend. The progressive radical movement was distinctive for its stress on nationalism, secularism (which it shared with the liberal movement), and socialism. In some instances, there were clear attempts to articulate a historical materialist interpretation. Representative of this movement during the formative period were Abd al-Rahman al-Kawakibi (1849–1902), Shibli Shumayyil (1850–1917), and Farah Antun (1874–1922).

Al-Kawakibi was perhaps the first Arab intellectual in modern times to theorize about democratic, secular, and socialist Arabism as an alternative to the Ottoman caliphate. He described the dominant order he wanted to destroy as despotic, absolutist, fatalistic, sectarian, exploitative, and traditional. He used even harsher terms as well—such as enslavement by illusions, fanaticism, ignorance, hypocrisy, and backwardness. The alternative order he envisioned would be based on the principles of Arab nationalism, secularism, democracy, socialism, scientific thinking, and tolerance. Al-Kawakibi was one of the first to provide a systematic view of Arabism based on culture and geography. In accordance with this view, he maintained that "nationalist ties are above every other tie." Based on what he called Turkish hatred of Arabs as reflected in their cultural discourse, he posed Arab unity as an alternative to the Ottoman caliphate and called for the separation of religion and the state. "Let us run our earthly lives and let religion rule in the other life only," he said, appealing to both Muslim and non-Muslim Arabs. [28]

It can be argued, based on his book *Umm al-qura* (The Mother of Villages), that Al-Kawakibi's main purpose, curiously, was to return the caliphate to the Arabs and establish their primacy within the Islamic *umma*. In fact, he lists several reasons why there should be a shift in the balance of power in the *umma* from Turks back to Arabs. Yet he was clear in his call for the separation of temporal political authority from religious authority. In support of his appeal to Muslim and non-Muslim Arabs, he argued for a separation between the management of religion and the management of the state, warning against the negative consequences of mixing the two. He even accused religious tradition-alists of attempting "to reinforce their authority over the simple-minded believers" by using religion as "an instrument of disunity" for the purpose of spreading the "spirit of submissiveness and compliance." [29]

Another issue for Al-Kawakibi was liberation from despotism. He clearly and systematically develops this argument in his book *Taba'i' al-istibdad* (The Nature of Despotism). As he defines it, despotism, *istibdad,* "means autocratic rule according to the ruler's own whims and inclinations." It also means "the despotism of governments," the "arbitrariness of some heads of religion, families, and classes," and "the disposal by some individuals of a whole group of people's rights without fear of the consequences or respecting any law, whether divine or human." Al-Kawakibi also examines in great detail how despotism distorts religion, knowledge, and education. Finally, he came to embrace socialism as a philosophy and a system for achieving equality and social justice. He argued that socialism freed the great majority of people from the grip of poverty, and liberated society from "social despotism protected by the citadels of political despotism." [30] He condemned the "unjust division of labor" and "the monopoly of the country's wealth by the few . . . political and religious elites and their associates," who, he said, totaled less than 5 percent of the population:

> The poor do not seek help from the rich nor charity; what they seek
> is justice. . . . Money is the value of labor and it accumulates in the

hands of the rich only through coercion and deception. Justice requires that a portion of the money of the rich be returned to the poor so as to achieve balance without undermining the desire for work. This formula is sought by . . . organized societies which . . . demand that land, stable properties and the machines of factories . . . be shared communally among all the people of the nation. . . . This socialist livelihood is the ultimate of what the mind envisions.[31]

Another representative of the progressive and radical movement during the formative period was Shibli Shumayyil, who is considered the first Arab intellectual to expound and articulate socialism as an ideology and program by following a scientific materialist approach. In his view, society could be revived not through religion but through science, which liberates humanity from ignorance and fanaticism. He viewed religion as an element of divisiveness, a product of primitive and superficial feelings and illusions and not of an advanced mind. Yet Shumayyil defended Islam in response to harsh criticism of it by Lord Cromer. From a socialist and secular perspective, Shumayyil accepted the nationalist idea, but he warned that narrow-minded definitions of nationalism might prove as divisive as the religious idea nationalism was supposed to replace. Shumayyil "was not simply trying to replace religious by national solidarity," Hourani observes. "All types of exclusive solidarity, he argued, had the same danger as religious, because they divided human society. National fanaticism was as bad as religious, and sooner or later loyalty to the limited watan must give way to the wataniyya of the world."[32]

Many of the abovementioned concepts were also being promoted around the same period by Farah Antun, whose openly progressive views put him in conflict with various groups, governments, and other intellectuals, including his old friends Muhammad Abdu and Rashid Rida. In 1896, Farah Antun founded the journal *Al-Jami'a* in Beirut, but he was obliged to flee to Egypt, where he reestablished it between 1899 and 1905. Exposed to persecution and censorship because of his strong criticism of British imperialism, he escaped once again to New York, where he resumed publication of *Al-Jami'a* between 1906 and 1908. Soon afterward, Antun returned to Cairo and reentered its debates. He published several works in defense of science and socialism (which he considered to be "the religion of humanity") and attempted to acquaint Arabs with key Western thinkers, including Marx, Nietzsche, and Tolstoy.

Antun published a detailed study of the life and philosophy of Ibn Rushd (Averroës). Influenced by Renan, he expounded his views on the conflict between faith and reason or religion and science, and on secularism in the context of national unity and mutual respect between religions. In his ensuing debate with Muhammad Abdu, Antun listed, among the reasons for the adoption of secularism, the contradiction between religious and political aims and functions, the desire for the equality of all citizens regardless of creed or belief, the unity of the *umma*, the changing conditions that make it impossible to manage the present by reference to the past, sectarian conflicts within the same religion, and the weakening of religion itself.

Antun also published several philosophical novels to convey his ideas and visions for the *umma*. His first novel, entitled *Ad-Din wal-'ilm wal-mal* (Religion, Science, and Money), published in 1903, depicts social contradictions and class conflict through lengthy debates, with speeches from representatives of workers, capitalists, clerics, and scholars. For example, the representative of the workers complains that "they serve capitalists as slaves serve their master" and calls on the reader to "listen to the opinion of the philosopher Karl Marx . . . the factories, the business, and the lands of the nation . . . should not belong to an individual, whoever he is, but to the nation as a whole." [33]

Of the three orientations explored in this first phase, the religious movement continued to prevail during this period. However, the collapse of the Ottoman Empire as a result of World War I, and the subsequent European fragmentation of the Arab world into artificial political entities and domination over it, created the necessary conditions for the rise of new forces of nationalism. What followed was the dominance of nationalist liberal thought in confrontation with, rather than in imitation of, the West.

Arab Thought and the Struggle for National Independence (1918–1945)

Arab thought in the first, formative period occupied itself mainly with the problems of revival. In the aftermath of the war, the issue became one of mobilization to confront European domination. Instead of gaining their independence and establishing a new nationalist order, Arabs found to their dismay that they faced a fierce European colonization bent on dismantling the society of the region. Forced to rethink their new situation, they had to mobilize whatever forces they could muster to confront the European assault. Among other results, this led to the rise of ideologies and political movements, in contrast to the cultural organizations that had marked the previous period. Nationalists took the lead in forming political parties. These included the Wafd party in Egypt, the League of National Action (the ideological parent of the Ba'th) and the Syrian Social Nationalist party in Syria, the Al-Ahali party in Iraq, and the Destour party and the Independence party in the Maghrib. Similarly, during this period communist parties were formed in several Arab countries. The Muslim Brotherhood movement was also formed at this time. Most of these parties emerged out of, or addressed themselves to, the middle classes and people in general rather than the elite as such. The dominance of nationalist ideas during this period must be explained in terms of the imperialist oppression that befell Arabs and not in terms of the emulation of European models.

Taken together, these developments—the formation of political parties, the expansion of popular involvement, and the dominance of the nationalist idea—represented a step forward in bridging the gap between intellectual debate and activism in support of liberation. Debate over issues pertaining to the meanings of nation and nationalism (*umma, qawmiyya, wataniyya*) was inseparable from the struggle to achieve independence and to build a new order. The collapse of the Ottoman Empire had encouraged some members of the elite to contemplate the possibility of reviving the Islamic caliphate by shifting its center to Arabia or Egypt. The great majority of Arabs, however, became convinced that given the prevailing conditions, this scheme was illusory. Reflecting this judgment, two critical works appeared at this time challenging this and other religion-based conceptualizations.

In 1925 'Ali 'Abd al-Raziq of Egypt (1888–1966) published a controversial book entitled *Al-Islam wa usul al-hikm* (Islam and the Bases of Authority), in which he argued as a *shaykh* of Al-Azhar University in Cairo, the world center of Islamic studies, that Islam did not impose a political order or form of government on Muslims. The caliphate, based on the incorrect belief that Muslim rulers since Abu Bakr, the first caliph, were the temporal representatives of God's Prophet, Muhammad, was nevertheless a political rather than a religious order. It had been in the interest of various rulers and sultans to propagate this error among the believers. In the name of religion, they had tyrannized over their subjects, imposing on them a narrow understanding of religion, and restricting their critical judgment and all free enquiry concerning the most suitable political system. There is nothing in Islam, Razik said, that forbids Muslims to overthrow a system of government that has humiliated them ever since they adopted it. Muslims are free to establish rules of government in keeping with the achievements of the human spirit. These views were vehemently rejected by the religious establishment embodied in Al-Azhar, and Abdel Razik was expelled from its ranks and persecuted for the remainder of his life.

The second controversial book, *Fi al-shi'r al-jahily* (On Pre-Islamic Poetry), published in 1926, was authored by the prominent literary and educational figure Taha Hussein (1889–1973). In the context of the battle between the old and the new, Hussein questioned the authenticity of the pre-Islamic poetry that, along with religious texts, had shaped Arab cultural thinking. In his criticism of this literary legacy, Hussein propagated principles of reason and skepticism in contrast to the doctrine of faith (which accepts whatever is transmitted without qualification). Based on the scientific principles of scrutiny and doubt, Hussein concluded that a significant majority of "pre-Isamic poems" had actually been composed after the appearance of Islam.[34]

In the same vein, ten years later, Taha Hussein published yet another controversial book, *Mustaqbal al-thaqafa fi Misr* (The Future of Culture in Egypt), in which he concluded that Egypt was culturally affiliated with Western rather than Eastern civilization. So when Khedive Isma'il (1863–79) had pronounced Egypt a part of Europe, he was not boasting but merely stating a fact. "It is meaningless to waste time to prove [the khedive's pronouncement], to cite evidence in support of its validity. People completed [this task] a long time ago," Hussein asserted, counter to his own principle of skepticism. "We must follow the path of the Europeans so as to be their equals and partners in civilization—in its good and evil, its sweetness and bitterness, what can be loved or hated, what can be praised or blamed."[35]

Another proponent of nationalism and modernization was Ahmed Lutfi al-Sayyid (1872–1963), who greatly influenced the Wafd party and its intellectuals, including Taha Hussein and Mahmoud Abbas al-'Aqqad (up to 1936). In a critique of traditionalism, al-Sayyid asserted that "man needs freedom no less than the soul needs a body." He defended those writers such as Taha Hussein who were accused of copying their European masters, and noted that "these Egyptian writers have set out to explicate the feelings and hopes they see beating in the hearts of our people. Even if you deny us everything else, you cannot take away the fact that we are human beings, that we too thirst for liberty and hope one day to recover a fitting place in the concert of nations; in any case, no nation has a higher claim to be called civilized than the Egyptian nation."[36]

In the Fertile Crescent, nationalists were less concerned with defining the place of their countries within world civilizations. Of utmost interest for them was the advancement of the nationalist idea in their communally divided societies. Amin Rihani (1876–1940) saw the predicament of the nation caused by a sectarian political system and European imperialism. In a collection of his "nationalist writings" (*Al-Qawmiat*), he characterized himself as "Syrian first, Lebanese second, Maronite third . . . respecting the source of my Arab language . . . I am [a] Syrian who . . . wishes to see a constitutional decentralized government in Syria whose pillar is nationalist geographical unity . . . I am [a] Syrian Lebanese who believes in the separation of religion from politics because I realize that the obstacle to national unity is religious partisanship."[37] He put Arabism (Al-'Uruba) first, before Islam and Christianity: "Al-'Uruba is before anything else and above everything else. . . . Each of our sects is a homeland on its own. Sunnism and Shi'ism in Iraq, Maronitism and its sisters in Lebanon, Al-Wahabiyya in Najd, and Zaydia in Yemen; they are all one and of the same sort in this respect. They all place their interests over and above the greater national interest. . . . Hence, my call for replacement of the sectarian idea with the nationalist idea." [38] Following World War I, Rihani warned against the partition of Syria as follows:

> There are two groups, in fact two parties, in our midst. One party drew a narrow circle around itself and said: This is our country; this is our circle, and whoever does not belong to our sect falls outside the circle. Another party drew a broader circle around the narrower one and said: This is our country; this is our circle that surrounds yours and protects it. . . . The first circle is Lebanon, and the second is Syria. The first is a symbol of the principle of the Lebanese awakening, and the second is the symbol of the principle of Syrian unity. . . . The first principle is based on the sectarian idea . . . whereas the second principle is based on the correct social idea that weak people cannot survive and prosper except through unity. . . . That is why we say that the Lebanese idea, in fact the national sectarian idea, is an old and impotent idea. If we adopt it, it will be a devastating blow to us. It was at the root of our defeat and misery in the past, and will be, if it prevails, the reason for our misery in the future. . . . What a narrow conception of Lebanon! [39]

Antun Saada (1904–1949) was born in Mount Lebanon and founded the Syrian Social Nationalist party in 1932. He is the author of *Nushu' al-umam* (The Evolution of Nations), in which he tries to define the concepts of nation (*umma*) and nationalism (*qawmiyya*) and to argue the case for Syrian unity. In other works, he addresses himself to the basic questions that must be answered to provide Syrian society with a new vision of and for itself. Saada called for liberation from all communal loyalties in favor of nationalist loyalty. He also argued that internal and external contradictions could be resolved only through secularism and the elimination of feudalism and "free individualistic capitalism," which contributed to "the formation of two oppressed classes: the spiritually crushed middle class and the materialistically crushed lower class." [40]

The views of the pan-Arab nationalist movement at this stage were expressed by Constantine Zurayk, who published a collection of articles entitled *Al-Wa'i al-qawmi* (The Nationalist Consciousness) in 1939, and by Sati' al-Husseri. Nationalist thought superseded both Islamic and socialist thought during this period, but both of the latter trends continued to be actively involved in the debate.

Hassan al-Banna (1906–49) founded the Muslim Brotherhood movement in 1928, carrying to the emerging middle classes the message of a need to return to the wellsprings of Islam. Restoration of the power and glory of Islam would make possible the reestablishment of a Muslim state and adherence to Islamic law. Al-Banna proclaimed the Qur'an to be the book of God, and

Islam to be a general law regulating the order of this world and the next. He believed that the reason for Muslim backwardness was estrangement from religion, and that the basis for reform should therefore be a return to the precepts of Islam and the revival of the power and glory of Islam.

At the time that Taha Hussein was pronouncing Egypt to be part of Europe, the Maghrib was engaged in a battle to assert its Arab-Islamic character against fierce French attempts to crush it. A key intellectual figure in this struggle was Abdul Hamid Ben Badis (1889–1940), leader of the Association of Algerian Muslim Scholars, whose motto was: "Islam is our religion, Arabic is our language, and Algeria is our homeland." He embraced the precepts of the *salafiyya* movement in calling for a return to the source of Islam, but he insisted on distinguishing between "subjective" Islam (that is, the Islam based on tradition, search, and contemplation), and the "inherited" Islam (that is, the Islam based on tradition and stagnation).

The Maghrib also had its liberal and progressive movements. In Algeria, there was the secular nationalist movement Najm Shamal Afriqia (The Star of North Africa), originally based among Algerian workers in France. Similarly, there emerged in Tunisia a trade unionist movement deeply embedded in a more comprehensive struggle for Tunisian and Arab national renaissance. A key figure in this movement was Al-Taher al-Haddad (1899–1935), an active militant in the Destour party from the time of its formation in 1920 and the author of a book entitled *Al-'Ummal al-tunisiyyoun wa dhuhur al-haraka al-naqabiyya* (Tunisian Workers and the Appearance of the Unionist Movement). He was also a pioneer of political democracy and the emancipation of women. As a nationalist and social reformer, he addressed himself to all Tunisians regardless of their class differences. Given the situation of Tunisia then and the struggle for independence, he advised against class struggle and called for unity between workers and nationalists.

Perhaps the most renowned socialist thinker at this time was Salama Musa of Egypt (1887–1958), who produced an extensive body of writings on socialism, political democracy, evolutionary theory, Egyptian nationalism, literature, and secularism. Being more a reformer and a modernist along Western lines, he preached a mild form of Fabian-style socialism and rejected Bolshevism and economic interpretations of history. He also condemned Arab and Muslim tradition as backward and called for the adoption of Western civilization in its totality, stating that although the sun rises in the East, the light comes from the West.[41] At the core of his theory of secular socialism is humanism in the tradition of Tolstoy and, among others, Voltaire, Bacon, G. B. Shaw, H. G. Wells, Karl Marx, Goethe, Darwin, and Nietzsche.

These were the major trends of thought that prevailed during the period of national struggle for independence between the two world wars. They should be viewed both as a continuation of the trends in the formative period and as a prelude to what followed in the independence and postindependence periods.

Independence and Postindependence, 1945–1992: Researching the Roots of Disaster

If the first period can be characterized essentially by its spirit of revival, and the second period by mobilization and national struggle, the independence and postindependence era has been distinguished by a search for the meanings and causes of the failure of Arabs to confront the challenges facing them. This period can be divided into an independence phase (1945–67) and a postindependence phase (from 1967 on). The first phase was characterized by the emergence of a secular nationalist movement and culminated in the devastating defeat of the 1967 Arab-Israeli war. In the aftermath of this war, a second phase was fueled by the great hopes prompted by the Palestinian resistance movement as a spearhead for Arab revolution. Gradually, however, the Palestinian movement changed into an organization and simply became part of the larger Arab system. The Gulf War, which led to the defeat and destruction of Iraq in early 1991, was an even more traumatic shock for Arabs. Throughout this period, Arab thought has been preoccupied with searching for the cause of this enduring crisis. Arab aspirations for national unity, social justice, democracy, comprehensive development, and genuine independence have been shattered. A situation closer to stagnation than to rejuvenation has continued to prevail.

Following World War II, Arab hopes were dashed by the destruction of Palestinian society and the establishment of Israel. Soon afterward, however, the 1952 Egyptian revolution revitalized the Arab world and generated new hopes among the masses. Moved by a new nationalist surge, Arabs regained a sense of pride and projected an optimistic view of the future. Besides challenging Western imperialism and Zionism, attempts were made to reconcile nationalism, secularism, and socialism. The nationalization of the Suez canal and the subsequent resistance to the British-French-Israeli invasion in 1956 inflamed the Arab world. The Algerian revolution (1954–62) inspired a great sense of involvement in shaping history and preparing for a new era. This optimism was shattered by the sudden defeat of the Arabs in the war of June 1967, followed by a rekindling of hope with the rise of the Palestinian resistance movement. It seemed that the battle waged by Arab governments had been lost, but popular armed struggle promised the beginning of the transformation of Arab society.

The June 1967 defeat could have ushered in a new stage in Arab history if the Arabs had decided to confront the challenge. Instead, they chose a course of acceptance of the status quo and ultimate resignation. The defeat of Iraq will usher in a gloomy new period, marked by the fear of further dismemberment of Arab society. It has shattered Arab dreams for some time to come. The evolution of Arab thought in response to these changing conditions and historical events can also be outlined in terms of the contending views and ideas of the three major tendencies that I identified earlier: the liberal, the religious, and the progressive.

Liberalism. Liberal thought has been most concerned with explaining and transcending the disasters that have afflicted Arab life throughout modern history. In their search for answers to the questions they have raised, liberal thinkers have tended to focus almost exclusively on cultural rather than social structural and economic situations. In their minds, there is one set of value orientations associated with stagnation and an opposite set associated with modernity. Their thinking is rooted in a sharp contrast between the vanquished Arab world and the triumphant West.

This liberal trend is most clearly represented in the works of the Syrian historian Constantine Zurayk, who in the early 1950s published *Ma'na al-nakba* (The Meaning of the Disaster), reflecting on the destruction of Palestinian society and the establishment of Israel. Less than two decades later, he published *Ma'na al-nakba mujaddadan* (The Meaning of the Disaster Revisited), which discussed the stunning defeat of 1967. His books all stress the urgent need to transform the Arab world "from an emotional, illusionary, mythological and poetic society into a practical achievement-oriented, rational and scientific one." Two reasons for the disaster are singled out by Zurayk— scientific underdevelopment and the weakness of the spirit of activism or militancy. The first lies in the "civilizational differences" between Arab and Israeli societies. He calls Israel a "modern civilization . . . in the area of science and rationality." [42] But being modern in this sense is not enough; the strength of the spirit of activism enabled Algeria and Vietnam to defeat their enemies in spite of their opponents' scientific superiority. Zurayk traces the lack of a spirit of activism among Arabs to their lack of clarity of purpose, which he attributes to divisiveness and fragmentation into "nationalist," "socialist," and "reactionary" camps.

Another representative of the liberal trend is Zaki Naguib Mahmud of Egypt, who preaches rationality in the context of renewal through reconciliation of authentic Arab culture and modernity. This process of Arab renewal and rebirth would require Arabs to take from their traditions what they can actually apply, and reject without regret whatever is not applicable. He recommends using the same standard for adoption of concepts from the West. His motto is open-mindedness to all experiences; the utility of such experiences should be gauged by the application of rationality and reason. From this perspective, he calls for liberation from the illusions of myth and the mistakes of ignorance, as well as from the shackles of imperialism and the despotism of rulers. [43]

The Religious Trend. For over three decades following World War II, the religious movement remained dormant and confined to a few narrow circles. Secular nationalist and socialist thought, thanks to the triumph of the 1952 Egyptian revolution, dominated the Arab world. A few religious voices, however, managed to be heard. Certainly, the most prominent of these voices was that of Sayyid Qutb (1906–66), who struggled to reactivate the Muslim Brotherhood following the death of its founder, Hassan al-Banna, in 1949. Upon his return from a visit to the United States that year, Qutb joined the movement and wrote several works in which he proposed an Islamic political system and ideology and rejected all other forms of government. He characterized the modern world as a new *jahiliyya* (a concept used in the Qur'an to refer to the pre-Islamic period of ignorance), which Muslims could transcend only through a divinely ordained Islamic system and a total Islamic view of life. From this perspective, indiscriminate borrowing and copying of alien and man-made models, including Western capitalism and communism, were anathema. Accused of conspiring to assassinate Nasser in 1954, Qutb was sentenced to fifteen years of hard labor; he was released ten years later, only to be rearrested and executed in 1966.

There were also less well known voices of Islamic revival in the Maghrib and the Mashriq. Malik Bin Nabi of Algeria wrote several works in French, calling for "the awakening of the Islamic community from its deep sleep" and arguing that the "divine word" or the "religious idea" is what actually moves history and constructs reality. He notes that "civilization is reformed only through religious ideology . . . and inspiration descending from Heaven." [44] In the eastern Arab world, there were a few voices that explained the defeat of the June 1967 war in religious terms. One of those was that of Salah al-Din al-Munajjid, who wrote *A 'midat al-nakba* (The Pillars of the Disaster), in which he argued that Arabs had been defeated in that war because they "gave up their faith in God, so He gave up on them." [45]

The Islamic resurgence, however, occurred only after the Iranian revolution of 1979. Since then there have been several conversions to the divine path by a younger generation of Arab intellectuals, as well as by some secular nationalists and socialists. Gradually, at least two trends besides the conservative Saudi version began to emerge within the religious movement. One followed the same path as the Muslim Brotherhood. Another was composed mainly of ex-nationalists and ex-socialists who followed a moderate divine path and tried to unify the old and the new forces within the framework of a leftist and nationalist version of Islam. Among those who have tried unsuccessfully to reconcile religious and nationalist forces have been such leftists as Muhammed 'Amara, Adel Hussein, Tariq al-Bushri, and Hassan Hanafi, whose main concern has been to reconcile Islamic and Arab nationalist forces and challenge the Western cultural invasion. These are often referred to as the Islamic left, or called the "new *salafiyyin.*" In their view, the primary contradiction is between Muslim societies and Western imperialism. So the most urgent task at present is to preserve the Arab-Islamic identity and revive its authenticity (*asala* or *khususiyya*). This position has led either to a stress on the application of Islamic law or to a complete rupture with the West in an attempt to put an end to dependency. What is common to all these intellectuals is the rejection of ideas in the name of authenticity, on the basis of their being "borrowed," "imported," or "alien." Many of these rejected notions were advanced by nationalists and socialists as early as the formative period—including secularism, nationalism, socialism, and even democracy. The net result has been a shift from confrontation with the West to a complete rupture with it, and from liberation from repressive traditions to accommodation, or at least silence, in the name of authenticity.

Muhammed 'Amara called for the progressive use of Islam and the Arab heritage, but ended up favoring the incorporation of Islamic law into Egyptian jurisprudence, pointing out that secularism was not a feature of Arab-Islamic civilization.[46] Similarly, Tariq al-Bushri advocated better relationships between Christians and Muslims within the framework of national cohesiveness, but ended up considering secularism to be *"nabt wafid"* (an alien plant).[47] Speaking from the point of view of the Islamic left, Hassan Hanafi has addressed himself to an ambitious project of *al-turath wal-tajdid* (heritage and renewal). For him, the left means social justice and improvement of the conditions of the poor; it is not a methodology for the study of social reality. He has been more of an idealist, insisting on the need to build a new man based on revelation before any social revolution can occur.

More recent exchanges of views between Islamists and secular nationalists have yielded very little. This was clearly demonstrated in a conference on "nationalist-religious dialogue" sponsored by the Center for Arab Unity Studies in Cairo in the fall of 1989. What the participants exchanged were apologetic niceties, with tendencies toward self-criticism on the part of nationalists and self-assertion on the part of Islamists. At this conference, Al-Bushri noted that the bone of contention between Islam and Arabism is secularism. If it distanced itself from secularism, Arabism could move closer to Islam.

There have been some critics of the religious movement. Muhammed Abed Jabri of Morocco has asserted in several works on classical and contemporary Arab thought that the prevailing Arab discourse is a discourse of memory rather than a discourse of reason. In the 1980s, he published a two-volume work entitled *Naqd al-'aql al-'arabi* (Critique of the Arab Mind), a critical analysis of the epistemological systems of Arab-Islamic culture as methods of perceiving reality. Deriving his categories directly from Michel Foucault, Jabri argues for the deconstruction of Arab thought, detached for the first time from social and political struggle. In his view, hegemony over culture has been the first item on the agenda of every religious or political movement aiming at political control. Hence, the integral relationship between ideological struggle and epistemological clashes in Arab culture. In the last analysis, Jabri does not practice criticism for its own sake, but to liberate Arab thought from the referential framework of the past (*namuzaj-al-salaf*), whether that past be seen as Arab-Islamic or European.[48] In other works, Jabri has attempted to reconcile *al-asala* (authenticity) and *mu'asara* (contemporaneity) through self-knowledge and critical analysis of all models. However, his attempt has been made without a clear definition of the concept of *asala* and how it might be differentiated from that used so often by the religious intellectuals.[49] He has also questioned secularism, although he sees Islam as merely one of the constituent elements of Arab nationalism. He contends that the relationship between religion and the state must be studied separately in each Arab country. The implication is that while secularism might be relevant in the Mashriq, it becomes a false issue when generalized to the rest of the Arab world, and particularly the Maghrib.[50]

Another prominent critic of the religious trend is Mohammed Arkoun, who has argued for liberation from ideological dogmas through historicity and the application of the multidisciplinary methodologies of the social sciences. The thrust of his argument is the deconstruction of dominant religious thought by freeing the "first text" (the revealed Qur'an) from the "second text" (the dominant interpretations of the Qur'an); being held captive by the "second text" has constituted a formidable obstacle to free thinking by Arabs.[51] Arkoun also uses the categories of epistemology, as developed by Foucault, to show how religion has been transformed into an ideological weapon in the hands of the ruling classes. Consequently, Arkoun has called for continuing the attempt of 'Ali 'Abd al-Raziq in 1925 to secularize Islamic thought in the light of political anthropology.[52]

Other critics of religious thought include Sadiq al-Azm, Fuad Zakariyya, and Muhammed al-Nuwayhi. In a far-reaching and defiant book entitled *Naqd al-fikr al-dini* (Critique of Religious Thought), quoted earlier (see p. 133 above), Al-'Azm shows how religiously oriented intellectuals grant Islamic legitimacy to the government they are linked to irrespective of its coloration.[53] Zakariyya characterizes Islamic discourse as a political ideology and speaks of the fundamentalist movement as "petro-Islam," suggesting it receives financial support from oil-producing countries.[54] In the late 1960s, Al-Nuwayhi spoke of the limitations of religious thought and the need to replace it with a broad secular view, basing his argument on the premises that (1) Islam neither grants any special group the right to monopolize the interpretation of its beliefs nor offers a final order, and (2) Qur'anic laws are not all equally binding; some have been disregarded in later periods.[55]

The debate between Islamists and progressive nationalists continues to rage in Egypt and other Arab countries. Meanwhile, the progressive movement desperately seeks to recapture the prominent position it occupied for a few decades following independence.

Progressivism. Arab progressive thought has been defined in terms of its critical stance, futuristic outlook, secular and socialist views, and scientific interpretation, with special emphasis on class analysis. What may be most distinctive about it is its future-oriented paradigm, which dismisses idealistic and purely cultural interpretations and examines things in their social and historical contexts. Beyond these shared general tendencies, however, all progressive thought is not the same. The progressive movement consists of three basic subtrends based on the analytical frameworks provided by classical and partisan Marxism, by dependency theory, and by social criticism.

Classical and partisan Marxist analysis is represented by Hussein Mroueh, Mahmud Amin al-'Alim, and Tayyib Tizzini. In the late 1970s, Mroueh of Lebanon published an impressive two-volume work entitled *Al-Naza'at al-maddiyya fi al-filsafa al-'arabiyya al-islamiyya* (Materialist Trends in Arab-Islamic Philosophy). This work uses the methodology of historical materialism to examine the Arab-Islamic heritage from pre-Islamic times to the middle of the thirteenth century, with particular emphasis on the conflicting origins of and roles played by ideas. A basic proposition in this work is his characterization of the dominant mode of production during this historical period as essentially feudal and undifferentiated from the Asiatic mode of production. More specifically, he defines the dominant mode as "feudal intertwined with remnants of the dissolved slavery and growing mercantile feudalism side by side with the growth of artisan manufacture."[56]

Mroueh's examination of the debates of the Mu'tazila and Sufi movements in the context of the socioeconomic and political transformation of Arab society at the time of their appearance and development is illustrative of his method and the scope of his analysis. Mroueh argues that Mu'tazila participation in the debate on the question of predestination, arguing in favor of free will, reflected class struggle. Mroueh also presents Sufism as a movement ideologically opposed to the dominant official ideology.

Mahmud Amin al-'Alim (b. 1922) of Egypt has been the leading Marxist critic of literary and broader cultural matters. His works include *Fi al-thaqafa al-misriyya* (On Egyptian Culture) in collaboration with A. A. Anis; *Ma'arik fikriyya* (Intellectual Battles); and *Al-Wa'i wal-wa'i al-za'if fi al-fikr al-'arabi al-mu'asir* (Consciousness and False Consciousness in Contemporary Arab Thought). In his introduction to this last work, a collection of articles written between 1974 and 1986, he says he considers it to be the second volume of *Ma'arik fikriyya*, which was written between 1950 and 1965 (although there are great differences between the two books). Al-'Alim concedes that the first volume was essentially political propaganda produced in the revolutionary period under Nasser. In contrast, he says, the second volume on consciousness and false consciousness is a critical analysis of Arab thought in the counterrevolutionary period under Sadat and Mubarak. What the two books have in common is their attempt to offer a dialectical historical materialist interpretation of culture.

Dialectical relationships shaping Arab-Islamic thought and cultural heritage have also been examined by Tayyib Tizzini of Syria, who has demonstrated a correspondence between economic and political conditions and intellectual trends. In the process of defining his scientific and progressive methodology, Tizzini presents his attempt as a constructive alternative to what he considers to be the ahistorical approaches of traditionalists, liberal eclectics, ultramodernists, and Orientalists. [57]

Another subtrend of progressive thought is represented by proponents of dependency theory such as Samir Amin, Mahmoud Abdel-Fadil, and Galal Amin. Dependency theory is not merely a critique of modernization theories; it provides an alternative understanding and redefinition of the process of development. This redefinition is based on several propositions. First, development as practiced aims at the integration of Third World countries into the world capitalist system. Second, the division of labor in the international economic order is one in which Third World or peripheral countries produce raw materials while Western or center societies produce industrial goods. This leads to asymmetrical and contradictory relationships between the center and periphery (that is, relationships of domination and exploitation). Finally, the emergence of multinational corporations (in alliance with the elites and ruling classes of the Third World) has exacerbated inequalities and political instability in the periphery, and thus leads to uneven development.

This theory was first conceived in the analysis of the plight of Latin America, but it was Samir Amin who contributed to its development as a highly sophisticated theory. In applying it to the Arab world, Amin characterizes the precolonial Arab mode of production as tributary, not feudal. He bases this characterization on the existence of long-distance trade, or mercantilism, and on the creation of a surplus drawn from the local exploitation of the peasantry. The unity of the Arab nation as a result of this tributary mode of production suffered a national regression because of the Crusades. The results of these wars and the shifting of the commercial center from Arab to Italian cities, the fall of Baghdad under the assault of the Mongols in the thirteenth century, the Ottoman conquest, and the shift of Mediterranean trade to the Atlantic continue to have a profound effect on the Arab world. Under present conditions of dependency, the Arab bourgeoisie is dependent on its foreign alliances and unable to overcome its internal contradictions. So the whole Arab region continues to suffer from both national and class oppression, with little hope of unity. As part of the periphery, it is forced into a subordinate and complementary role in the dominant world order. [58]

Mahmoud Abdel-Fadil has investigated several crucial aspects—employment, income distribution, and class structure—of the political economy of Egypt under Nasser. He argues that the ultimate objective of Nasser's socialism was not to create a classless society but rather to dissolve class distinctions, leaving intact some of society's basic contradictions. By the end of the Nasser era, a new bourgeoisie composed of an amalgam of the upper stratum of the bureaucratic and managerial elites, wholesale traders, contractors, capitalist entrepreneurs, and top members of the liberal professions had developed. Great disparities continued to exist along with great temptations to copy Western consumption patterns. [59] It is these very conditions that explain, at least partly, the resurgence of the Islamic movement.

In 1976, Galal Amin published a paper critical of the development philosophy underlying the United Nations Declaration on the Establishment of a New International Economic Order (1974). As an alternative, he advocated a strategy of independent development and self-reliance, to be achieved by detaching the Arab effort from the international economic system controlled by multinational corporations. At the base of his rejection of the international economic system lies the assumption that it inevitably leads to accentuation of social and economic dualism and inequalities within developing societies, as well as to further integration into the Western economic and value systems. Amin also expressed concern about the great danger of losing cultural identity in the interaction between unequal parties. So rather "than sing praises of cooperation and interdependence, Third World countries would be better advised to follow a policy of isolation." [60] In 1990 Amin published a book entitled *Misr fi muftaraq al-turuq* (Egypt at a Crossroads), in which he shows that Egypt has reached an impasse. The right has failed miserably at achieving a just and balanced economic development. The religious movement is in crisis, and the left needs to reassess its goals and aspirations. [61]

The third subtrend of progressive thought is represented by social critics such as Hisham Sharabi, Abdallah Laroui, Sadiq al-Azm, Abdelkebir Khatibi, and others who have benefited from the ideas of Marxism, European structuralism, and social analysis. Hisham Sharabi explains the June 1967 defeat in terms of child-rearing practices. He suggests that children in the feudal-bourgeois Arab family have been socialized into dependency and escapism. The principal techniques of child-rearing in the Arab family are shaming, physical punishment, and *talqin* (rote-learning) rather than intellectual persuasion and reward. Generalizing the patriarchal nature of the Arab family to other institutions has been more fully and broadly developed by Sharabi in a later major work, *Neopatriarchy: A Theory of Distorted Change in Arab Society* (1988). By *patriarchy,* Sharabi understands "a universal form of traditional society," in contrast to modernity (which "occurred in its original form in Western Europe)". He further argues that the Arab renaissance in fact deformed rather than displaced the patriarchal structure of Arab society, in the sense that modernization produced a hybrid society and culture. What developed was neopatriarchy, a system that is neither traditional nor modern. The central feature of this new system has continued to be "the dominance of the father (patriarch), the center around which national as well as the natural family are organized. Thus between ruler and ruled, between father and child, there exist only vertical relations: in both settings the paternal will is the absolute will, mediated in both society and the family by a forced consensus based on ritual and coercion."[62]

A central theme in the works of Abdallah Laroui (b. 1933) is the failure of the Arab intelligentsia to develop a realistic and comprehensive theory of history. One manifestation of this "historical retardation" is the opposition of Arab culture to liberal culture in both its classical and contemporary expressions. This may be particularly true of the 1980s—a period that witnessed a process of retraditionalization even within the Arab nationalist movement. This process was reinforced by internal and external influences. To the extent that outside pressures and threats to Arabs persist and intensify, traditionalization may also be expected to intensify. Laroui has also argued that the crisis of the Arab intellectual reflects the crisis of the society as a whole and bears witness to its inefficiency and stagnation. In analyzing the nature of the crisis itself, Laroui notes that "Arab intellectuals think according to two rationales. Most of them profess the traditionalist rationale (*salafi*); the rest profess an eclecticism. Together, these tendencies succeed in abolishing the historical dimension." This is what Laroui calls "ahistorical thinking," which he sees as leading to alienation through medievalization and westernization. Thus from Laroui's perspective, both the religious *salafi* movement and westernization constitute forms of alienation.[63]

It is in the religious form of alienation that Sadiq al-Azm finds the roots of Arab failures. He has argued from a revolutionary Marxist perspective that it is necessary to bring about radical changes in life, as well as in society, because the causes of defeat lie in traditional loyalties, the dominance of religious thought, and the negative attributes of the "Fahlawi personality" (see Chapter 9).[64]

Another critic is Abdelkebir Khatibi of Morocco, who has called for the development of a new Arab sociology to follow a methodology that will lead to "double criticism" by rejecting both Western and ethnocentric paradigms. This would constitute a deconstruction of the dominant forms of discourse. Like any sociology of liberation and decolonization, "that of the Arab world would consist of carrying out two tasks: (1) a deconstruction of 'logocentrism' and of ethnocentrism, that speech of self-sufficiency par excellence which the West, in the course of its expansion, has imposed on the world . . . [and] (2) [a] criticism of the knowledge and discourses developed by the different societies of the Arab world about themselves."[65]

The approach of these progressive Arab critics emanates from a commitment to transcendental change in Arab society through the achievement of democracy, national unity, secularism, and socialism. The challenges confronting them are immense and formidable. Meanwhile, the debate continues, rekindled by the Gulf War and the destruction of Iraq. Will this debate transform the nature of Arab discourse or merely add to its intensity and fragmentation?

Conclusion

These are the major currents of thought that have been competing for priority in contemporary Arab culture. They seem unable to converge to reach a common understanding of Arab reality or to determine the direction needed to achieve change. They all emanate from a full-fledged realization and unwavering conviction that the prevailing situation is totally unacceptable. The battle continues. It will have to be resumed more intensely after every failure or defeat. This also requires a greater commitment to change, and therefore a renewed search for new explanations and solutions, calling for creative rethinking and visionary analysis in a lengthy process of transformation. It is this process to which the concluding chapter will address itself.

PART FOUR

The Crisis of Civil Society Approaching the Horizon of the Twenty-First Century

12   Conclusion

This concluding chapter addresses the fundamental issues that have emerged repeatedly in the preceding analysis of the prospects for the transformation of Arab society and the achievement of comprehensive development. The upheavals in the socialist system, the sudden unraveling of the old world order, and the devastating Gulf War make this summation even more relevant. These historical events at the beginning of the last decade of the twentieth century signal the end of one era and the beginning of a new one for the whole world. Such drastic changes may finally dare Arabs to free themselves from their deeply rooted skepticism about the possibility of remaking society. Despite Arab apprehensiveness that the current upheavals may reinforce the Western sense of self-righteousness, and consequently the uncontested dominance of the capitalist world system over Arabs and other peoples of developing societies, Arabs share a growing awareness that a new era is in the making. After all, Arab society is an integral part of the changing world order and cannot be insulated from its dynamism. The question therefore becomes, how can the Arabs remake their society to fit their dreams for it?

The Gulf War seems to have shattered the conviction of Arabs that they can bridge the gap between reality and dream to make a fresh start. Suddenly, they find themselves in a situation not unlike the one they experienced at the end of World War I: instead of a new era of independence and unity, they are overwhelmed by Western domination and threats of further fragmentation. Disturbing nightmares seem to have replaced their hopeful dreams, leaving them disoriented. The changes that have actually taken place in Arab society during the past century are truly immense, especially if measured in quantitative terms. Yet somehow the Arab struggle to transcend alienating conditions and achieve the *nahda* has not been reflected in these changes.

Throughout this book one can see clearly the perplexing inability of Arabs to achieve the basic goals to which they have aspired. What is most discouraging is that Arabs continue to wrestle with the same old dilemmas, exacerbated by the added burdens of greater dependency and the marginalization of movements for revolutionary change. They are keenly aware of the successive defeats and failures they have suffered, and they expect more to come; but they also realize that nothing can diminish their resolve to restructure their society, to rethink their visions and options. Arabs blame the West for their defeats and failures, but they also blame themselves. In fact, Arab intellectuals and popular movements have critically, boldly, and perhaps even harshly examined their internal problems, seeking explanations of their plight in the nature of their society and culture. All sorts of explanations have been articulated, particularly in times of defeat. Successive defeats and failures did bring many disappointments and frustrations, but they also stimulated intense intellectual debates and generated new movements for change.

The 1991 Gulf War will generate its own discourse and movements, but unlike previous wars, it has failed to produce a shared sense of agony. Emerging from disputes among Arabs themselves, this conflict undermined the dream of a common destiny. While some Arabs became engulfed by a sense of loss, others celebrated victory together with their long-term enemies. Owing to this collapse of Arab consensus on basic principles, collaboration to overcome the present malaise promises to be much more elusive than in previous crises.

During the last half of the twentieth century, various Arab intellectuals and movements have sought to explain their plight by focusing on certain key characteristics. These have included class disparities and dependency resulting from Western penetration and the integration of the area into the world capitalist system;[1] social and political fragmentation;[2] the centrality of religion,[3] or, conversely, the loss of religious faith and return of the *jahiliyya*;[4] the absence of scientific and future-oriented rationalism;[5] repressive family socialization and neopatriarchy;[6] the subjugation of women;[7] the dominance of traditionalism over creativity and modernity;[8] the duality of westernization and *salafiyya*;[9] disequilibrium in the Arab ego;[10] and the prevalence of a traditional mentality.[11] Will the Gulf War and its aftermath generate other explanations? Feelings of uncertainty, lack of confidence, postwar vindictiveness, fears of prolonged feuds, and receding hopes will take their toll, but will not prevent Arabs from reexamining the sources of their difficulties.

Indeed, formal and informal gatherings assessing the current situation and rethinking deeply held premises have already been reported in all the major cities of the Arab world. Simply stated, there is a deep conviction that lingering aimlessly in a state of retreat will only exacerbate the sense of weakness and the difficulties Arabs face in everyday life. What is expected, therefore, is more rather than less reflection on the conditions that have rendered them so powerless and divided.

One manifestation of the profound agonizing among Arabs over what happened in the Gulf War was a national conference of Arab intellectuals from all over the Arab world held in Amman, Jordan, in May 1991 to discuss the state of the *umma* in the aftermath of the war. A statement to the *umma*, signed by sixty-four Arab intellectuals, noted the absence of democratic life and the violations of human rights in Arab countries, as well as Western hegemony and its aim to destroy Arab capacities. It condemned Arab rulers for monopolizing political decisions and held them accountable.

By exploring the prevailing crisis of civil society in this chapter, I wish to reiterate the thesis that a devastating condition of alienation is responsible for the current Arab plight.[12] My basic argument is that Arab citizens have been rendered powerless because they have been excluded from the political process. Marginalized, and isolated from the human and material resources civil society should place at their disposal, the people of the area suffer from state tyranny over society. The most vital functions of society in "progressive" as well as "conservative" Arab states have been constantly undermined by authoritarian rule. Citizens of Arab countries have been denied the basic right to participate in the political process. The affairs of the community and society have ceased to be their own. The annual reports of local and international human rights organizations tell us that Arab governments do not guarantee their citizens the fundamental human rights of freedom of conscience, expression, association, and assembly. Thousands of people have been detained without charge or placed on trial under state-of-emergency legislation; they are being held incommunicado, tortured, and executed. The basic goals in the name of which human rights have been violated—such as national unity, comprehensive development, liberation, and socialism—have been sacrificed by denying people access to the very sources of their strength, and by prohibiting them from freely conducting their affairs and those of the society. Instead of achieving these popular objectives, Arab states and rulers have become a force against and over society. No wonder, then, that the Arab people experience acute feelings of alienation, fearing that their dreams may have been extinguished for a long time to come.

Arabs have also been denied the right to influence decisions on how to utilize oil resources and the immense revenues they generate. Economic power, not unlike political power, has become the privilege of a few families and tribal chiefs. Hence the feeling among so many Arabs that the discovery of oil has, directly or indirectly, brought misery upon them. On March 9, 1991, an Arab observed in a personal journal:

> Because we own oil, we are being subjected to the control of
> corporations, foreign armies, and tribal chiefs. No nationalistic,
> religious, cultural, or ethnic affinities will spare us the wrath of little

gods. Because we own oil, we lost control over our very destiny. The shedding of our blood has been legitimized. . . . They extract the oil from our land and bury our hopes in its place. Is there a future to dream of? How many disasters shall we have to undergo before we find our way? What way?

Though confronted with pressing challenges, Arabs cannot give up. Feelings of alienation, prevalent prior to the latest upheavals, have only intensified a growing realization that the most urgent task is the emancipation—perhaps along the model of the Palestinian *intifada*—of Arabs from the grip of their coercive rulers and regimes. As the Palestinian *intifada* demonstrates, sooner or later subjugated people will reassert themselves in one way or another. Many have begun to wonder how Arab governments have managed so far to contain Arab public anger and how, in the words of Mohammed Arkoun, "all Arab governments find themselves obeyed notwithstanding their lack of legitimacy." [13]

The extent to which people are actively and freely involved in conducting their affairs and those of society determines the health of civil society. In other words, civil society exists and functions properly so long as the destiny of the society is shaped by the people themselves and not merely by the state and its rulers. Indicative of the existence of a civil society is active and free participation by citizens in political parties, grass-roots popular and labor movements, voluntary organizations, and professional associations. These institutions must function within a framework of accountability, due process, free self-reflection, respect for human rights, and genuine opposition and debate.

Political sociology tells us that "social organization has a two-fold nature. One aspect consists in the concrete community-life. . . . The other . . . in a system of institutions for the protection, domination, and governance of the entire human and territorial complex. This side of the organization we call the political, the other, the social. Seen from one vantage point, the whole is perceived as the state; seen from the other, it is perceived as society." [14] We are further told that in the course of history, state and society intertwine to such an extent that they become inseparable. For Marx, civil society is "the true source and theater of all history." [15] This must be what prompted Henri Lefebvre to observe that for Marx the "truth of politics, and hence of the state . . . is to be found in society: social relationships account for political forms. They are the living, active relationships among people (groups, classes, individuals). Contrarily to what Hegel thought, . . . 'civil society' has more truth and more reality than political society." [16] Yet, lest it be thought that the state is the sole source of alienation, Marx traced some of its forms to the predominance of "egoistic" and "physical" needs under industrial capitalist systems.

He located the immediate source of alienation in the nature of civil society under such systems, and more particularly in the nature of the exploitative private system. He concluded that the eradication of alienation and the greed that prevails in such civil societies could only be accomplished by replacing their very socioeconomic orders—that is, by the transformation of civil society itself. From this vantage point, one can understand Marx's call for the emancipation of humanity from subjection to "mere utility," and from the "despotism of egoistic and physical needs." The reasons behind his emphasis on "the categorical imperative to overthrow all those conditions in which man is an abased, enslaved, abandoned, contemptible being"[17] become ever clearer. It is obvious that democracy itself has become distorted under these conditions.

True democracy can thus not be achieved merely by overcoming political alienation or by freeing society from the grip of the state. In fact, civil society is arguably subordinate to the state even in industrialized societies; the crisis of civil society characterizes both developed and developing regions of the world. If it is true that civil society has been overwhelmed by marketplace values in the West, and by state control and one-party systems in the East,[18] it may even more convincingly be argued that civil society in the Arab world is overwhelmed by both state control and marketplace values. In the course of modern Arab history, it is becoming more difficult to speak of an Arab world with a will and a social system of its own, even as conceptualized by Western functional theory. Such a social system implies that constituent units function in terms of one another.[19] Instead, the Arab world seems to be closer to being a multiple society—that is, one consisting of separate states clearly functioning in opposition to each other, rather than in concert and constituting a society as a whole.

The malfunctioning of civil society is most visible in times of disaster, when there is a pressing need to confront trying historical challenges, and in fact, Arab thought has been shaped by the experience of several failures and defeats, which Arabs call *nakbat*, disasters. The fact that these circumstances may have been created by Arabs themselves does not mollify their feelings of frustration, and the gap between dream and reality is acutely perceived as a widening one, notwithstanding a handful of successes that have kept the flame of hope alive, such as the Algerian revolution, the heroic confrontation of the 1956 Suez invasion, the emergence of the Palestinian resistance movement following the 1967 defeat, the Lebanese national resistance of the 1982 Israeli invasion, and the ongoing Palestinian *intifada*.

Arabs have struggled desperately for the past century and a half for such basic goals as national unity, institution-building, and the ability to overcome socioeconomic disparities. They have worked for social emancipation through an emphasis on secularization, democratization, and national liberation. The proper utilization of Arab resources, comprehensive development, and an end to dependency have all preoccupied the best Arab thinkers. However, both external and internal threats to these goals are formidable. We have seen how regimes have appropriated the vital functions of civil life and sacrificed these goals in order to remain in power.

Although subjugated peoples inevitably struggle to reassert themselves, the hegemony of Arab states may continue for some time. They have managed to expand their powers by controlling both traditional and modern institutions. Here, our understanding of the crisis of civil society in Arab countries can be enhanced by introducing the lucid distinction Antonio Gramsci made between those institutions the state uses to establish its hegemony over society, and other institutions of civil society through which the people try to free themselves from the grip of the state in order to resume control over their affairs. For Gramsci, civil society is "at once the political terrain on which the dominant class organizes its hegemony and the terrain on which opposition parties and movements organize, win allies and build their social power." He also points out that his very distinction between political society and civil society is "methodological" or analytical rather than "organic." In practice, the two must be seen as being intertwined. Yet "civil society is a site of consent . . . in conceptual opposition to the state . . . which is a site of coercion." [20]

By seeking legitimacy in traditional loyalties, and by consolidating their control through intermediate groups and corporations, Arab governments have tried to impose consent by justifying coercion and using religion as a mechanism of control. Besides the use of coercive measures to stay in control, Arab governments have increasingly sought legitimacy in traditional loyalties. They have particularly cultivated religious, sectarian, and tribal orientations. The destruction of those modern institutions that exist outside the framework of full state control (such as secular political parties, labor unions, popular movements, and voluntary associations) has left the people with very limited options except to seek refuge in their traditional institutions (that is, religion, sect, tribe, family, ethnicity) to express their discontent.

Already these governments have managed not only to destroy or prevent the emergence of modern institutions, but also to replace them with corporations directly or indirectly linked to government bureaucracy. The role of these corporations in a society characterized by strong intermediate and primary groups—families, tribes, neighborhoods, and local communities—has been to facilitate the efforts of the state to assert its control over its citizens. Examples of these corporations are the higher councils for tribal, religious, ethnic and local affairs, which serve as interest and pressure groups, often at the expense of comprehensive social development. Reinforcing one another and bolstered by the government's deliberate manipulation, the focus on these special interests has resulted in the emergence of religious fundamentalism and tribalism at the expense of civil society and even true religion itself. To the extent that people have sought refuge in traditional institutions, they have become more rather than less overwhelmed by alienation. While they may have derived personal satisfaction from the closeness and security provided by these old ties, they have failed to cope with accumulating problems. The more they have attributed power to divine forces outside themselves, the weaker they have become within themselves. Form has been confused with substance, means with ends, and medievalization with renewal. Unable to align religion with sect and tribe, these identities have contributed to further social and political fragmentation—that is, to the emergence of a multiple rather than a unified society. These recent developments and others have solidified rather than diminished the conditions of dependency, patriarchal and authoritarian relationships, socioeconomic disparities, and alienation that have endured throughout the postindependence period.

Several studies have shown that the transitional nature of Arab society has made it neither traditional nor modern. It is worthwhile summarizing the overall pattern delineated by these studies. Khaldoun al-Naqeeb has shown that Arabian and Gulf society between the sixteenth century and the middle of the nineteenth century existed in what he calls a natural state (*al-hala al-tabiʿiyya*). In Arabia, there was advanced mercantilism, along with other marginal economic sectors such as simple agriculture, pastoralism, and fishing. The center of political control was located in the commercial coast cities, and the economy was controlled by patriarchal aristocratic tribal rulers. However, there was a constant circulation of tribal elites in power. This natural condition collapsed as a result of the hegemony of British imperialism (1839–1920) and the integration of the area into the capitalist world system. This meant a shift of the center of political control from the commercial coastal cities to the tribal areas of the interior, the end of the rotation of tribal elites, and the emergence of a ruling family system based on sectarian-tribal alliances. This system of ruling families and states defined by artificially established national boundaries has been maintained by foreign interference. Rentier states emerged in the 1950s as a result of the great increases in oil revenues that the ruling families received from oil companies in the form of taxes. Full control by ruling families over economic life, and the absence of diversified sources of income, rendered these ruling families relatively independent of the society's declining centers of power and authority. The majority of the national labor force worked for the government. In the mid 1960s, an authoritarian state began to emerge. As a modern form of a despotic state, it sought to achieve effective monopoly over the sources of power and authority in society for the benefit of the ruling elites. This authoritarian state could achieve such a monopoly only by undermining civil society, whose institutions were transformed into corporations functioning as an extension of the state apparatus. Notwithstanding these difficulties, progressive and nationalist movements continued to oppose the ruling families in the Gulf and to articulate popular demands. They called for legislation to limit the powers and privileges of the ruling elites; to establish constitutional and democratic rule; to ensure equal treatment of all citizens, guaranteeing fundamental human rights; to stop the waste of natural and human resources; to plan for comprehensive development; and to achieve the project of national unity. [21]

Hisham Sharabi's *Neopatriarchy* shows that the state in Arab society as a whole had gained the overwhelming power necessary to regulate totally the life and activities of the people. Here, too, the legacy of Europe's colonization provided the structures of what Sharabi calls the etatist patriarchy:

> What made *etatism* so natural to neopatriachal society is the fact that the former was essentially nothing but the medieval sultanate in modern form. For the distinctive characteristic of *etatism*, like that of the sultanate, is personalized (legal and extralegal) power, which finds expression in the coercive and suppressive apparatus of the state and derives its legitimacy not from some formal (constitutional or even traditional) sources, but from the reality and possession of power. In this kind of polity the ordinary person is a passive entity, a subject not a citizen, with no human or civil rights or power to influence decisions concerning society as a whole. [22]

In a society that is neither modern nor traditional, the state—by restricting public involvement and appropriating the vital functions of society—has become a force against, rather than for, the people and society. Society, failing to develop a vision for the future, seems to lack a core and a will of its own. It drifts at the mercy of historical challenges and events, while its material and human resources have been harnessed for the benefit of a small segment of the population and for antagonistic external forces.

The net outcome has been the sacrifice of democratic rights without the realization of popular aspirations for political unity, comprehensive development, and social justice. In all instances, authoritarian regimes were imposed on society in the name of such popular demands. While these regimes may be threatened by the recent upheavals in the world order, they still derive legitimacy from very real external threats, concretely represented by Zionism and Western hegemony. They also derive self-deceptive encouragement from the fact that civil society is still subordinate to the state even in industrialized and developed countries.

Is there a way out, then? What is to be done, and by whom? What sorts of prospects await Arabs?

Visions for the Future

In the first chapter of this book, I argued that Arabs were essentially faced with two alternative visions of the future. One vision limits its ambition for the area to the management of existing conflicts, barring the possibility of finding just and permanent solutions to deep problems. The other, alternative vision is the radical transformation of present reality by addressing the root of the conflicts and aiming at the establishment of a unified, democratic, and egalitarian Arab nation-state or federation of states. This second, alternative vision could be easily dismissed as unrealistic were it not for the dismal nature of the present reality and the urgent need for transcendence. Externally, Arabs suffer from Western-Zionist hegemony. Internally, they suffer from lack of freedom and dignity. These humiliating conditions in themselves constitute a great impetus for a general Arab *intifada* to regain control over their destiny and to remake society.

Although the present situation continues to look bleak, perspicacious observers can see signs of coming upheavals. Even prior to the profound changes in Eastern Europe, there had been growing apprehensions on the part of Arab governments about the spread of the Palestinian *intifada*. Indeed, uprisings have already taken place in several Arab countries, and the causes that brought them about continue to intensify. Here, however, we need to keep in mind the distinction between foreign occupation and indigenous despotic rule. It is much easier to mobilize people against the former than against the latter. Indigenous despotic rule, resulting from the struggle for independence, has managed to silence people in the name of national and popular goals. This distinction explains the widespread and intense mass participation in the preindependence period, and the demoralizing resignation afterward. It may also explain why what happened in Eastern Europe at the beginning of the last decade of the twentieth century may *not* happen in the Arab world. The difference is that East Europeans rebelled against a system externally imposed during the aftermath of World War II. They lived for about half a century in the shadow of a superpower. Only when this superpower began to look inward in an attempt to renew itself did Eastern Europeans begin to rebel against their governments, which they did with the encouragement of the Soviet leadership itself. By contrast, Arab despotic rule resulted from the popular struggle for independence and in the name of the people's aspirations. That is why it is wrong to expect that the Arabs will as easily depose their rulers and dismantle the indigenously established order. Furthermore, the changes in the world order have already proved to have negative consequences for Arabs. As long as the West continues to subjugate the area and to protect despotic ruling families, prospects for democracy will continue to be dim.

Nevertheless, Arabs share with the rest of the world the conclusion that there can be no true revolution, no national unity, no liberation, no socialism, and no comprehensive development without democracy and respect for human rights. In a series of interviews conducted with leading scholars by the Moroccan newspaper *Al-Itihad al-ishtiraki*, there seems to be a developing consensus that democracy may head the list of popular demands in the Arab world. Muhammed Guessus asserts that "the question[s] of democracy and human rights occupy at the beginning of the 1990s the same significance and level of concern as the question of independence in the thirties, forties, and fifties of this century."[23] In the same series of interviews, Samir Amin points out that "by becoming undemocratic, the state in the Soviet Union . . . encouraged the emergence of the new bureau-technocratic class that monopolized decision-making . . . [but] the open admission that the ways of socialism are many constitutes an important achievement for progressive forces . . . that is why we should welcome the new developments [in the Soviet Union]."[24] A third prominent interviewee, Abdelkebir Khatibi, says, "We Arabs . . . must link socialism and democracy, and make democracy the basic element of socialism."[25]

This consensus and the progress of the democratic cause in the Arab world are manifested in several other developments, signs of the presence of a civil society in the making. First, some indigenous human rights organizations have been established and continue to expand and assert their credibility. Special reference may be made to the Arab Organization for Human Rights, and the Arab Lawyers' Union, whose reports have systematically exposed violations of human rights by Arab governments. They address such issues as constitutional guarantees and emergency legislation and measures, as well as violations of political, civic, social, economic, and cultural rights.[26] Second, there have been spontaneous popular uprisings in countries such as Sudan, Egypt, Algeria, Tunisia, Jordan, and Morocco. The most inspirational and heartening is the Palestinian *intifada*, but special reference should be made to the Sudanese *intifada* of April 1985, which demonstrated the existence of civil society and its ability to depose a repressive military regime through the mobilization of political parties, labor unions, professional organizations, and student groups. Third, some Arab governments, as if in a preemptive gesture, have begun to reform their systems in response to popular pressures. These minimal reforms have included restricted elections, limited pluralism, and the broadening of the bases of ruling fronts.

In spite of these and other developments, civil society continues to be weak. Arab states have extended their control over both traditional and modern social institutions, as well as over the public sector and private business. They managed to do so in the postindependence period in the name of nationalist demands and under the pressure, or perhaps the pretext, of external threats.

The public sector expanded at the expense of the private sector, and then began to be re-privatized as a result of abuses by certain groups and communities.

At the present time, Arab society does not function properly. Its vital functions have been constantly undermined and curtailed. The failures of nationalist and socialist experiments have reinforced the conditions that contribute to the development of strong, primordial affiliations. A deep and enduring sense of dissatisfaction with, and rejection of, the status quo permeates Arab consciousness. Untold resentments and grievances have been suppressed for too long and threaten to explode at any moment; this is likely to be followed by a period of great turmoil. Arabs seem to be going through a nightmare rather than a dream. For a long time, they have been besieged, and the circle of siege is getting increasingly smaller. The question, then, is whether Arabs will continue to adjust to a life of insignificance and historical oblivion, or break the barriers and surge beyond predictability.

Attempts at development and reform have failed to achieve their stated goals. A wide variety of concepts describing Arab aspirations have been proposed and re-proposed, defined and redefined, and ardently argued and re-argued to no avail. These include *al-nahda* (awakening, renaissance), *al-taqqadum* (progress), *al-tajdid wa al-hadatha* (renewal and modernity), *al-asala wal mu'asara* (authenticity and contemporaneity), *al-islah* (reform), *al-tahrir wa al-taharur* (liberation and liberalization), *al-tanmiyah* (development), *al-tahawwol* (transformation), *al-thawra* (revolution).

Conservative regimes and ruling classes or groups have followed a slow, selective, partial, gradual, and evolutionary process of development. For them, development has meant economic growth without concern for the fair distribution of wealth. They have adopted selected items of Western technology while rejecting the principles and values that brought it about. They have raised standards of living without combating economic disparities, and expanded education while overlooking its relevance and utilization. The necessary infrastructures have been built, but this has been accomplished under the control of multinational corporations, and with an emphasis on consumption rather than production. The net result has been continued, increasing dependency, social class disparities, repression, elitism, and alienation.

The Arab national bourgeoisie, based in the old and the new emerging middle classes, refracts development through one of three lenses: Western liberalism and modernization; Arab socialism and nationalism; or *salafiyya*. Those who have opted for Western liberalism define development as a modernizing process involving the cultivation of new values: rationality, achievement, looking toward the future, tolerance, and individuality. This process aims at promoting local nationalism and independence, and it places an emphasis on economic growth and efficiency, but with symbolic concessions to the deprived classes so as to prevent radicalism. At the heart of this form of development is the transfer of technology and consumer products. Concomitant with these economic strategies is the modernization of the political system, allowing for seemingly Western-style democracy and free elections.

The national bourgeoisie in some Arab countries opted for what they called "Arab socialism"—Egypt under Nasser, Syria, Iraq, Algeria, Libya—selectively borrowing some Marxist concepts and slogans, without integrating them into a comprehensive theory shaped by the particular Arab situation. Their version of development involved land reform, nationalization, expansion of the public sector, and the restriction of economic relations with the West.

The *salafiyya* movement has so far failed to achieve power in the Arab world, but it is gaining momentum by providing a refuge for people seeking to express their discontent after the failure of nationalism and socialism. It preaches authenticity and rejects both capitalism and socialism as borrowed concepts from the West, but does not offer an alternative program for change.

The failure of both the conservative ruling classes and the national bourgeoisie leaves Arabs with limited options, given the disarray and marginality of the impoverished classes of the Arab world. Hopes for the future center on the emergence of civil society in some central Arab country, from which it may spread to others. Initially, the achievement of comprehensive development requires the emergence of an acute awareness by the people of the need to depend on their own resources. This will lead, in turn, to mobilization and ultimate confrontation with their oppressors. Real development takes place only when people get actively involved in changing their conditions. Consciousness, mobilization, and active involvement, in this order, would lead to the establishment of a humane, egalitarian democracy, to rejuvenate rather than undermine civil society. What Arabs must keep in mind is that civil society is the last guarantee of both democracy and socialism, neither of which can be fully achieved without the other.

At this moment in history, Arabs may theoretically have all sorts of options for the future. In reality, however, they have reached an impasse rather than a crossroads. Ruling regimes have clearly demonstrated their inability to cope with the overwhelming present calamities and challenges. Thus, the Arabs are left with two options or visions for the future: the traditional religious vision, and the progressive secular vision.

The religious vision has as a starting point an absolutist and medieval frame of reference, without a clear program for solving the complicated problems from which people have suffered for so long—that is, poverty, social and political fragmentation, lack of freedom, the monopolization of power and wealth by the elite, colonialism, and dependency. Burdened by the impoverished social and cultural legacy of the immediate past, the religious vision seems to possess very little of that revolutionary ethos that marked the formative era of Islam. It fails to realize that ideas emerge out of a certain social reality, and that one cannot impose notions borrowed from the distant past, given the dissimilarities between the two periods.

The first impulse of religious fundamentalists is to impose Islamic law, to deprive women of the few rights they have earned, and to abandon pluralism. These strategies are explained by the claim that there is no solution to contemporary problems other than Islam (as the Islamists interpret it). By claiming to implement God's will, although they are more politically than religiously oriented, they create an order that cannot tolerate dissent or even different interpretations of religious texts. New ideas are dismissed as *wafida*, *nabt ghareeb*, *mustajlaba* (borrowed, "alien plant," inauthentic). The concept of authenticity (*asala*) is meant not only to assert national identity and a genuine search for roots, but also to restrict free discussion. Once in power, past experience has shown us, the moderates among the religious absolutists are most likely to become sacrificial lambs. The lack of tolerance of this kind of regime derives also from a perception of religion itself as something requiring externally enforced conformity to tradition, rather than as being an enriching spiritual experience. The method is one of coercion rather than persuasion. This tendency is clearly visible in social areas such as women's rights. In an interview (1990) on Algerian television the supposedly moderate leader of the Islamic Salvation Front, Abbassi Madani, showed some flexibility and diplomatic skill when confronted with controversial political questions. However, when the discussion shifted to social issues and women's rights, all signs of flexibility vanished completely. Serious questions were met with accusations, threats, and evasive generalities. He called Algerian women activists, including two of his interviewees, "eagles of neocolonialism" and "the daughters of Jeanne d'Arc," and warned one of them quite explicitly, saying, "If your demands [such as the right of women to seek divorce] conflict with the requirements of the shari'a, then I do not believe that a Muslim woman could say there is no god but God and Muhammad is the Messenger of God and still reject the application of the Islamic shari'a."[27] No wonder, then, that religious fundamentalists have launched a growing number of attacks against women. So much for the religious vision, which is more political than spiritual, a reaction rather than a solution, an impasse rather than a way out, and a threat rather than a promise.

The second, alternative vision for the Arab future is the progressive secular vision. The basic shortcoming of this approach has been a distorted understanding of democracy and the emphasis on some essential elements at the expense of others. Equality, social justice, the redistribution of wealth, and central planning have been emphasized at the expense of freedom, basic human rights, pluralism, true elections, and genuine dissent. The Arab left, like its counterparts across the globe, is in utter crisis. Classical socialism has collapsed, and its forces seem to be in deep disarray. John Keane traces its demise to the centralized state bureaucracy and the subjection of private life to the public sphere—that is, to a lack of democracy.[28]

It should be pointed out, however, that progressive secular forces have not themselves seized power in Arab countries. In fact, they have been oppressed and cannot be held responsible for the rampant abuses of human rights that occur. What they can be criticized for is speaking on behalf of the people without reaching out to them: not unlike the rest of the educated elite, they have maintained their distance and spoken about, rather than to, the masses. They have gallantly defended the cause of the people, but somehow they have done very little to involve them in the struggle.

Now and then, particularly in times of defeat, these secular forces for change have reassessed their strategies and tried to make a fresh start. That is the sort of process they are undergoing at the present time, but they may not be able to prevent the shift from the hegemony of the state to the hegemony of religious fundamentalism over civil society. The biggest challenge for them is to continue to struggle for social justice and the democratization of the society and its institutions. Just as Arabs cannot afford to emulate a Western democracy that excludes notions of equality and social justice, so they cannot accept the Eastern version of socialism—a system devoid of freedom, pluralism, opposition, free expression, due process, and representation. They realize that the demand for democracy is closely associated with the struggle for social justice, hence the need for an imaginative redefinition of democracy.

The collapse of socialism in Eastern Europe has led many Western leaders and intellectuals proudly to declare "the triumph of capitalism," while overlooking its shortcomings. Political repression in the United States has managed to marginalize leftists and to deny them a place on the map of American pluralism. Even liberalism may no longer have a place on such a map. The mainstream has shifted from the center to the right. So the political discourse in America is presently unbalanced and unrepresentative of the existing social forces. What is lacking is a balance between freedom and equality.

Some critiques have, surprisingly, managed to emerge from the citadel of the mainstream press. E. J. Dionne, Jr., tells us that American society has lost its faith in egalitarianism and that the impact of its demise is just beginning to be felt. The concept that "government has a responsibility to narrow the gap between rich and poor . . . no longer guides the design of American economic policies. Instead, inequality is now being widely defended as a source of productivity, economic growth and individual striving for excellence."[29] According to one survey based on which Dionne reaches this conclusion, only 29 percent of Americans see redistribution of income as a government responsibility, in comparison to 43 percent in Switzerland, 61 percent in West Germany, 64 percent in Britain, 81 percent in Austria, and 82 percent in Italy. If the highest priority in American culture is economic growth, it is no wonder that respondents choose the market system and that the intellectual climate is hostile to egalitarianism. Another critic, Paul Taylor, says that "at a time when democracy is flourishing around the globe, it is losing ground in the U.S. . . . In light of the fact that two-thirds of the American electorate do not care to vote, a congressman admitted, 'I get so embarrassed when I see elections in Central America where . . . they vote at twice the rate we do in this country.' " Taylor proffers a variety of explanations for this high rate of noninvolvement. One is: "People don't feel any sense of ownership over the federal government. It isn't them, and it isn't theirs." Others are "the atomization of the popular culture—the segmentation of the population by forces of modern marketing and technology into demographic ghettos"; "loss of faith in the future"; "apathy"; the "strong and growing class dimension to nonvoting," inasmuch as the people "in the highest 20 percent of income are almost twice as likely to vote as people in the lowest 20 percent"; the "profound . . . feeling of disconnection" from the system; self-serving materialism; lack of a sense of common purpose; and an "impoverished notion of citizenship," since a "democracy that does not value citizenship is not a very healthy place."[30]

In their search for democracy, Arabs, the great majority of whom suffer from poverty, cannot afford to adopt the Western definition of democracy if it excludes equality and social justice as constituent elements. Simply put, a certain balance has to be found between freedom and equality. This is the challenge that awaits the Arab progressive secular movement. In this sense, progressives are likely to agree with Czechoslovakia's writer-president, Vaclav Havel, who said in a speech to the U.S. Congress: "As long as people are people, democracy, in the full sense of the word, will always be no more than an ideal. One may approach it as one would the horizon in ways that may be better or worse, but it can never be fully attained. In this sense, you, too, are merely approaching democracy."[31]

It remains to be seen whether the U.S. Congress grasped the message. The great majority of its members never think in terms of transcending their system, for they strongly believe that they have already achieved full democracy. For some of them, there is no longer a horizon beyond the one they passed two hundred years ago.

Arabs are deeply dissatisfied with their present condition and place in history. It is not clear, however, which of the two alternative visions they will follow as they approach the twenty-first century. Some of the most active of them—the religious fundamentalists—seem to be absolutely convinced that they passed the last horizon of human seeking over fourteen centuries ago. They therefore strive to reverse history, moving backward when they are not fully certain in what direction "backward" lies. Others, particularily progressive nationalist Arabs, feel that precisely at the time when they were confronting the challenges of the twenty-first century, the catastrophic Gulf War pushed them back into a period similar to the aftermath of World War I, when the victorious European powers preempted the Arabs' drive for independence and unity and fragmented Arab society in accord with their own interests.

Have Arabs, then, lost their sense of direction? For the present, the answer is "perhaps." What remains certain is the intensity of the Arabs' struggle to transform their society and determine their place in history.

Notes

1. SOCIAL AND POLITICAL INTEGRATION: ALTERNATIVE
VISIONS OF THE FUTURE

1. Gamal Hamdan, *Shakhsiyyat Misr* (Egyptian Personality) (Cairo: Maktabat an-nahda al-misriyyah, 1970), pp. 494, 513, 514, 15.

2. Laila Shukri El-Hamamsy, "The Assertion of Egyptian Identity," in Saad Eddin Ibrahim and Nicholas S. Hopkins, eds., *Arab Society in Transition: A Reader* (Cairo: American University in Cairo, 1977), pp. 50, 75; originally published in George DeVos and Lola Romanucci-Ross, eds., *Ethnic Identity: Cultural Continuities and Change* (Palo Alto: Mayfield, 1975).

3. El-Sayyid Yassin, *Al-Shakhsiyya al-'arabiyya* (The Arab Personality) (Beirut: Dar at-Tanwir, 1981), p. 147.

4. Saad Eddin Ibrahim, "Al hiwar hawl 'urubat Misr wal qawmiyya al-'arabiyya" (The Debate on the Arabism of Egypt and Arab Nationalism), *Al-Fikr al-'arabi* (Beirut) 1, nos. 4–5 (September–November 1978): 185–268.

5. 'Ali Eddin Hilal, "A-tajzi'a wat-taqsim fi al-watan al-'arabi" (Division and Fragmentation in the Arab Homeland), *Qadaia 'arabiyya* (Beirut) 3, nos. 1–6 (1976): 43–52, p. 45.

6. Jonathan C. Randal, *Going All the Way: Christian Warlords, Israeli Adventurers, and the War in Lebanon* (New York: Viking Press, 1983), p. 188.

7. Livia Rokach, *Israeli's Sacred Terrorism: A Study Based on Moshe Sharett's Personal Diary and Other Documents* (Belmont, Mass.: Association of Arab-American University Graduates, 1980), pp. 24–25, 28.

8. Pierre Gemayel, *Lubnan waqi' wa murtaja* (Lebanon: Reality and Hope) (Beirut: Manshurat al-kata'ib al-Labnaniyya, 1970), p. 32.

9. Anne Sinai and Chaim Waxman, in *Middle East Review* 9, no. 1 (Fall 1976): 5.

10. R. Hrair Dekmejian, "The Armenians: History, Consciousness and the Middle Eastern Dispersion," *Middle East Review* 9, no. 1 (Fall 1976): 26.

11. Thomas Collelo, ed., *Syria: A Country Study*, 3d ed. (Washington, D.C.: Library of Congress, 1988), p. 51.

12. Eric A. Nordlinger, *Conflict Regulation in Divided Societies* (Cambridge, Mass.: Harvard University, Center for International Affairs, 1972), p. 20.

13. Arend Lijphart, "Consociational Democracy," *World Politics* 21, no. 2 (January 1979): 207–25.

14. Samir Amin, "The Historical Foundations of Arab Nationalism," in Saad Eddin Ibrahim and Nicholas S. Hopkins, eds., *Arab Society in Transition: A Reader* (Cairo: American University in Cairo, 1977), p. 8.

2. ARAB SOCIETY: BASIC CHARACTERISTIC FEATURES

1. Abdelkebir Khatibi, "Arabs between Post-Modernity and Modernity" (paper presented at Arab-American University Graduates Annual Convention, Boston, November 1986). For an Arabic version of this paper, see *Al-Moukaddima,* 1, no. 2 (June 1987): 4–5.

2. Abdelkebir Khatibi, "Double Criticism: The Decolonization of Arab Sociology," in Halim Barakat, ed., *Contemporary North Africa: Issues of Development and Integration* (Washington, D.C.: Center for Contemporary Arab Studies, Georgetown University, 1985), pp. 9–19.

3. Taher ben Jelloun, "Decolonizing Sociology in the Maghreb: Usefulness and Risks of a Critical Function," in Ibrahim and Hopkins, eds., *Arab Society in Transition,* p. 605.

4. Hamdan, *Shakhsiyyat Misr,* pp. 7, 494.

5. Hussein Fawzi, *Sindibad misri* (Egyptian Sinbad), 2d ed. (Cairo: Dar al-ma'arif, 1969), pp. 10, 311.

6. For details, see Halim Barakat, *Lebanon in Strife: Student Preludes to the Civil War* (Austin: University of Texas Press, 1977); "The Social Context" (i.e., of the Lebanese civil war), in P. E. Haley and L. W. Snider, eds., *Lebanon in Crisis: Participants and Issues* (Syracuse, N.Y.: Syracuse University Press, 1979), pp. 3–20; and *Toward a Viable Lebanon* (London and Washington, D.C.: Croom Helm and Center for Contemporary Arab Studies, Georgetown University, 1988).

7. For details on these conflicts, see Mohammed Beshir Hamid, "Confrontation and Reconciliation within African Context: The Case of Sudan," *Third World Quarterly* 5, no. 2 (April 1983): 320–29, and Mohamed Omer Beshir, *Southern Sudan: Regionalism and Religion: Selected Essays* (Khartoum: University of Khartoum Publications, 1984).

8. Turki Rabih, *Al-Ta'lim al-qawmi wal-shakhsiyya al-jaza'iriyya* (National Education and the Algerian Personality), 2d ed. (Algiers: Al-Sharika al-wataniyya lil-nashr wal-tawzi', 1981), p. 54.

9. Elbaki Hermassi, *Leadership and National Development in North Africa* (Berkeley and Los Angeles: University of California Press, 1972), p. 8.

10. Abdallah Laroui, *The History of the Maghrib: An Interpretive Essay*, trans.

from the French by Ralph Manheim (Princeton: Princeton University Press, 1977), p. 384.

11. Hanna Batatu, *The Old Social Classes and the Revolutionary Movements of Iraq* (Princeton: Princeton University Press, 1978), p. 9.

12. C. A. O. van Niewenhuijze, *Social Stratification and the Middle East* (Leiden: E. J. Brill, 1965); James A. Bill, "Class Analysis and the Dialectics of Modernization in the Middle East," *International Journal of Middle East Studies* 3, no. 4 (1972): 417–34.

13. Iliya Harik, "Lebanon: Anatomy of Conflict," *American Universities Field Staff Reports,* no. 49 (1981): 8.

14. Bryan S. Turner, *Marx and the End of Orientalism* (London: George Allen & Unwin, 1978), pp. 49, 48–49.

15. Nicholas S. Hopkins, "The Emergence of Class in a Tunisian Town," *International Journal of Middle East Studies* 8, no. 4 (1977): 456–57, 479.

16. Pierre L. van den Berghe, *The Ethnic Phenomenon* (New York: Elsevier, 1981), p. 17.

17. Ibid., pp. 18–19, 37, 35.

18. Barakat, *Lebanon in Strife*, pp. 115–18.

19. Here reference is made to out-of-context interpretation by Fuad Ajami of poems by the modern Arab poets Adonis and Qabbani. See Fuad Ajami, "The Silence in Arab Culture," *New Republic*, April 6, 1987, pp. 27–33.

20. Menahem Milson, ed., *Society and Political Structure in the Arab World* (New York: Humanities Press, 1973), p. xiv.

21. Hisham Sharabi, *Neopatriarchy: A Theory of Distorted Change in Arab Society* (Oxford: Oxford University Press, 1988).

22. Ibid., p. 35.

23. For details, see Saad Eddin Ibrahim, *The New Arab Social Order* (Boulder, Colo., and London: Westview Press and Croom Helm, 1982), ch. 6.

24. For details, see Halim Barakat, "Socio-Economic, Cultural and Personality Forces Determining Development in Arab Society," *Social Praxis* 2, nos. 3–4 (1976): 179–204.

25. For details of the variation in environmental settings, see Hassan Haddad and Basheer Nijm, eds., *The Arab World: A Handbook* (Wilmette, Ill.: Medina Press, 1978); W. B. Fisher, *The Middle East: A Physical, Social and Regional Geography*, 5th ed. (London: Methuen, 1963); Daniel Bates and Amal Rassam, *Peoples and Cultures of the Middle East* (Englewood Cliffs, N.J.: Prentice-Hall, 1983); Alasdair Drysdale and Gerald H. Blake, *The Middle East and North Africa: A Political Geography* (Oxford: Oxford University Press, 1985).

26. See Fawzi Girgis, *Dirasat fi tarikhi Misr as-siassi* (Studies in the Political History of Egypt) (Cairo: Dar an-Nadim, 1959), p. 39; and Ibrahim and Hopkins, eds., *Arab Society in Transition*, p. 305.

27. For these quantitative and qualitative improvements, see Munir Bashshur, *Itijahat fi at-tarbiyya al-'arabiyya* (Trends in Arab Education) (Tunis and Beirut: Al-Munazzama al-'arabiyya lil-tarbiyya wal-thaqafa wal-'ulum, 1982).

28. Fred Halliday, "Labor Migration in the Arab World," *Middle East Research and Information Project Reports* 14, no. 4 (May 1984): 3, 4.

29. For more details, see *Middle East Research and Information Project Reports* 14, no. 4 (May 1984); Ibrahim, *New Arab Social Order;* and J. S. Birk and C. A. Sinclair, *Arab Manpower* (London: Croom Helm, 1980).

30. Frederic C. Shorter and Huda Zurayk, eds., *Population Factors in Development Planning in the Middle East* (New York and Cairo: Population Council, 1985), p. 45.

3. ARAB IDENTITY: E PLURIBUS UNUM

1. Albert Hourani, *Arabic Thought in the Liberal Age, 1798–1939* (Oxford: Oxford University Press, 1970), p. 1.

2. Jacques Berque, *The Arabs: Their History and Future,* trans. Jean Stewart (London: Faber & Faber, 1964), pp. 25, 191, 51.

3. See Saad Eddin Ibrahim, "Nahwa dirasat sociologiyya lil-wahda: Al-'Aqaliat fi al-'alam al-'arabi" (Toward a Sociological Study of Unity: Minorities in the Arab World), *Qadaia 'arabiyya* (Beirut) 3, nos. 1–6 (1976): 5–24; id., *Itijahat al-ra'i al-'am al-'arabi nahwa mas'alat al-wahda: Dirasa midaniyya* (Trends of Arab Public Opinion toward the Question of Unity: A Field Study) (Beirut: Center for Arab Unity Studies, 1980).

4. Abd al-Aziz Duri, *Al-Juzur at-tarikhiyya lil-qawmiyya al-'arabiyya* (Historical Roots of Arab Nationalism) (Beirut: Dar al-'ilm lil-malayyin, 1960).

5. Abd al-Aziz Duri, *The Historical Formation of the Arab Nation,* Center for Contemporary Studies, Georgetown University, Occasional Papers Series (Washington, D.C.: Center for Contemporary Studies, 1983), p. 1.

6. Sati' al-Husari, *Ma hia al-qawmiyya?* (What Is Nationalism?) (Beirut: Dar al-'ilm lil-malayyin, 1959), pp. 252, 57.

7. Samir Amin, "The Historical Foundations of Arab Nationalism," in Ibrahim and Hopkins, eds., *Arab Society in Transition,* pp. 9–10.

8. Philip S. Khoury, *Urban Notables and Arab Nationalism: The Politics of Damascus, 1860–1920* (Cambridge: Cambridge University Press, 1983), p. 64.

9. Abd al-Aziz Duri, "Hawla at-tatawur at-tarikhi lil umma al-'arabiyya" (Historical Development of the Arab Nation), in Center for Arab Unity Studies, *Al-Qawmiyya al-'arabiyya fi al-fikr wal-moumarassa* (Arab Nationalism: Thought and Practice) (Beirut: Center for Arab Unity Studies, 1980), pp. 221–27.

10. Duri, *Historical Formation of the Arab Nation,* p. 1.

11. Constantine K. Zurayk, *Tensions in Islamic Civilization,* Center for Contemporary Arab Studies, Georgetown University, Seminar Paper no. 3 (Washington, D.C.: Center for Contemporary Arab Studies, 1978), pp. 8, 6.

12. Duri, *Historical Formation of the Arab Nation,* p. 8.

13. Muhammed Rumayhi, *Mu'auuqat at-tanmiyya al-ijtima'iyya wal-iqtisadiyya fi mujtama'at al-khalij al-'arabi al mu'asira* (Obstacles to Social and

Economic Development in the Contemporary Gulf States) (Kuwait: Dar as-siyassa, 1977), p. 37.

14. 'Allal al-Fassi, *An-Naqd al-dhati* (Self-Criticism), (Beirut: Dar al-kashshaf, 1966), p. 139.

15. Roger Owen, "Arab Nationalism, Unity and Solidarity," in Talal Asad and Roger Owen, eds., *Sociology of "Developing Societies": The Middle East* (New York: Monthly Review Press, 1983), p. 21.

16. El-Sayyid Yassin, "Ash-Shakhsiyya al-'arabiyya: An-Nasaq ar-ra'issi wal-ansaq al-far'iyya" (Arab Personality: Primary and Secondary Patterns), *Al-Mustaqbal al-'arabi* 1, no. 3 (September 1978): 145.

17. Muhammed Mahdi Shamseddin, "Nadhrat al-Islam ila al-usra fi mujtama' mutatuir" (Islam's View of Family in a Changing Society), *Al-Fikr al-Islami* 6, no. 5 (May 1975): 8.

18. Muhammed 'Amara, "Min huna bada't masiratuna lil-wahda al-'arabiyya," (The Beginnings of Our March for Arab Unity), *Qadaia 'arabiyya* (Beirut) 3, nos. 1–6 (1976): 63–75, 67–68.

19. Zurayk, *Tensions in Islamic Civilization*, p. 5.

20. Donald P. Cole, *Nomads of the Nomads: The Al-Murrah Bedouin of the Empty Quarter* (Arlington Heights, Ill.: AHM Publishing, 1975), p. 109.

21. Hermassi, *Leadership and National Development in North Africa*, p. 38.

22. Kamal Salibi, "Tribal Origins of the Religious Sects in the Arab East," in Barakat, ed., *Toward a Viable Lebanon,* pp. 15–26.

23. Beshir, ed., *Southern Sudan,* p. 26.

24. Abdelaziz Abbassi, "A Sociolinguistic Analysis of Multilingualism in Morocco" (Ph.D. diss., University of Texas, Austin, 1976), p. 13.

25. Hermassi, *Leadership and National Development in North Africa*, p. 73.

26. For a review of plans of accommodation and recurrent uprisings, see Edmund Ghareeb, *The Kurdish Question in Iraq* (Syracuse, N.Y.: Syracuse University Press, 1981).

27. Albert Hourani, *Minorities in the Arab World* (Oxford: Oxford University Press, 1947), p. 1.

28. Tariq al-Bushri, "Al-Ta'ifiyya ghair al-mandhura" (Invisible Sectarianism), *Al-Youm as-sabi'*, no. 28 (October 8, 1984).

29. Muhammed Abed Jabri, *Al-Khitab al-'arabi al-mu'asir* (Contemporary Arab Discourse) (Beirut: Dar at-tali'a, 1982), pp. 61–63.

30. Al-Husari, *Ma hia al-qawmiyya?* p. 153.

31. Adib Nassur, *Al-Naksa wal-khata'* (Beirut: Dar al-katib al-'arabi, n.d.).

32. Samir Amin, *The Arab Nation: Nationalism and Class Struggle* (London: Zed Press, 1978), p. 81; id., "Historical Foundations of Arab Nationalism," in Ibrahim and Hopkins, eds., *Arab Society in Transition*, p. 20.

33. Walid Kaziha, "Fikrat al-wahda al-'arabiyya fi matla' al-qarn al-'ishrin" (The Idea of Arab Unity at the Beginning of the Twentieth Century), *Al-Mustaqbal al-'arabi* 1, no. 4 (November 1978): 12.

34. Constantine Zurayk, *Nahnu wal-mustaqbal* (We and the Future) (Beirut: Dar al-'ilm lil-malayyin, 1977), p. 221.

35. Ibrahim, *New Arab Social Order*, ch. 6.

36. Khoury, *Urban Notables and Arab Nationalism*, p. 23.

37. See Lewis A. Caser, *The Functions of Social Conflict* (New York: Free Press, 1954); id., ed., *Continuities in the Study of Social Conflict* (New York: Free Press, 1967).

38. Nadim Bitar, "Dawr al-makhater al-kharijiyya fi tajarub at-tarikh al-wahdawiyya" (The Role of External Dangers in History in Unification Experiences), *Al-Mustaqbal al-'arabi* 1, no. 3 (September 1978): 121–30.

39. See Ajami, "Silence in Arab Culture."

4. THE CONTINUITY OF OLD CLEAVAGES: TRIBE, VILLAGE, CITY

1. Abu Zaid 'Abdel Rahman Ibn Muhammad Ibn Khaldun, *Al-Muqaddimah* (Prolegomena) (Tunis: Al-Dar at-Tunisiyya, 1984), 1: 165.

2. Ali al-Wardi, *Mantiq Ibn Khaldun* (The Logic of Ibn Khaldun), (Tunis: Ash-Sharika at-Tunisiyya, 1978–79), pp. 81–82.

3. Mahmoud 'Awda, *Al-Fallahun wal-dawla* (The Peasants and the State) (Cairo: Dar al-thaqafa, 1979), pp. 179–88.

4. Abdul-'al al-Saqban, *Nahwa nizam iqtisadi 'arabi jadid* (Toward a New Arab Economic Order) (London: Arab Research Center, 1981), p. 32.

5. Al-Wardi, *Mantiq Ibn Khaldun*; Faruq al-Kilani, *Shari'at al-'asha'ir fi al-watan al-'arabi* (Tribal Law in the Arab Homeland) (Beirut: Dar al-'ilm lil-malayyin, 1972).

6. Wayne Eastep, *Bedouin: Photography and Text* (United Technologies Corporation, [1983?]).

7. Ibn Khaldun, *Muqaddimah,* 1: bk. 2.

8. M. T. Abu al-'Ula, *Jighrafiat al-'alam al-'arabi* (The Geography of the Arab World) (Cairo: Anglo-Egyptian Press, 1977), pp. 65–67.

9. William Lancaster, *Changing Cultures: The Rwala Bedouin Today* (Cambridge: Cambridge University Press, 1981), p. 73.

10. Ibid., p. 28.

11. Muhammed al-Marzuqi, *Ma' al-badu fi hallihim wa-tirhalihim* (Bedouin: Their Settlement and Movement) (Tunis: Al-Dar al-'arabiyya lil-kitab, 1980), p. 137.

12. Lancaster, *Changing Cultures*, p. 129.

13. Fadl Ali Ahmed Abu Ghanim, *Al-Bunia al-qabaliyya fi al-Yemen* (The Tribal Structure in Yemen) (Damascus: Matba'at al-katib al-'arabi, 1985), pp. 115, 138.

14. Ibn Khaldun, *Muqaddimah* 1: 174.

15. Al-Wardi, *Mantiq Ibn Khaldun*, p. 274.

16. See Norman N. Lewis, *Nomads and Settlers in Syria and Jordan, 1800–1980* (Cambridge: Cambridge University Press, 1987).

17. Al-Marzuqi, *Ma' al-badu fi hallihim wa-tirhalihim*, p. 7.

18. Kamal Abu Jaber et al., *Bedouins of Jordan: A People in Transition* (Amman: Royal Scientific Society Press, 1978), pp. 5–7.

19. Ibrahim, *New Arab Social Order*, p. 7.

20. Saad Eddin Ibrahim and Donald Cole, *Saudi Arabian Bedouin*, Cairo Papers in Social Science, vol. 1, no. 5 (April 1978), pp. 4, 42, 104.

21. Lancaster, *Changing Cultures*, p. 131.

22. See Afif Tannous, "Social Change in An Arab Village," *American Sociological Review* 6, no. 5 (1941): 650–662; "Group Behavior in the Village Community of Lebanon," *American Journal of Sociology* 48, no. 2 (September 1942): 231–39; and "Emigration: A Force of Social Change in an Arab Village," *Rural Sociology* 7 (March 1942): 62–74.

23. Abu Ghanim, *Al-Bunia al-qabaliyya fi al-Yemen*, pp. 89–90.

24. Rosemary Sayigh, *Palestinians: From Peasants to Revolutionaries* (London: Zed Press, 1979), pp. 14, 21, 24.

25. Mahmoud 'Awda, *Al-Fallahun wal-dawla*, p. 108.

26. Beshara Doumani, "Merchant Life in Ottoman Palestine: Its Hinterland, 1800–1860" (Ph.D. diss., Georgetown University, 1990).

27. For a description of these different categories of land tenure in a specific village, see Richard Antoun, *Arab Village: A Social Structural Study of a Transjordanian Peasant Community* (Bloomington: Indiana University Press, 1972), pp. 19–20.

28. Hamdan, *Shakhsiyyat Misr*, p. 133.

29. Mahmoud 'Awda, *Al-Fallahun wal-dawla*, p. 133.

30. Bates and Rassam, *Peoples and Cultures of the Middle East*, p. 136.

31. All these images are found in one of his several collections of poetry: Mahmoud Darwish, *A'ras* (Weddings) (Beirut: Dar al-'awda, 1977).

32. Janet Abu-Lughod, "Migrant Adjustment to City Life: The Egyptian Case," *American Journal of Sociology* 47, no. 1 (July 1961): 22–32, at pp. 22, 23.

33. Hanna Batatu, *The Egyptian, Syrian and Iraqi Revolutions* (Washington, D.C.: Center for Contemporary Arab Studies, Georgetown University, 1984), p. 4.

34. Anis Frayha, *Al-Qaria al-lubnaniyya: Hadara fi tariq al-zawal* (The Lebanese Village: A Civilization on the Way to Extinction) (1957; 2d ed., Beirut: Dar an-nahar, 1980), p. 1.

35. Ibn Khaldun, *Muqaddimah*, 1: 165–66.

36. Albert Hourani, "Introduction: The Islamic City in Light of Recent Research," in A. Hourani and S. M. Stern, eds., *The Islamic City* (Philadelphia: University of Pennsylvania Press, 1970), p. 9.

37. Janet Abu-Lughod, *Cairo: 1001 Years of the City Victorious* (Princeton: Princeton University Press, 1971), ch. 12.

38. Cited in Janet Abu-Lughod, "The Islamic City—Historic Myth, Islamic Essence, and Contemporary Relevance," *International Journal of Middle East Studies* 19, no. 2 (May 1987): 155–76, at p. 168.

39. Abdulkarim Ghallab, *Dafanna al-madi,* 4th ed. (Rabat: Matba'at al-rissala, 1966), p. 119.

40. Abu-Lughod, "Islamic City," p. 172.

41. Ahmed Banani, *Fas fi sab' qassas* (Fez in Seven Short Stories) (Rabat: Matba'at al-rissala, n.d.), p. 66.

42. Ghallab, *Dafanna al-madi,* p. 38.

43. As-Sayyid al-Husseini, *Al-Madina: Dirastun fi 'ilmi al-ijtima'i al-hadari* (The City: A Study in Urban Sociology) (Cairo: Dar al-ma'arif, 1981), p. 51.

44. Frank H. Stewart, "Tribal Law in the Arab World: A Review of the Literature," *International Journal of Middle East Studies* 19, no. 4 (November 1987): 473–90, at p. 473.

45. Fadil al-Insari, *Al-Jugrafia al-ijtima'iyya* (Social Geography) (Damascus: Manshurat jami'at dimashq, 1978), p. 298.

46. Al-Wardi, *Mantiq Ibn Khaldun,* p. 289.

47. Berque, *The Arabs,* pp. 29, 164.

48. Stewart, "Tribal Law in the Arab World," p. 475.

49. Banani, *Fas fi sab' qassas,* p. 46.

5. SOCIAL CLASSES: BEYOND THE MOSAIC MODEL

1. Carlton S. Coon, *Caravan: The Story of the Middle East* (New York: Holt, Rinehart & Winston, 1961).

2. Van Niewenhuijze, *Social Stratification and the Middle East,* esp. pp. 7–9; id., ed., *Commoners, Climbers, and Notables* (Leiden: E. J. Brill, 1977), esp. pp. 579–80.

3. Bill, "Class Analysis and the Dialectics of Modernization in the Middle East," pp. 420, 422, 430.

4. Manfred Halpern, *The Politics of Social Change in the Middle East and North Africa* (Princeton: Princeton University Press, 1963), pp. 46, 59, 69.

5. Turner, *Marx and the End of Orientalism,* p. 49.

6. Hopkins, "Emergence of Class in a Tunisian Town," p. 456.

7. Erik Olin Wright, *Class, Crisis, and the State* (1978; London: Verso, 1979).

8. Ibid., pp. 41–42.

9. Mahmoud Abdel-Fadil, *The Political Economy of Nasserism: A Study in Employment and Income Distribution Policies in Urban Egypt, 1952–72* (Cambridge: Cambridge University Press, 1980), pp. 92–94.

10. Batatu, *Old Social Classes and the Revolutionary Movements of Iraq,* p. 7.

11. Zuhair Hatab, *Tatowor buna al-usra al-'arabiyya* (The Evolution of the Structures of the Arab Family) (Beirut: Ma'had al-inma' al-'arabi, 1976), pp. 109, 130–31.

12. Abd al-Aziz Duri, *Muqaddimah fi at-tarikh al-iqtisadi al-'arabi* (Introduction to Arab Economic History) (Beirut: Dar at-tali'a, 1969), pp. 139–48.

13. Abdul Karim Rafiq, *Buhuth fi at-tarikh al-iqtisadi wal-ijtima'i libilad ash-*

sham fi al-'asr al-hadith (Studies in the Economic and Social History of Syria in the Modern Period) (Damascus: Jami'at Dimashq, 1985), pp. 241, 253.

14. Khoury, *Urban Notables and Arab Nationalism*, p. 4.

15. Judith E. Tucker, "Taming the West: Trends in the Writing of Modern Arab Social History in North America and England," in Hisham Sharabi, ed., *Power, Theory and the Arab World* (New York: Routledge, 1990), pp. 198–227.

16. Roger Owen, *The Middle East in the World Economy, 1800–1914* (London: Methuen, 1981).

17. Amin, "Historical Foundations of Arab Nationalism," in Ibrahim and Hopkins, eds., *Arab Society in Transition*, p. 19.

18. Khoury, *Urban Notables and Arab Nationalism*, p. 5.

19. Ibid., p. 6.

20. Raphael Patai, *Society, Culture and Change in the Middle East* (Philadelphia: University of Pennsylvania Press, 1971), pp. 372–73.

21. Ibrahim, *New Arab Social Order*, pp. 132–39.

22. See Al-Saqban, *Nahwa nizam iqtisadi 'arabi jadid*, pp. 8–9, 27.

23. Samir Amin, *Arab Economy Today* (London: Zed Books, 1982), p. 57.

24. Charles Issawi, review of Tarif Khalidi, ed., *Land Tenure and Social Transformation in the Middle East*, Proceedings of a conference held at the American University of Beirut in February 1983, *Journal of Palestine Studies* 17, no. 1 (Autumn 1987): 144.

25. Khoury, *Urban Notables and Arab Nationalism*, pp. 5, 26–44.

26. Pamela Ann Smith, *Palestine and the Palestinians, 1876–1983* (New York: St. Martin's Press, 1984), p. 13.

27. Afaf Lutfi al-Sayyid Marsot, *Egypt in the Reign of Muhammed Ali* (Cambridge: Cambridge University Press, 1984), p. 160.

28. Hamed Ammar, *Growing Up in an Egyptian Village* (London: Routledge & Kegan Paul, 1954), p. 41.

29. Charles Issawi, *Egypt in Revolution: An Economic Analysis* (Oxford: Oxford University Press, 1963), p. 160.

30. Anouar Abdel-Malek, *Egypt: Military Society*, trans. Charles L. Markmann (New York: Random House, Vintage Books, 1968), p. 72; Hamdan, *Shakhsiyyat Misr*; Iliya Harik, *Distribution of Land, Employment and Income in Rural Egypt* (Ithaca, N.Y.: Cornell University, Center for International Studies, 1975).

31. Abdul-Basit Abudl-Mu'ti, *Al-Sira' at-tabaqi fi al-qaria al-misriyya* (Class Struggle in the Egyptian Village) (Cairo: Dar al-thaqafa al-jadida, 1977), p. 122.

32. Mahmoud 'Awda, *Al-Qaria al-misriyya* (The Egyptian Village) (Cairo: Maktabat Said Ra'fat, 1983), p. 135.

33. 'Awda, *Al-Fallahun wal-dawla*, p. 152.

34. Batatu, *Old Social Classes and the Revolutionary Movements of Iraq*, pp. 54–55.

35. Ibid., p. 11.

36. Yusif A. Sayigh, *The Economics of the Arab World: Development since 1945* (London: Croom Helm, 1978), p. 487.

37. Amin, "Historical Foundations of Arab Nationalism," in Ibrahim and Hopkins, eds., *Arab Society in Transition*, p. 19.

38. George Abed, "Oil and Development in the Arab Oil-Exporting Countries," in Michael C. Hudson, ed., *The Arab Future: Critical Issues* (Washington, D.C.: Center for Contemporary Arab Studies, Georgetown University, 1979) pp. 41–62, at p. 42.

39. Rumayhi, *Mu'auuqat at-tanmiyya al-ijtima'iyya wal-iqtisadiyya fi mujtama'at al-khalij al-'arabi al mu'asira*, pp. 16–18.

40. Abdalla S. Bujra, *The Politics of Stratification: A Study of Political Change in a South Arabian Town* (Oxford: Oxford University Press, 1971), p. xiii; and see also pp. 13–18.

41. Batatu, *Old Social Classes and the Revolutionary Movements of Iraq*, p. 153.

42. Ibid., p. 160.

43. See, e.g., Paul Rabinow, *Symbolic Domination: Cultural Form and Historical Change in Morocco* (Chicago: University of Chicago Press, 1975); Dale F. Eickelman, *Moroccan Islam* (Austin: University of Texas Press, 1976).

44. Hamdan, *Shakhsiyyat Misr*, p. 133.

45. Abdel-Malek, *Egypt: Military Society*, pp. 58–59.

46. Ibid., p. 14.

47. Abdel-Fadil, *Political Economy of Nasserism,* p. 92.

48. See Khoury, *Urban Notables and Arab Nationalism*, ch. 2.

49. Batatu, *Old Social Classes and the Revolutionary Movements of Iraq,* pp. 53–57, 63, 95, 210.

50. Abdel-Malek, *Egypt: Military Society,* p. 60.

51. Henry Habib Ayrout, *The Egyptian Peasant,* trans. John A. Williams (Boston: Beacon Press, 1963), pp. 16, 21, 150.

52. For the latter two works, see Chap. 9 n. 41 and Chap. 2 n. 5.

53. Gabriel Baer, *Studies in the Social History of Modern Egypt* (Chicago: University of Chicago Press, 1969), pp. 93–108; Ayrout, *Egyptian Peasant,* pp. 33, 2, 18.

54. Franz Fanon, *The Wretched of the Earth,* trans. C. Farrington (New York: Grove Press, 1963), p. 129.

55. Sayigh, *Palestinians: From Peasants to Revolutionaries,* p. 6.

56. Karl Marx, *The Economic and Philosophic Manuscripts of 1844* (New York: International Publishers, 1964), pp. 106–19.

57. Elisabeth Longuenesse, "The Class Nature of the State in Syria: Contributions to an Analysis," *Middle East Research and Information Project Reports* 9, no. 4 (May 1979): 3–11.

58. Batatu, *Egyptian, Syrian and Iraqi Revolutions,* p. 16.

59. Sadir Younis, "Al-Haraka an-niqabiyya al-lubnaniyya wa-hatmiyyat al-bunia al-ijtima'iyya" (The Lebanese Union Movement and the Inevitabilities of the Social Structures), *At-Tariq* 39, no. 3–4 (1980): 38–52.

60. Abdullatif al-Mununi, "At-Tatour al-siassi lil haraka an-niqabiyya bil-Maghrib" (The Political Evolution of the Union Movement in Morocco), *Al-Thaqafa al-jadida* 4, no. 13 (1979): 7.

6. THE ARAB FAMILY AND THE CHALLENGE OF CHANGE

1. Naguib Mahfouz, *Zuqaq al-Midaqq* (Midaq Alley), 6th ed. (Cairo: Maktabat Misr, 1965), p. 58. See the translation by Trevor Le Gassick (Beirut: Khayats, 1966; also published by Heinemann and Three Continents Press).

2. Naguib Mahfouz, "The Mistake," an excerpt from *Baina al-qasrain* (Between Two Palaces), in E. W. Fernea and B. Q. Bezirgan, eds., *Middle Eastern Muslim Women Speak* (Austin: University of Texas Press, 1977), p. 97

3. Hisham Sharabi, *Muqaddamat li-dirast 'al mujtama' al-'arabi* (An Introduction to the Study of Arab Society) (Jerusalem: Manshurat Salahad Din, 1975), p. 112.

4. 'Abbas Mahmoud al-'Aqqad, *Al-Mar'a fi al-Qur'an* (The Women in the Koran) (Cairo: Dar al-hilal, 1971), pp. 29–33; Sheikh Hassan Khalid, "Al-mar'a fi 'irf al-Islam" (The Woman in Islam), *Majallat al-fikr al-islami* 6, no. 5 (May 1975): 3–5.

5. Ahmed Shalabi, "Al-Wiratha wal-wassiyya" (Inheritance and Will), *Majallat al-fikr al-islami* 6, no. 5 (May 1975): 24–25

6. Aminah al-Sa'id, "The Arab Woman and the Challenge of Society," in Fernea and Bezirgan, *Middle Eastern Muslim Women Speak*, pp. 373–90.

7. Hourani, *Arabic Thought in the Liberal Age*, p. 168.

8. Salama Moussa, *Laisat al-mar'at lu'bat al-rajul* (The Woman Is Not a Man's Toy) (Cairo: Salama Moussa lil-nashr wa at-tawzi', 1953); Fadela Mrabet, *Les Algériennes* (Paris: Maspero, 1967); Layla Ba'albaki, *Ana ahya* (I Live) (Beirut: Dar shi'r, 1958); Ghadah al-Samman, "The Sexual Revolution and the Total Revolution," in Fernea and Bezirgan, *Middle Eastern Muslim Women Speak*, pp. 391–99; Khalida Sa'id, "Al-Mar'a al-'arabiyya: Ka'in bi-nafsihi" (The Arab Woman: An Alienated Being), *Mawaqif* 2, no. 12 (1970): 91–100; Nawal El-Saadawi, *The Hidden Face of Eve* (Boston: Beacon Press, 1982); Fatima Mernissi, *Beyond the Veil: Male-Female Dynamics in a Modern Muslim Society* (New York: Schenkman, 1975).

9. Markaz dirasat al-wahda al-'arabiyya (Center for Arab Unity Studies), *Al-Mar'a wa-dowruha fi harakat al-wahda al-'arabiyya* (Woman and Her Role in the Arab Unity Movement) (Beirut: Markaz dirasat al-wahda al-'arabiyya, 1982).

10. Sa'id, "Al-Mar'a al-'arabiyya," pp. 91–93.

11. Halim Barakat, "An-Nizam al-ijtima'i wa 'alaqatuhu bi mushkilat al-mar'a al-'arabiyya" (Arab Social Order and Its Relationship to the Question of Arab Woman), in Center for Arab Unity Studies, *Al-Mar'a wa-dowruha*, pp. 53–67, and in *Al-Mustaqbal al-'arabi* 4, no. 34 (December 1981): 51–63.

12. Sharabi, *Muqaddamat*, ch. 2.

13. Barakat, *Lebanon in Strife*, p. 79.

14. E. T. Prothro and L. N. Diab, *Changing Family Patterns in the Arab East* (Beirut: American University of Beirut, 1974).

15. Ihsan Muhammed al-Hassan, *Al-'A'ila wal-qaraba wal-zawaj* (Family, Kinship Ties, and Marriage) (Beirut: Dar at-tali'a, 1981), pp. 82, 106, 116.

16. Emile Habiby, *Sudasyyiat al-ayyam as-sittat* (The Six-Day War in Six Parts) (Beirut: Dar al-'awda, 1969), p. 72.

17. Ahmed Shalabi, *Al-Hayat al-ijtima'iyya fi at-tafkir al-islami* (Social Life in Islamic Thought) (Cairo: Maktabat an-nahda al-misriyya, 1968), p. 35.

18. Jabra I. Jabra, *Hunters in a Narrow Street* (London: Heinemann, 1960), p. 141.

19. Tayeb Salih, *Season of Migration to the North* (London: Heinemann, 1969), p. 82

20. Sahar Khalifa, *As-Sabbar* (Wild Thorns) (Jerusalem: Galilio, 1976), pp. 208, 216.

21. Nura S. Alamuddin and Paul D. Starr, *Crucial Bonds: Marriage among the Lebanese Druze* (Delmar, N.Y.: Caravan Books, 1980), pp. 34–39.

22. Hatab, *Tatowor buna al-usra al-'arabiyya*, p. 17.

23. Shakir Salim, *Al-Jibayish: Dirasa anthropologiyya li-garia fi ahowaz al-Iraq* (An Anthropological Study of an Iraqi Marsh Village) (Baghdad: Al-'Ani Press, 1970), pp. 119–21.

24. Al-Hassan, *Al-'A'ila wal-qaraba wal-zawaj,* p. 115.

25. Eickelman, *Moroccan Islam*, pp. 203–4.

26. Fuad Khuri, "Parallel Cousin Marriage Reconsidered: A Middle Eastern Practice That Nullifies the Effects of Marriage on the Intensity of Family Relationships," *Man* 5, no. 4 (December 1970): 597–618.

27. Muhammed Safouh al-Akhras, *Tarkib al-'a'ila al-'arabiyya* (The Structure of the Arab Family) (Damascus: Ministry of Culture, 1976).

28. Salim, *Al-Jibayish,* pp. 105–6.

29. Antoun, *Arab Village*, pp. 118–25, 169.

30. Safouh al-Akhras, *Tarkib al-'a'ila al-'arabiyya*, p. 131.

31. Buali Yassin, *Azamet az-zawaj fi Suriyya* (Marriage Crisis in Syria) (Beirut: Dar ibn Rushd, 1979), p. 23.

32. Alamuddin and Starr, *Crucial Bonds,* pp 63–83.

33. Prothro and Diab, *Changing Family Patterns in the Arab East,* pp. 29–33.

34. Safouh al-Akhras, *Tarkib al-'a'ila al-'arabiyya,* pp. 181–82. The greatest gap was for husbands aged 60–64, whose wives' ages ranged from 50 to 54 in 44 percent of the marriages; those with wives aged 40–44 constituted 28 percent, and those with wives aged 40 or less accounted for 11 percent. The study also found that 40 percent of husbands whose ages ranged between 55 and 59 had wives who were less than 45 years old. In comparison, half of the husbands aged 30–34 had wives ranging in age from 25 to 29.

35. Abdel Karim al-Jahayman, *Min asatirina ash-sha'biyyah fi qalb al-jazira al-'Arabiyya* (Folktales in the Heart of Arabia) (Beirut: Dar ath-thaqafa, 1969), 3 vols.

36. Ahmed Muhammed Ibrahim, "The Family System in Islam," *Al-Fikr al-islami* (Islamic Thought) 6, no. 5 (May 1975): 43–48, 46.

37. Abdul Nasser Tawfiq al-'Attar, *Ta'dod az-zawjat* (Polygamy) (Jidda: Dar as-shurouq; Damascus and Beirut: Mou'assat ar-Rissalah, 1976), pp. 126–31.

38. Ali Shalaq, "At-Tatour at-tarikhi li-awdha' al-mar'a al-'arabiyya fi al-watan al-'arabi" (Historical Development of the Conditions of Arab Women in the Arab Homeland), in Markaz dirasat al-wahda al-'arabiyya, *Al-Mar'a wa-dowruha fi harakat al-wahda al-'arabiyya*, p. 20.

39. Al-'Aqqad, *Al-Mar'a fi al-Qur'an*, p. 84.

40. Al-'Attar, *Ta'dod az-zawjat*, pp. 14–15.

41. Khalid Chatila, *Le Marriage chez les musulman en Syrie* (Paris: Librairie orientaliste, 1934).

42. Al-Hassan, *Al-'A'ila wal-qaraba wal-zawaj*, p. 79.

43. *Wa'i al-'ammal* (Iraq), no. 460 (1978).

44. Hatab, *Tatowor buna al-usra al-'arabiyya*, p. 93.

45. Abdalla Lahoud, *Az-Zawaj al-madani* (Civil Marriage) (Beirut: An-Nadi ath-thaqafi al-'arabi, 1966), p. 3.

46. Mohammed Barhoum, "Divorce and the Status of Women in Jordan" (MS, 1980).

47. Amira Abdul Mun'im al-Bassiouni, *Al-Isra al-misriyya* (The Egyptian Family) (Cairo: Dar al-katib al-'arabi, 1964), pp. 59–74.

48. Sharabi, *Neopatriarchy*, p. 7.

7. RELIGION IN SOCIETY

1. G. E. von Grunebaum, *Islam: Essays in the Nature and Growth of a Cultural Tradition* (1955; New York: Barnes & Noble, 1961), p. 127

2. Manfred Halpern, *The Politics of Social Change in the Middle East and North Africa* (Princeton: Princeton University Press, 1963), p. 119.

3. Von Grunebaum, *Islam*, pp. 74, 29.

4. Sayyid Qutb, *This Religion of Islam*, trans. "Islamdust" (Palo Alto, Calif.: Al-Manar Press, 1967), pp. 2, 6.

5. Berque, *The Arabs*, esp. pp. 25, 54, 55, 262, 281.

6. Wilfred Cantwell Smith, *Islam in Modern History* (New York: Mentor Books, 1957), p. 14.

7. E. Gellner, "A Pendulum Swing Theory of Islam," in Roland Robertson, ed. *Sociology of Religion* (Harmondsworth: Penguin Books, 1969), pp. 127–38, at p. 127.

8. Mohammed Arkoun, *Rethinking Islam Today* (Washington, D.C.: Center for Contemporary Arab Studies, Georgetown University, Occasional Papers Series, 1987).

9. Bryan S. Turner, *Weber and Islam* (London: Routledge & Kegan Paul, 1974), p. 23.

10. Max Weber, *The Sociology of Religion*, trans. E. Fischoff (London: Methuen, 1966), pp. 1, 2.

11. Al-Marzuqi, *Ma' al-Badu fi hallihim wa-tirhalihim,* pp. 142–43.

12. Max Weber, "Major Features of World Religions," in Robertson, ed., *Sociology of Religion,* p. 20.

13. Emile Durkheim, *The Elementary Forms of Religious Life,* trans. J. W. Swain (New York: Free Press, 1965), pp. 62, 53.

14. Ibid., pp. 466, 468.

15. Karl Marx, "Contribution to a Critique of Hegel's Philosophy of Right," cited in T. B. Bottomore and M. Rubel, eds., *Karl Marx: Selected Writings in Sociology and Social Philosophy* (London: Watts & Co., 1956), pp. 26–27.

16. J. Milton Yinger, *Religion, Society and the Individual* (New York: Macmillan Co., 1965), pp. 110–15. For Freud's interpretations, see his *Totem and Taboo* (1918), *Future of An Illusion* (1927), *Civilization and Its Discontents* (1930), and *Moses and Monotheism* (1939).

17. A. R. Radcliffe-Brown, "Religion and Society," in Louis Schneider, ed., *Religion, Culture and Society* (New York: John Wiley, 1964), p. 66.

18. Rafiq, *Buhuth fi at-tarikh al-iqtisadi wal-ijtima'i libilad ash-sham fi al-'asr al-hadith,* pp. 59, 160–64.

19. Salibi, "Tribal Origins of the Religious Sects," pp. 15–26.

20. Marsot, *Egypt in the Reign of Muhammed Ali,* p. 139.

21. Nassif Nassar, *Nahwa mujtama' jadid* (Toward a New Society) (Beirut: Dar al-nahar, 1970), p. 135.

22. Khaldoun al-Naqeeb, *Al-Mujtama' wal-dawlah fi al-khalij wal-jazira al-'arabiyya* (Society and State in the Gulf and Arabian Peninsula) (Beirut: Markaz dirasat al-wahda al-'arabiyya, 1988), pp. 74–78.

23. Gellner, "Pendulum Swing Theory of Islam."

24. Hassan S. Haddad, " 'Georgic' Cults and Saints of the Levant," *NVMEN: International Review for the History of Religions* (Leiden) 16, no. 1 (April 1969): 21–39.

25. Muhammed al-'Abdalla, "Al-Mazar: Dhalik al-wassit al mas-hur" (The Shrine: That Enchanted Mediator), *Al-Nahar al-'arabi wal-duawali,* February 2–8, 1981, p. 50.

26. Al-Marzuqi, *Ma' al-Badu fi hallihim wa-tirhalihim,* pp. 161, 162–63.

27. Rabinow, *Symbolic Domination,* p. 1.

28. Eickelman, *Moroccan Islam,* p. 237.

29. Michael Gilsenan, *Recognizing Islam* (New York: Pantheon Books, 1982), p. 12.

30. Michael Gilsenan, *Saint and Sufi in Modern Egypt: An Essay in the Sociology of Religion* (Oxford: Oxford University Press, 1978), chs. 3 and 6.

31. Sayyid Oweiss, *Min malamih al-mujtama' al-misri al-mu'assir* (Features of Contemporary Egyptian Society) (Cairo: Al-Markaz al-qawmi lil-buhuth al-ijtima'iyya wal-jina'iyya, 1965).

32. *Karl Marx: Selected Writings in Sociology and Social Philosphy,* ed. Bottomore and Rubel, pp. 26–27.

33. This sketch of the evolution of the concept of God is based on Leonard Broom and Philip Selznick, *Sociology: A Text with Adapted Readings*, 6th ed. (New York: Harper & Row, 1977), p. 380, and Joseph Henninger, "Pre-Islamic Bedouin Religion," in Merlin L. Swartz et al., *Studies on Islam* (Oxford: Oxford University Press, 1981), pp. 3–22.

34. 'Allal al-Fassi, *Al-Naqd al-dhati*, p. 206.

35. Sadiq al-'Azm, *Naqd al-fikr al-dini* (Critique of Religious Thought) (Beirut: Dar al-tali'a, 1969), pp. 45–46.

36. Richard L. Chambers, "The Ottoman Ulama and the Tanzimat," in N. R. Keddie, ed., *Scholars, Saints, and Sufis: Muslim Religious Institutions since 1500* (Berkeley and Los Angeles: University of California Press, 1978), p. 33.

37. Afaf Lutfi al-Sayyid Marsot, "The Ulama of Cairo in the 18th and 19th Centuries," in Keddie, ed., *Scholars, Saints, and Sufis*, p. 163.

38. Weber, *Sociology of Religion*, p. 46.

39. Tawfiq al-Hakim, *'Usfour min ash-sharq* (Bird from the East) (1938; Cairo: Dar al-ma'arif, 1974), pp. 45, 78–80.

40. Faysal Mulawi, *Al-Shihab* 7, no. 4 (July 15, 1973), p. 5.

41. Ayman al-Yassini, *Religion and State in the Kingdom of Saudi Arabia* (Boulder, Colo.: Westview Press, 1985).

42. John L. Esposito, ed., *Voices of Resurgent Islam* (Oxford: Oxford University Press, 1983), p. 4.

43. Hassan Turabi, "The Islamic State," in Esposito, ed., *Voices of Resurgent Islam*, p. 242.

44. Eric Davis, "The Concept of Revival and the Study of Islam and Politics," in Barbara Freyer Stowasser, ed., *The Islamic Impulse* (Washington, D.C.: Center for Contemporary Arab Studies, Georgetown University, 1987), p. 37.

45. Philip S. Khoury, "Islamic Revivalism and the Crisis of the Secular State in the Arab World: An Historical Appraisal," in Ibrahim Ibrahim, ed., *Arab Resources: The Transformation of a Society* (Washington, D.C.: Center for Contemporary Arab Studies, Georgetown University, 1983), pp. 214–15.

46. Qutb and Rahman quoted in Tamara Sonn, "Secularism and National Stability in Islam," *Arab Studies Quarterly* 9, no. 3 (Summer 1987): 284.

47. "Declaration of the Council of 'Ulama in Lebanon on Secularism," in *Islamic Law and Change in Arab Society*, Center for the Study of the Modern Arab World [St. Joseph University, Beirut] Reports, no. 4 (Beirut: Dar El-Mashreq, 1976), pp. 85–92; taken from *Al-Anwar*, March 26, 1976.

48. Von Grunebaum, *Islam*, p. 60.

49. Cited in Herbert J. Liebesny, *The Law of the Near and Middle East: Readings, Cases and Materials* (Albany, N.Y.: State University of New York Press, 1975), pp. 93–94.

50. Ibid., pp. 79–81.

51. L. Carl Brown, ed., *State and Society in Independent North Africa* (Washington, D. C.: Middle East Institute, 1966), p. 111.

52. Cited by Sonn, "Secularism and National Stability in Islam," p. 288.

53. Cited by Nassar, *Nahwa mujtama' jadid*, pp. 19–26.

54. Abd al-Rahman al-Kawakibi, *Al-'Amal al-kamila* (Complete Works) (Beirut: Al-Mu'assa al-'arabiyya lil-dirasat wal-nashr, 1975), pp. 206–8.

55. For more details, see Barakat, "A Secular Vision of Lebanon," in *Toward a Viable Lebanon*, pp. 361–77.

56. Cited in Joseph Mughayzil, *Al-'Uruba wa al-'almaniyya* (Arabism and Secularism) (Beirut: Dar al-Nahar, 1980), p. 171.

57. Muhammed al-Nuwayhi, *Nahwa thawra fi al-fikr al-dini* (Toward a Revolution in Religious Thought) (Beirut: Dar al-adab, 1983).

58. Gamal Hamdan, *Al-'Alam al-islami al-mu'asir* (The Contemporary Muslim World) (Cairo: 'Alam al-kitab, 1971), p. 112.

59. Quoted in Donald E. Smith, ed., *Religion, Politics, and Social Change in the Third World* (New York: Free Press, 1971), pp. 26–28.

60. *Al-Nahar*, February 5, 1969.

61. *Al-Nahar*, December 22, 1985.

62. Peter L. Berger, *Elements of a Sociological Theory of Religion* (Garden City, N.Y.: Doubleday, Anchor Books, 1969), pp. 95–96.

63. Ibid., pp. 87, 89.

64. Abdallah Laroui, *The Crisis of the Arab Intellectual* (Berkeley and Los Angeles: University of California Press, 1976), p. 156.

65. Yinger, *Religion, Society and the Individual*, p. 299.

66. Berger, *Elements of a Sociological Theory of Religion*, p. 100.

67. Adonis, *Al-Thabit wal-mutahawwil: Bahth fi al-ittiba' wa-al-ibda' 'ind al-'arab* (The Permanent and the Changing: A Study of Arab Conformity and Creativity) 3 vols. (Beirut: Dar al-'awda, 1974–78).

8. ARAB POLITICS: ITS SOCIAL CONTEXT

1. For instance, see Ernest Gellner, *Saints of the Atlas* (Chicago: University of Chicago Press, 1969); E. E. Evans-Pritchard, *The Sanusi of Cyrenaica* (Oxford: Clarendon Press, 1949); Coon, *Caravan*.

2. Ghassan Salame, *Al-Mujtama' wal-dawlah fi al-Mashriq al-'arabi* (Society and State in the Arab East) (Beirut: Markaz dirasat al-wahda al-'arabiyya, 1987), ch. 2.

3. Elbaki Hermassi, *Al-Mujtama' wal-dawlah fi al-Maghrib al-'arabi* (Society and State in the Maghrib) (Beirut: Markaz dirasat al-wahda al-'arabiyya, 1987), p. 8.

4. Ahmed Sadiq Saad, *Tarikh Misr al-ijtima'i al-iqtisadi fi dau' al-namat al-asiawi lil-intaj* (The Socioeconomic History of Egypt in the Light of the Asiatic Mode of Production) (Beirut: Dar Ibn Khaldun, 1979); *Tarikh al-'Arab al-ijtima'i: Tahhawoul al-takwin al-Misri min al-namat al-asiawi ila al-namat al-rasmali* (The Social History of the Arabs: The Transformation of Egypt from Asiatic to Capitalist Mode) (Beirut: Dar al-hadatha, 1981); "Misr shibh al-sharqia"

(Egypt the Semi-Oriental), *Qadaia fikria* (Cairo), 3, no. 4 (August–October 1986): 11–19.

5. Sharabi, *Neopatriarchy*, pp. 3, 7.

6. Michael C. Hudson, *Arab Politics: The Search for Legitimacy* (New Haven: Yale University Press, 1977), p. 25.

7. Batatu, *Old Social Classes and the Revolutionary Movements of Iraq*, p. 9.

8. Amin, *Arab Nation*, p. 81, and "Historical Foundations of Arab Nationalism," in Ibrahim and Hopkins, eds., *Arab Society in Transition*, p. 20.

9. Al-Naqeeb, *Al-Mujtama' wal-dawlah fi al-khalij wal-jazira al-'arabiyya.*

10. Karl Marx and Frederick Engels, *The German Ideology*, ed. C. J. Arthur (New York: International Publishers, 1970), p. 57.

11. Khoury, *Urban Notables and Arab Nationalism*, p. 2.

12. Philip Khoury, *Syria and the French Mandate: The Politics of Arab Nationalism, 1920–1945* (Princeton: Princeton University Press, 1987), p. 22.

13. Al-Naqeeb, *Al-Mujtama' wal-dawlah fi al-khalij wal-jazira al-'arabiyya,* p. 112.

14. Hermassi, *Leadership and National Development in North Africa*, p. 8.

15. Ibid., pt. 3.

16. Saad Eddin Ibrahim, *Al-Mujtama' wal-dawlah fi al-watan al-'arabi* (Society and State in the Arab Homeland) (Beirut: Markaz dirasat al-wahdah al-'arabiyya, 1988), p. 119.

17. Marsot, *Egypt in the Reign of Muhammed Ali*, pp. 100, 160–61.

18. Khoury, *Syria and the French Mandate*, pp. 251–62, 147–48.

19. Batatu, *Old Social Classes and the Revolutionary Movements of Iraq*, pt. 2.

20. Ibid., p. 200.

21. Hermassi, *Al-Mujtama' wal-dawlah fi al-Maghrib al-'arabi*, p. 90.

22. Bujra, *Politics of Stratification*, p. 33.

23. Batatu, *Old Social Classes and the Revolutionary Movements of Iraq*, ch. 7.

24. See, e.g., Sheikh Abdul Aziz bin Baz, *Naqd al-qawmiyya al-'arabiyya 'ala daw' al-Islam wal-waqi'* (A Critique of Arab Nationalism in Light of Islam and Reality) (Beirut: Al-Maktab al-islami, 1983).

25. Cited in Al-Naqeeb, *Al-Mujtama' wal-dawlah fi al-khalij wal-jazira al-'arabiyya*, p. 152.

26. Hermassi, *Leadership and National Development in North Africa*, p. 17.

27. See Batatu, *Old Social Classes and the Revolutionary Movements of Iraq*, p. 28.

28. For a condensed review of such structural changes in the Third World societies, see Alexei Levkovsky, *The Developing Countries' Social Structure* (Moscow: Progress Publishers, 1987).

29. Constantine Zurayk, *Nahnu wal-mustaqbal* (We and the Future) (Beirut: Dar al-'ilm lil-malayyin, 1977), p. 350.

30. Khoury, *Syria and the French Mandate*, p. 626. The story of the earliest stirrings of Arab awakening in the nineteenth and early twentieth centuries was told by George Antonius in his famous book, *The Arab Awakening* (Philadel-

phia: Lippincott, 1939). Later, the Iraqi historian Abd al-Aziz Duri traced Arab nationalism to its earliest pre-Islamic beginnings.

31. Khoury, *Syria and the French Mandate,* pp. 626–27.

32. Cited in Batatu, *Old Social Classes and the Revolutionary Movements of Iraq,* pp. 298, 299.

33. Beshara Doumani, "The Syrian Social Nationalist Party: An Analysis of Its Social Base" (MS, 1983) indicates that of 71 of its top leaders between 1948 and 1958 26 were Greek Orthodox, 14 Sunni, 9 Druze, 8 Maronite, 7 Shi'ite, 5 Alawite, and 2 Christians of another denomination; 42 of the leaders were Lebanese, 23 Syrians, and 5 Palestinians. In terms of occupation, they were all well-educated and highly trained—16 were teachers, 11 lawyers, 7 doctors, 7 merchants, 4 intellectuals, 2 journalists, 2 engineers, and 4 career officers, with the remainder from other professions. The overwhelming majority came from villages and small towns.

34. Batatu, *Old Social Classes and the Revolutionary Movements of Iraq,* p. 730. The three groups were: the Arsuzi group, named after its leader, Zaki al-Arsuzi, a teacher and the son of a lawyer and owner of medium-sized land-holdings who was an Alawite from the Alexandretta district; the group of students and teachers who formed a party in the early 1940s around Michel 'Aflaq and Salah ad-Din Bitar (both of whom were born in Damascus, sons of middling grain merchants, Sorbonne-educated, and teachers); and the group of Akram Hourani, a lawyer born to an affluent landowner of Hama who was always lacking money because an older brother had squandered the family fortune. (Hourani founded his group after two years of affiliation with the Syrian Social Nationalist party [1936–38] as a reaction against big landlords in Hama.)

35. Ibid., pp. 746–48.

36. Hermassi, *Al-Mujtama' wal-dawlah fi al-Maghrib al-'arabi,* p. 38.

37. Michel 'Aflaq, *Fi sabil al-ba'th* (For the Sake of Renaissance) (Beirut: Dar at-tali'a, 1963), pp. 26, 204.

38. Abdel-Fadil, *Political Economy of Nasserism,* 69.

39. Marnia Lazreg, *The Emergence of Classes in Algeria: A Study of Colonialism and Socio-political Change* (Boulder, Colo.: Westview Press, 1976), p. 175.

40. Elbaki Hermassi, *The Third World Reassessed* (Berkeley and Los Angeles: University of California Press, 1980), pp. 80–81.

41. *Al-Mithaq al-watani* (The National Charter) (Algiers: Ministry of Culture, 1979), pp. 33, 29.

42. Saad Eddin Ibrahim, "Al-Mas'alatu al-ijtam'iyyu baina at-turath wa tahadiat al-'asr" (The Social Question between Legacy and Contemporary Challenges), *Al-Mustaqbal al-'arabi* 7, no. 71 (1985): 50, 65.

43. Batatu, *Old Social Classes and the Revolutionary Movements of Iraq,* pp. 374–75.

44. See *Qadaia fikria* (Cairo) 5, no. 5 (May 1987), special issue on the Egyptian working class; Rifa't as-Said, *Tarikh al-haraka al-ishtirakiyya fi Misr*

(History of the Socialist Movement in Egypt) (Beirut: Dar al-farabi, 1972); Amin ʿIzzedin, *Tarikh at-tabaqa al-ʿamila mundh nash'atiha* (History of the Working Class since Its Inception) (Cairo: Dar al-katib al-ʿarabi, 1970; Cairo: Dar ash-shaʿb, 1972).

45. Batatu, *Old Social Classes and the Revolutionary Movements of Iraq*, pp. 377, 380–81.

46. Jamal ash-Sharqawi, "An-Nashat wat-tawor" (The Beginning and Development), *Qadaia fikria* (Cairo) 5, no. 5 (May 1987): 13–25.

47. Batatu, *Old Social Classes and the Revolutionary Movements of Iraq*, p. 427.

48. Al-Mahdi Bin Baraka, *Al-Ikhtiar al-thawri fi al-Maghrib* (The Revolutionary Alternative in the Maghrib) (Beirut: Dar at-taliʿa, 1966), pp. 136 and 145 respectively.

49. Hanna Batatu, "Some Reflections on the Decline of the Arab Left and Iraq Communists" (Paper, Center for Contemporary Arab Studies Reports, Georgetown University, 1983), p. 5.

50. Ibid., p. 1.

9. NATIONAL CHARACTER AND VALUE ORIENTATIONS

1. Raphael Patai, *The Arab Mind* (New York: Charles Scribner's Sons, 1976).

2. Sonia Hamady, *Temperament and Character of the Arabs* (New York: Twayne, 1960).

3. Fuad M. Moughrabi, "The Arab Basic Personality: A Critical Survey of the Literature," *International Journal of Middle East Studies* 9 (1978): 99–112.

4. El-Sayyid Yassin, *Al-Shakhsiyya al-ʿarabiyya*.

5. Patai, *Arab Mind*, p. 18.

6. Patai, *Society, Culture and Change in the Middle East*, pp. 3, 381.

7. Ibid., p. 359.

8. Morroe Berger, *The Arab World Today* (New York: Doubleday, Anchor Books, 1964), p. 136. In a chapter on personality and values, Berger attempts to "delineate a group of traits encompassing the Arabs in their variety, a kind of modal point which they approximate in varying degrees." To do that he has to ignore what he has recognized about variety and change and to avoid serious analysis or explanation of the phenomena under study in their social and historical contexts. Realizing that the idea of an "Arab personality" is a "formidable abstraction" to which he must resort in order to say what "kind of person" an Arab is, he has to make several sweeping generalizations: "The Arab seems to harbor two major contradicting impulses: egotism and conformity. The first takes the forms of extreme self-assertion before others, pride, and sensitivity to criticism. The second is reflected in obedience to certain group norms which are resented, and an inability to assert independence as an individual with confidence or finality" (p. 136). "The individual Arab's self-assertiveness has been directed not only

against other groups but also against his own" (p. 137). "In a society in which interpersonal relations are so marked by tender egos, hostility, display, and suspicion, it is not surprising to find a great deal of personal and group rivalry" (p. 148). "By providing ready-made phrases, it [speech] obviates the need for thought and originality" (p. 155). "Arab views of the external world of nature and of the arts display a similar rigidity, formalism, and disinclination to look into the unknown" (p. 158). "Even in their science the Arabs were wary of abstract ideas" (p. 159).

9. Fanon, *The Wretched of the Earth*, p. 41.

10. Albert Memmi, *The Colonizer and the Colonized* (Boston: Beacon Press, 1967), p. 79.

11. Janet Abu-Lughod, "The Islamic City—Historic Myth, Islamic Essence, and Contemporary Relevance," *International Journal of Middle East Studies* 19, no. 2 (May 1987): 155.

12. Edward Said, *Orientalism* (New York: Pantheon Books, 1978), p. 5.

13. E. Terry Prothro and Levon Melikian, "The California Public Opinion Scale in an Authoritarian Culture," *Public Opinion Quarterly* 17 (Fall 1953): 355, 360–61.

14. Levon H. Melikian, "Authoritarianism and Its Correlates in the Egyptian Culture and in the United States," *Journal of Social Issues* 15, no. 3 (1959): 58.

15. Ammar, *Growing Up in an Egyptian Village*, p. xi.

16. Hamed Ammar, *Fi bina' al-bashar* (On Building Human Character) (Cairo: Sirs Allayan Publication, 1964), pp. 79–91.

17. Sadiq Jalal al-'Azm, *An-Naqd al-dhati ba'd al-hazima* (Self-Criticism after the Defeat) (Beirut: Dar at-tali'a, 1968), p. 69–89.

18. Hichem Djait, *Al-Shakhsiyya al-'arabiyya al-islamiyya wal-masir al-'arabi* (Arab-Islamic Personality and Arab Destiny) (Beirut: Dar at-tali'a, 1984), p. 177.

19. Moughrabi, "Arab Basic Personality," pp. 105, 109.

20. Yassin, *Al-Shakhsiyya al-'arabiyya,* pp. 59–60. Yassin cites J. H. Schaar, *Escape from Authority: The Perspective of Erich Fromm* (New York: Harper Torchbooks, 1961), and Erich Fromm, *Marx's Concept of Man* (New York: F. Mear Publishing Co., 1970).

21. Ibid., pp. 65, 216.

22. Berger, *Arab World Today*, pp. 156–57, 159.

23. Von Grunebaum, *Islam*, pp. 67, 70.

24. Patai, *Arab Mind,* p. 147.

25. Ibid., pp. 150–51.

26. Abd al-Rahman al-Kawakibi, *Al-'Amal al-kamila* (Complete Works) (Beirut: Al-Mu'assa al-'arabiyya lil-dirasat wal-nashr, 1975), p. 68.

27. See Patai, *Arab Mind,* pp. 106–7, 111–12; David P. Ausubel, "Relationship between Shame and Guilt in the Socialization Process," *Psychological Review* 62, no. 5 (September 1955); Hamady, *Temperament and Character of the*

Arabs, pp. 34–39; Jean G. Peristiany, ed., *Honour and Shame: The Values of Mediterranean Society* (London: Weidenfeld & Nicolson, 1965); Harold W. Glidden, "The Arab World," *American Journal of Psychiatry* 128, no. 8 (February 1973): 984–88.

28. Patai, *Arab Mind,* p. 106.

29. Glidden, "Arab World," pp. 98–100.

30. Erica Jong, *Fear of Flying* (New York: A Signet Book, 1973), p. 245.

31. Amos Elon, *The Israelis: Founders and Sons* (New York: Bantam Books, 1972); "Two Arab Towns that Plumb Israelis' Conscience," *New York Times Magazine,* October 22, 1972, p. 69.

32. See *Middle East International* (London), March 9, 1984, and *Arab Studies Quarterly* 7, no. 2–3 (Spring–Summer 1985): 95.

33. Von Grunebaum, *Islam,* p. 67.

34. Berger, *Arab World Today,* p. 155.

35. Laroui, *Crisis of the Arab Intellectual,* pp. 153–54.

36. Adonis, *Al-Thabit wal-mutahauwil,* 3: 9–11.

37. Constantine Zurayk, "Cultural Change and the Transformation of Arab Society," in Hudson, ed., *Arab Future* p. 11.

38. 'Allal al-Fassi, *Al-Naqd al-dhati,* p. 94.

39. See *Al-Mustaqbal al-'arabi* 4, no. 71 (December–January 1985), a special issue on authenticity.

40. Adonis, *Transformation of the Lover,* trans. Samuel Hazo (Pittsburgh: International Poetry Forum, Byblos Editions, 1982), pp. 11, 25, 27.

41. Tawfiq al-Hakim, *'Awdat ar-ruh* (The Return of the Spirit) (1933; Cairo: Maktabat al-adab, n.d.), 2: 45, 55.

42. Yahya Haqqi, *Qindil umm Hashem* (The Lamp of umm Hashem) (Cairo: Dar al-ma'rif, 1944).

43. Nazik al-Mala'ika, "Al-Qawmiyy al-'arabiyya wal-hayat," *Al-Adab* 8, no. 5 (May 1960): 1.

44. Berque, *The Arabs,* pp. 25, 51, 191.

45. Hourani, *Arab Thought in the Liberal Age,* p. 1.

46. Patai, *Arab Mind,* pp. 48–49, 211.

47. Halim Barakat, *'Awdat at-ta'ir ila al-bahr* (Beirut: Dar an-Nahar, 1969), trans. Trevor Le Gassick as *Days of Dust* (1974; Washington, D.C.: Three Continents Press, 1983), p. 126.

48. E. Shouby, "The Influence of the Arabic Language on the Psychology of the Arabs," *Middle East Journal* 5, no. 3 (1951): 291, 295.

49. Halim Barakat, "Arab-Western Polarities: A Content Analysis Study of the Tunisian Journal *Al-Fikr,*" in Barakat, ed., *Contemporary North Africa: Issues of Development and Integration* (Washington, D.C.: Center for Contemporary Arab Studies, Georgetown University, 1985), pp. 45–59.

50. Djait, *Al-Shakhsiyya al-'arabiyya al-islamiyya,* p. 9.

51. Daniel Bliss, *The Reminiscences of Daniel Bliss* (New York: F. H. Revell Co., 1920), p. 200.

10. CREATIVE EXPRESSION: SOCIETY AND LITERARY
ORIENTATIONS

1. Philip K. Hitti, *History of the Arabs from the Earliest Times to the Present*, 6th ed. (1937; New York: Macmillan Co., 1958), p. 90.

2. Kamal Boullata, "Modern Arab Art: The Quest and the Ordeal," *Mundus artium* 10, no. 1 (1977): 107–25, at p. 107.

3. Cited in Jabra I. Jabra, "Modern Arabic Literature and the West," in Issa Boullata, ed., *Critical Perspectives on Modern Arabic Literature* (Washington, D.C.: Three Continents Press, 1980), pp. 7–22, p. 8.

4. Barakat, *Days of Dust*, p. 126.

5. R. Wuthnow, J. D. Hunter, A. Bergesen, and E. Kurzeil, eds., *Cultural Analysis* (Boston and London: Routledge & Kegan Paul, 1984), p. 21.

6. Adonis, *Zaman ash-shi'r* (Time of Poetry), 2d ed. (Beirut: Dar al-'awda, 1978), p. 9.

7. Khalida Sa'id, "Al-Hadatha au 'iqdat Gelqamesh" (Modernity, or the Gilgamesh Complex), *Mawaqif*, no. 51/52 (Summer/Autumn 1984): 11–51.

8. See Matti Moosa, *The Origins of Modern Arabic Fiction* (Washington, D.C.: Three Continents Press, 1983); Muhammed Yusuf Najm, *Al-Masrahiyya fi al-adab al-'arabi al-hadith, 1847–1914* (Drama in Modern Arabic Literature) (Beirut: Dar Beirut, 1967); Ali 'Uqla 'Ursan, *Al-Zawahir al-masrahiyya 'ind al-'arab* (Damascus: Itihad al-kuttab, 1981).

9. Abdelkebir Khatibi and Mohammed Sijelmassi, *The Splendour of Islamic Calligraphy* (London: Thames & Hudson, 1976), p. 192.

10. Boullata, "Modern Arab Art."

11. For an original exploration of these folk arts, see Bert Flint, *Forme et symbole dans les arts du Maroc* (Tangier: Dépôt Légal Eté, 1973–74).

12. Edmond J. Mousally, "Introduction to Arab Music," *Arab Perspectives* 4 (February 1984): 20–22.

13. Al-Hakim, *'Awdat ar-ruh*, 2: 37–40.

14. Al-Hakim, *'Usfour min ash-sharq*, p. 45.

15. David Caute, *The Illusion: An Essay on Politics, Theatre and the Novel* (New York: Harper & Row, 1972), p. 53.

16. Tawfiq al-Hakim, *Yaumiat na'ib fi al-ariaf* (Maze of Justice) (1937; Cairo: Maktabat al-Adab, n.d.), p. 154.

17. Quoted in Caute, *Illusion*, pp. 143–46.

18. Themes of reconciliation are also reflected in the literary works of other writers. In fact, preceding the novels of Al-Hakim is the well-known novel *Zainab* (1913) by Muhammed Hussein Haykel (of feudal family origin) in which peasants are depicted as living in a state of harmony with their deprivation and servitude. Another well-known novel is *Sarah* (1938) by 'Abbas Mahmoud al-'Aqqad (1889–1964). A more recent novel representing this orientation is *Dafanna al-madi* (We Buried the Past) by the Moroccan writer Abdulkarim Ghallab.

19. Naguib Mahfouz, *Zuqaq al-Midaqq* (Middaq Alley), 6th ed. (Cairo: Maktabat Misr, 1965), pp. 6, 57, 312.

20. Naguib Mahfouz, *Awlad haratina* (The Children of Geblawi) (Beirut: Dar al-adab, 1967), pp. 7, 476, 548, 552.

21. Naguib Mahfouz, *Al-Liss wal-kilab* (The Thief and the Dogs), 4th ed. (Cairo: Maktabat Misr, 1966), pp. 10, 14, 154, 8.

22. Naguib Mahfouz, *As-Samman wal-kharif* (The Quail and Autumn), 4th ed. (Cairo: Maktabat Misr, 1967), pp. 84, 121, 83.

23. Naguib Mahfouz, *Ash-Shahhadh* (The Beggar), 2d ed. (Cairo: Maktabat Misr, 1966), p. 146.

24. Naguib Mahfouz, *Hubb taht al-matar* (Love in the Rain), 1st ed. (Cairo: Maktabat Misr, 1973), p. 22.

25. Naguib Mahfouz, *Al-Karnak* (Cairo: Maktabat Misr, 1974), pp. 33, 28.

26. Naguib Mahfouz, *Al-Tariq*, 2d ed. (Cairo: Maktabat Misr, 1965), p. 123.

27. Naguib Mahfouz, *Al-Harafish* (The Despondent Ones) (Cairo: Maktabat Misr, n.d. [1978?]), pp. 208, 260.

28. Naguib Mahfouz, *Baina al-qasrain*, 7th ed. (Cairo: Maktabat Misr, 1970), p. 9.

29. Mahfouz, *Zuqaq al-Midaqq*, pp. 58, 106.

30. Ibid., p. 185.

31. Georg Lukács, *Studies in European Realism* (New York: Universal Library, 1974), p. 52.

32. Ibid., p. 22.

33. Mahfouz, *Al-Karnak,* p. 52.

34. Naguib Mahfouz, *Tharthara fawq an-Nil* (Chattering on the Nile) (Cairo: Maktabat Misr, 1965), pp. 126–27.

35. Georg Lukács, *The Theory of the Novel* (Cambridge, Mass.: MIT Press, 1971), pp. 113–14.

36. Mahfouz, *Tharthara fawq an-Nil,* p. 28.

37. Ibid., pp. 25, 60, 75, 147.

38. Jabra I. Jabra, *As-Safina* (The Ship) (Beirut: Dar an-nahar, 1970), p. 22.

39. Ibid., pp. 24, 84.

40. Lukács, *Theory of the Novel,* p. 135.

41. Georg Lukács, *Realism in Our Time: Literature and Class Struggle* (New York: Harper Torchbooks, 1971), p. 21.

42. Layla Ba'albaki, *Ana ahya* (I Live) (Beirut: Dar majallat shi'r, 1958), pp. 226, 46.

43. Jabra I. Jabra, *Hunters in a Narrow Street* (London: Heinemann, 1960), pp. 78, 111–22.

44. Ga'ib Tou'ma Faraman, *Khamsat aswat* (Five Voices) (Beirut: Dar al-adab, 1967); id., *Qurban* (Holy Offering) (Baghdad: Al-Adib Press, 1975).

45. Tayyib Salih, *Mawsim al-hijra ila ash-shamal* (Season of Migration to the North) (Cairo: Riwait al-hillal, 1969), p. 32; originally published in *Hiwar,* no.

24/25 (1966); trans. Denys Johnson-Davies as *Season of Migration to the North* (London: Heinemann, 1969).

46. Quoted in Caute, *Illusion,* pp. 143–44.

47. Abdel Rahman al-Sharqawi, *Al-Ard* (The Earth) (Cairo: Nadi al-qissat, al-kitab al-zahabi, 1954), 2: 153.

48. Ibid., 2: 165, 1:78.

49. Abdel Hakim Qassem, *Ayyam al-insan as-sab'a* (Man's Seven Days) (Cairo, Dar al-kitab al-'arabi, n.d.).

50. Yusuf Idriss, *Al-Haram* (The Sin) (Cairo: Riwaiat al-hillal, 1965), p. 17.

51. Yusuf Idriss, *Qa' al-medina* (The Dregs of the City) (Cairo: Markaz kutob as-sharq al-awsat, 1958).

52. Yusuf Idriss, *Qissat hubb* (Love Story) (Cairo: Dar al-kitab al-'arabi, 1967), pp. 62, 63.

53. Ibid., pp. 28, 29.

54. Halim Barakat, *Sittat ayyam* (Beirut: Dar majallat shi'ir, 1961), trans. Bassam Frangieh and Scott McGehee as *Six Days* (Washington, D.C.: Three Continents Press, 1990).

55. Barakat, *Days of Dust,* p. 28.

56. Ghassan Kanafani, *Rijal fi ash-shams* (1962), trans. Hilary Kilpatrick as *Men in the Sun* (Washington, D.C.: Three Continents Press, 1983).

57. Ghassan Kanafani, *Umm Saad* (Beirut: Dar al-'awda, 1969), pp. 21, 92.

58. Habiby, *Sudasyyiat al-ayyam as-sittat,* pp. 72, 36–37, 91.

59. Emile Habiby, *The Secret Life of Saeed, the Ill-Fated Pessoptimist* (New York: Vantage Press, 1982).

60. Abdelkebir Khatibi, *Le Roman maghrebin* (Paris: Maspero, 1968).

61. Mohammed Dib, *Ad-Dar al-kabir, al-hariq, an-nawk* (The Great Mansion, The Fire, The Looms) (Beirut: Dar at-tali'a, 1968).

62. At-Tahir Wattar [Tahar Ouettar], *Al-Laz* (*L'As*), 2d ed. (Algiers: As-Sharika al-wataniyya lil-nashr, 1978), p. 257.

11. ARAB THOUGHT: PROBLEMS OF RENEWAL, MODERNITY,
AND TRANSFORMATION

1. Hourani, *Arabic Thought in the Liberal Age.*

2. Hisham Sharabi, *Arab Intellectuals and the West* (Baltimore: Johns Hopkins Press, 1970) p. 2.

3. Ibid., p. 3.

4. See Sharabi, *Neopatriarchy,* chs. 7 and 8.

5. Ra'if Khuri, *Modern Arab Thought: Channels of the French Revolution to the Arab East,* trans. from Arabic by Ihsan Abbas (Princeton, N.J.: Kingston Press, 1983).

6. Anouar Abdel-Malek, ed., *Contemporary Arab Political Thought* (London: Zed Books, 1980).

7. Issa Boullata, *Trends and Issues in Contemporary Arab Thought* (Albany: State University of New York Press, 1990).

8. Laroui, *Crisis of the Arab Intellectual.*

9. Alaine Touraine, *Return of the Actor: Social Theory in Postindustrial Society,* trans. Myrna Godzich (Minneapolis: University of Minnesota Press, 1988).

10. See Halim Barakat, "Ideological Determinants of Arab Development," in Ibrahim, ed., *Arab Resources,* pp. 169–183.

11. Khuri, *Modern Arab Thought,* p. 122.

12. For a review of this controversy, see Rudi Matthee, "Jamal Al-Din Al-Afghani and the Egyptian National Debate," *International Journal of Middle East Studies* 21, no. 2 (1989): 151–69.

13. Hourani, *Arabic Thought in the Liberal Age,* p. 158.

14. Farah Antun, *Ibn Rushd wa-falsafatuhu* (Ibn Rushd and his Philosophy) (Beirut: Dar al-tali'a, 1981), p. 125.

15. *Al-Manar* 11, no. 12 (January 22, 1909): 937–38.

16. Cited in von Grunebaum, *Islam,* p. 190.

17. Sharabi, *Arab Intellectuals and the West,* p. 27.

18. Hourani, *Arabic Thought in the Liberal Age,* p. 81.

19. Cited in ibid., p. 79.

20. A. L. Tibawi, "The Genesis and Early History of the Syrian Protestant College," *Middle East Journal* 21, no. 2 (Spring 1967): 199–212.

21. Nassar, *Nahwa mujtama' jadid,* pp. 19, 26, 28.

22. B. Dodge, *The American University of Beirut* (Beirut: Khayat, 1958), p. 22.

23. *Al-Muqtataf* 9, no. 8 (May 1885): 468–72.

24. Ibid., no. 10 (July 1885): 633–36.

25. *Al-Abhath* 20, no. 4 (1967): 341.

26. Tibawi, "Genesis and Early History of the Syrian Protestant College."

27. Hourani, *Arabic Thought in the Liberal Age,* p. 168.

28. Abd al-Rahman al-Kawakibi, *Al-'Amal al-kamila* (Complete Works) (Beirut: Al-Mu'assa al-'arabiyya lil-dirasat wal-nashr, 1975), pp. 48, 208.

29. Ibid., pp. 80–148, and 12.

30. Khuri, *Modern Arab Thought,* pp. 132, 169.

31. Ibid., pp. 169–72.

32. Hourani, *Arabic Thought in the Liberal Age,* p. 252.

33. In Farah Antun, *Al-Mu'allafat al-rua'iyya* (Fictional Works) (Beirut: Dar al-tali'a, 1979), pp. 60–62.

34. Taha Hussein, *Fi al-shi'r al-jahily* (On Pre-Islamic Poetry) (Cairo: Dar al-ma'rif, 1926).

35. Taha Hussein, *Mustaqbal al-thaqafa fi Misr* (The Future of Culture in Egypt) (Cairo: Dar al-ma'arif, 1938), pp. 14, 45.

36. Ahmed Lutfi al-Sayyid cited in Abdel-Malek, *Contemporary Arab Political Thought,* pp. 112–13.

37. Amin Rihani, *Al-Qawmiat,* vol. 1 (Beirut: Dar al-rihani, 1956), p. 152.

38. Ibid., pp. 160–61.

39. Ibid., pp. 145–48.

40. Adel Daher, *Al-Mujtama' wal-insan: Dirasat fi falsafat Antun Saada al-ijtima'yya* (Society and Man: Studies of the Social Philosophy of Antun Saada) (Beirut: Manshurat mawaqif, 1980), pp. 275–76.

41. Cited in Ibrahim A. Ibrahim, "Salama Musa: An Essay on Cultural Alienation," *Middle Eastern Studies* 15, no. 3 (October 1979): 348.

42. Constantine Zurayk, *Ma'na al-nakba mujaddadan* (The Meaning of the Disaster Revisited) (Beirut: Dar al-'ilm lil-malayyin, 1967), pp. 17, 14.

43. For the views of Zaki Naguib Mahmud, see "Milad Jadid," *Mawaqif* 1, no. 1 (1968).

44. Malik Bin Nabi, *Shurut al-nahda* (Conditions of Awakening) (Beirut: Dar al-fikr, 1969), p. 75.

45. Salah al-Din al-Munajjid, *A'midat al-nakba* (The Pillars of Disaster) (Beirut: Dar al-kitab al-jadid, 1967), p. 17.

46. Muhammed 'Amara, "Al-Dawlah fi turath al-Islam" (State in Islamic Heritage), *Al-Hayat*, no. 9,761 (September 2–3, 1989): 5.

47. Tariq al-Bushri, *Al-Muslimun wal-Aqbat* (Muslims and Copts) (Cairo: Al-Hai'a al-misriyya, 1980), and "Al-Ta'ifiyya ghair al-mandhura."

48. Muhammed Abed Jabri, *Naqd al-'aql al-'arabi* (Critique of the Arab Mind) (Beirut: Markaz dirasat al-wahda al-'arabiyya, 1984).

49. Muhammed Abed Jabri, *Al-Khitab al-'arabi al-mu'asir* (Contemporary Arab Discourse) (Beirut: Dar al-tali'a, 1982).

50. Muhammed Abed Jabri, "Al-Din wal-dawlah fi al-marja'iyya al-nahdawiyya" (Religion and State in the Renaissance Referential Framework), *Al-Yawm al-sabi'*, December 9, 1985.

51. Mohammed Arkoun, "Al-Nass al-awal / al-nass al-thani" (The First Text / The Second Text), *Mawaqif*, no. 54 (Spring 1988): 4–12.

52. Mohammed Arkoun, *Tarikhiat al-fikr al-'arabi al-islami* (The Historicity of Arab-Islamic Thought) (Beirut: Markaz al-inma' al-qawmi, 1986), pp. 279–80.

53. Al-'Azm, *Naqd al-fikr al-dini*, pp. 45–46.

54. Fuad Zakariyya, *Al-Haqiqa wal-wahm fi al-haraka al-islamiyya al-mu'asira* (Fact and Illusion in the Contemporary Islamic Movement) (Cairo: Dar al-fikr, 1986), and *Al-Sahwa al-islamiyya fi mizan al-'aql* (Islamic Resurgence in the Scale of Mind) (Cairo: Dar al-fikr, 1987).

55. Al-Nuwayhi, *Nahwa thawra fi al-fikr al-dini*.

56. Hussein Mroueh, *Al-Naza'at al-maddiyya fi al-falsafa al-'arabiyya al-islamiyya* (Materialist Trends in Arab-Islamic Philosophy) (Beirut: Dar al-farabi, 1978–79), 1: 38.

57. Tayyib Tizzini, *Mashrou' ru'ia jadida lil-fikr al-'arabi* (A Project for a New Vision of Arab Thought) (Beirut: Dar Ibn Khaldun, 1978).

58. Amin, *Arab Nation*.

59. Abdel-Fadil, *Political Economy of Nasserism*, pp. 94, 68–69.

60. Galal A. Amin, "Dependent Development," *Alternatives* 2, no. 4 (December 1976): 379–403, at p. 400.

61. *Misr fi muftaraq al-turuq* (Egypt at a Crossroads) (Cairo: Dar al mustaqbal al-'arabi, 1990).

62. Sharabi, *Neopatriarchy*, pp. 5, 7.

63. Laroui, *Crisis of the Arab Intellectual*, pp. 43, 153–54.

64. Al-'Azm, *Al-Naqd al-dhati ba'd al-hazima*, pp. 69–89.

65. Khatibi, "Double Criticism," in Barakat, ed., *Contemporary North Africa*, pp. 9–10.

12. CONCLUSION

1. Samir Amin, *Arab Nation*; Galal Amin, "Dependent Development"; Mahmoud Abdel-Fadil, *Al-Tashkilat al-ijtima'iyya wal-takwinat al-tabakiyya fi al-watan al-'Arabi* (Social and Class Formations in the Arab World) (Beirut: Markaz dirasat al-wahda al-'arabiyya, 1988).

2. Halim Barakat, *Lebanon in Strife*; id., *Al-Mujtama' al-'arabi al-mu'asir* (Contemporary Arab Society) (Beirut: Markaz dirasat al-wahda al-'arabiyya, 1984).

3. Al-'Azm, *Al-Naqd al-dhati ba'd al-hazima;* id., *Naqd al-fikr al-dini.*

4. Al-Munajjid, *A'midat an-nakba*; Sayyid Qutb, *Ma'alim fi at-tariq* (Cairo: Maktabat wahba, 1964).

5. Constantine Zurayk, *Ma'na al-nakba mujaddadan*; Zaki Maguib Mahmoud, "Milad jadid" (Rebirth), *Mawaqif* 1, no. 1 (1968): 5–14; and "Al-'Arab wa ma'na at-tahawol" (Arabs and the Meaning of Transformation), *Mawaqif* 1, no. 4 (1969): 47–57.

6. Sharabi, *Neopatriarchy*.

7. El-Saadawi, *Hidden Face of Eve;* Mernissi, *Beyond the Veil*.

8. Adonis, *Al-Thabit wal-mutahawwil*.

9. Laroui, *Crisis of the Arab Intellectual*; Khatibi, "Double Criticism," in Barakat, ed., *Contemporary North Africa*.

10. Ali Zay'our, *Tahlil al-dhat al-'arabiyya* (Analysis of the Arab Ego) (Beirut: Dar al-tali'a, 1977).

11. Al-Jabri, *Al-Khitab al-'arabi al-mu'asir*.

12. Halim Barakat, "Al-ightirab wal-thawra fi al-hayat al-'Arabiyya al-mu'asira," *Mawaqif* 1, no. 5 (1969): 18–44.

13. Mohammed Arkoun, "Al-Muthaqqaf fi al-'alam al-'arabi al-islami" (Intellectuals in the Arab Muslim World), *Al-Moukaddima* 1, no. 6 (October 1987): 5.

14. Otto Hintze, "The State in Historical Perspective," in Reinhard Bendix, ed., *State and Society: A Reader in Comparative Political Sociology* (Boston: Little, Brown, 1968), p. 155.

15. Marx and Engels, *The German Ideology*, ed. Arthur, p. 57.

16. Henri Lefebvre, *The Sociology of Marx* (New York: Pantheon Books, 1968), pp. 4–5.

17. Richard Schacht, *Alienation* (New York: Doubleday, Anchor Books, 1970), p. 117.

18. *The Nation*, May 7, 1988, pp. 630–31.

19. Wolfram Eberhard, "Problems of Historical Sociology," in Bendix, ed., *State and Society*, p. 16.

20. *A Gramsci Reader: Selected Writings, 1916–1935*, ed. David Forgacs (London: Lawrence & Wishart, 1988), p. 224.

21. Al-Naqeeb, *Al-Mujtama' wal-dawlah fi al-khalij wal-jazira al-'arabiyya.*

22. Sharabi, *Neopatriarchy*, pp. 65–66.

23. *Al-Itihad al-ishtiraki*, March 30, 1990.

24. Ibid., January 19, 1990.

25. Ibid., February 8, 1990.

26. See Al-Munazzama al-'arabiyya li-huquq al-insan (Arab Organization for Human Rights), *Huquq al-insan fi al-watan al-'arabi* (Human Rights in the Arab Homeland) (Cairo, 1988).

27. *Al-Itihad al-ishtiraki*, April 8, 1990.

28. John Keane, *Times Literary Supplement*, June 21, 1991.

29. E. J. Dionne, Jr., "Loss of Faith in Egalitarianism Alters U.S. Social Vision," *Washington Post*, April 30, 1990, section A.

30. Paul Taylor, "For Disconnected Americans Citizenship Fades," *Washington Post*, May 6, 1990, "Outlook" section.

31. *Washington Post*, February 22, 1990, p. A28.

Glossary

AHL: extended family

AHL AL-DHIMMA: "People of the Book," mainly Christians and Jews

'AILA: extended family

AKHDAM: a menial caste in Yemen (sing. *khadim*)

AKRAH AL-HALAL: the most hated of lawful practices: divorce

AMIN: term for local officials in North Africa

'AQILA: a wife

'ARAF: tribal customary laws (sing. *irf*)

'ASABIYYA: tribal cohesion or solidarity

ASALA: authenticity

'ASHIRA: bedouin clan, composed of four to six subtribes

ASHRAF: a subclass composed of those who claim descent from the family of the Prophet Muhammad; see also *sadah*

AWLIA': saints

AWQAF: religious endowments (sing. *waqf*)

BADAWA: the nomadic style of life

BADIA: the beginning of life in the desert

BADU-HADAR: bedouin-sedentary

BARAKA: blessedness, divine grace

BATN: bedouin subtribes

BEDOON: an outcast group in Kuwait

BEIT: extended family; also used to the family home

BID'A: departure from orthodox custom

BINT 'AMM: patrilineal parallel cousin

CASBA: old city in the Maghrib

DAWLAH: modern state bureaucracy

DHIKR: a mystical practice designed for the remembrance of God that induces a trancelike state in the believer

DIN: religion

DUNUM: a quarter of an acre

FAKHDH: bedouin subtribe

FATWA: a formal religious opinion

FEDDAN: (sing. and pl.) Egyptian unit equaling 1.038 acres (0.42 ha)

FELLAH: peasant (pl. *fellahin*)

FITNA: dissent, social disorder, rebellion

FURUSSIYYA: chivalry

GOURBIVILLE: an indigenous form of shantytown in North Africa

HADAR: city dwellers

HAI: neighborhood

HALAL: allowed by Islamic law

HAMULA: subtribe, lineage

HARA: subneighborhood

HIJRA: relocation (in relation to control of bedouins)

HUKUMA: government

ILTIZAM: a land grant connected to the Ottoman tax-farming system

INTIFADA: Palestinian uprising

ISRA: nuclear family

JAHILIYYA: a Qur'anic concept: the pre-Islamic period of ignorance

KAFA'AH: legal principle calling for the equality and suitability of marriage partners

KHUWA: protection money

MAHR: a dowry designated by the bridegroom to the bride on the date of the marriage; of two types, *muqaddam* and *mu'akhkhar*

MAWALI: non-Arab converts who were clients of the Umayyad dynasty in Damascus, A.D. 661–750

MEDINA: city

MILLA: religious community

MIRI (AL-ARD AL-AMIRIYYA):   form of land tenure, state-owned land

MU'AKHKHAR: dowry (*mahr*) payment, deferred

MUKHTAR: term for local officials in the Fertile Crescent

MULK: privately owned land

MUQADDAM: dowry (*mahr*) paid in advance

MUSHA':   communal land

NAHDA: attempts to achieve an Arab "renaissance," dating from the mid nineteenth century and reflecting the effort to redefine the Arab world after the demise of the Ottoman Empire; in the context of this book, the essence of the *nahda* would include national liberation and unity, the achievement of social justice, institution and state-building, democratization, and the cessation of dependency

NAJDA: support

NASAB: ascribed status, based on tribal ancestral origins, and reckoned by kinship ties

NIDR: offerings and sacrifices to a shrine

ORIENTALISM: Western scholarship on "the Orient" from the perspective of "the Occident," and thus rooted in relations of domination

QABILA: tribe

QAWMIYYA: nationalism or loyalty to the larger nation

RA'IYYAH: the shepherded; traditional term for citizens of Arab polities

SADAH: landed elite whose ascribed status is based on claims of descent from the Prophet Muhammad; see also *ashraf*

SALAFIYYA: revivalist movement, evoking apparently authentic and indigenous classical Arab-Islamic culture

SHAYKH: sheikh, tribal or religious leader

SHARIʿA: Islamic law

SHUʿUBIYYA: ethnic solidarity, ethnicity

AL-TALAQ AL-BAʾIN: clear divorce, lasting for more than three months; to resume married life would require a new contract and *mahr*

AL-TALAQ AL-RAJʿI: revocable divorce; marriage may resume within three months

TAQIYYA: dissembling, denial of one's religious affiliation out of fear, concealment

TAʾWIL: allegorical interpretation of the revealed texts for their concealed meanings

TIMAR: resumable land grant for service to the Ottoman state

ʿULAMA: men learned in Islamic law; status group

ʿUMDA: term for local notables in Egypt and Sudan

UMMA: nation, community in the larger sense

AL-ʿURUBA: Arabism

WALI: saint, pious founder of a Sufi order

WAQF: religious endowment (pl. *awqaf*)

WATAN: country, homeland

WATANIYYA: patriotism

ZAʿIM: leader

Select Bibliography

I. WORKS IN ARABIC

Abudl-Mu'ti, Abdul-Basit. *Al-Sira' at-tabaqi fi al-qaria al-misriyya* (Class Stuggle in the Egyptian Village). Cairo: Dar al-thaqafa al-jadida, 1977.

Abu Ghanim, Fadl Ali Ahmed. *Al-Bunia al-qabaliyya fi al-Yemen* (The Tribal Structure in Yemen). Damascus: Matba'at al-katib al-'arabi, 1985.

Adonis. *Al-Thabit wal-mutahawwil: Bahth fi al-ittiba' wa-al-ibda' 'ind al-'arab* (The Permanent and the Changing: A Study of Arab Conformity and Creativity). Beirut: Dar al-'awda, 1977.

————. *Zaman ash-shi'r* (Time of Poetry). 2d ed. Beirut: Dar al-'awda, 1978.

'Aflaq, Michel. *Fi sabil al-ba'th* (For the Sake of Renaissance). Beirut: Dar at-tali'a, 1963.

'Ali, Muhammed Kurd. *Al-Islam wal-hadara al-'arabiyya* (Islam and Arab Civilization). 3d ed. Cairo: Lijnat at-ta'lif wat-tarjama wan-nashr, 1968.

al-'Aqqad, 'Abbas Mahmoud. *Al-Mar'a fi al-Qur'an* (The Women in the Koran). Cairo: Dar al-hilal, 1971.

'Awda, Mahmoud. *Al-Fallahun wal-dawla* (The Peasants and the State). Cairo: Dar al-thaqafa, 1979.

————. *Al-Qaria al-misriyya* (The Egyptian Village). Cairo: Maktabat Said Ra'fat, 1983.

al-'Azm, Sadiq Jalal. *An-Naqd al-dhati ba'd al-hazima* (Self-Criticism after the Defeat). Beirut: Dar at-tali'a, 1968.

————. *Naqd al-fikr al-dini* (Critique of Religious Thought). Beirut: Dar al-tali'a, 1969.

Bashshur, Munir. *Itijahat fi at-tarbiyya al-'arabiyya* (Trends in Arab Education). Tunis and Beirut: Al-Munazzama al-'arabiyya lil-tarbiyya wal-thaqafa wal-'ulum, 1982.

Bin Baraka, Al-Mahdi. *Al-Ikhtiar al-thawri fi al-Maghrib* (The Revolutionary Alternative in the Maghrib). Beirut: Dar at-tali'a, 1966.

Bin Baz, al-Sheikh Abdul Aziz. *Naqd al-qawmiyya al-'arabiyya 'ala daw' al-Islam wal-waqi'* (A Critique of Arab Nationalism in Light of Islam and Reality). Beirut: Al-Maktab al-islami, 1983.

Bin Nabi, Malik. *Shurut al-nahda* (Conditions of Awakening). Beirut: Dar al-fikr, 1969.

al-Bushri, Tariq. *Al Muslimun wal-Aqbat* (Muslims and Copts). Cairo: Al-Hai'a al-misriyya, 1980.

Daher, Adel. *Al-Mujtama' wal-insan: Dirasat fi falsafat Antun Saada al-ijtima'yya* (Society and Man: Studies of the Social Philosophy of Antun Saada). Beirut: Manshurat mawaqif, 1980.

Djait, Hichem. *Al-Shakhsiyya al-'arabiyya al-islamiyya wal-masir al-'arabi* (Arab-Islamic Personality and Arab Destiny). Beirut: Dar at-tali'a, 1984.

Duri, Abd al-Aziz. *Al-Juzur at-tarikhiyya lil-qawmiyya al-'arabiyya* (Historical Roots of Arab Nationalism). Beirut: Dar al-'ilm lil-malayyin, 1960.

———. *Muqaddimah fi at-tarikh al-iqtisadi al-'arabi* (Introduction to Arab Economic History). Beirut: Dar at-tali'a, 1969.

al-Fassi, 'Allal. *An-Naqd al-dhati* (Self-Criticism). Beirut: Dar al-kashshaf, 1966.

Fawzi, Hussein. *Sindibad misri* (Egyptian Sinbad). 2d ed. Cairo: Dar al-ma'arif, 1969.

Hamdan, Gamal. *Al-'Alam al-islami al-mu'asir* (The Contemporary Muslim World). Cairo: 'Alam al-kitab, 1971.

———. *Shakhsiyyat Misr* (Egyptian Personality). Cairo: Maktabat an-nahda al-misriyyah, 1970.

Hatab, Zuhair. *Tatowor buna al-usra al-'arabiyya* (The Evolution of the Structures of the Arab Family). Beirut: Ma'had al-inma' al-'Arabi, 1976.

Hermassi, Elbaki. *Al-Mujtama' wal-dawlah fi al-Maghrib al-'arabi* (Society and State in the Maghrib). Beirut: Markaz dirasat al-wahda al-'arabiyya, 1987.

al-Husari, Sati'. *Ma hia al-qawmiyya?* (What is Nationalism?). Beirut: Dar al-'ilm lil-malayyin, 1959.

Hussein, Taha. *Fi al-shi'r al-jahili* (On Pre-Islamic Poetry). Cairo: Dar al-ma'rif, 1926.

———. *Mustaqbal al-thaqafa fi Misr* (The Future of Culture in Egypt). Cairo: Dar al-ma'arif, 1938.

Ibn Khaldun, Abu Zaid 'Abdel Rahman Ibn Muhammad. *Al-Muqaddimah* (Prolegomena). Tunis: Al-Dar at-Tunisiyya, 1984.

Ibrahim, Saad Eddin. *Itijahat al-ra'i al-'am al-'arabi nahwa mas'alat al-wahda: Dirasa midaniyya* (Trends of Arab Public Opinion toward the Question of Unity: A Field Study). Beirut: Markaz dirasat al-wahda al-'arabiyya, 1980.

———. *Al-Mujtama' wal-dawlah fi al-watan al-'arabi* (Society and State in the Arab Homeland). Beirut: Markaz dirasat al-wahdah al-'arabiyya, 1988.

Idriss, Yusuf. *Al-Haram* (The Sin). Cairo: Riwaiat al-hillal, 1965.

———. *Qa' al-medina* (City Dregs). Cairo: Markaz kutob as-sharq al-awsat, 1958.

———. *Qissat hubb* (Love Story). Cairo: Dar al-kitab al-'arabi, 1967.

Jabri, Muhammed Abed. *Buniat al-'aql al-'arabi* (The Structure of Arab Mind). Beirut: Markaz dirasat al-wahda al-'arabiyya, 1986.

———. *Ishkaliyat al-fikr al-'arabi* (The Problematics of Arab Thought). Beirut: Markaz dirasat al-wahda al-'arabiyya, 1989.

———. *Al-Khitab al-'arabi al-mu'asir* (Contemporary Arab Discourse). Beirut, Dar at-tali'a, 1982.

———. *Takwin al-'aql al-'arabi* (The Formation of Arab Mind). Beirut: Markaz dirasat al-wahda al-'arabiyya, 1984.

al-Jahayman, Abdel Karim. *Min asatirina ash-sha'biyyah fi qalb al-jazira al-'Arabiyya* (Folktales in the Heart of Arabia). Beirut: Dar ath-thaqafa, 1969.

al-Kawakibi, Abd al-Rahman. *Al-'Amal al-kamila* (Complete Works). Beirut: Al-Mu'assa al-'arabiyya lil-dirasat wal-nashr, 1975.

Khalifa, Sahar. *As-Sabbar* (Wild Thorns). Jerusalem: Galilio, 1976.

Mahfouz, Naguib. *Awlad haratina* (The Children of Geblawi). Beirut: Dar al-adab, 1967.

————. *Bayn al-qasrain* (Between the Two Palaces). Cairo: Maktabat Misr, 1970.

————. *Zuqaq al-Midaqq* (Midaq Alley). Cairo: Maktabat Misr, 1965.

al-Marzuqi, Muhammed. *Ma' al-badu fi hallihim wa-tirhalihim* (Bedouin: Their Settlement and Movement). Tunis: Al-Dar al-'arabiyya lil-kitab, 1980.

Moussa, Salama. *Laisat al-mar'at lu'bat al-rajul* (The Woman Is Not a Man's Toy). Cairo: Salama Moussa lil-nashr wa at-tawzi', 1953.

Mroueh, Hussein. *Al-Naza'at al-maddiyya fi al-falsafa al-'arabiyya al-islamiyya* (Materialist Trends in Arab-Islamic Philosophy). Beirut: Dar al-farabi, 1978–79.

al-Naqeeb, Khaldoun. *Al-Mujtama' wal-dawlah fi al-khalij wal-jazira al-'arabiyya* (Society and State in the Gulf and Arabian Peninsula). Beirut: Markaz dirasat al-wahda al-'arabiyya, 1988.

Nassar, Nassif. *Nahwa mujtama' jadid* (Toward a New Society). Beirut: Dar al-Nahar, 1970.

al-Nuwayhi, Muhammed. *Nahwa thawra fi al-fikr al-dini* (Toward a Revolution in Religious Thought). Beirut: Dar al-adab, 1983.

Oweiss, Sayyid. *Min malamih al-mujtama' al-misri al-mu'assir* (Features of Contemporary Egyptian Society). Cairo: Al-Markaz al-qawmi lil-buhuth al-ijtima'iyya wal-jina'iyya, 1965.

Rabih, Turki. *Al-Ta'lim al qawmi wal-shakhsiyya al-jaza'iriyya* (National Education and the Algerian Personality). 2d ed. Algiers: Al-Sharika al-wataniyya lil-nashr wal-tawzi', 1981.

Rafiq, Abdul Karim. *Buhuth fi at-tarikh al-iqtisadi wal-ijtima'i libilad ash-sham fi al-'asr al-hadith* (Studies in the Economic and Social History of Syria in the Modern Period). Damascus: Jami'at Dimashq, 1985.

Salame, Ghassan. *Al-Mujtama' wal-dawlah fi al-Mashriq al-'arabi* (Society and State in the Arab East). Beirut: Markaz dirasat al-wahda al-'arabiyya, 1987.

Salim, Shakir M. *Al-Jibayish: Dirasa anthropologiyya li-garia fi ahowaz al-Iraq* (An Anthropological Study of a Marsh Village in Iraq). Baghdad: Al-'Ani Press, 1970.

Shalabi, Ahmed. *Al-Hayat al-ijtima'iyya fi at-tafkir al-islami* (Social Life in Islamic Thought). Cairo: Maktabat an-nahda al-misriyya, 1968.

Sharabi, Hisham. *Muqaddamat li-dirast al-mujtama' al-'arabi* (An Introduction to the Study of Arab Society). Jerusalem: Manshurat Salahad Din, 1975.

al-Sharqawi, Abdel Rahman. *Al-Ard* (The Earth). 2 vols. Cairo: Nadi al-qissat, al-kitab al-zahabi, 1954.

Tizzini, Tayyib. *Mashrou' ru'ia jadida lil fikr al-'arabi* (A Project for a New Vision of Arab Thought). Beirut: Dar Ibn Khaldun, 1978.

al-Wardi, Ali. *Mantiq Ibn Khaldun* (The Logic of Ibn Khaldun). Tunis: Ash-Sharika at-Tunisiyya, 1978–79.

Yassin, Buali. *Azamet az-zawaj fi Suriyya* (Marriage Crisis in Syria). Beirut: Dar Ibn Rushd, 1979.

Yassin, El-Sayyid. *Al-Shakhsiyya al-'arabiyya* (The Arab Personality). Beirut: Dar at-tanwir, 1981.

Zakariyya, Fuad. *Al-Haqiqa wal-wahm fi al-haraka al-islamiyya al-mu'asira* (Fact and Illusion in the Contemporary Islamic Movement). Cairo: Dar al-fikr, 1986.

Zay'our, 'Ali. *Tahlil al-dhat al-'arabiyya* (Analysis of the Arab Ego). Beirut: Dar al-tali'a, 1977.

Zuraiq, Constantine. *Ma'na an-nakba* (The Meaning of Disaster). Beirut: Dar al-'ilm lil-malayyin, 1948.

—————. *Ma'na an-nakba mujaddadan* (The Meaning of Disaster Revisited). Beirut: Dar al-'Ilm lil-malayyin, 1967.

—————. *Nahnu wal-mustaqbal* (We and the Future). Beirut: Dar al-'ilm lil-malayyin, 1977.

II. WORKS IN ENGLISH

Abdel-Fadil, Mahmoud. *Development, Income Distribution and Social Change in Rural Egypt, 1952–1970: A Study in the Political Economy of Agrarian Transition.* New York: Cambridge University Press 1975.

—————. *The Political Economy of Nasserism: A Study in Employment and Income Distribution Policies in Urban Egypt, 1952–1972.* Cambridge: Cambridge University Press, 1980.

Abdel-Malek, Anouar. *Egypt: Military Society.* Translated by Charles L. Markmann. New York: Random House, Vintage Books, 1968.

Abu-Lughod, Janet. *Cairo: 1001 Years of the City Victorious.* Princeton: Princeton University Press, 1971.

Alamuddin, Nura S., and Paul D. Starr. *Crucial Bonds: Marriage Among the Lebanese Druze.* Delmar, N.Y.: Caravan Books, 1980.

Amin, Samir. *The Arab Economy Today.* London: Zed Books, 1982.

—————. *The Arab Nation: Nationalism and Class Struggle.* London: Zed Press, 1978.

Ammar, Hamed. *Growing up in an Egyptian Village.* London: Routledge & Kegan Paul, 1954.

Arkoun, Mohammed. *Rethinking Islam Today.* Washington, D.C.: Center for Contemporary Arab Studies, Georgetown University, 1987.

Ayrout, Henry Habib. *The Egyptian Peasant.* Boston, Mass.: Beacon Press 1963.

Baer, Gabriel. *Studies in the Social History of Modern Egypt.* Chicago: University of Chicago Press, 1969.

Barakat, Halim. *Lebanon in Strife: Student Preludes to the Civil War.* Austin: University of Texas Press, 1977.

—————. *Visions of Social Reality in the Contemporary Arab Novel.* Washington D.C.: Center for Contemporary Arab Studies, Georgetown University, 1977.

—————, ed., *Contemporary North Africa: Issues of Development and Integration.* Washington, D.C.: Center for Contemporary Arab Studies, Georgetown University, 1985.

Batatu, Hanna. *The Egyptian, Syrian and Iraqi Revolutions.* Washington, D.C.: Center for Contemporary Arab Studies, Georgetown University, 1984.

—————. *The Old Social Classes and the Revolutionary Movements of Iraq.* Princeton: Princeton University Press, 1978.

Bates, Daniel, and Rassam, Amal. *Peoples and Cultures of the Middle East.* Englewood Cliffs, N.J.: Prentice-Hall, 1983.

Berger, Morroe. *The Arab World Today.* New York: Doubleday, 1964.

Berger, Peter L. *Elements of a Sociological Theory of Religion.* Garden City, N.Y.: Doubleday, Anchor Books, 1969.

Berque, Jacques. *The Arabs: Their History and Future.* Translated by Jean Stewart. Preface by Sir Hamilton Gibb. London: Faber & Faber, 1964.

Beshir, Mohamed Omer. *Southern Sudan: Regionalism and Religion.* Khartoum: University of Khartoum Publications, 1984.

Boullata, Issa J. *Trends and Issues in Contemporary Arab Thought*. Albany: State University of New York Press, 1990.

Bujra, Abdalla S. *The Politics of Stratification: A Study of Political Change in a South Arabian Town*. Oxford: Oxford University Press, 1971.

Cole, Donald Powell. *Nomads of the Nomads: The Al-Murrah Bedouin of the Empty Quarter*. Arlington Heights, Ill.: AHM Publishing, 1975.

Coon, Carlton S. *Caravan: The Story of the Middle East*. New York: Holt, Rinehart & Winston, 1961.

Drysdale, Alasdair, and Gerald H. Blake. *The Middle East and North Africa: A Political Geography*. Oxford: Oxford University Press, 1985.

Duri, Abd al-Aziz. *The Historical Formation of the Arab Nation*. Washington, D.C.: Center for Contemporary Arab Studies, Georgetown University, 1983.

Eickelman, Dale F. *Moroccan Islam: Tradition and Society in a Pilgrimage Center*. Austin: University of Texas Press, 1976.

El-Saadawi, Nawal. *The Hidden Face of Eve*. Boston: Beacon Press, 1982.

Esposito, John L., ed. *Voices of Resurgent Islam*. Oxford: Oxford University Press, 1983.

Fanon, Franz. *The Wretched of the Earth*. Translated by Constance Farrington. Preface by Jean-Paul Sartre. New York: Grove Press, 1963.

Gellner, Ernest, and Charles Micaud, eds. *Arabs and Berbers: From the Tribe to Nation in North Africa*. Lexington, Mass.: Heath, 1972.

Gilsenan, Michael. *Recognizing Islam: Religion and Society in the Modern Arab World*. New York: Pantheon Books, 1982.

———. *Saint and Sufi in Modern Egypt: An Essay in the Sociology of Religion*. Oxford: Oxford University Press, 1978.

Haddad, Hassan, and Basheer Nijm, eds. *The Arab World: A Handbook*. Wilmette, Ill.: Medina Press, 1978.

Haddad, Yvonne Yazbeck. *Contemporary Islam and the Challenge of History*. Albany: State University of New York Press, 1982.

Halpern, Manfred. *The Politics of Social Change in the Middle East and North Africa*. Princeton: Princeton University Press, 1963.

Harik, Iliya. *Distribution of Land, Employment and Income in Rural Egypt*. Ithaca, N.Y.: Cornell University, Center for International Studies, 1975.

Hermassi, Elbaki. *Leadership and National Development in North Africa: A Comparative Study*. Berkeley and Los Angeles: University of California Press, 1972.

———. *The Third World Reassessed*. Berkeley and Los Angeles: University of California Press, 1980.

Hourani, Albert. *Arabic Thought in the Liberal Age, 1798–1939*. Oxford: Oxford University Press, 1970.

———. *Europe and the Middle East*. Berkeley and Los Angeles: University of California Press, 1980.

Hudson, Michael C. *Arab Politics: The Search for Legitimacy*. New Haven: Yale University Press, 1977.

Ibrahim, Ibrahim, ed. *Arab Resources: The Transformation of a Society*. Washington, D.C.: Center for Contemporary Arab Studies, Georgetown University, 1983.

Ibrahim, Saad Eddin. *The New Arab Social Order: A Study of the Social Impact of Oil Wealth*. Boulder, Colo.: Westview Press; London: Croom Helm, 1982.

———, and Nicholas S. Hopkins, eds. *Arab Society in Transition: A Reader*. Cairo: American University in Cairo, 1977.

Issawi, Charles. *Egypt in Revolution: An Economic Analysis*. Oxford: Oxford University Press, 1963.

Jabra, Jabra Ibrahim. *Hunters in a Narrow Street*. London: Heinemann, 1960.

Kanafani, Ghassan. *Men in the Sun*. Washington, D.C.: Three Continents Press, 1983.

Khatibi, Abdelkebir, and Sijelmassi, Mohammed. *The Splendour of Islamic Calligraphy*. London: Thames & Hudson, 1976.

Khoury, Philip. *Syria and the French Mandate: The Politics of Arab Nationalism, 1920–1945*. Princeton: Princeton University Press, 1987.

———. *Urban Notables and Arab Nationalism: The Politics of Damascus 1860–1920*. Cambridge: Cambridge University Press, 1983.

Khuri, Ra'if. *Modern Arab Thought: Channels of the French Revolution to the Arab East*. Translated by Ihsan Abbas. Princeton, N.J.: Kingston Press, 1983.

Lancaster, William. *Changing Cultures: The Rwala Bedouin Today*. Cambridge: Cambridge University Press, 1981.

Laroui, Abdallah. *The Crisis of the Arab Intellectual: Traditionalism or Historicism*. Translated by Diarmid Commell. Berkeley and Los Angeles: University of California Press, 1976.

———. *The History of the Maghrib: An Interpretive Essay*. Translated by Ralph Manheim. Princeton: Princeton University Press, 1977.

Lazreg, Marnia. *The Emergence of Classes in Algeria: A Study of Colonialism and Socio-Political Change*. Boulder, Colo.: Westview Press, 1976.

Lefebvre, Henri. *The Sociology of Marx*. New York: Pantheon Books, 1968.

Lewis, Norman N. *Nomads and Settlers in Syria and Jordan, 1800–1980*. Cambridge: Cambridge University Press, 1987.

Liebesny, Herbert J. *The Law of the Near and Middle East: Readings, Cases and Materials*. Albany: State University of New York Press, 1975.

Lukács, Georg. *Realism in Our Time: Literature and Class Struggle*. New York: Harper Torchbooks, 1971.

———. *Studies in European Realism*. New York: Universal Library, 1974.

———. *The Theory of the Novel*. Cambridge, Mass.: MIT Press, 1971.

Marsot, Afaf Lutfi al-Sayyid. *Egypt in the Reign of Muhammed Ali*. Cambridge: Cambridge University Press, 1984.

Marx, Karl. *Contribution to the Critique of Political Economy*. New York: International Publishers, 1989.

———. *The Economic and Philosophic Manuscripts of 1844*. New York: International Publishers, 1964.

———, and Frederick Engels. *The German Ideology*. Edited by C. J. Arthur. New York: International Publishers, 1970.

Memmi, Albert. *The Colonizer and the Colonized*. Boston: Beacon Press, 1967.

Mernissi, Fatima. *Beyond the Veil: Male-Female Dynamics in a Modern Muslim Society*. New York: Schenkman Publishing, 1975.

Patai, Raphael. *The Arab Mind*. New York: Scribner's, 1976.

———. *Society, Culture and Change in the Middle East*. Philadelphia: University of Pennsylvania Press, 1971.

Prothro, Edwin Terry, and Lutfi Najib Diab. *Changing Family Patterns in the Arab East*. Beirut: American University of Beirut, 1974.

Qutb, Sayyid. *This Religion of Islam*. Palo Alto, Calif.: Al-Manar Press, 1967.

Rabinow, Paul. *Symbolic Domination: Cultural Form and Historical Change in Morocco*. Chicago: University of Chicago Press, 1975.

Rodinson, Maxime. *Islam and Capitalism*. Translated by Brian Pearce. Austin: University of Texas Press, 1978.

Said, Edward. *Orientalism*. New York: Pantheon Books, 1978.

Salih, Tayeb. *Season of Migration to the North*. London: Heinemann, 1969.

Sayigh, Rosemary. *Palestinians: From Peasants to Revolutionaries*. London: Zed Press, 1979.

Sayigh, Yusif A. *The Economies of the Arab World: Development since 1945*. London: Croom Helm, 1978.

Sharabi, Hisham. *Arab Intellectuals and the West: The Formative Years, 1875–1914*. Baltimore.: Johns Hopkins Press, 1970.

———. *Neopatriarchy: A Theory of Distorted Change in Arab Society*. Oxford: Oxford University Press, 1988.

Smith, Donald E., ed. *Religion, Politics and Social Change in the Third World*. New York: Free Press; London: Macmillan, 1971.

Smith, W. Robertson. *Kinship and Marriage in Early Arabia*. Boston, Mass.: Beacon Press, 1903.

Smith, Wilfred Cantwell. *Islam in Modern History*. New York: Mentor Books, 1957.

Swartz, M. L., et al. *Studies on Islam*. Oxford: Oxford University Press, 1981.

Touraine, Alaine. *Return of the Actor: Social Theory in Postindustrial Society*. Translated by Myrna Godzich. Minneapolis: University of Minnesota Press, 1988.

Turner, Bryan S. *Marx and the End of Orientalism*. London: George Allen & Unwin, 1978.

———. *Weber and Islam*. London: Routledge & Kegan Paul, 1974.

Van Niewenhuijze, C. A. O. *Social Stratification and the Middle East*. Leiden: E. J. Brill, 1965.

Von Grunebaum, G. E. *Islam: Essays in the Nature and Growth of a Cultural Tradition*. New York: Barnes & Noble, 1961.

Weber, Max. *The Sociology of Religion*. Translated by E. Fischoff. London: Methuen, 1966.

al-Yassini, Ayman. *Religion and State in the Kingdom of Saudi Arabia*. Boulder, Colo.: Westview Press, 1985.

Zurayk, Constantine K. *Tensions in Islamic Civilization*. Washington, D.C.: Center for Contemporary Arab Studies, Georgetown University, 1978.

III. ARTICLES IN ARABIC

'Amara, Muhammed. "Al-Dawlah fi turath al-Islam" (State in Islamic Heritage). *Al-Hayat*, no. 9,761 (September 2–3, 1989).

———. "Min huna bada't masiratuna lil-wahda al-'arabiyya" (The Beginnings of Our March for Arab Unity). *Qadaia 'arabiyya* (Beirut) 3, nos. 1–6 (1976).

Barakat, Halim. "An-Nizam al-ijtima'i wa 'alaqatuhu bi mushkilat al-mar'a al-'arabiyya" (Arab Social Order and Its Relationship to the Question of Arab Woman). *Al-Mustaqbal al-'arabi* 4, no. 34 (December 1981): 51–63.

———. "Ath-Thawra wal-ightirab fi al-hayat al-'arabiyya al-mou'asira" (Revolution and Alienation in Contemporary Arab Life). *Mawaqif* 1, no. 5 (1969): 18–44.

Ibrahim, Saad Eddin. "Al-Mas'alatu al-ijtam'iyyu baina at-turath wa tahadiat al'asr" (The Social Question between Legacy and Contemporary Challenges). *Al-Mustaqbal al-'arabi* 7, no. 71 (1985): 48–89.

———. "Nahwa dirasat sociologiyya lil-wahda: Al-'Aqaliat fi al-'alam al-'arabi" (Toward a Sociological Study of Unity: Minorities in the Arab World). *Qadaia 'arabiyya* (Beirut) 3, nos. 1–6 (1976): 5–24.

Sa'id, Khalida. "Al-Hadatha au 'iqdat Gelqamesh" (Modernity, or the Gilgamesh Complex). *Mawaqif*, no. 51/52 (Summer/Autumn 1984): 11–51.

———. "Al-Mar'a al-'arabiyya: Ka'in bi-nafsihi" (The Arab Woman: An Alienated Being). *Mawaqif* 2, no. 12 (1970): 91–100.

Shamseddin, Muhammed Mahdi. "Nadhrat al-Islam ila al-usra fi mujtama' mutatuir" (Islam's View of Family in a Changing Society). *Al-Fikr al-islami* 6, no. 5 (May 1975).

Yassin, El-Sayyid. "Ash-Shakhsiyya al-'arabiyya: An-Nasaq ar-ra'issi wal-ansaq al-far'iyya" (Arab Personality: Primary and Secondary Patterns). *Al-Mustaqbal al-'arabi* 1, no. 3 (September 1978): 144–155.

IV. ARTICLES IN ENGLISH

Abu-Lughod, Janet. "The Islamic City—Historic Myth, Islamic Essence, and Contemporary Relevance." *International Journal of Middle East Studies* 19, no. 2 (May 1987): 155–76.

———. "Migrant Adjustment to City Life: The Egyptian Case." *American Journal of Sociology* 47, no. 1 (July 1961): 22–32.

Amin, Galal A. "Dependent Development." *Alternatives* 2, no. 4 (December 1976): 379–403

Barakat, Halim. "Ideological Determinants of Arab Development." In Ibrahim Ibrahim, ed., *Arab Resources: The Transformation of a Society*, pp. 169–183. Washington D.C.: Center for Contemporary Arab Studies, Georgetown University, 1983.

———. "Socio-Economic, Cultural and Personality Forces Determining Development in Arab Society." *Social Praxis* 2, nos. 3–4 (1976): 179–204.

Bill, James A. "Class Analysis and the Dialectics of Modernization in the Middle East." *International Journal of Middle East Studies* 3, no. 4 (1972): 417–34.

Boullata, Kamal. "Modern Arab Art: The Quest and the Ordeal." *Mundus artium* 10, no. 1 (1977): 107–25.

Haddad, Hassan S. " 'Georgic' Cults and the Saints of the Levant." *NVMEN: International Review for the History of Religions* (Leiden) 16, no. 1 (April 1969): 21–39.

Halliday, Fred. "Labor Migration in the Arab World." *Middle East Research and Information Project Reports* 14, no. 4 (May 1984): 3–10.

Harik, Iliya. "Lebanon: Anatomy of Conflict." *American Universities Field Staff Reports*, no. 49 (1981).

Hopkins, Nicholas S. "The Emergence of Class in a Tunisian Town." *International Journal of Middle East Studies* 8, no. 4 (1977): 453–91.

———. "Modern Agriculture and Political Centralization: A Case from Tunisia." *Human Organization* 37, no. 1 (Spring 1978).

Ibrahim, Ibrahim A. "Salama Musa: An Essay on Cultural Alienation." *Middle Eastern Studies* 15, no. 3 (October 1979).

Longuenesse, Elisabeth. "The Class Nature of the State in Syria: Contributions to an Analysis." *Middle East Research and Information Project Reports* 9, no. 4 (May 1979): 3–11.

Mernissi, Fatima. "Virginity and Patriarchy." *Women's Studies International Forum* 5, no. 2 (1982).

Owen, Roger. "Arab Nationalism, Unity and Solidarity." In Talal Asad and Roger Owen, eds., *Sociology of "Developing Societies": The Middle East.* New York: Monthly Review Press, 1983.

Tibawi, A. L. "The Genesis and Early History of the Syrian Protestant College." *Middle East Journal* 21, no. 2 (Spring 1967): 199–212.

Tucker, Judith E. "Taming the West: Trends in the Writing of Modern Arab Social History in North America and England." In Hisham Sharabi, ed., *Power, Theory and the Arab World,* pp. 198–227. New York: Routledge, 1990.

Index

Abdel-Fadil, Mahmoud, 75, 168, 262, 263
Abdel-Malek, Anouar, 87, 88, 90, 240
Abdu, Muhammad, 243, 244–45, 250
Abu-Lughod, Janet, 60, 62, 63–64, 185
Adonis, 146, 197–98, 207
al-Afghani, Jamal Eddin, 243–44
Afghanistan, 160, 170
'Aflaq, Michel, 165–66, 167, 302n34
Agriculture: decline of, 30, 80; in Egypt, 16–17, 28, 56, 77, 87; and irrigation systems, 28, 57, 80, 155; market-oriented, 66, 84, 87; mechanization of, 19, 66, 74; nationalization of, 168; and peasant society, 55, 56; precolonial, 275; in Tunisia, 19
Ahl al-dhimma, 76
Akhdam, 86, 87
al-Akhras, Muhammed Safouh, 110, 111
Alawites, 6, 7, 31, 34, 37, 42, 124, 125, 127, 166
Algeria: Berbers in, 40; capitalism in, 18; civil society in, 18; class structure in, 20; democracy in, 17, 18, 278; divorce law in, 115; divorce rates in, 114; education in, 29; elites in, 17, 65, 88, 168; French colonialism in, 18, 40, 158; income levels in, 80; Islamic religion in, 18, 169, 258, 281; legal system in, 139; literature of, 230, 237–38; military in, 168, 176; nationalism in, 17, 155, 255; nationalization of enterprises in, 168; political relations in, 17, 18, 168–69; polygamous marriage in, 112, 113; revolution in, 18, 37, 44, 92, 158, 168, 237, 256, 273; rural-urban interdependence in, 66; secularism in, 255; social diversity in, 16, 17; socialism in, 169, 280; and unity with Arab world, 18; workers' self-management in, 168, 169
Alienation, 11, 14, 46, 79, 264; and civil society, 26–27, 151, 177, 273; and class struggle, 91, 94; and family relations, 26, 100, 106; literary representations of, 216, 222, 223; and *nahda*

Compositor: ComCom, Division of Haddon Craftsmen, Inc.
   Printer: Haddon Craftsmen, Inc.
   Binder: Haddon Craftsmen, Inc.
     Text: 10/13 Bembo
  Display: Bembo